MY WIFE AND I

THE MACMILLAN COMPANY
NEW YORK · BOSTON · CHICAGO · DALLAS
ATLANTA · SAN FRANCISCO

MACMILLAN AND CO., Limited
LONDON · BOMBAY · CALCUTTA · MADRAS
MELBOURNE

THE MACMILLAN COMPANY
OF CANADA, Limited
TORONTO

OUR FORTIETH ANNIVERSARY

My Wife and I

THE STORY OF LOUISE AND SIDNEY HOMER

By

SIDNEY HOMER

NEW YORK

THE MACMILLAN COMPANY

1939

PRINTED IN THE UNITED STATES OF AMERICA
AMERICAN BOOK—STRATFORD PRESS, INC., NEW YORK

To My Wife

PREFACE

EVERY child should have an opportunity to learn to play some musical instrument and should be taught to sing. All schools, including the lower grades, should have teachers of music of high standard. For children with special aptitude for music, more intensive teaching should be provided, including the study of the counterpoint and form of Bach and Mozart, and more time for practice should be allowed.

The study of music greatly increases a child's sensibility, his sensitiveness to balance and form and to beauty of every kind, and his consciousness of the more subtle meanings. The playing of an instrument demands concentration, coordination and self-control. In playing great music a child comes under the influence of men of the highest genius—men who arouse ideals, create standards, and inspire confidence. In playing in an orchestra or singing in a chorus he takes part in a work which demands perfect cooperation and the highest discipline.

Thus the study of music meets every requirement of education and can do its part towards preparing the child for the years of maturity. It will make his hours of work easier and more interesting (as all culture does), and will make his hours of leisure happier and more profitable.

Men who see our daily life as a sort of glorified prize ring, and who want their boys to be tough and aggressive, may get what they want, but they may not have the gratitude of their sons. Life is not a prize ring, and many a hard, tough character has found himself stranded in a society that had other standards.

The music of the great masters is not abstruse or obscure. It was written from the human heart in its most exalted and inspired state, with all the powers of expression at their very height, at white heat. These composers did not disdain their hearers, but with passionate honesty strove to reach them. They bared their hearts and poured out their feelings before all the world, and the finest and truest consciousness within them guided their music. They have communicated their sincerity to their interpreters, and thus this music stands inflexible in its purity, and inexorable in its demands on the nobility and rectitude of its hearers. In its presence all those who can hear are elevated and made whole. The consciousness of the ability to share in this wonderful art has had much to do with the development of self-confidence.

Music knows no limitations. A tune is a tune wherever born, and nothing can destroy its appeal. Regardless of barriers of race, space, and time, it travels cheerfully throughout the world and is loved everywhere.

There is more to music than many men, including many educators, realize. Teachers wish to arouse a love for lyric poetry: composers have done much to give lyric poetry a place in daily life. Teachers wish to instill a reverence for the higher forms of the drama: composers have given the drama new glories and verities. Teachers wish to develop nobility in their pupils: nowhere will they find greater help than in music. Great composers have given their lives for the expression of the noblest emotions of which man is capable. Educators have in music a tremendous power, ready to hand.

Every city and town should have a small fund for the higher musical education of those rare young people who show positive genius for music. The expense would be a trifle, but the returns would be enormous. A musical genius belongs to the people and should be educated by the people. To place the responsibility for the training of such children on their parents is wrong. Fine performances of great musical works should be made possible, and they should be accessible to all. This, too, is a public responsibility.

We are slowly becoming aware of the fact that, if humanity does not insist on going right, it will go dangerously wrong. We are gradually acquiring a desire to cooperate with those men of genius of every kind who labored to elevate mankind. So long as we were not afraid, we were willing to keep art to ourselves. Exclusiveness had a glamour, and we fondly thought it enhanced art. But now we are afraid, and we want to use art for the softening and appeasing of all mankind. If we had begun earlier, perhaps we need never have known fear.

However, the business at hand is to use music in a great way. For that we need great artists; and fortunately we have them. But now is the time to prepare the artists of the next generation; in the enjoyment of what we have, we must not forget the future. Nothing is more fatuous than the easy assumption that we shall always have plenty of artists. We may not. Artists have a way of disappearing off the face of the earth so that all the King's horses cannot find them. Liszt provided most of the concert pianists for the generation which followed him.

Men will ask: Will the outlay and effort necessary for great performances bring adequate return? Yes. Bayreuth, Salzburg, Bethlehem, Pennsylvania, and Worcester, Massachusetts—to mention but a few of the smaller cities—have had great performances; and every inhabitant, down to the last man, has known what it has meant to his city. There need be no qualms. Art is the greatest investment the world has ever known.

CONTENTS

ILLUSTRATIONS

MY WIFE AND I

I

MY MOTHER, BY EXAMPLE AND PRECEPT, taught me that the world was a fascinating place in which to live, that love played a great part in it, that humanity could be trusted, that a physical handicap need not be discouraging, that courage and a determination to make the most of oneself would always meet with recognition and opportunity, that boredom and a fear of the commonplace led to distortion and artificiality.

These convictions have lasted throughout my life; there have been no disillusionments, and I feel that her instincts and judgment were infallible.

She was one of those magnetic, dynamic souls that make life interesting, not only for themselves but for others. I sometimes think that humanity is made up of suns and planets, radiating personalities and grateful satellites.

All that I know of my mother's early life is what she told me. She had a most dramatic way of telling a story, and her mind was so impressionable that what she told became vivid in the telling. Her name was Anna Maria Swift. She was born in Rochester, New York, in 1827. Her father, John Dean Swift, came from Virginia and was at one time a friend of Stephen Girard. He died in 1828, while she was still in infancy. Her mother was a Hun. This fact she impressed on me very carefully. The Huns and Lansings intermarried. They were old Dutch families. President Van Buren was in some way a connection. I have an old pastel, very beautiful, of Katharine Hun, who was a famous beauty more than a hundred years ago.

When I think of my mother's life, I cannot wonder that she felt she was under Divine protection. When she was three years old she had a severe attack of scarlet fever which left her totally deaf. As a consequence she never learned to talk. Soon after this illness her mother died.

Such a situation would seem to promise only a narrow, circumscribed life. And when I think of her joy as she sat in the Théâtre Royal de la Monnaie, Brussels, in Covent Garden, London, and the Metropolitan in New York, watching my wife in such roles as Amneris, Ortrud, and Azucena—I realize what miracles the vicissitudes of life can lead to.

My mother was educated at the New York Institute for the Deaf, which was at Fifth Avenue and Fiftieth Street, where St. Patrick's Cathedral stands today. Those were the thrilling days when the beautiful sign language and one-hand alphabet, created in France by the great humanitarian and genius, the Abbé Sicard, was spreading throughout the world. Laurent Clerc had come to the United States from Paris to teach this language; Gallaudet was teaching it at Hartford, Dr. Sharpe and others in New York.

This sign language was so full of grace and beauty that it even had a fascination, pantomimic of course, for those who could not understand it. I have seen people moved to tears by watching the rendering in signs of the Lord's Prayer. This grace and beauty had a cultural effect on all who used it. It was adopted in all western countries and became the first international language.

Its power can be shown by the following incident: A few days after we arrived in Munich (this was during my student period) a young German baron, a deaf mute, asked the privilege of calling on my father and mother. Although I knew German fairly well I rather dreaded the translating I should have to do. When he came I was amazed to see with what ease he and my parents carried on a long conversation. He knew no English, they knew no German, and yet, except for an occasional word for which there was no sign equivalent (which I, of course, translated) they talked away merrily and without embarrassment.

After seven years of study at her New York alma mater my

mother was graduated. Then came a decisive change in her life. Her five older brothers, all of whom, by the way, played various instruments in the famous old Dodsworth amateur band, were marrying and migrating to remote parts of the country; so she went to live with her mother's sister in Waltham, Massachusetts. I love to think of this great-aunt. Any woman who undertakes the charge of a young and beautiful deaf-mute girl must have a wonderful spirit. Perhaps it was the Hun spirit, that my mother loved so much. Anyway it is things like this that keep our old world moving. An infinite number of kindly acts occur every moment of every day, everywhere, and these, in their sum total, make up the truest picture of human life.

This aunt was very jolly, big-hearted, beloved by all. Bless her memory!

Moving to Waltham, in those days, meant saying good-bye forever to one's family, friends, and associates. Distances were great, travel expensive. The motto of the day was rigid economy; not one cent must be wasted, and all unnecessary travel was taboo. It used to be several days' journey for my father from Boston to his school at Hartford, Connecticut. There were no Christmas or Easter holidays at home in those days. When missionaries started out for foreign lands they did not expect to return. It does no harm to think of the heroic courage which was a commonplace thing then.

Life was quiet in Waltham. There were no other deaf mutes. Boston was far away (fully fifteen miles) unless one owned fast horses. One day the village was stirred by the arrival of a handsome turnout—black horses and coachman. It stopped at my aunt's house, and inquiries were made for Miss Swift. Mother was hurried upstairs to don her best silk dress, and when she came down she was presented to two dignified ladies, in black silk, and a tall man with brown hair and merry, blue eyes. He was a deaf mute. After a short visit he asked Miss Swift if he might call on her again.

When the engagement was announced the dear aunt's happiness was complete. Old Boston family, fine man, fine character! In the midst of the wedding preparations she suddenly became ill and died. Perhaps her noble heart could not bear quite so much joy.

My father was born in 1811. His name was George Homer. His father, Joseph Warren Homer, built his house on Pinckney Street, Boston, back of the Statehouse. The bricks were brought from England, and the old house, Number 41, still stands. Grandmother's maiden name was Sally Rea. The old Rea mansion was torn down to make room for part of the Statehouse. There were thirteen children, of whom my father was one of the younger. The objectives of the family seem to have been dignity, loyalty to the family name, commercial success, and a quiet life. Several brothers became importers and amassed what in those days were called fortunes.

One of my father's brothers, Sidney, made a great fight for Free Trade, his opponent being Amos Lawrence. Lawrence and tariff won. Peter was Democratic candidate for mayor of Boston and was defeated.

In the early days the boys played along the Charles River. There were cows on the Common. In the crowd were Motley, the future historian, and others who became famous in later years. Any boy would dive to the bottom of the Charles River, with his clothes on, if a passing philanthropist would toss in a silver coin.

The rarest thing in those days was coin, something a boy almost never possessed. It was customary to drop copper pennies into the contribution box on Sunday morning, and you dropped them so that they would jingle and sound like a lot. Even in my boyhood, when the government issued ten-cent scrip, a boy with one of these pieces of paper in his pocket was regarded with respect by the other boys. Five cents was the usual limit.

There seemed to be almost a conspiracy among the elders to prevent boys from spending money, or even having any.

On one of our many trips downtown, when I acted as interpreter for my father, we met my famous uncle Peter. "Sidney," he said impressively, "save your pennies." I nodded. "Do you know how long I have worn this hat?" He pointed to his high, white silk hat, the long nap of which was turning yellow. I shook my head. "Ten years!" he said, and looked anxiously into my face to see if he had driven home the great lesson of the day: Save! I thought he didn't have the winning smile and the look of calm on his face that I was so used to in my father. Perhaps his great wealth was a burden to him.

When my father was ten years old he gradually lost his hearing. It may have been the diving into the Charles. He retained his ability to talk all his life. If lip reading had been understood in those days he need never have been educated as a deaf mute. But there was no such thing then, and so he was sent to Hartford to study with Dr. Gallaudet.

After graduation he followed in his father's footsteps and went to work for Uncle Sam, first in the Customhouse and then in the Post Office—forty years, all told.

There was a dignity in those days superior to wealth. Wealth was a new thing, dignity was a heritage. I have often heard that when the family gathered on Sunday afternoons at Number 41, as was the weekly custom, Grandfather presided with calm sureness, unaffected by the importance and wealth of some of his children. Discussions verging on disputes were not allowed; only gentleness and kindness were tolerated.

My father had the finest character I have ever known. His life was entirely at the service of others. If he had any personal desires I never knew it. His interests seemed to be wholly outside himself. His was the happiest nature one could imagine, and the sunniest. He was fifty-four when I was born, so that I really knew him only when he was old.

Always on our trips downtown old friends of earlier days would stop us and I would have to hear those tales of how wonderful he had been all his life. They seemed really to love him, and I was constantly astonished to see how many had learned the deaf-mute language just on his account.

My parents' first child, George, was born in 1856. The great question was: Could he hear? There was suspense. All the relations waited anxiously—it takes time to find out these things. Finally the answer came: Yes, he could! When he was three, a beautiful boy, he was accidentally scratched on the eye by a playmate. After much severe medical treatment he died of inflammation of the brain.

I have never been able to conceive of what my father and mother must have suffered, but I do know they never allowed this sorrow to darken the lives of my sister and myself. Only once did my mother ever tell me the whole story.

My sister was born some time after George's death. Yes, she too could hear. She became the sunshine of the family. She was called Georgiana.

In 1864 I was born. More suspense. Yes, I had good, big, healthy ears and could hear wonderfully! All our relations rejoiced over these children who could hear, and each member wanted to be the one who taught us to talk. It was rather trying. But the language of parents comes first, and I know I could talk in the sign language before I could speak.

In 1869 my uncle Sidney died. As an importer he had traveled much in Europe. Family tradition represents him as often acting for the United States government, unofficially. He left annuities of two thousand dollars each to his poorer brothers and sisters, and five hundred dollars a year to each of their children, the bulk of his estate to be divided after fifty years among his three nephews who bore the name of Homer, in the hope that one of them would make the name of Homer distinguished.

So far as his circle was concerned, music was apparently nonexistent. There had been a distinguished amateur musician in the family in the preceding generation. Daniel Rea was the best singer of his day and was the first in America to sing the tenor arias from the Handel oratorios. He sang the Welcoming Ode, when Washington made his famous visit to Boston in 1791. Yet, until the Boston Symphony Orchestra was founded, and listening to music became a social obligation, I never heard him mentioned.

When I was three, my father bought a little house at 27 Appleton Street, the first we had ever owned. The joy of my parents in this tiny house was without limit and unending. Uncle Sidney held the mortgage, which he canceled at his death. Then the improvements began. Father's passion was for the outside of the house—new basement entrance, new concrete cellar, new rear extension, new roof, etc. Mother loved the inside—new pearl paper with crimson border, Gothic rosewood parlor furniture, a Miller square piano. For fifteen years these little changes went on. The house was my parents' great joy—and also my sister's and mine; we acquired that wonderful sense of the sanctity of home, which has had such a great part in the forming of American character. To make a home in a wilderness was the first American job; no other civilized people had ever had this task, and home took on a new meaning in our country. In European countries land had been preempted and homes were held on sufferance. Here, no nobility parceled out its vast estates; land was free and ownership was complete. We should do well to study the things that have made us what we are, and guard our heritage. Americans are famous homemakers. They make real homes in every country in the world. It took an American to write "Home, Sweet Home." There is nothing accidental about this, and creating a love for home in their children is the first traditional task American parents have.

Our little family was a close corporation. Perhaps the fact that our parents could not talk freely with their neighbors had something to do with this, but there were other things. They were so proud of their speaking children that they forgot to assume that pose of superiority which so many parents think necessary. They treated us as companions, often deferred to our judgment, and frankly showed us that respect and confidence which all children crave. In my father's case this companionship was to continue for twenty years, in my mother's, for forty, and the fact that it began in this spirit of intimacy was an unspeakable blessing to us all.

When I was eleven father retired from his government position (he was then sixty-five), and that brought us all still closer together. Having their father home most of the time is an unusual experience for young children. It gives a different tone to family life. I believe that many children suffer from lack of intimate contact with the balanced mind of a man, and even when they mature and take their place in the world they still have to learn the point of view of men. In musical education the pupils often have during lessons the undivided attention and close personal influence of a great master, but in general education this is rare.

Father's interest was almost entirely concentrated on his family. He knew that his annuity would cease with his death, and he wished to make provision for mother, who was seventeen years younger and would, of course, live much longer than he. But he never allowed this problem to affect the joyous carefree life of his children. It was his problem, not theirs. His other interests lay in politics and current events. He read three newspapers every day.

Mother's interests were entirely different. Blessed with a romantic nature and unbounded enthusiasm, she sought out everything that had emotional color or sensation. She took us to every spectacular play—and there were many in those days—every circus, every important exhibition of pictures. I remember at the time of the great Boston fire, she got a special police permit and took me, a boy of seven, inside the fire lines into the heart of the burning district. Father, of course, was helping the government night and day.

She made us stand on corners or high steps for hours, to see processions, parades, great men, and national figures pass by. Her religious faith was absolute, and her telling of Bible stories in the sign language was intense with grace and beauty.

The truth is that she was naturally musical. Her sense of rhythm was perfect. While at school she had been taught to dance, and the climax of all children's parties came when we induced her to do the national dances of different countries for our little guests.

Later, when I was forming my class in Boston, she went with me every Saturday night to the Boston Symphony concerts. Every nuance of the conductor's baton and the bowing of the string players, and, also, the vibrations, to which she was peculiarly sensitive, held her spellbound. She would sit motionless for two hours, her eyes glued on the orchestra, an enraptured expression on her face. It was very moving. Some folk are musical, some are not, and nothing can change either sort.

Some weeks after my brother George was born, came the news of the birth of the Prince Imperial of France. This event was hailed by the whole world, but to my mother it had a special significance. He was born on the same day, almost at the same hour as George! From this moment began an intensive study of the crowned heads of Europe, beginning with Napoleon and Eugénie. I remember albums filled with photographs of kings, queens, princes, and princesses, in various costumes, singly, in tender family groups, some as heroic military leaders, others as exemplars of domestic virtue. Mother became a royalist snob. She never doubted the divinity of kings. She knew all the intermarriages of royal families. Years later, when we were visiting some obscure German palace, she would explain the distant relationship of the owner to Queen Victoria.

Once, in London, I took her to the Crystal Palace. A chorus
of ten thousand sang *The Messiah*, but our seats were close to
the royal box. Prince Edward and Princess Alexandra were
there, and royalty won over music. It was a night of nights for
mother! Years later, when Louise sang Amneris at Covent Garden and the Prince and Princess were again present, Louise won
out. To visit a performance by my wife was, to mother, the
ultimate experience.

As we children grew up it was my sister who set the pace. I
copied her in everything. She became a great reader, and I
followed suit. She had piano lessons, and I learned to play all of
her pieces. Very soon she became a "high-brow," a real one. The
British writers became our passion. First Dickens, then Thackeray, then Shakespeare—the whole of Shakespeare. As she grew
older we turned to the Romantic poets—Byron, Burns, Moore,
Keats; then to translations—Chapman's Homer, Carlyle's translations of Jean Paul Richter and E. T. A. Hoffmann. Then the
essays of Emerson and Carlyle became all-absorbing. This led to
a struggle with philosophy, and finally Herbert Spencer came
along to show us that we were living in an abyss of ignorance.
George Eliot appeared, and the world was breathless.

All this took many years. Always school had second, third,
or fourth place in our thoughts. School was an interruption
which took away our precious reading time. Lessons were done
in a rush in order to save time.

We little realize what time means in a young life, how important a half-hour can be. We older ones ask a favor or suggest an
errand, interrupt in some way, and misunderstand the reluctance,
the tragedy of giving up time. Youth has very little time in
which to do those things it most longs to do. In that crowded
period of life fascinations beckon seductively from every side.
They must be sternly resisted. Why? The injustice of this insistent monopoly of a child's whole time sinks deep in the young
heart.

After a year in the Boston Latin School came a year at Andover Academy, which was disappointing. The teachers seemed distant and aloof in manner, and the pupils resentful. No boy that I knew understood why he was made to work so hard. No mention was made of music, and I saw no musical instrument. The atmosphere was dry and bleak. There was no charm, no romance. Youth without romance! What a distortion! I believe that what the pupils needed was closer personal contact with their teachers.

In the study of music, charm, romance, imagination, vistas, goals just ahead, conscious progress—all lead the fascinated pupil on to joyous, almost superhuman efforts. The fact that he is usually alone with his teacher during his lessons has much to do with this. Music students practice six or seven hours a day and are happy.

I think all educators can learn something from the spirit in which music is taught.

At Andover there was a theological seminary with a wonderful library. Two or three of us knew of it, and to us it was a green oasis in a dreary waste. The librarian understood boys and helped us.

I was now sixteen and was beginning to realize that life was a problem. I expected enthusiasm everywhere. My parents were enthusiastic, my sister even more so; everything we did together was done in this spirit. My idea of a teacher was of one filled with enthusiasm for his subject, and able to infuse his pupils with this same sacred fire.

Instead, I found all subjects treated as mechanical tasks to be gone through with patiently for the sake of something beyond. What was that something beyond? None of us seemed to know. It was called Education, and could, perhaps, have been called Discipline. It seemed to presuppose the necessity of our spending our time at something irksome, tiresome, and disagreeable. Discipline must be bought at the cost of the joy of living, cheerfulness, enthusiasm. Unless one could suppress these unnecessary and irritating attributes of Youth, one could not discipline the mind and arrive at education.

Suppression of these vital forces cannot endure forever. Wise age has always dictated to foolish youth, but youth has a wisdom of its own, an irrepressible creative genius of which joy is an essential part, and this must finally find full expression. Youth, with its keen sense of values, aesthetic and practical, will win out in the long run!

I had two wonderful experiences before this time—two revelations, as it were. In 1878 Dwight L. Moody built a tabernacle a few blocks from our house. The entire neighborhood joined his congregation of many thousands. We boys could not understand his theology; but, with the almost unerring instinct of childhood, we could feel his sublime love of humanity. It won us. It is always this way. When a man's love for others goes far beyond his love of himself, he becomes a magnet for those around him. William Booth, Karl Marx, Tolstoi, Lenin, Gandhi, Ibsen, Shaw —all men of this kind have the same experience. We boys loved Moody's self-forgetfulness and came to feel that it was incarnate in Jesus.

The other great experience was the art of Edwin Booth. The old Boston Museum Stock Company had been a joy; Warren, Mrs. Vincent, Charles Barron, Annie Clarke, and the rest, we adored. The old *Evangeline* cast, Crane, Goodwin, Dixey, Golden, Eliza Weathersby, and the favorites from England— Willie Edouin, Marie Williams, and others—all were beloved.

But with Booth it was different. He transformed the stage into life.

What went on on that stage was really happening; the street outside the theatre, the theatre, we ourselves, might or might not be real; there was some doubt about that. The art of making the unreal more real than life; the psychology of an imaginary character more important than one's own personality; the period of another century more truly existing than our own faded day; the tragic destiny of Hamlet, Lear, Macbeth, more excruciatingly vital than the happenings to any mere hundred or thousand living beings, imagination, art—what are they? We didn't know; we do not yet know.

Many of us went to every performance, including the two weekly matinees, during Booth's seasons in Boston, hung on every word, knew every inflection. We talked about it through the rest of the year. To us he was a revealer of profound truth, of things which could not be known in any other way, of mysteries which would lie hidden from humanity, not for a space but for all eternity, if we did not seize them in these precious moments. The earnestness of children is almost pathetic, but they have a vital sense of truth, of the value of the moment. They seek reality and try to catch it on the wing. They do not know the meaning of complacency, and struggle painfully in the darkness. A gleam of light is a ray from heaven. The written word—yes, wonderful, but the spoken word from Booth, oh, hold it, grasp it, do not let it go!

How those who listened to Jesus must have felt! I think it was the young who never forgot.

II

1881–1882

I WAS SIXTEEN AND THOUGHT THINGS
over. There was Boston—it was cold, material. There was Harvard
—that meant Greek. I had read the Greek plays in translations;
in five years I would read them in Greek. Five years! It was a
lifetime.

Browning went to the University of London. To be sure, he
only stayed there one year, but he went to the University of
London. He was, at that moment, our wisest man, our prophet,
and there must be some reason why he went to the University
of London.

I went to my father and told him that I wanted to go to London, that I thought there was some other way to get that prized
thing, an education. My father was a very great man. He did not
want me to go; he would miss me. But he understood my desire
and sympathized with my passionate feelings. He looked at
things in a broad way and was not sure I must be wrong because
I was young.

I sailed from New York on the *Bolivia*, Anchor Line, toward
the end of October, 1881. I had never known anyone who had
crossed the ocean; it was an almost unheard-of experience in
those days. I was leaving the New World and going to the Old
World, a totally different world, strange, surprising, superior,
older, and wiser. I was very ignorant and wholly unaccustomed
to meeting people outside of our narrow circle. But I felt that
a country that could produce such writers must be a marvelous
place, and that is why I went.

The *Bolivia*, a large steamer of five thousand tons, was bound
for the port of London. So alive were my senses that every mo-

ment was packed with adventure. Each roll of the ship had a
thrill; the waves were mountainous; the precision of the English
sailors fascinated, the officers awed me. I had never seen an
ocean steamer or an Englishman.

> Sing me a song of a lad that is gone;
>   Say, could that lad be I?
> Merry of soul he sailed on a day
>   Over the sea to Skye.

What intense meaning in Stevenson's verse! The soul of a boy!
A very kind and very strong-willed young Englishman ordered my immediate future. I must not live in a hotel in London.
I must live in a residential club that he knew of. He would introduce me. It was at the corner of Cursitor Street and Chan-
cery Lane. Magical names! I could see them on the printed page
of this or that book of Dickens and Thackeray. Names coming
to life—that was to be my experience for the next few months.

It was an inexpensive club where a number of professional
men lived. I had my September quarterly annuity of one hundred and twenty-five dollars in my pocket. The next installment
would reach me in London about January 1. I felt as rich as
Croesus. My father had saved a part of my annuity each year,
ever since it began. We had a tacit understanding that I was not
to touch this fund except in extreme necessity. I had drawn
sixty dollars for my steamship fare.

At the club I was eyed from under bushy eyebrows and
through monocles for several days. I felt very humble. Then I
was adopted. A barrister took me to the law courts, an army
officer took me to see the Guards, a reporter, who became a real
friend, made me his companion on his assignments. We took
strange trips to forbidding places and mysterious quarters, always at night.

All day I hunted out places for myself, haunts of Goldsmith, streets where heroes and heroines of beloved novels had lived. It was strange to look at a house and imagine Becky Sharp or Captain Rawdon Crawley coming out of the door, when these personages had never really lived. Fiction is not fictitious to the young; it is reality.

Pendennis and Colonel Newcome really lived in London. If they didn't, then London wouldn't be the same place.

At the club there lived a Mr. Green, who was the music critic of the London *Daily News*. We gradually became acquainted. There was a piano in the dining room, and as the room was empty in the afternoon he began playing for me. He grew more interested and gave more and more time to it. He played the whole of *The Messiah* through. It was enthralling. I didn't know such things could be. After several weeks he took possession of the situation. I must study music. I should go straight to Leipzig where he had studied. I should give my life to music, it was my sacred duty, I was born for that and nothing else!

Music! I could understand books, but music—it was a strange, exotic land, a far-away world where no common American boy could expect to live and breathe. Music! The very last thing I should ever think of knowing anything about. Musicians were like Martians, beings from another planet, magicians gifted with marvelous powers which could not be explained.

It is wonderful, the way those Europeans feel about us, prosaic Americans that we are. We can do anything! Many years later, when my wife and I arrived in Paris, the Frenchmen who heard her sing said, "An opera singer!" The last thing we had heard before leaving Boston, and this from a great authority, was, "Sidney, you know there are no roles in opera for Louise's voice."

It would be interesting to know how many Americans—doctors, surgeons, painters, sculptors, singers, pianists, violinists, and composers—owe their careers to European encouragement, to the confidence created in them by some European, or by some European public. Are we cowards in our approach to artistic life? Are we so oppressed by the banality we see around us that we lose all power of perception and must ever remain blind to the ineffable spark of talent or genius which glows fitfully in our midst, glows only to be crushed out?

Are we so oppressed by distorted religious conceptions that we are convinced that in this life we must grub, only in the next can we fly?

If so, let us remember, with a shock, that the first great thing Jesus did was to prove to all the world that men had genius, common men, fishermen, even a taxgatherer and a persecuting fanatic. Hope, not hopelessness, was his good tidings. A religion which crushes is no religion.

Or are we so soaked in barter that we can see nothing until we see the dollar beyond it? Does genius look like fantastic abnormality, freakish, abortive, until we discover its relation to some market? Good business. Is that the only eye we have? Is that the overdeveloped sense which deadens all others?

If so, let us wake up. The world is full of things that in their conception, creation, and fulfillment have no relation to barter and business—things too precious to be priced. No currency has been devised to measure them. If such surpassing things be, we cannot afford to lose the chance of finding them in our midst. They may be there, they must be there. Let us search diligently, hope, foster, encourage, develop that sixth sense of discovery— discovery of genius.

This English gentleman had given up a part of every day, for several weeks, for the purpose of looking me over, testing me out, not because I could do anything but because he thought he saw something. In all my nine years at school I had never had one word of personal conversation with a teacher, not even in the year when I did two years' work in one. Personal interest is what boys need. It might take time away from business, there might be fewer automobiles, but there would be better boys.

There are no magic mirrors in which boys can discover their subtle qualities, their hidden potentialities. And if there were, boys would not use them. They are far too diffident; besides, it is not their job. It is no one's job to think about himself. The less of this the better. We must think about one another; it is healthier and the surest way to results. Personal interest from another means more strength, courage, comfort, for the boy.

His elders say to the boy: "Discover your talent, develop it, find your job. If you make a mistake, you suffer." At the threshold of life we give him the most difficult task that exists. We wash our hands of it. We even create obstacles and establish a barometer of success, called "education," which does not fit all temperaments. Is it strange that an inferiority complex so often attacks youth?

It may seem surprising that I never found an inferiority complex among deaf mutes. Their mental attitude was always the same: joy and gratitude at being able to share in the life of their speaking brethren, and humility before the frankly acknowledged superiority of five full senses. Gratitude and humility make for character, and I have never known happier people. All of them (and I knew many) had had a great deal of personal interest showered upon them, love, solicitude, attention—all those things that give strength and courage.

Mr. Green's dictum troubled me. I had no illusion about music, and I knew something of its difficulties. I knew I was too old to begin such a study and that, at best, I could only look forward to very mediocre success, that I should always be handicapped by the time I had lost. But I had been very much moved by the music I had just heard, and it was something to be told that you showed talent for anything. Finally, I decided to go to Leipzig and try the matter out.

My plan became known about the club, and our little German waiter, Emil, came to me and begged me, with tears in his eyes, to take him with me to Germany. He had come to England to learn English. His salary was but six shillings a week, and he had to buy his own dress suits. He had no money and wanted to go back to his home in Thuringia. He asked me to visit his family in their peasant home. "Peasant" had a primitive and remotely suggestive sound to my American ears.

I went on a cheap steamer to Hamburg; he went on a cheaper. Suddenly a foreign language began to rattle around me, the first I had ever heard. No boy can stand hearing strange noises like that; he simply learns the language.

We traveled fourth class on a slow train. Fourth class meant a boxcar without seats: you sat on your bag. All night long peasants got in, carrying their live fowl, eggs, cheeses, to the next market town. The men did all the talking, and just as they seemed about to fight they all laughed! Irritating not to know this language; I resolved to learn it. If you want a boy to learn something, put him where ignorance of that thing is a handicap: he will learn it.

Every few hours the peasant costumes changed. Emil could tell where we were by the costumes. These peasant girls are willing to dress like every girl in town, but not like a girl from another town.

The next afternoon we arrived at Weissenfels, in the heart of the Thuringian Forest. Emil's sister met us. She dragged my big Saratoga trunk onto her sled. I tried to help, but Emil said she would feel hurt if I did: it was woman's work. She harnessed herself in with the big dog, chattering and laughing all the while, and together they dragged our baggage over the snow to Emil's village home, three miles away. Three days from London, and a totally different world! Inconceivably different. All that I knew went by the board. I might be quite a boy in Boston; here I was a heathen in a carefully regulated civilization.

Emil's home was one of fifty tiny, plastered houses, packed tightly together in a circle. Everyone walked a distance to the patch of ground which he tilled. The real objective was sociability, and to gain this they lived close together. The inn was the village clubhouse and was filled every night. The women knit and whispered, the men played games and talked and laughed. A mug of beer, with a pewter cover, lasted an hour. At ten o'clock they went home. I thought of the lonely farmers on the New Hampshire hills, cut off from their distant neighbors by snowdrifts, reading their weekly papers and turning in at eight o'clock to save the kerosene. Sociability is a good objective, after all.

The second afternoon, Emil's older brother, a giant, staggered into the kitchen, his eyes almost closed. He hardly noticed me and went at once into a little room off the kitchen, threw himself on a cot with his clothes on. There he slept for fourteen hours without moving. Such fatigue I have never seen. He worked in a sugar factory in the near-by town. His hours were eighteen hours on, eighteen hours off. The work was hard and only a very strong man could do it. He had four very happy hours the next morning, and, strangely, was one of the jolliest fellows I have ever seen. But it broke your heart to see him go off to work again; you knew he would come home almost blind and speechless with fatigue, a pitiable sight.

Our meals were always the same: black bread, boiled potatoes, cottage cheese, with occasional beets or carrots. On Sunday we had a pot of bean soup out of which each one of us fished one small piece of meat. It was a kind of ceremony, and no one spoke. There was an atmosphere of intense thankfulness at having *meat*, a thing no one should expect.

After three weeks Emil and I went up to Leipzig, he to find a job, I to look into this thing called music.

I had learned a great deal in three weeks. Men have often asked me this question: "How do you teach children the value of money?" I have only one answer. I say: "Bring them into close association with the poor, either through social service work or in some better way. Once they realize what one dollar, five dollars, ten dollars, will do for the very poor, their idea of the real meaning of money will rest solidly on this basis."

I had seen real happiness in the simplest surroundings. Cheerfulness, patience, industry—this was the atmosphere. The daughter's village costume, her best dress, would last for many years, perhaps a lifetime. The father and mother asked nothing but to finish their lives as they had always lived them. There were no unfulfilled desires, no sad regrets, no wish for wealth or ease. I have always been intensely grateful for the privilege of knowing these people and living with them.

Leipzig, the home of music! It had at that moment a prestige above all cities of the world. This was the heritage of Schumann, Mendelssohn, and Ferdinand David, but I knew nothing of this. I simply knew there was something here and I must find it. My money was almost gone, and it would be two months before the next installment came. I should have to do some careful planning.

I rented a room in the apartment of a business man. He and his wife took me very seriously. They had never seen an American before, or a grown boy of any kind who couldn't speak German. It was a disgrace (*eine Schande*) and should not be! They took it to be their solemn obligation to teach me German. At all odd moments of the day they taught me, and in the evenings we often went out to restaurants. It was a continuous lesson. Their joy at my progress was boundless. In three months I talked German fluently.

Bayard Taylor, I believe, tells of acquiring a practical command of a new language in a month. It is a simple matter of ear training.

I prowled around the crooked, narrow streets and quaint restaurants of old Leipzig. One day I came across a group of American boys. They were music students and gave me a royal welcome. They asked me to join their *Stammtisch*. (The *Stammtisch* is a wonderful German institution. It is simply a reserved table in a restaurant, around which the same friends gather every day. I have heard old men boast of their *Stammtisch* at which the same group had met for thirty and forty years. I was still learning that sociability, *Gemütlichkeit*, was always the great objective.)

I explained my purpose in coming to Leipzig. My new friends were sympathetic, but they knew the difficulties. There were discussions and conferences lasting several days. It was a serious and delicate subject: a boy's whole future was involved.

Finally, they decided it was too late. It would take me one year, perhaps two, to prepare for the entrance examinations of the Leipzig Conservatory of Music. It was already too late to do much that year; besides, my money had given out, and I had no piano. Only one boy, Carl Hauser of New York, held out any hope. I think his gentle nature could not bear to inflict such disappointment.

But why all this hesitation and fine feeling? Because music is such a lofty art. Only perfection is recognized, and musicians dedicate themselves to music in humility and grateful service. If architects rebuilt in each town, year by year, the historic masterpiece of architecture they would feel humble. Musicians rebuild the cathedrals of Beethoven, the Saintes Chapelles of Mozart, the Parthenons of Bach every year in every city.

How would our painters feel if the great pictures of Leonardo, Rembrandt, and the rest were painted, in their midst, in all their perfection? They would feel humble, and their own pictures would not seem so important. Musicians repaint exquisitely, wherever they go, the tone pictures of Schubert, Schumann, and Brahms.

Preachers, doctors, and lawyers would feel a proper humility if the greatest masters of all time worked with them daily in their churches, hospitals, and courts of law.

Musicians are always in the presence of the Most High. They give their lives to making the Gospel of Music known throughout the world, and their anxious, their only thought is: Can they do it well enough! If they reap fame in the doing, they are happy enough; but the central purpose remains the same. It is not they but the masters who count.

The fact that some men have discovered that they can exploit this purpose commercially should confuse no one. These men open up new fields for musicians, and in doing so they may advance the missionary work or they may retard it. Always the true nature of music will remain the same: a sublime message of infinite power, to be spread throughout the world in a spirit of humility and devoted service.

Although I was a hopeless case, technically, my new friends determined to do everything in their power that would help me musically. They had come to Leipzig to study with Schradieck, the world-famous teacher of the violin. John Beck of Cleveland would specialize in quartet playing, Schramm of St. Louis hoped to be a violin soloist, etc. They all had the entrée to the rehearsals of the Gewandhaus Orchestra, and they planned to smuggle me in. I met them outside the hall, and we all walked in together talking loudly in English. If I could not be a music student I could at least look like one. There in the dark gallery of the old Gewandhaus a new life began, a new and endless world slowly unfolded.

The boys, with bated breath, told me that Karl Reinecke was the conductor. He raised his stick, and they played a Beethoven symphony. I had never heard a symphony or an orchestra. Oh, the grandeur, the power, the beauty, the infinite meaning of this new world! I had, literally, suddenly arrived in heaven! It would be profanation for me to attempt to write more on this personal and, to me, holy experience, and I shall not do so.

From this moment I haunted the Gewandhaus. My face became known, and I walked in boldly. To this day I prefer rehearsals to concerts. Audiences are a disturbing factor, a disconcerting influence, often an intrusion in an atmosphere of sanctity.

It is a mistake to think that music was written for audiences: it was written for kindred souls. Audiences are merely people who are allowed the privilege of sharing in the mysteries, if they can. In fairness to the art, they should prove their fitness, or be educated to some point of intelligent apprehension. Music should be as exclusive as the Communist Party in Russia. Educational facilities can always be provided, but they should be recognized as such.

The sight of a bored tourist in an old cathedral is no worse than that of a bored, soul-seared listener at a great performance of great music. The audience I love is the one that goes to the Metropolitan Museum of Art to hear David Mannes and his orchestra. Although ten thousand may be standing (there are no seats) it is rarely that one sees an indifferent or blasé face.

At the Gewandhaus, Beethoven, Mozart, Schubert, Schumann, and Mendelssohn made up most of the programs. Symphonies, overtures, and concertos followed in rapid succession. Hearing rehearsals meant hearing many of the works played two or three times. Orchestras required more rehearsing in those days. The technique of the modern orchestra is quite a new thing. Instrumental virtuosity is one of the marvels of our age, and I only wish the world could realize it. The miracles we hear in our concerts are too often accepted as a matter of course. Fortunately, there is, in musicians that eternal love of art to spur the effort on to higher and higher achievement.

Music is volcanic in its nature and goes on and on of its own volition, regardless of sunshine or rain, social patronage, popular applause or condemnation. The efforts of society to take unto itself responsibility for these musical outbursts are tragically funny. Music, like the earthquake, has an origin all its own, and happens when least expected. Musicians are simply willing slaves of this magnetic and mystical power and partake of its nature.

I was surely the happiest boy in the world that spring. I

walked on air. My money gave out; but my landlady brought me a hearty breakfast every morning, and at noon I went to the restaurant where Emil worked. We had a little pantomime. He led me to one of his tables, hung up my coat, showed me the bill of fare and, with my approval, brought me the regular dinner. He then brought the bill, wrote the amount (seventeen cents) in his little black book, helped me on with my coat, and bowed me to the door. Later in the spring Emil went to Switzerland and sent me back the balance of the money I had spent for him.

Years afterward in Boston one of my fellow music teachers came back from a trip through Europe with a tale that I had a great friend at the Frankfurter Hof, the biggest hotel in Frankfurt am Main. He was a tall, handsome fellow with a flowing blond beard. He was head porter of the hotel and paid ten thousand dollars a year for his position. He had nearly wept when he found my friend knew me, and sent all kinds of messages. He was married, had two children, was doing well. The next year another friend had the same experience. The last I heard of him was that he had become part owner of a big hotel. Good old Emil! I hope the War didn't break his heart.

In April my money came, and I was rich again.

In the spring another great event took place. The Leipzig Opera gave a Wagner festival which included the Nibelungen Ring. Anton Seidl was the conductor and the great Hedwig Reicher-Kindermann was the dramatic soprano. Scaria, the great bass, was brought from Vienna, and Lederer, the tenor, from somewhere else. The excitement was intense. All everyday things seemed to cease. We American boys banded together and rushed the top gallery; center seats, front row, every time. No one could climb stairs as we could. Another new world burst forth! Not so subtle and poetic, not the tragedy of the inner life, as revealed by some of the music I had heard at the symphony rehearsals, but most intense, vivid, overwhelming in its grandeur, overpowering in the truths it drove home: the tragedy of human relationships, the fatality of gold lust, the beauty of purity of character, the inevitability of love!

We boys were in a dream; we talked over each performance till all hours of the night. We met the next day and began it all over again. We knew we should never hear these works again, all at one time. I, for one, never did. The stories, characters, and problems were real, and the music—the music was truth itself, an unveiling of fundamentals, a revelation of the primitive impulses and sources of all things. Music went beyond, where words could not go. It was all too wonderful. Life would never be the same again, the commonplace was banished from our several lives forever! Thus youth—always settling things for all time, jumping at immovable conclusions, disposing of age-long problems in a minute with cold, fixed inexorable finality! Blessed youth!

This was the end. I must hurry home before my money gave out and because my family looked for me. We renewed our *Brüderschaft*, my landlady wept, and the old towers of Leipzig, the Peterskirche, disappeared in the darkness.

I arrived in Boston early in June. The little street looked smaller, our house had shrunk to tiny proportions. My mother, father, and sister looked grander than ever! Such a reunion! It took days to tell it all. No one questioned my judgment. Music meant nothing in our home, but that made no difference. It had come to mean something to me, and that was all that mattered to them. I could talk German, and that meant nothing. Nobody ever talked German in Boston. But if I said it meant something, then it meant something. In our small family mutual trust was supreme.

We had four happy months together. My sister told me of the books she had read during my absence. I had traveled far, but I had seen no one half as beautiful as she was, and no one who lived in such a world of detached idealism. (We build worlds around ourselves as the caterpillar builds his cocoon, and we always hope to fly. Many things may intervene, but hope unfulfilled is better than no hope at all, and some part of our self-constructed world stays with us and sustains us.)

I had plenty of time to think things over. I struggled with that question which haunts many young men: had I wasted a year of my life? I was now hopelessly behind my class in school, and what had I in place of that? I finally decided that I had something and, with the encouragement of my family, I determined to see it through.

III

1882–1888

IN OCTOBER I WAS BACK AGAIN IN LEIPZIG,
hard at work. I was still only seventeen and had high hopes of
making up the time I had lost. I rented a room at the top of the
old Hôtel de Pologne in the Peterstrasse (fifteen dollars a month
with breakfast). It was up five long flights of stairs. This time
I had a piano, a Blüthner upright with a tone that sang like angel
voices.

Carl Hauser was my teacher, and I worked all day at piano
and harmony. Some of our crowd had gone home, and some
new boys had come. One friend, Charley Davidson, took the
room next to me. He was a disillusioned music student who had
given up in disgust, and looked on my efforts with cynical pity.

But he was a great pal, a philosopher, and a voracious reader.
His father was editor of a Detroit newspaper, and his sister,
who lived with their mother in another part of town, was studying with Schradieck. Maud Powell and Geraldine Morgan were
also in the class. This was the beginning of that wonderful succession of women fiddlers. All honor to these pioneers with their
great courage and great art! Some years later Schradieck came
to the United States. In Germany he was a great master, revered
by all; in America he was only a violin teacher known to a very
few. He died in Brooklyn. The indifference of Americans to
fine teachers is unique. One would suppose they could be bought
at any time with money like a commodity.

Two things happened this fall. I heard my first song recital.
The great Lieder singer, Herr Gustav Walter, came from Vienna
and gave a Schubert evening at the Gewandhaus, singing the
whole of the Winterreise. We were transported. What is a song

28

anyway? Why is it so powerful? What is the magic of lyric art? A thousand people held spellbound by an inexplicable beauty. A very small work just as potent as a symphony or a music drama. It seems a joy that lyric beauty will ever remain a mystery. Only an insensitive mind can attempt to explain, and to the sordid nature it will always be nonexistent. But to many it will be what it always has been, a secret and everlasting source of comfort—consolation, if you will—hope, inspiration, a beckoning star. From that evening, song had a new and infinite meaning.

The other experience was very personal. I was standing at my window watching the black crowd, far below, pushing along the narrow sidewalk. Suddenly I sank to my knees and prayed to God that I might do something, however small, for humanity. I was not in the habit of praying and could not explain my action. But from that moment human beings seemed but helpless souls, grouped around their homes, unaware of gathering storm clouds and unable to protect themselves from subtle forces and cruel destinies. The very poor seemed inarticulate; those better off, blinded in complacency; those still more powerful, hopelessly engulfed in selfishness and isolation. Humanity seemed a pitiful thing, needing help but unable to cry out; filled with desire but without hope or strength. These feelings have remained with me, and I always see mankind struggling in bonds.

Individually, men seem kind and considerate; in masses, they seem cold and implacable. Is it the consciousness of collective strength that breeds these qualities? Must cruelty always be the child of power? The problem to be solved by humanity appears to be the translating of the idealism of the individual into the life force of the mass.

In 1882 the shadow of the Great War was already on the earth. I did not know a German who did not speak of it with horror. Men hate war as many drug fiends hate drugs, with a desperate and ineffectual hate. It takes more than hate to change world habits. Nothing was known in those days of the fallacy of victory, the futility of war, community of interests and economic interdependence. A boy of today cannot possibly realize how new is the world in which he lives. This is a day of questioning and discussion. In 1882 boys did not question holy crusades and national destinies. These things lay like ether cones over a stupefied humanity; and fatalism held the world in a vise.

This new questioning suggests a possible road out of the morass of fetishisms in which we live; but questioning will not be enough. Questions must have answers. It may be that the day of wisdom is dawning, and that a new light is about to flood the world. If so, it will be glorious to be among the first to see it. The young have the best sight.

I worked on merrily for four months. Harmony was very easy and logical, and seemed to be merely a matter of good taste. Piano was difficult. My clumsy hands, gnarled and thickened from baseball and rowing, were obstinate. But at last they showed signs of yielding to the hours of practice, and Carl Hauser looked pleased and encouraged.

Then something happened. I came down with a queer sickness. It was really shingles, I believe, but I had no way of knowing this. Boys do not resort to doctors if they can help it. Finally the symptoms became alarming, and I was taken to a specialist, a Herr Professor with fifty patients waiting in his anterooms. When I lay on his table stripped to the waist, and he saw the little pink blisters at the end of each nerve, his eyes gleamed with joy. He threw open the double doors. "Herein, meine Herrschaften!" he cried, and the fifty patients came trooping in. "This is what Bismarck has!" he announced triumphantly. Bismarck! Magic name! Any American boy ought to be proud to lie still and suffer if he can show fifty Germans what Bismarck has! He ought to be glad to have this illustrious disease. The Germans looked at me admiringly. Americans went up in their estimation: they couldn't all have Indian blood—there must be a little blue blood mixed in. The Herr Professor held a clinic: the opportunity to lecture was too valuable to be lost.

Finally, when he was exhausted, he condescended to do something for me. As I was about to go he asked what had brought me to Leipzig and to him. Perhaps he thought I had come from New York to seek his advice; you can never tell what goes through a Herr Professor's mind. "Music student," I said.

"Music! Thou God in heaven! Music! Never! *Never!!* Your nervous system will never bear it, never support it. Impossible! It is finished!" he shouted, with all the emphasis, all the sublime finality and authority, which only a Herr Professor has at his command.

After a while I was well again, weak but free from pain. The blisters were little scars. It never occurred to anyone to doubt the truth of the Professor's death warrant.

The Germans knew. They were always right. They knew all about music, and all about health, too. My friends condoled with me—all except Charley Davidson. He congratulated me heartily. He had discovered that music was an hallucination, a very pretentious one, but really empty and insincere.

I was not merely disappointed; there was a sense of shock in my heart which I tried to cover up. The study of music is often very dangerous. Undoubtedly the good doctor was quite aware of this. The language of notes is so flexible and lends itself so easily to speed and intensity that emotional temperaments are often led into excesses which result in prostration. The great masters have shown that temperament must be balanced by a sense of proportion, a feeling for form, intellectual purpose, and fine command of oneself. Students are apt to ignore everything but emotional intensity, and the consequences are, sometimes, disastrous.

I had attempted a difficult thing and failed. The place for me was at home. I had only left home in order to study at a music center. Now that I must find some other vocation there was no further reason to stay away. The call of home was very strong.

As this would probably be my last trip to Europe, I went with my chuckling Charley to see Paris and its art. His amusement at my dilemma was a life-saver, and I soon learned to accept my fate good-naturedly.

A wonderful month in Paris, and then home. Again a joyful reunion. No reproaches or regrets; only concern for my happiness.

Now ensued one of those struggles which are, often, so tragic in a young man's life; the choosing of a life work. I knew that this time my decision would be final, and I was anxious not to make a second mistake. There was, of course, always a faint hope of being a writer, and I resumed my literary studies more passionately than ever. I worked in Bates Hall, in the old Boston Public Library. That dear, classic hall had more charm and good cheer than any other place I have ever known. You left all doubt, all care behind as you climbed the stairs and entered its door. The silence and peace made it a sanctuary. Books are the most steadying influence in human life. Other things may excite and disturb, but books bid one go slowly, think deeply, and be willing to learn from others. They abide and outlive the passing turbulence and suggest eternity.

Another possible choice was architecture. Richardson had recently built the new Trinity Church, and a new hope was in the air; just such a hope, in a small way, as must have filled Italy in the early Renaissance. I read Fergusson through, and some of Viollet-le-Duc.

My father was concerned about my future and took me to see his old friends, Charles Hovey, the dry-goods merchant, and W. W. Clapp, the brilliant editor of the Boston *Journal*. Both were sympathetic, because of their affection for my father.

At that time a young man had come to Boston and shown the musical world that it was possible to be a great artist, and yet be perfectly natural, sincere, original, and free from affectation of any kind. It was a thrilling event. The Boston Symphony had been founded, and music had become respectable; but it was still an exotic art born of the passions of foreign lands. Could New England have anything to say? George Chadwick had quietly shown that it could, that there was a poetry in prosaic, repressed New England which could find expression in that strange medium called music. The performance of his *Rip van Winkle* overture by the Boston Symphony Orchestra can be called a landmark in American musical life.

Young men were swept away by the new vista suddenly opened to them. Music had always been a question of execution, technique, interpretation. Now, overnight, it became a creative art in which a poet might, possibly, have a place.

There had always been many poets in New England, but very few technicians. I could not resist this new hope, and my decision was made for me.

I was nineteen when I began studying with Mr. Chadwick. He wanted me to enter Rheinberger's class at the Royal Music School at Munich the following September, and planned my studies accordingly. I could not enter without an instrument, so he taught me to play the organ. Theory was my principal study, and in that winter we did harmony, counterpoint, double counterpoint, all forms of canon and simple fugue. Music is an easy study under a great master, and by summer I was firmly on my feet. No problem in harmony or counterpoint could disturb me.

What a change! The confidence and assurance given me by one man, to whom music was an art, not merely technique.

Europe again, but this time not alone! My father, mother, and sister should go with me. I knew I could show them amazing things, surprise them in a thousand ways and make them happy. The weeks before our sailing were hectic, and on the steamer I came down with rheumatic fever.

But this did not spoil our trip. Sickness is only a passing nuisance to the young. I limped around Antwerp and gloried in the awe and thrills of my family. Then we went up the Rhine to Wiesbaden, where I took the cure. I must be ready for those entrance examinations, and get the stiffness out of my legs.

In September we were settled in Munich, and I passed the examinations. Three cheers! I was launched, and nothing could stop me now.

The next three years were those of a conventional music student. Rheinberger's class was simply a place where beautiful counterpoint was written. If you were wise, you could learn. No home work was assigned beyond the careful study of what was done in the class. All original work done by a student was self-imposed. What he wrote at home was read in silence in the class by Rheinberger and was never heard by his twenty classmates. All the classwork was done on a blackboard, and the piano was rarely touched.

In that silence the most exquisite counterpoint was written on the board either by Rheinberger or by one of the students. The tension was tremendous, and after two hours (our class was from eight to ten in the morning) we were exhausted.

What a strange sight for an outsider who should occasionally look in! A long bare room badly lit by gas. A small gray-bearded man with burning eyes and expressive hands; twenty absorbed students watching a blackboard on which notes were being written, waiting breathlessly in absolute silence for the next progression: a beautiful passage in the alto, a thrilling touch in the tenor, a delicate, satisfying melodious step in this or that voice —the whole *sounding* wonderful. Sounding! When you could hear a pin drop? Yes, every student was listening, and the little white notes were sounding out clearly as they were written.

This class is typical of the *real* world of music, in which everyone waits anxiously for the next beautiful work, and cherishes, zealously, every beautiful work ever written. It is not in the public arena or amid the struggling tides of popular favor or disfavor that this little world lives and does its work. It lives in privacy and works in secrecy. Works of art are dragged into the limelight as diamonds are displayed in shop windows, but they are born and made in the recesses of the soul as diamonds are formed in the bowels of the earth.

Those who know music only in the bright light of publicity may easily mistake its true character. The bright light may even become more important than the work of art itself, and many who think they are worshiping art may find they are kneeling at the shrine of publicity. Paste and false pearls may seem more dazzling in the bright light than real jewels in obscurity, but the great music will ever remain true to itself, a music of genuineness and quality, in the creation of which humility, devotion, and gratitude are the dominating passions.

It would be interesting to know how many orchestral performances of their symphonies Beethoven and Brahms ever heard, how many times Bach heard his Passion According to St. Matthew, or Wagner his own music dramas. Was it frequency or quality of performance they valued most? Was it size of audience or sensitiveness of individuals that mattered? Surely, mere familiarity with a work means nothing. It may even dull the senses and breed indifference.

Ministers, dissatisfied with the way Jesus has been presented, are seeking truer ways of revealing him. Fine musicians are ever striving to present the works of the masters in a more convincing way. Wagner designed a Festspielhaus which he hoped would eliminate distracting influences. Certainly great works can be easily cheapened, even vulgarized, and it is probable that we have much to learn about the true conditions under which the message of music should be spread.

This little group of twenty lads from five countries, studying with a great master, striving for a touch of beauty in a simple exercise, and not caring which one found it, glorified the humble, dimly lit room in which they worked, and did their bit for music. They had no illusions about musical composition. I doubt

if a single member expected to write an original piece of music.
They were simply trying to develop the sense of the beautiful
within themselves and acquire, in humility, a little of the technique of the masters.

Composing was like climbing mountains; unless you climbed
one that had never been scaled you had not climbed at all. Of
course Everest and certain dizzy, sharp-pointed *aiguilles* were
always there—but who could attain the impossible? It was ef-
frontery even to attempt it.

Music was to them the newest religion, and its Bible was a
strong, well bound book, with no room left between the covers.
Who could ask that his little epistle be added? Lest any approach on such a course of folly, self-appointed watchdogs,
guardians of this new Scripture, sprang up all over the world
and infested every city. How they barked! Fortunately they
had no teeth and could not actually destroy, much as they might
wish to. But they could spread alarm!

In Boston, later on, I remember one loud bark, in particular,
when a little thief began climbing into the Symphony programs.
The good citizens trembled—an interloper, a destroyer of the
sanctity of Symphony Hall! Keep him out!

The trouble was, he had a friend on the inside, a crony, who
seemed to think more of him than he did of Boston itself. Good
Boston, dear Boston, which fed this crony and gave him something besides. Ungrateful servant! But you couldn't touch him
because he had a conductor's contract, and then, too, he was
deaf. That is, he couldn't hear the dogs barking.

Only one thing remained, Boston's last and proudest resource,
a chilling silence, a distant aloofness, a pained endurance. Too
bad that a few who loved this music disturbed the atmosphere
of this final and tremendous squelching! It might, otherwise,
have been effective. And who was this thief? He was a little
man who lived in far-off Vienna, a presumptuous upstart who
thought he could compose because he lived in the town where

Beethoven had lived, who tried to hide the poverty of his work in a murky, dusty cloud of noise. He couldn't fool Boston.

The name of this upstart was Johannes Brahms.

Such is the organized world of music—not the real but the outward world. The time to destroy the potential composer is in the beginning! Crush him—lest he, like the Communist, arise to disorganize a carefully constructed and complacent society.

I know nothing sadder than the welcome that awaits the young composer. We say to him: "Of course you know that you are ranking yourself with the masters. You are usurping the place on the program that one of them would otherwise fill."

If a famous Velásquez and a magnificent Rembrandt were to be shown, would we ask a young painter to hang his picture between theirs? He would resent it if we did. But the young composer must be heard just after Beethoven and just before Brahms, or not at all. We force an appearance of pretentiousness on him and give him no alternative.

We had a young composer in Munich that year who was a sort of Lochinvar. He saw through the powers that were and ignored them. They hated him bitterly and thoroughly, and felt badly for his father who was a fine musician. This tall and dreamy-looking young man was just my age, and I used to see him as I left my organ practice late in the afternoon. He was not a member of the faculty of the school but often used one of the rooms that I had to pass through. If he happened to be improvising he would smile but would not stop. He was a sort of champion: youth in revolt, as it were—all wrong, of course, but courageous.

One night he conducted a new work of his own, *Aus Italien*, at the Symphony concert. Bad enough to compose, but to conduct—with Hermann Levi, our great conductor, sitting right there! There was bitter feeling, and during the performance three of our music professors got up at the same moment and stalked out of the hall. Condemnation of the pseudo composer, and a feeling that an act of desecration had taken place, seemed to be everywhere. I am sure there were hopes in some quarters that he had been finally crushed. If he had had a more tender skin he might have been; but he was wise and had work to do. His name was Richard Strauss.

We have dragged art into the open and put the spotlight on it. We have honored it with publicity and put the yardstick of sensationalism on it. But art, like a sly wild animal, prefers the jungle and the shade. Art cannot be coaxed with a loud shout and gong. It has a way all its own and wanders where it will. Large bodies of directors seem to lose their authority, and society seems sheepish when there is a little thing, just a little thing, which cannot be found and cornered.

Art is a perfectly sane thing. It does not bow to pretension, condescension, hypocrisy, or commands. It is a law unto itself and, like religion, responds only to a sincere and simple faith. Unless we meet it halfway in its own spirit we cannot have it. Fortunately, there is plenty of faith in the world, and so there will be plenty of art. It may not be the kind society craves, but it will be the kind humanity needs.

Bach's carefully written copies of earlier masters, Beethoven's tribute to Handel—"The greatest of us all!"—Schumann's passionate search for Schubert's works, Mendelssohn's tireless labor for Bach, Liszt's loving devotion to the renegade, Wagner, Wagner's glorification of Beethoven, Schumann's impressive tribute to the young and unknown musical poet, Brahms, are classic examples of the brotherhood, the loving bonds of understanding and enthusiasm, the self-effacement and true humility of spirit that have made music what it is.

Those who look on music merely as an egotistical expression are far from the truth. It is not born of a desire for admiration, but of a passion for service. The beautiful thing is that real music can only spring from the purest sources. A skeptical and suspicious world that tries to read itself into art cannot change this fact; and until we change and meet the young in a spirit of trust and sympathy we shall not be doing our part toward the creation of great works. A cynical Cyclops eye in the middle of the public forehead is not a pretty sight or one of which to be proud.

Our class disbanded and started out. Many of its members attained distinction: Berwald at Syracuse University; Louis Victor Saar at Cincinnati; George Hamer at Lawrence; Pommer in Philadelphia; Cajani, the great pianist, in Florence, Italy; Howard Pierce, an equally great pianist in Dayton, Ohio; and Otto Singer as a world-famous musician.

The idealism of Rheinberger spread over the world. Such are the life and influence of a great teacher, underrated individual that he is.

Some of us went to Bayreuth, where we heard *Parsifal* and *Die Meistersinger*—an unforgettable experience, a wonderful last remembrance of Germany.

IV
1888–1895

I HURRIED HOME. I HAD NOT SEEN MY FAMily for two years, and during that time my sister had married Frederick L. Diman, a fine singer and conductor, and settled in New Bedford. My father and mother were, of course, living with her. Separation was undreamed of. Father had developed heart trouble, and we were anxious; but not until I arrived home did I realize how serious it was. His condition had been carefully concealed from me. I had intended returning to Rheinberger (my education was very incomplete—all I knew was how to write counterpoint), but I immediately gave this up and started in to organize a class in harmony, something they had not had in New Bedford.

Father, though feeble, was the same jolly soul he had always been; we resumed our nightly games of whist and picked up the other scattered threads. I convinced father that mother's future was assured, and he was satisfied.

Then our first sorrow came. Mother and sister had been closely confined and so, at my urging, they went to New York on a four days' trip. I slept with father, and one night he got up to walk up and down the room telling me, softly, not to let it disturb me. Suddenly he called in a loud voice, "Sidney, great pain!" I sprang out just in time to catch him in my arms. In a moment he was dead.

At a later time, when I was able to think about it, I could realize what a shock mother had been spared, and be glad it had come to me.

Our greatest concern, now, was mother. Father was seventy-seven when he died, but she was now only sixty. This shock and loss might break her down. Deaf mutes are very close to one another and it is not easy to realize the depth of their feelings.

Finally, I conceived a great plan. Mother and sister, who were tired out, should go to Italy and then travel through other European countries. Fred would join them in London in the spring, have lessons with William Shakespeare, the famous teacher of singing, and later they could all see the great Exposition in Paris, which would surely make mother happy. I would continue with my new classes and keep Fred company until he sailed.

It was a great plan and met with great success. Mother came back restored and ready for a new life which was to continue for twenty years. My sister and Fred came back thrilled and sparkling as a result of their experience.

It was now high time for me to turn what I had learned to account. New Bedford was too limited a field, although I had found some interesting pupils there. Two high-school boys, in particular, became fine musicians. James Corey is one of our best organists, and Winfred Goff, who worked with me for six years, became the leading baritone of the Savage Opera Company. He was such a fine musician that the entire production of *Die Walküre* was put into his hands. It was an achievement to adapt the theatres throughout the country to this difficult music drama, and to sing Wotan, too.

I planned to teach harmony in Boston. Mr. Chadwick thought very few pupils would pay anything for harmony lessons and advised me to take a church position as organist. This was the very thing I wished to avoid. I had substituted at one of the churches in New Bedford and loathed the sentimental, sanctimonious atmosphere that music was supposed to create. After the Bach preludes and fugues and the sonatas of Mendelssohn and Rheinberger, anything less majestic and profound than these seemed a profanation of that great and holy instrument, the organ.

At last we took the step. In the fall of 1889 my mother and I went to Boston and established ourselves in two studio rooms in the old Hotel Pelham at the corner of Tremont and Boylston streets. We rigged up a kitchenette and kept house.

I advertised in the Boston Symphony program and the Boston *Transcript*, "Harmony, Counterpoint and Composition"—and waited. It was an anxious time, but we had plenty of hope and knew the impossible would happen. And suddenly it did. Carl Baermann, our foremost pianist, who had been brought from Munich, sent for me and told me he had been advised from Munich to send his pupils to me for harmony lessons.

I knew this was Rheinberger doing something for me. I was filled with a deep and overwhelming sense of gratitude. The little gas-lit room and the three long years came back to me, and I felt repaid for all the hard work I had done. And so it is. As we go through life we meet a few great souls whose idealism stands as pure and immovable as a snow-clad peak. A word from them is enough. This recommendation from Rheinberger, four thousand miles away, meant everything. I felt this way, years later, when Puccini met me on the stairs, backstage, of the Metropolitan and told me what he thought of my wife's Orfeo.

In this way my class began; and soon I had pupils from a number of the best teachers—pianists, violinists, and singers. It was an interesting, devoted, and hard-working class. I soon found that each pupil had to be handled in an individual way. No set formula would do for all. Musical minds all vary, and the problem was to discover what would strengthen each pupil where he was peculiarly weak.

Violinists and singers, often, would think melodically, yet would be unable to think harmonically. Pianists would sometimes have a feeling for chords but very little sense of melodic flow. Rhythm, taste, fine feeling for form—each had to be emphasized as needed.

My class progressed. With those who advanced rapidly I used a little course in score reading. They bought the Bach chorals, arranged for piano, Peters edition, and wrote them out in score using the old soprano, alto and tenor clefs. These old clefs, which are such a bugbear for American students, were used for most of the work in Rheinberger's classes. They should be used freely here. The pupils played the chorals from the open score, and this answered a double purpose. They came under the influence of Bach's technical mastery and, most important of all, under the spell of the infinite beauty of this music. The Bach chorals are the pinnacle of all existing works in this form.

After this we took up the string trios of Beethoven, Opus 8, the string quartets of Mozart, and then went on to orchestral scores.

I soon found myself cramped for time in these short lessons, and organized a group for the study of symphonies. My pupils and a number of outsiders made up the class. The plan followed was so simple that I will venture to decribe it. We began with the last three symphonies of Mozart, and each member bought the piano score, arranged for two hands, Peters edition. With the score in hand they could follow intelligently and make marginal notes.

The first theme of a symphony was played and discussed. We tried to discover its beauties. Then the connecting passage leading to the second theme was taken up, and this much was played from the beginning. Then the second theme, and so on. The key succession and formal structure were sketched on a blackboard. It was interesting to see thirty copies of a Mozart symphony covered with guiding marks and marginal notes. I found that untrained amateurs could follow the study quite intelligently. The only novel features were the blackboard and the insistence on each pupil having a copy of the score. It is to these things that I attribute the clearness and success of the work. In three years we did all the symphonies of Beethoven, two of Schubert, four each of Mendelssohn, Schumann, and Brahms. By the time we came to the Brahms symphonies the class was able to do most of the analyzing.

During the following two years we took up Wagner's music dramas in the same way, studying the text and the evolution of the leading motives. We did *Tristan und Isolde* and the Nibelungen Ring. It was amazing to see twenty copies of the *Götterdämmerung* at one time. Scores of the Nibelungen Ring were comparatively rare in Boston in those days.

By this time our family was united again. We had sold the little house in Appleton Street and built a new house in Arlington, a few miles from Boston. We chose Arlington because my sister was living there. Mother was supremely happy in her new home.

In September, 1893, I was sitting one morning in my studio waiting for pupils to reappear, after the long summer, and cheerfully declare their intention of continuing their work. We music teachers used to meet every day at lunch and condole with one another on the dilatory, careless ways of pupils. They always kept us on the anxious seat.

I was particularly anxious this morning as I was to take my mother to the Chicago Exposition the following week, and might lose pupils by my absence. But expositions were almost a religion to mother, and the pilgrimage had to be.

Suddenly there was a knock at the door, and in walked one of my Arlington neighbors, a very beautiful and gracious matron whom I knew slightly. Behind her came a sort of younger edition of the same clan. They took my teaching chair and piano stool and monopolized the studio. There was a little chair by the door intended for hats, and I sat on that. I felt rather out of it. My neighbor explained that her sister had come to Boston from Philadelphia or some place, to study singing, but that she wanted to learn "all about music"; so she, my neighbor, had brought her sister to me. I smiled. Right place, of course.

We discussed lessons merrily until Sister suddenly asked my

neighbor: "What will it cost?" This was a dampener. We had quite forgotten that trifle as we talked of learning "all about music."

I murmured something about three dollars a lesson and Sister said abruptly to my neighbor: "Oh, I cannot pay that!" She never spoke to me. This was a dilemma. She had a little, Irish, turned-up nose, and a Scotch way of doing business.

She might be a good pupil, and it was September, the anxious month. Hanging on to my dignity, I finally told her she could have forty-minute lessons for two dollars each. She accepted this as no favor at all, and told her sister she thought she'd come.

I never did succeed in getting those lessons down to forty minutes. In a canny, Scotch way she brought more work than I could handle in that time and showed a wicked glee in all the overtime she got for nothing. To get even with her I made her work very hard, and this made it necessary for me to give her an extra lesson occasionally, without charge, to give me time to correct her work. She always won out in the end.

She was the alto in George Chadwick's choir, at the First Universalist Church, which was the best choir in Boston at that time. Elizabeth Hamlin was the soprano, Herbert Johnson the tenor, and young Myron Whitney, Jr., the bass. The choir took a modest pride in its excellent singing. It is useless for the great opera stars who live on the heights to think that they have any monopoly of the lovely pride which music engenders.

Music is glorious in its impartiality and distributes pride all up and down the line. All those who have anything to do with music share in this beautiful feeling. You can see it on the face of the man who sings in a parlor or around a campfire, and it seems quite right and appropriate. If he looked that way doing anything else you would think things about him. Even those who write about music seem to live in a celestial atmosphere. And as for the man who publishes a song—words fail!

Only the initiated know the glow of satisfaction which comes with the playing of a difficult horn passage in a symphony or a tricky rhythm. The joy of living is inherent in music, and honest, unblushing pride its most natural expression. Long life to it!

On Sundays I used to go to hear my pupil sing. She had a good voice, and after a while I felt it my duty to coach her on some songs. Almost everyone feels it to be his duty to coach a singer, and I was no exception. Of course I made no charge for this although it took more and more of my time.

We worked on the Brahms songs, quite new at that time, and then went back to Schumann and Schubert. It was extraordinary to hear how well placed her voice was. There were no breaks or weak tones, and the range was astonishing. It seemed to go down like a cage into a mine and up like a balloon. And then it had a haunting quality, a little like some orchestral instruments and yet really quite different from any of them. It was not like the contralto voices I had heard. It had none of the sepulchral quality which I associated with low voices. It was low but it had the sparkle and the brilliance of a great dramatic soprano.

It made me want to write songs. I had begun to write songs in Munich eight years earlier, always using German poems, or poems from eastern countries translated into German. I associated music with the German language. There were a sonority and emphasis and an emotional sincerity in German that seemed to demand music. But with this new pupil who knew no foreign languages I sometimes used English translations in order to get at the sentiment of a text. We also did songs by Chadwick, Arthur Foote, and Horatio Parker, and I began to understand that there was a vast field for song writing in English and American poetry. But I was destined to consider this and work at it for another eight years before publishing any songs.

Miss Beatty (for this was my new pupil's name) was determined to learn "all about music"; so I took her to the Boston Symphony concerts and to the Kneisel Quartet concerts. She joined the St. Cecilia Society which Mr. Lang conducted.

She wanted to read good books and asked me about it. I recommended Chapman's translation of the Iliad as a start. She read it, and we talked about Hector and Menelaus; but she was secretly amused and has joked me about it since. It was a rather funny choice, considering the little time she had for reading.

Miss Beatty boarded at 355 Boylston Street, next door to the Arlington Street Church. I began to take my meals at that boarding house, which was not far from my studio. I have been told since that we talked so loud about music in the dining room that the twenty old ladies who lived there couldn't talk about anything. Of course we didn't know it, and I suppose that made it worse.

The climax of the winter came in March when Mr. Maurice Grau brought the Metropolitan Opera Company to Boston for a two weeks' season at the Mechanics Hall. I had heard very little Italian or French opera, and Miss Beatty had never heard opera of any kind. Here was a chance to help along that "all about music" matter that she had come to me to learn. I became excited and bought two seats in the front row on the floor for alternate nights through the season. Miss Beatty's brother-in-law took the seats for the other nights.

It was like a dream. The opening opera was *Faust*, with Emma Eames, Jean and Edouard de Reszke and Lassalle in the cast. We were so near we could touch the first violins with our hands. We could see right through the make-up and the wigs, and could see the scene-shifters behind the scenes. The illusion should have been destroyed but it wasn't! That old Faust became young, as sure as you were born! No one but a real Faust could sing like that, and no one but the devil himself could act like that; and when Emma Eames tore her heart out in the Prison scene, why you just had to climb on the stage and rescue her and carry her back to Bath, Maine, where she came from! These foreign fellows weren't fit to associate with anyway—they couldn't be trusted.

We talked about it as we walked home after the performance, down Huntington Avenue and Boylston Street. Those men! Such voices! Of course the hall was vast. With seven thousand seats on the floor and in the gallery, they had to make their voices carry to the last seat—and we were in the front row. And how they acted! They were like panthers, so lithe and vital. They didn't seem human at all; superhuman, rather; embodied spirits from another world. And then the American girl in opera. That seemed strange. Somehow she suggested Boston, in that far-away medieval setting. The voice had a familiar ring.

I had been to the farewell concert which that fine musician, John K. Paine, had planned and given several years before for Emma Eames. She was about to go to Paris and try her fortune. I remembered her well—tall, beautiful, poised, reserved. And here she was back again, throwing herself on the stage, pleading, raving, her hair down her back.

It was a triumph, a triumph for America. It might all be natural enough for foreigners, but it was not natural for American girls; it was just exactly contrary to all their bringing up.

Miss Beatty had had a great evening and had heard her first opera. I was a "high-brow" and in one way looked down on it. She was a singer and looked up to it—way, way up to it. She had a great sense of humor and an infectious laugh, and if anyone had ventured to suggest that in five years she would be singing with these same great artists, she would have roared, and you would have roared with her.

In May Miss Beatty's mother announced our engagement. Yes, Miss Beatty had made up her mind she could get along with me. One thing I remember distinctly: she never took another harmony lesson after we were engaged, and there is something funny about that. I cannot exactly reconcile it with my *amour propre*.

In the following January (January 9, 1895, to be exact) we were married, amid pomp and circumstance, at her sister's house

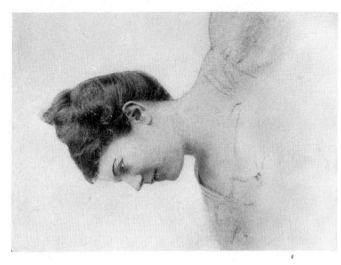

Photographs Litchfield, Arlington, Mass.

BOSTON, MAY, 1894

in Arlington. Her blessed mother was there and seemed to rejoice. Dr. Paxton, who came on from Philadelphia with his wife, married us. Miss Beatty had sung in his church, and his wife was her dearest friend. Two musical waifs threw their fortunes in together. As we drove across country in the old-fashioned coach on runners to the train that was to carry us to the snowy wilds of the Baldpate Inn at Georgetown, Massachusetts, I wondered why all the world seemed to know who we were and smiled on us so fondly—even waved. A little shoe, neatly perched on the top of the coach, explained it.

By great good fortune the dear old house at 355 Boylston Street had been converted that fall into a semibusiness building. We took the top floor for our home, and a large room on the third floor for my teaching studio. My mother, who fell in love with her new daughter, gave us all her best furniture. It was a precious home. The top floor wasn't well heated, but there was a fireplace, a coal grate, in the large front living room where Louise had her piano. One of the back rooms was fitted up as a kitchen, and the little side room overlooking the church next door made a fine dining room for two, or even three on occasion. We had no maid, but Tillie came up from the basement to clean.

The studio was fine and was a busy place. I spent one day each week at New Bedford, where I had a class in symphony study and one in harmony. My wife worked steadily with her great singing teacher, William L. Whitney, and made rapid progress. She began to sing in little occasional concerts and was so free from embarrassment that she disarmed criticism.

It really seemed that we had found our life work. I would go on teaching indefinitely. Dr. Anagnos asked me to take the music department of the Perkins Institute for the Blind, and another school made a similar offer, but this would mean giving up my fine class and I couldn't do that. My wife would probably become known as a local concert singer. Of course there were comparatively few concerts, and most of them went to the older singers with established reputations. Nordica, Eames, and Max Heinrichs came from New York to sing at the Symphony concerts.

In November our Louise was born. Everything changed. It seemed beyond belief that so much happiness could come into the lives of two people. Why is it that happiness cannot be imagined? Yet it is true. Happiness can only be truly known through experience. Imagination has its limitations. It is suggestive, but it is not reality. We may as well be honest and acknowledge that mental concepts can do no more than give a faint and inadequate picture of such elemental things as love, parenthood, and faith. If it were not so, life would soon degenerate into a succession of cerebral substitutes.

It seems to me that the new contribution of our age to human life is its growing distrust of imagination as a guide and its demand for truth and reality through experience. This is one reason why music has grown so in power. Music is not imagination; it is the real experience of a human soul, crystallized and transmuted into an art form. Through it we not only share the deepest experience of another, but we also discover something new and undreamed of within ourselves.

V

1896–1897

WE HAD A GREAT THANKSGIVING AND
Christmas. Early in January the class reassembled, and then
something happened. Momentous things have the tiniest begin-
nings, apparently. We were sitting before our little grate fire
one evening. We had turned out the gas light, and the fire lit up
the room. My wife sighed. This was unusual. I think I had never
heard her sigh before. I soon discovered that she did not feel
altogether happy about her studies. Music study is often discouraging. Progress is so imperceptible, and the monotony of routine
becomes oppressive. My wife had the happiest nature in the
world, but she also had tremendous energy and needed a chance
for expansion. Students need to do things, not simply learn. All
she thought she could look forward to was mere repetition of
what she had been doing for two years.

I began to think things over, and during the next two weeks
I went through what might be called a struggle. Then I announced my great plan. If she would borrow some money from
her friends in Pittsburgh, I would borrow from my relatives in
Boston. We would finish the season with my class and her
church, and then go to Paris for two years. I had had five years
in Germany, and she ought to have two years with the great
masters in Paris. We would then come back to Boston and resume our work. Louise was horrified! The thought of giving
up what we already had seemed too tremendous, too foolhardy,
too much like tempting Fate. I had to advance every argument.
My mother and sister, with her husband and two darling little
boys, had a happy home in Arlington. There were no reasons in
my wife's family to deter us.

51

The fifty thousand dollars which would come to me in 1920 from my Uncle Sidney's estate justified our borrowing. I began to consult my friends and met only with discouragement, except in one instance. My fellow teachers warned me that it had taken eight years to build up my class, and that it would take eight years more after we returned to get back to where I then was. I had about eighty pupils in all my classes. I remember the day we walked down Boylston Street with George Chadwick, who was our father-confessor, and whose opinion we valued most. He was walking between us and seemed very anxious. Finally he stopped and said: "Sidney, the trouble is there are no roles in opera for Louise's voice!"

He seemed to think we aspired to opera. He knew that my wife rarely sang above G flat in those days, and of course opera roles ran higher than this. The one exception was Mr. Whitney, who, of course, knew Louise's voice as no one else did. He approved my plan. But he and I disagreed on one point. He wanted her to go to his old teacher, Vannuccini, in Florence. I wanted her to go to Paris. I simply argued that, as the great singers of the day, Jean and Edouard de Reszke, Lasalle, Calvé, Melba, and Eames, had just come from Paris, that must be the place to study.

After three weeks my wife consented—because she wanted to get me away from my work. I was so exhausted at night that she became alarmed.

Three cheers! We were going—that is, if we could borrow the money! She wrote letters, and I saw my cousins and one of my friends. We waited, and then the responses came. Yes, it was all right; glad to do it; hoped it was the right thing, etc. Such excitement! We worked harder than ever, and, strangely enough, work grew easier. Work is always easy if it does not stretch out before one in an endless vista. One can walk rapidly toward a mountain, but it is difficult to hurry over an apparently interminable plain.

Perhaps, when we are wiser, all jobs will have an interesting change in sight, and disheartening monotony will be taken out of labor. We may even alternate in drudgery and relieve one another.

My wife sang a recital in Arlington and another at the Y.M.C.A. Hall in Boston. Brahms' "Sapphische Ode," "Mon cœur s'ouvre à ta voix," from *Samson et Dalila*, etc., were on her programs.

George Stewart, that astute manager who always knew a voice, engaged her for a symphony concert at the Newton Club House. She sang "Il est doux, il est bon," from *Hérodiade* and a group of songs. He gave her a check for twenty-five dollars and, years later, had it framed and hung on the wall alongside one for the same amount which he had given to Emma Eames. Stewart, like Calabresi of Brussels, never made a mistake. These men, who, with limited means, made young artists famous, engaging them when they were young and inexperienced, deserve the gratitude of all. The true story of public success, in music, will never be told. When Calabresi patiently trained and brought out such debutantes as Calvé, Melba, Alvarez, Gilibert, Journet, and Renaud, he showed wonderful intuition and performed a public service. George Stewart had much of this intuition.

At last the season was over and we were ready to go. We had no illusions and aspired to nothing but two years of study. The fond expectation of operatic success, of fame, fortune, idolatry, which haunts the minds of so many young singers, is nothing less than a tragedy. Not only does it prepare the soil for bitter and unnecessary disappointment, but it causes a paralysis of those abilities which the young people actually have and prevents all progress. It hangs like a blighting pall over their lives.

My wife had none of this silly nonsense. Sufficient to the day was the work thereof. The joy of work and progress filled her life. The present was her concern, not the future. She would meet that when it came.

We had our tickets and a letter of credit for twenty-five hundred dollars, a hard hair pillow and a lot of condensed milk for the baby. I think neither of us had ever had more than one or two hundred dollars at one time. The future looked rosy. Think of just resting, and then studying and composing! We had worked hard for a number of years, and I suppose we were tired out. Anyway, this venture brought us a happy sense of relief. Supreme bliss, perfect contentment: nothing in the world to ask for! We knew nothing of luxury, and the simplest comfort was sufficient. All we wanted was a chance to work and study, and that we were sure to have. Our chief problem was to make our money last as long as possible, and not one cent would be spent for anything but the barest necessities.

We landed at Rotterdam, then went up the Rhine to Cologne on a little Dutch river boat, which delivered mail and packages at the prim little farmhouses along the banks. The boat would whistle, and a skiff, rowed by a neatly dressed boy, or a girl with a white cap, large stiff bows and a black silk apron, would come out to collect the mail. No careless clothes or untidiness. Everything correct and formal and clean as a whistle.

It was all so quaint and new. My wife, who had never stirred from home, watched and marveled, while I watched her and gloried in the triumph of my big idea. Europe was an old story to me, but I was sure it was going to be a revelation to her. This was her trip, not mine.

We dreamed in the Cologne Cathedral. Oh, the glorious past! Bonn, the birthplace of Beethoven. Was he really ever born? Then on to Lucerne: snow-clad mountains. Think of it—eternal snows! Then to St. Beatenberg, nearly two thousand feet above Lake Thun, where we were to rest for the summer.

In Lucerne we had picked up a maid, fifteen years old, to whom we paid three dollars a month. She was a devoted treasure who saw us through all our struggles for two years. Such joy, such beauty all around us! It was a privilege to live and breathe. At our little hotel (one dollar a day apiece, wine twenty-five cents a bottle), we met Antonin Savard, the French composer, and his wife. They talked French to us every day. We received word recently of Madame Savard's death. How she loved my wife! For thirty years she followed her life with unchanging devotion.

Savard heard Louise sing and immediately began writing something for her. There is where Europeans differ from us. They see something and act. We see something and wait. They love the possibilities of the bud, and long to help. We wait, immobile, for the bud to unfold and then lose ourselves in ecstasy. But we have a severe climate, and our buds need much care.

Savard heard some of my songs, and again he thought he saw something. He did not call them "very dainty." Arthur Schmidt, the publisher, whose daughter was in my class in Boston, and who had at one time wished to publish them, gave them this inspiring description. Savard was the first composer to see them, except Rheinberger who had seen a few. What he said was straightforward and positive, and made it easy for me to go on.

The French are very decided in their views and do not mince their words. This decisiveness inspires confidence. It seems to me that Americans are full of faint praise. It is not that they do not appreciate, but they are afraid they don't know. They need to be reassured, which is sad. Perhaps so much publicity has made them timid, or perhaps they have had too many disappointments.

Our wonderful summer came to an end, and we started for Paris. I carried the baby on the hair pillow, and Louise carried the can of Swiss milk. We tried a furnished apartment which was so tiny that when my wife sang a note the baby woke up. Here was a serious problem, but we found a happy solution. In the rue de Lubeck, between the home of ex-President Carnot and that of some countess, was a simple old apartment house of primitive type with a workmen's restaurant on the ground floor. Upstairs on the third floor was a *grand appartement*, two rooms fronting on the street, two rooms at the back on the garden, and a kitchen between. Louise could sing, baby could sleep. Thirteen dollars a month by the year. Perfect! At the Bon Marché, a Paris department store, we bought our furniture—white iron beds and hair mattresses for fifty dollars, rattan chairs, chaise-longue, and other things for fifty. The total cost of our house furnishings was a hundred dollars. Packing cases draped in chintz were bureaus. It was a fight of time against money.

Anna, our Swiss maid, came on from Lucerne. We were in clover! We had the Trocadéro Gardens, a block away, for the baby. We could have our own plain American cooking. (French food has ruined many a beautiful American voice!) There were two coal grates to heat the four rooms, and we loved open fires. The little shops around the corner on the rue de Longchamp would sell the smallest quantity of anything. We had an eighth of a pound of delicious sweet butter each morning. The bus line from downtown ran by the door.

We were ready to assault the vast and complicated problem of learning to sing, and the simpler, more naïve task of composing. For I was a composer now, whether I wanted to be or not; I must justify my existence.

We found a studio for me around the corner in the Avenue Kléber, at four dollars a month, up six flights, a healthy walk-up. It overlooked the chimneypots and the Eiffel Tower. A table, a chair, a rented piano and my books, and my factory was equipped.

A composer is a nuisance to have around, and should be discouraged by his friends and gently led into some harmless occupation. He must have absolute quiet, makes a lot of noise; he must have a lovely view, nothing disagreeable in sight, and can go about looking like the dickens himself. If he has an idea, he needn't eat on time or keep engagements. If he has a brooding look on his face you mustn't mention casual topics to him. Above all things, you mustn't speak of his compositions or inquire about his work. He knows how rotten his work was that morning and thinks you know it, too. Isolate him and have nothing to do with him—that's my advice!

We went to Jacques Bouhy and arranged lessons (four dollars each!), found a French teacher, and, a stroke of real luck, discovered the Yersin sisters for French diction; eight lessons a week in all. The campaign was on!

I prided myself on what I knew about the study of music. My theory was that, time being the precious element, any skimping of lessons was false economy. We spent eleven hundred dollars of our tiny capital on lessons during that first year. We met students who had been in Paris for years who were taking one lesson a week and picking up French without cost. After my wife had sung two years in opera we came back to Paris and found many of these students still studying. Intensive study with plenty of lessons is the better plan in musical work.

Much of the work that a music student does by himself is wrong and injurious. He often merely undoes the work of his teacher. Therefore, constant and vigilant supervision is necessary.

My wife attracted immediate attention with her voice. Within a few weeks Frenchmen pronounced it "an opera voice." The French are always sure they are right. If they say it, it's so! And you are tempted to agree with them!

Everything went swimmingly. In a few short weeks my wife spoke and sang French with an accent that the French people themselves marveled at. Delicious, they called it. Diction was their passion.

Savard finished the work he was writing for my wife. It was a rhapsody for a contralto voice and orchestra on a poem of Paul Verlaine, *Le Crépuscule*. He wanted her to sing it at a concert which his society intended to give. This society was a ridiculous sort of thing in Parisian eyes. It was made up of a few disgruntled young composers who could not get their works performed at the Lamoureux or Pasdeloup Symphony concerts. Once or twice a year they hired a theatre, got together a scratch orchestra and solemnly produced their own works for their friends.

We were much excited! The work was beautifully written for the voice, and had haunting sustained passages for the most beautiful contralto tones. There was a mixed-up rehearsal, all confusion, so many new works, mistakes in the orchestral parts, composers conducting, much shouting; the French language took on a new picturesqueness! I wish I had a record of it.

Then the evening came. My wife wore her made-over wedding dress, the only evening dress she owned, and put her hair up high in a pompadour. She looked like a sweet American girl, very un-French in that intensely Gallic atmosphere. I sat in a box with Savard. All around, men in full dress, many with their opera hats on, were chattering excitedly. It was evidently quite an occasion. There were very few ladies present. I suspected many of the men had their knives out and were prepared to slice up gleefully these new unpublished compositions. An audience of secretly gloating friends is the worst of all.

The first composer appeared, and the chatter simmered down to a hum. He finished, and his friends clapped their hands. Then another composer came out. He was a thin, little man with a pointed beard. His name was Dukas and he was going to give his new work called *L'Apprenti Sorcier*. Rather funny to try to tell a story with an orchestra. The string players sawed, the wind instruments howled, the composer waved and jumped. It was hilarious, but somehow it was good. You forgot to reserve your judgment and pounded your hands when it finished. Of course you realized afterward that you had been foolish—a little unfaithful to the masters.

Then a tall young man came out to conduct Savard's composition. He was evidently quite a favorite and they gave him a hand. His name was Vincent d'Indy.

Then my wife came on the stage! She looked beautiful, naïve, quite unprofessional and out of place. There was a patter of applause for the only woman on the program. When she sang her voice rang out with great beauty and she seemed to feel the deep intensity of Paul Verlaine's poem. The long low notes held you spellbound, and as she finished the audience was hushed and intent. It was grand! There was an ovation, and Savard had to stand up and bow with her, several times. There were flowers for Louise presented by the society.

After this a fine tenor sang several songs by Fauré, who was an older man and the only recognized composer on the program. Something by Chausson, I think, closed the concert. It was a great evening! Of course it was not a regular symphony concert, such as society patronized. You might say it was semi-dilettante, and naturally most of the critics had to treat it as such. The dignity of recognized institutions had to be preserved, and impromptu affairs could not be confused with them.

Such is the world of music. I often wonder how they regarded the concerts which Beethoven used to get up in Vienna. They were also impromptu affairs. On the other hand the Royal Opera where they gave works by Rossini was a recognized institution.

Everything moved on smoothly, and apparently we had nothing more to wish for. Our friends Dr. and Mrs. James D. Paxton had come to Paris. He was holding studio services in the Latin Quarter every Sunday evening. My wife used to sing for him very often. Through him and Mrs. Paxton, we met a number of American painters. It was all very pleasant and homelike.

It is remarkable how many hidden obstructions lurk in the way of the student of voice culture. You must watch every step. I knew enough to keep my hands off this delicate matter and leave it entirely to the master. But I could, and must, listen, and after five months the conviction became stronger and stronger that my wife's voice was growing smaller, was so covered that the brilliance was diminishing fast.

That was a real tragedy! We had come to Paris to gain, not lose. We were devoted to Mr. Bouhy and venerated him. After a painful and prolonged struggle with ourselves, we finally decided to change teachers. Louise began lessons with Juliani, a retired Italian tenor who had become a popular teacher.

There is nothing more strange than this question of voice teachers. I have, long since, made up my mind that when a pupil does not make progress it is not, necessarily, a reflection on his teacher. Another pupil will do wonderfully under his care, and the unsuccessful pupil will get on famously under another master. There is an alchemy about it, a reaction of personalities, a mysterious mutual helpfulness, an unexplainable sympathy.

Juliani was a comical genius. He could open his mouth so wide that you couldn't see his face at all. He soon had my wife's voice bright and free again. He was jolly and she was jolly, and the studio used to ring with laughter. Bouhy had been formal and most reserved; Juliani loved to act like a clown and make his pupils feel at ease. They adored him. The whole class was like a happy family.

Summer was approaching, and there was very little time left, a bare three months. I insisted on taking my wife to the country for a two months' vacation. The other pupils were aghast. They followed their masters to their summer places and went on working. I said that rest was essential to all progress.

Alas, the voice! The cantankerous, obstinate, inconsiderate instrument that persists in inventing new and devilish defects! Before the three months were over, my wife's voice began to sound peculiar on the lower medium notes. The timbre was gone and there were a breathiness and throaty quality. This opening the mouth so wide might be overdone; anyway, it wasn't all there was to singing.

We started on our vacation with misgivings in our hearts, but they soon disappeared. Life was too glorious. Baby Louise was walking and beginning to talk—French, of course. We went to Freiburg near the Black Forest. It was beautiful. I was thrilled to be in Germany again, and took my wife to the hotel garden and ordered some real Munich beer. She liked it. I gravely explained the great difference between the beer exported from Munich and that which was drunk in Munich itself.

Beer is an endless topic of conversation in Munich, as wine is in France. Every time a Münchener tastes a fresh glass of beer he comments on the flavor, and everyone answers. There are several hundred words that express the delicate differences of flavor, and the choice of the right word is a weighty matter.

We went on to Schönwald in the heart of the Black Forest. There we had two months of perfect rest. Even after thirty-eight years the wondrous peace of that summer comes back to me. The beautiful forest, the absolute stillness, the sense of restored strength after such exhausting efforts, the gentle kindliness of the people around us and their simplicity and contentment—all this gave us new courage.

In September we were back in Paris. It was a critical time. We were doubtful about the value of Juliani's teaching for my wife, much as we respected his sincerity and experience. Our funds were low, and there was no assurance that we could get through another winter. The prospect was disheartening, and there was a kind of irritating stagnation in the air which we could hardly bear. We were deep in a rut, and we wanted to do something; but we did not wish to decide hastily. Many music students will recognize what I mean.

One morning a young American woman, who had married a French musician, came to see us. She begged my wife to study with her husband, and was sure he could do wonders for her. He had done great things for Suzanne Adams who had made her debut in opera, and he was sure he could do as much for my wife whose glorious voice he had heard.

It was very embarrassing. We had met her husband, a tall blond Frenchman with a pleasant smile and a jolly disposition. He had a broken vocal chord, and his voice cracked when he talked. We knew he was a fine pianist, had taken the Grand Prix at the Conservatoire and had been *chef de chant* at the Opéra for many years. But he had no reputation as a voice teacher beyond the fact that he had coached Suzanne Adams. We hesitated while his wife urged and pleaded. Finally, we said that my wife would study some roles with him at five francs a lesson but would continue her voice culture with Juliani.

Fidèle Koenig, that great man and consummate musician, with his passion for a beautiful voice, put his pride into his pocket and said, "For sure! Come on, let us try and see what we can do!"

And so the marvelous thing that was to decide my wife's whole life came about! She took her first lesson, and the change began. In two weeks she stopped her lessons with Juliani. At last, for the first time, she could confide her voice without fear or reservation to the guidance of another, trust everything to him without thought or care.

We were supremely happy! From this moment on not a shadow appeared. My wife's art went onward and upward; and all our affairs went with it. To see my wife so happy was enough for me. My piano quintet and a lot of little songs went booming ahead. For those who do not know, I will confide that in a singer's family the voice is the barometer of happiness. When the voice is fine, the sky is blue, the sun shines, and the birds sing. When the voice is bad, the gloomy fog comes down and only the tree toads croak. Those who are not willing to submit to such conditions should keep away from singers. A man who can be happy when his wife is out of voice is a brute.

Fidèle Koenig, like a great general, looked over the field and planned his campaign. The time was short, the money almost gone. My wife's voice was rich and heavy and did not run high easily; she had never sung coloratura, she had no repertoire and in one whole year had only learned parts of *Samson et Dalila*. It was necessary to work quickly, decisively, and to the point.

He gave her a lesson every day, and allowed only fifteen minutes' vocalizing at home. He concentrated on head tones and brought them down into the medium of the voice. He selected the great scene of Fidès in the fourth act of *Le Prophète,* as the number which would secure a possible engagement for her. It ran from low G to high C, over two octaves and a half, and had coloratura and sustained cantabile.

My wife said she could never sing it. He said they would work on it for fifteen minutes at every lesson, and in a short time she would be able to sing it. He was supremely confident, and there was no gainsaying him.

It was most exciting! How strange it was for my wife not to be singing at home by the hour, wearing her voice out in futile efforts! Resting the voice seemed such a queer way to make progress.

How inspiring he was when he touched the piano, what an atmosphere of art filled the room, how lightly and easily he smoothed out each difficulty, how quickly and deftly he increased her repertoire! It was thrilling and entrancing. My wife and I looked at each other with thanksgiving in our eyes, a lump in our throats, and deep gratitude in our hearts. I went to every lesson and shared in the whole, wonderful experience.

In November, just six weeks after these lessons began, I read in the Paris edition of the New York *Herald* that Mr. Maurice Grau was in town and that he had decided not to open the Metropolitan Opera House in New York during the season of 1897–98. I was fascinated by the thought of his being in Paris, this famous man who had the courage to bring so many artists to America, and who had such an uncanny intuition for great voices and great art. Suddenly I thought, "Why shouldn't he hear my wife sing?"

He was an American, and he should be interested in hearing her because she was an American, if for no other reason. He was not giving opera, and there would be no question of hinting for an engagement or anything of that kind. He would advise her as no one else could.

That afternoon I spoke to M. Koenig about it. He was immediately sympathetic, said he was acquainted with Mr. Grau and would see him. The next day he said that Mr. Grau would be glad to hear Mrs. Homer but that he wanted to hear her in a small hall, not in a room. M. Koenig knew of a small hall in the Boulevard Haussmann which he could get; and he would fix the appointment and make all arrangements.

Tremendous! Just the most impossible, inconceivable things seemed to come to pass! We were in a dream as we went down to the hall. My wife's unfailing courage supported her as it always did. Mr. Grau greeted us in the most affable way and almost made us feel that we were conferring a favor, not he. Louise and M. Koenig went up on the stage and Mr. Grau and I sat together at the back of the hall. The hall was dark, but there was a small light on the stage by the piano. Calmly and simply my wife sang a number of arias and songs. There was no comment, and the two artists went on from one thing to another. After an hour they stopped.

To our surprise Mr. Grau asked them to continue and suggested several numbers, some of which, fortunately, they had with them. Afterward we stood outside the hall where it was light, and talked. Mr. Grau was very definite. She had a beautiful voice, she must have at least one year's experience in a provincial opera house; the conditions would not be very pleasant, but it was necessary to go through with it; he never took debutantes at the Metropolitan; she should not, in any case, sign one of the five-year contracts which the Paris Opéra insisted on. Would we write him and tell him how she got along?

He wished her every good fortune, and, with the kindest of smiles, he said good-bye.

The dream was not over, and we walked home almost in silence. Men in high places shape the course of many lives. They have very little conception of the happiness they distribute as they go along.

VI

1898

MY WIFE MADE RAPID PROGRESS, AND IN
January M. Koenig announced that he wanted her to sing for
the head of the Roberval Agency, the principal one in Paris.
It was there that most of the engagements were made for the
provincial opera houses. He would make the appointment and
would go with her and play for her.

This was exciting and interesting. There would be no harm in
singing for them even if nothing came of it. I made up my mind
not to go along. Why have an auditor sitting around, who might
be a little nervous in strange surroundings? This was M. Koenig's
affair, his pupil who was to sing, his glory if she did well.

It was a gray afternoon. There was no snow on the ground,
but the stones looked frozen. I came home earlier than usual
from my studio and waited for my wife to return from her
audition. I knew she would have an interesting story to tell, and
she could tell a story better than anyone ever born. It grew dark.
This was the hour when I always played my new work for her
and she tried it out and made it sound like something. I wished
she would come.

Suddenly the door opened, and in she hurried. She was smiling and had a twinkle in her eye. She waited until she was close
to me and then suddenly cried, "I have an offer!"

An offer! A bomb through the wall couldn't be more startling.
An offer! What, how, when, why! Who ever heard of such a
thing? Only three hours before, we were looking forward to
a calm student life, and a trip home—the usual thing. An offer
was a kind of will-o'-the-wisp. You heard it mentioned, but no
one ever saw one. Students often spoke of it: "I wouldn't accept

66

an offer for the provinces"; "I wouldn't accept an offer from any place but the Paris Opéra"; "I wouldn't accept an offer from the Paris Opéra—I would rather go to La Monnaie"—these were common remarks. In the year and a half we had been in Paris no student, American, French, English, or any other kind, had ever had an offer, and here was Louise saying she had one! The room was hot, but she forgot to take off her coat, hat, and gloves. She told me the story.

They had gone to the agency, a large place up one flight, and the manager had met them—no, not M. Roberval; there was no M. Roberval; that was just a name. His name was M. Perrez. He was a short fat man, very bright and alert, and walked with quick short steps. "What did he—" "Now, Sidney!" You cannot interrupt my wife when she tells a story. She puts a little lace on here, a bit of embroidery there; she loves suspense and always makes a climax, often quite unexpected. So you have to take it as it comes, "quick short steps" and all. He took them into another room where there were a grand piano, a large window, and a couple of chairs. She took off her coat, and he sat down in a chair directly in front of her.

It was funny singing to a business man. She felt like a piece of silk or a box of apples being examined for the market. But there was always M. Koenig with his sensitive face and poetic touch. That helped. While she was singing her first number the door opened, and a tall man, not very old but with gray hair, came in and walked over to the window and stood there looking out into the court, with his back to her. It seemed a little rude, but the agency was a funny place anyway, the last place in the world for making music. It was rather ridiculous. But she must do her best for M. Koenig's sake, and tried to forget the surroundings.

She sang five or six arias, ending with her great *tour de force*, the scene from the fourth act of *Le Prophète* on which she and M. Koenig had worked so long and so hard.

As she finished, the tall man at the window turned and came

forward and was presented. He was M. Bussac. He said that he was the director of the summer season of opera at Vichy; that his company was made up of the best singers from the Paris Opéra, the Opéra Comique, and La Monnaie; that they hadn't had a debutante in fifteen years; that he would be glad to offer her a contract for the approaching season if she cared to consider it.

She controlled her emotions as best she could and murmured something about me. The agency manager, M. Perrez, grew voluble and excited, but M. Bussac quietly stopped him. "Let me write the conditions on a piece of paper," he said. "Take it home and consult your husband, and give your answer to the agency in two or three days." He was so courteous, so calm and considerate! A true French gentleman. He did not show that he knew the agitation that was in my wife's heart, nor did he suggest by the slightest word that he thought she should feel honored by his offer.

On the way home M. Koenig told my wife that, next to the two opera houses in Paris, Vichy ranked highest of all opera houses in France. The audience was made up of the élite of French society. He thought it was a good offer but did not wish to influence her too strongly.

She stopped and took the paper out of her muff. No subsequent contract ever looked like that one. We sighed as we read it, together, and thought of our families at home and the friends who had helped us.

A three months' season, beginning June 15, 1898; repertoire, *La Favorite* (Léonore), *Hamlet* (the Queen), *Samson et Dalila* (Dalila), *Lohengrin* (Ortrud), *Tannhäuser* (Venus), *Le Roi d'Ys* (Margared), *Thaïs* (Albine, the nun), and *L'Attaque du Moulin;* ample rehearsals with at least one orchestral rehearsal for each opera; the artist to supply all her own costumes; compensation 450 francs ($90) a month. We read the contract three or four times and said nothing. Our hearts were too full.

It was time to play with the baby before she went to bed. She must be looking for us, and her happy coos and French nonsense were worth all the contracts in the world.

If there is anything more beautiful than the first steps of young people in professional or business life, I do not know it. The big strides of later life are commonplace in comparison. It is the confidence in them which some one feels, before they have proved their worth, that is so big with sentiment.

Conference, discussion, consultation. Could my wife prepare the repertoire in that short time? M. Koenig and Paul Lhérie, that great artist with whom my wife had already begun her lessons in acting, said she could! They knew her talent, speed, fearlessness, and directness. Ever since she had learned to do two hundred words a minute on the typewriter she had been a human dynamo of energy. She was as quick as her husband was slow; but it was a terrific repertoire.

What would the costumes cost? We visited Julien, the famous costumer. His enameled face and the black wig that hung in curls over his ears surprised me. He was kind and smooth and coaxing. He calculated. With little changes and extra *tabliers* by which this costume could be made to do for two different operas, and that for two others, he could do the whole, with crowns and jewels, for 5,000 francs ($1,000). He would trust us, and simply insert a clause in our opera contract by which the management paid him so much a month, and deducted this amount from my wife's salary. We did not like this idea and hoped we could borrow some of the money at home.

Would Vichy be a good place for the baby? It was hot, we were told; but there was a fine park, and we could easily get a little villa with a garden. Babies thrived in Vichy. We thought and thought, and on the third day the contract was signed. The die was cast. My wife would sing in opera! We knew nothing about it; behind the scenes was a hidden world. It was a little

like walking into the Lions' Den or the Fiery Furnace; you had
to have tremendous faith.

And now to work! Such work! Paul Lhérie, that consummate
master, could act every part. He had a stage in his studio, and as
my wife acted Léonore he circled around her as Inez, Fernand,
or Alphonse, changing his voice, gait, face, and manner with
each character. Or if she did Ortrud, he was the pure Elsa, the
divine Lohengrin, the fretful Frederick or the judicial King, by
turn, all with such art that you could only wonder in amazement. You could not help acting in his presence. His imagination was irresistible.

In February, the Agence Roberval asked my wife to come to
the office to meet some gentlemen who were interested. An appointment was made, and this time I went with her. Things
were becoming serious. It was a question of taking no false steps.
We arrived at the agency, where we were presented to a distinguished group of Frenchmen, several of them in frock coats and
high hats. It was most formal.

My wife sang gloriously. There was no applause or comment;
there never is on such occasions. The gentlemen conferred in
low voices. Finally one of them, a tall man with a bald head
and a kind face, constituted himself spokesman and stood up.
"Madame Homer," he said, "we are planning to have an opera
season next winter at Angers, on the Loire. I have been chosen
manager, the Comte de Romain," pointing to a distinguished
gray-haired man, "is chairman of our board, the Vicomte ——
is vice-chairman. There is no question of earning any profit; any
profit that might accrue will be turned into a fund designed to
perpetuate the project. Frankly, one of our purposes is to have
a series of symphony concerts, and we look to the opera to
cover the main cost of the orchestra and thus make it possible.
The company will consist of distinguished artists from La Monnaie, the Opéra Comique, and so on. We hope that you will join
us and are prepared to offer you a contract for six months, be-

ginning October 10th, your honorarium to be 1,000 francs
[$200] a month. The only additions to your repertoire which
we shall ask for will be *Aida* and the *Princesse d'Auberge*."

We listened in silence and retired to another room to confer.
There were reasons for and against. The sudden increase in
salary before my wife had even made her debut was undoubtedly due to the Agence Roberval. In my opinion, all the financial prosperity of public artists is created by the brokers, financiers, and astute business men who are interested in them. Left
to themselves many gifted and truly moving artists live and die
in obscurity and poverty.

Angers seemed a remote place, but the conditions surround-
ing the altruistic venture were attractive. We decided to accept.

After the contract was drawn up and signed, the atmosphere
of formality disappeared, and we all joined in an animated discussion of the great undertaking, the great things we would do,
what all this glorious music, including, of course, the symphony
concerts, would do for the people of Angers, separated as they
were from distant Paris with its advantages. I never saw a more
disinterested and cultured group of men than those I met that
afternoon.

Just as we were leaving an old gentleman introduced himself.
He had long gray hair that fell over his collar, and a gray beard.
His face was gentle and fatherly. He said he had listened to the
audition but did not belong to the group from Angers. He was
M. Stumont, one of the two directors of the Théâtre de la Mon-
naie at Brussels.

"You have a beautiful voice, madame," he said, "and you will
have great success. You must sing for my codirector, M. Calabresi."

To say that we were thrilled is but a trite and tame expression.
La Monnaie! The goal of all artists, the place that conferred the
hallmark of first excellence on all singers! As we went home we
thought only of this: La Monnaie, La Monnaie!

The winter was most interesting and most exciting. Augustus Saint-Gaudens came to Paris to live. His wife was my cousin, née Augusta Homer, and we knew them well. As a small boy I had been present at their wedding, and we children bet that the minister would get mixed up on their first names. To our great delight he did!

The Dreyfus affair was raging, and I read six French papers every day. Zola and Clemenceau were superb. I was near the Palais de Justice when an attack was made on Zola. Only a dozen of us witnessed it. Paris was literally at war. It is terrific to realize what passions lie beneath the surface in a great city, and that every great city is a dormant volcano.

My wife was asked to sing at the Baroness de Hegerman's house for the American Ambassador. She had no proper dress, and Helen Paxton gave her one of hers, black lace over rose silk. Mrs. Gray engaged her to sing in the evening, and again she had no dress; but a rich American had left a large wardrobe to be given to students, and a beautiful one was given to her.

The Paris Opéra announced a first performance of Wagner's *Les Maîtres-Chanteurs*, and I organized a class in the study of this music drama. It was very successful although most of the members were amateurs. During this period my little annuity was a godsend! It was nip and tuck and it hardly seemed that we could make it. We wrote home, with embarrassment, for small additional loans, and one morning a cable came from our Boston friend: "Am mailing one thousand dollars for costumes." My wife wept; it was too much. Why was everyone so good to her?

We saved on everything, even bus fare. In the two years we did not go once to the theatre. We went three times to the top gallery of the Opéra, once to hear Madame Héglon as Dalila, which we did not enjoy, and twice to hear the great Marie Delna as Fidès in *Le Prophète*, which sent us into a seventh heaven! We did not know such a voice could exist!

Once a month we went to a moderate-priced restaurant with the Savards, and dined. It was a ceremony, and on these occasions Savard and I each smoked a cigar. Otherwise we rolled our cigarettes. There must be a joy in simple living, for I cannot remember that we had a single unhappy moment or a single unfulfilled desire. We had our baby, our health, and our engagement and felt rich and blessed.

May came, and we must soon go to Vichy. It was necessary to buy a dress. My wife had bought only one dress (and I not even a necktie) since we were married, and that she had bought in Boston before the baby was born. Our clothes had lasted wonderfully and were still presentable. We went to the Trois Quartiers, a famous place, and they made my wife a beautiful "pearl-gray dress piped with white satin," my wife says, for twenty-five dollars, and a street costume. They also made over the evening gown that had been given to her. She felt ready for Vichy or any place.

The costumes were finished, and they were gorgeous. No other word described them! Such lines and colors, such jewels, so true to period and yet such grace! She wore some of them for fifteen years.

The roles were all tucked away in her little head: she could do any of them at a moment's notice.

June came, and we went to Vichy, that quaint sophisticated French town which was to be for us so full of adventure.

We looked for that villa, and, sure enough, there was half a villa we could have at a very low price. We could also have Marie, the French maid, who went with it, and that was a great blessing. There was a lovely garden around the villa, and we felt at home in a minute. So did the baby. We all developed a technique for feeling at home wherever we went. It was a part of our new profession.

Only one thing troubled me. There was a bullfight arena on the outskirts of Vichy, and the Spanish matadors and picadors had taken the house directly across the street from us. They spent much of their time sitting on their front steps, in their picturesque costumes, smoking cigarettes, and naturally noticed us; they had no other place to look. That, alone, would not have bothered me; but this was the summer of the Spanish-American War, and the telegraphic reports were not favorable to Spain! There was the baby! I thought I saw sullen looks, and we would be away in the evening at the Opéra. Nothing ever happened. People are never at war, only governments.

We went to the Casino to report, but M. Bussac was out. He returned our call immediately and seemed glad to see us. He was all smiles and very reassuring. He told us he had planned two symphony concerts for Mrs. Homer to introduce her to his *abonnés* and create still more interest in her approaching debut, which would be in *La Favorite* on the evening of Sunday June 23rd. We were rather surprised at its being on Sunday, but he told us that was the most popular night for opera in Vichy.

The symphony concerts were most enjoyable and easy. They were held in the afternoon, and my wife sang the *Hérodiade* aria in one and the scene from *Le Prophète* in the other, in addition to a group of songs in each. M. Amadou, the conductor of the orchestra, proved to be a most refined and sensitive musician. We were in a French atmosphere where purity of tone and delicacy and restraint in interpretation counted for so much.

Then the rehearsals for the grand debut began. The artists all lived in little houses with their families on the outskirts of Vichy, and spent their days fishing in the tiny streams. It was vacation time for them, and since they knew all the operas backwards it is conceivable that they may have begrudged rehearsing them all over again for a debutante. If so, they never allowed us to know it. On the contrary, they rehearsed with fervor, sang usually in full voice and left nothing to chance. All singers will know how much this meant to my wife. The stage manager fussed around; the scenes were changed on time, and everything regulated to the last detail. On Friday the orchestral rehearsal took place, and everything went without a hitch. As I look back I can realize how happy everyone must have been to hear my wife sing in such perfect French and with such command of her music. Trained artists have a horror of singing with uncertain or frightened young singers. It is difficult enough to sing, at all times, but doubly difficult under such conditions.

Scaremberg, the heroic tenor from the Paris Opéra, Montfort, the fine baritone from Lille, and Boussa, the white-haired bass, gathered around my wife and told her she was just fine! Just fine! Not to change a thing, only rest and get a good sleep, eat simply, and so on.

They were fine fellows and never changed in the three months that we knew them. I grow sentimental as I wonder how they got on in life, how their voices fared, and what the war did to them.

We rested as well as we could, took walks, and talked very little so as to save the voice. It was all rather trancelike.

Finally Sunday night came.

My wife went early to her dressing room, and I watched the crowd pour into the theatre. M. Bussac had given me an aisle seat two-thirds back on the floor; he said it was the best place to hear.

At last I went in. The house was crowded. There were many more men than women; some still had their opera hats on. Such jabbering! They were all excited—or was it because they were French, or was it just I? Some stood up and talked to other men four rows away; yes, there was surely something in the air.

I waited, and the noise increased; then the lights went down. Amadou raised his stick. I thought of what a fine musician he was, so sure, so steady. The singers could rely on him, and nothing could disturb him. He was like a great pilot steering the ship through narrow channels. I felt the deepest gratitude that he was there; so calm and unobtrusive, unnoticed and yet with such responsibility. He would carry my wife along just as he had done in rehearsal. At that time he had known she was hearing the orchestra for the first time and how confusing it was, but he had supported her at every moment.

The curtain went up. I could hardly wait! When—oh, when!

They brought Scaremberg on (I mean Fernand) and unbandaged his eyes and now— My wife sailed on from the wings, arms outstretched: "Mon idole! Mon idole!" It was great! She looked beautiful, dressed in a pink satin *tablier* from throat to feet, over white satin. She looked American all right, just as much so as she did on Boston Common, but she sounded French! How the words rolled out, how the voice rang! It was a long duet; they sang and sang; Scaremberg was great, Louise's voice soared up and up. It was over at last. She waved good-bye to him and was gone!

To my amazement the audience broke out in thunderous applause. It was only a duet, it wasn't a solo. They kept it up, on it went, the dramatic effect was spoiled, Scaremberg looked embarrassed and half bowed; then he went to the wings and led my wife on. They bowed. All wrong! The noise grew worse. Amadou put up his stick and motioned to my wife. She hurried over to the side, threw out her arms: "Mon idole! Mon idole!" And they sang it over again.

I was the happiest man in the world. I rolled around in my seat and smiled in all directions. I wanted to make a speech. I didn't listen to the music—what did I care for the old duet! I didn't care how they sang it or if they sang it! It was over, they had made a success! I could throw my hat to the ceiling!

From that moment on I could listen to opera sanely and enjoy it. Nothing like that duet ever happened again. She had proved herself, she had done it, and that was all there was to it. From that moment she was, in my eyes, a complete opera singer, just like any of them, as good as any of them.

I settled back and laughed. I went behind the scenes and told

AS LEONORE AT HER DEBUT, VICHY, JUNE 23, 1898

her how great she was! We almost wept. She didn't quite agree
with me. She still had the second act ahead of her, and the third.
I didn't care. Ask anyone in the audience. My anxiety had gone
over the horizon, like a bad dream, never to come back. Bussac
and Amadou came to back me up. I was right, and that was all;
there were no ifs and buts! We had a jollification meeting.

The second act was fine. Montfort sang with great tenderness;
my wife's voice was beautiful. I could listen now. The third act
was exciting. The pink *tablier* was gone, and the same white
satin dress looked like a new court costume—one of Julienne's
tricks of economy. My wife, alone on the stage in the bright
light, sang her solo, "Oh, mon Fernand!"

It was a crucial moment, and I held my breath; but I was confident, sure, almost triumphant. The audience was emphatic. For
me the ordeal was over, and I knew my wife felt the same way.
She was happy as a child with school over and vacation beginning.

The lights went down for the fourth act. I felt as if I had been
in that theatre for hours and hours. It was then that I discovered something new. This fourth act of *La Favorite* has been
admired by musicians as having unexpected power. Wagner
speaks of it.

When Léonore, disguised in the white robe of a novice, enters
the monastery with the despairing hope of receiving Fernand's
forgiveness before she dies, a new realism takes the place of the
conventionality of the earlier acts. When my wife came in,
leaning against the cloister pillars to control her weakness, it was
a new picture. When she prayed on her knees against the inexorable chant of the monks behind the scenes, it was most moving. When Fernand appeared and she threw herself into a desperate passion, imploring mercy for her dying soul, rising higher
and higher, finally sweeping opposition aside with her irresistible
insistence, it was truly great—no longer opera, just a naked soul.
Scaremberg rose to great heights. The curtain dropped on an

astonished audience, no one more so than I. I realized that I had a precious and unusual something in my charge, a power that could move and help. I had a duty to fulfill toward others.

It sobered and impressed me. Up to that scene it had been only a question of singing and deportment, and this new thing was unexpressed.

Behind the scenes all was animation and gaiety. Congratulations, laughter, relief, wisecracks, old street clothes, au revoirs, rehearsal of *Hamlet* on Tuesday, at ten o'clock, don't forget! One opera over and another immediately begun! It was a factory, a workshop, without rest or time for reliving.

We went home—my wife just a piece in the operatic picture puzzle which had to be put together over and over again, and I just a helper, the husband of a singer. We were happy and humble; proud that she had gotten through so successfully, and very conscious of the greatness of the art and the infinite distance that lay ahead of us.

But it was great fun, very exciting and thrilling. We had many funny incidents to recall, little things that had happened, this tone and that, this singer and that. I told about the audience; my wife hardly knew there was any. We loved the artists and Amadou. I realized what work it all was and made her promise she would never go on singing when the pleasure did not outrank the work a hundredfold.

Monday was a day of rest. There were fine newspaper notices —"Hear this!" Yawns and laughter and a comfortable feeling of something done. A walk in the park with the baby. No one noticed us; it was fun to be incognito; we even saw people sitting on the benches reading the account of the debut. My wife has a wicked sense of humor and rebounds from excitement like a rubber ball. She even takes the solemnity out of her Boston husband. We talked of everything but the night before. That was past history and gone in the limbo.

Artists may lift audiences to the heights and leave them there, but they themselves drop back to earth and enjoy the common, solid ground. They have no use for peaks and pinnacles except when they are working. Blessed compensation! It means new strength and sanity, human fellowship, and no silly nonsense, devastating pose or cross-eyed, inflating egotism!

Hamlet was a fine performance. Mlle. Merguilles, the Ophélie, had been a favorite for twenty years. It seemed funny to have a debutante as the Queen Mother. The audience broke into applause at one of my wife's low tones, a simple note in a recitative passage. The French applaud single low tones, Americans never do. Montfort was wonderful as Hamlet.

Then came *Samson et Dalila*, the favorite opera of all France. This was difficult; there was the soft, exposed solo in the first act, the dance and poses, the thrill of singing "Mon Cœur" with the tenor instead of as a solo—all new and exciting. Julienne had outdone himself on these costumes, the roses hanging to the floor, the long black wig which had cost so much and which she wore for the first time.

She made Dalila a religious fanatic dominated by a high purpose, using the power of her beauty for her god and her people. The whole performance, artists, chorus, ballet and orchestra, was fine and made a great hit.

Then came a great event, a Wagner opera in Vichy—very difficult on a small stage. It was *Lohengrin,* and Madame Adiny, a great American prima donna well known in Europe, was imported for the occasion, from Germany, I think, to sing Elsa. She was very large and had a most beautiful voice. It is sad to think of the Americans who have made great successes in Europe only to remain unknown in their own country.

My wife struggled with Ortrud, a soprano part, which was then, and was to be forevermore, her most difficult role. Her costume weighed a ton, and she was on her feet an hour in the first act.

The second act was thrilling. Her voice rang out in the darkness in that small theatre and had a sinister sound. Again she made her character a fanatic, justified in all she did through her devotion to her gods. Nothing wicked about *her!* Just triumphant womanhood venturing all and failing magnificently.

At this time we learned the truth about Mrs. Homer's "grand debut." It had been carefully concealed from us, but now that she had become such a favorite there was no harm in telling us the story.

It seems that about two months before the opening of the opera season the plans for the season had been announced. Immediately a protest arose at having a debutante in the company. Such a thing had not happened in a generation and was unworthy of anything so choice and important as the Vichy season.

It would jeopardize the success of the performances and meet with the disfavor of the *abonnés*, that valuable clientele on which Vichy depended for its prosperity. The city had voted a small subsidy toward the support of the opera, and some of the city fathers took the matter up.

M. Bussac stood by his guns and virtually staked his position and reputation on the accuracy of his judgment. The town split into two factions, and the battle raged furiously right up to this night of the debut. This accounted for the excitement which I felt but could not understand. It is amusing to think of our complete ignorance of this tempest in a teapot, and our innocent concentration on notes, tones, inflections, sincerity, memory, and other such trifles. And it is a wonderful commentary on the fellowship behind the scenes that everyone should try so hard to keep us from knowing the least thing of what was going on.

I wish the public knew more of this fellowship. I think of Caruso, sinking his voice to a whisper in the *Gioconda* duet to help out my wife who was suffering from a terrible cold, and singing only to oblige a desperate management; of the difficulty in inducing him ever to take a curtain call alone; of all the *Gioconda* cast gathering in my wife's dressing room that night in

Cincinnati when her trunk was lost, Nordica with her box of jewels, Plançon with his make-up things, Caruso with his box of shoes, chagrined because they were a shade too large (he knew he had some in New York that would just fit her) and Edyth Walker sewing furiously away on substitute costumes.

In August M. Bussac said he had just received a request from the director of La Villa des Fleurs, Aix-les-Bains, for Madame Homer in one performance of *La Favorite*.

They would pay her two hundred francs and all expenses. He advised accepting. We were gone four days and were glad to get back. The performance was enthusiastically received, but I did not like it. The hastily gathered company, the scratch orchestra, crude scenery, and glaring light, made me realize how artistically managed our own opera was. A singer is the victim of his surroundings. One inefficient member can almost ruin a cast. They say that a battleship fleet has only the speed of its slowest unit. Something like that obtains in opera. I have often heard some one say, "I didn't like X so well tonight." X may have been at his best; but if Y was out of voice, or Z succeeded in destroying the illusion, X must suffer. It is a very wise listener who really knows why performances vary.

A small role in *Thaïs*, a fine one in *Le Roi d'Ys*, repetitions of the repertoire, farewell performances, good-byes and regrets at the breaking up of the company just as it had reached real excellence, and the season was over. We hurried to La Boule-Escoublac on the coast of Brittany, where we had two weeks with the baby in the sand.

We thought the season over and agreed that it had been a most wonderful experience. Audiences think of opera in performances, but artists think in seasons. Good or bad health, good or poor repertoire, fine or indifferent company, handsome or slim pay—these make up the season.

My composing had gone by the board. This going to rehearsals almost every morning and performances two or three times a week, listening constantly to music that one did not always care for or got tired of, was going to make it difficult to get down to my own work.

I thought of my queer, new position as husband of a successful singer and felt uneasy, as any American would. No one around the opera knew I was a musician; if they heard it they immediately forgot it. No one counted who did not take an actual part in the performance—except the director and the treasurer. You can hang around a race track or racing stables and say you grow flowers, but it doesn't make much impression; only horses matter. But the whole thing was grand and worth any sacrifice and any inward struggles with pride.

VII
1898–1899

WE WENT TO ANGERS–BLACK ANGERS, AS
it is called—where the English Plantagenets came from; a strange
austere city in the heart of the royalist part of France. This was
no cosmopolitan place, such as Vichy, bright and busy with
transient life, but a cold, carefully regulated town, buried in old
French customs. Many of the inhabitants awaited the return of
the King.

I remember that a month later, when the Comte de Romain
took us to his château, he showed us the apartment reserved for
the King. The sheets and towels were changed every day, and
the rooms swept and dusted. "He may come any day," said the
Count. The pathos of this forlorn hope was too apparent.

Our noisy rooms on the stone-paved main street disheartened
us. We must have a quiet home. There was not one furnished
house in the town which could be rented. Houses were sancti-
fied heirlooms and were carefully guarded. Desperately we
walked the streets; there must be some way!

Half a block from a beautiful park we found an empty stucco
house with a fine garden, with a sign *"A Louer"* on it. We hurried to the owner; yes, we could have it for six months, at ten
dollars a month. We almost ran to the big furniture store; yes,
they would furnish it throughout and charge us ten dollars a
month rental, plus damages. We found a dear, old French "lady"
to cook for us, at four dollars a month, and in three days we
were installed. When the opera company assembled and found
that we already had a cozy home they were amazed. They lived
for six months in small furnished rooms and cheap hotels and

complained constantly, while we, at less cost, were in clover. "*Sapristi*, these clever Americans!" they said.

The Angers season demonstrated what every American city can have, with ease: a moderate-sized theatre (large houses are fatal to young voices and real illusion), a fine company, and an interesting repertoire. The orchestra and artists can be used for bimonthly symphony concerts, and even a string quartet and chamber concerts are not beyond possibility.

A modest endowment to keep the ticket prices within the popular reach and a wise director, with sure artistic instincts, insure success. Tickets beyond the reach of the popular purse, or an inartistic director, spells failure. Gifted young singers and players abound. Almost every great artist now before the public was at one time a member of some small company. They were all young once.

A little more courage and a hundred American cities will have such institutions. Forty cities in little France had them, when we were there, and could not live without them.

The people of Angers thrilled as the opera season opened. M. Breton, the director, presided like a father over his family of brilliant children, every one of whom made a success. Gauthier, the tenor, was young and not too experienced; but his voice was beautiful and he improved with each performance. He was later the leading tenor at the Opéra Comique in Paris, for, I believe, twenty years. Seveilhac, the baritone, was very fine, and years later came to Hammerstein, at the Manhattan Opera House in New York.

These people were young; only a little patience is necessary with young people who are gifted, and of course it is a pleasure to see them grow. Only by giving singers a chance while they are young, before they have eaten their hearts out with weary waiting, can we expect great artists.

My wife made her debut in *La Favorite* and sang her repertoire. In December *Aida* was added. This was a great event.

Amneris gave her new opportunities and seemed to bring out new qualities. She had studied this role a little with Lhérie, but had to work out most of it by herself. Our little stucco house became Pharaoh's palace, and baby Louise and Anna made a good audience. Even then little Louise was a regular *claqueur*.

In January came *Samson et Dalila,* and this was the success of the season. M. Breton engaged the score and parts (it was very expensive) for four performances and increased the number to twelve. He was supremely happy.

One day, for no reason at all, I suddenly thought of Maurice Grau, and determined to report to him as he had asked us to do. I recalled the audition in the Boulevard Haussmann to his memory and gave him a simple account of our experience at Vichy and Angers. The letter called for no answer. I had a thrill when I wrote the address: The Metropolitan Opera House, New York.

We were still a thousand miles from any opera house of first rank and would, apparently, continue in provincial theatres until we grew tired of it; then we would go back to Boston and renew our old life. Offers from small towns were coming in, and M. Breton began to talk about terms for the next year.

Our performance of *Samson et Dalila* became so famous that we had to go, *en masse,* to several French cities and give it. (I say "we," which shows how the husbands and wives of singers feel themselves a part of every performance. It is always thus. They take part, rejoice and suffer, vicariously.)

At last Tours insisted on a performance. At the same time the Agence Roberval asked my wife to come to Paris to meet M. Calabresi of La Monnaie. La Monnaie! A vibrating name! She secured one day's leave of absence.

The performance at Tours was a tremendous affair. It was an annual gala, with the Senator, deputies, and entire city government present. All performances look alike to the artist; but to the audience they vary with the solemnity and grandeur of the trimmings. A function is a function and not merely art.

During the performance a delegation waited on Mrs. Homer and requested our presence at an official banquet after the performance. We thought of the appointment with M. Calabresi the next morning, with sinking hearts; but we could not decline. It meant too much to M. Breton and the Comte de Romain. From twelve to three each official, in turn, solemnly wished my wife, the only lady present, a very long life and a most brilliant career. We—all but she—arose and sat down after every wish. She had that painted smile on her face which I tell her is the greatest fake which I, personally, have ever seen. I knew she was thinking of Calabresi.

After two hours of sleep she was on the train, and at nine the next morning she was at the Agence Roberval. M. and Mme. Koenig met her there. I went back to Angers; we were always uneasy away from the baby.

At noon came a telegram: "Have signed for La Monnaie." That night she was back home again and told me the story. She had had a compartment to herself all the way up to Paris, and had practiced her voice. It was fine, in spite of the night before. She met Calabresi at nine and sang the great scene from *Le Prophète*. He looked very solemn and said she had better sing at Angers the following winter and then come to him.

But you just cannot fool an American girl, with Scotch-Irish blood in her veins! She looked at him sharply, and instantly said:

"Monsieur Calabresi, I do not know where I shall sing next winter; but one thing I do know: I shall not sing at Angers!"

He roared with laughter, and his little fat body shook like jelly. "Bring the contract!" he shouted.

His tender feelings for his comrade, Breton, his consideration for a fellow director, had kept his mouth shut until my wife's final dictum released him from those secret bonds of honor. She read him like a book: she is a great reader!

We were happy beyond words! The news spread through the company and congratulations poured in. The town was disturbed, and M. Breton was criticized, openly, for allowing this to happen. The Comte de Romain wrote a tribute to my wife which was published in the papers. He explained that their opera could not hope to compete with an institution like La Monnaie.

A symphony concert was organized, and my wife sang the *Prophète* scene; and there was a great fuss, and it was all great fun.

At this moment the second great sorrow came to our family. My dear brother-in-law, Frederick Diman, had been suddenly killed in a railway accident. It was terrible. I thought of my poor sister and mother. And then of my poor wife, tied by her contract, and suffering almost as much as I. Finally, I thought of the only solution and cabled my mother and sister to sell the house and come immediately to us; bring the boys, of course, and break forever from such sad surroundings. It was all I could do. Our one great desire was to have them with us, so that we could help them.

The performances went on. Nothing is quite so inexorable, impersonal, and insistent as opera. In almost everything else some one can take your place and do your work. In opera there is no one, particularly in a small company. You simply put your personal life aside, and give your duty to your director and your fellow artists first place.

It was now late in March, and the end of the Angers season was approaching. The directors were happy over the success of the first year of their public-spirited venture. Not only the opera but the symphony orchestra had been enthusiastically received. Their policy regarding the latter had been unique. They gave ten concerts, and instead of engaging an expensive conductor for whom there would have been too little to do, they invited eminent composers from Paris to assist, each composer conducting a classical program and also one of his own works in larger form.

Vincent d'Indy came for one concert, Widor for another, and Leroux for another. It was an interesting experiment as it brought living composers into intimate relationship with the public of Angers. It all had a progressive and public-spirited nature, and the general feeling was jubilant.

Behind the scenes and in the orchestra pit, it was quite different. I know nothing sadder than the false glamour in which artists are placed. To the public they appear the spoiled children of fortune; and the bright lights, wondrous costumes, and endless applause all seem to bear this out.

But among themselves there is much anxiety. How will they manage to live through the spring and summer, what will happen next winter? These are the questions they ask themselves. "Have you an Easter engagement?" "Are you singing anywhere this summer?" "Madame Homer, if you know any place where I could get in, do speak for me!" This from a singer of small parts. She appears on the stage in royal robes and then rushes to her dressing room to stitch furiously on tinsel embroidery, her mother and grandmother stitching with her. She earns more by sewing than by singing, and can only live by working fourteen hours a day at both. She will be maid to a leading artist, help the wardrobe lady, run errands, or do any odd job to earn a few francs, and at the end of any short season may find herself adrift and helpless.

And all the public sees is a beautiful young girl, very graceful and with a sweet voice. "I like her very much," "She is charming," "Her voice was very lovely in that little scene"—these are her pay, her reward, but this praise will not support her, and, alas, may not even reach her ears.

I would not dare to express my feelings about the neglect, humiliation, and struggles often endured by these people, whom the public really admires and for whom it would gladly do something to show its appreciation. No solution for this absurd situation has been found. Directors and managers are helpless; they fight against odds to keep their doors open. A wisely administered endowment or foundation is the only thing that would solve this problem. The world has become aware of the plight of the teacher and professor, but that of the "small artist" is quite unknown.

One satisfaction they have which cannot be taken from them, and which is very dear to them. They can print on their cards: Mlle. D—— of the Grand Théâtre de Lyon, Théâtre d'Angers, M. B—— of the Théâtre Royal de la Monnaie, Théâtre d'Ostende, Théâtre d'Amiens, Miss Q—— of the Metropolitan Opera House!

Our situation was exciting: we were rich in success and had been able, with care, to meet our expenses each month, including the payment to Julien, the costumer. Each new opera, *Hérodiade, Princesse d'Auberge* and so on, had required new costumes and fresh outlay. We had an eight months' contract with La Monnaie, beginning September 15th, at one thousand francs a month, and had sublet our little furnished apartment in Paris. We faced six months of idleness. Small offers from small places came in, but the prestige of our Brussels engagement prevented us from accepting. Prestige is the soul of opera!

At that moment a kind and wondrous bolt came down from the blue! A letter arrived from Mr. Higgins, director of the Royal Opera, Covent Garden, London. He had received a letter from Mr. Grau of the Metropolitan Opera in New York, who was also going to manage the Covent Garden season, asking him to communicate with Madame Homer about a possible engagement. Would it be possible for her to meet Lord and Lady de Grey, his codirectors, in Paris, some time within two weeks? This was Mr. Grau's answer to my letter! My wife and I looked at each other. We couldn't speak. What was this thing that was shaping our lives in ways that we would not dream of as even possibilities? We didn't know, but we felt it. Gratitude filled our hearts, inarticulate and undefined, just simple gratitude and that was all.

Mrs. Homer wrote, telegrams were exchanged, M. Breton granted leave, deeply moved and impressed. A few weeks before, he had been raising his offer for the next year, a hundred francs at a time.

Mrs. Homer went to Paris on the morning train. M. Koenig had wisely secured a gorgeous hall in the Paris Opéra for the audition. He was sure it would impress the directors of Covent Garden. At two o'clock my wife sang Amneris's great scene in the fourth act of *Aida* for Lord and Lady de Grey. They offered her a contract for eleven weeks at five hundred francs ($100) a week. The repertoire was discussed. "You know we do *Aida* in Italian and *Lohengrin* in German," remarked Lady de Grey. "Certainly," replied my wife, casually and cheerfully. She had never sung a role in Italian or German and would have only two weeks in which to prepare them, but why disturb the pleasant atmosphere of this quasisocial gathering in the lovely Paris Opéra?

In the evening she was back in Angers with the agreement in her pocket; the contract was to follow.

It was April now, and the farewell performances took place. My wife said adieu as Dalila. Our baritone was provoked at this as he disliked the role of High Priest and wanted to do Hamlet. He took revenge by mumbling the role in a weak voice that could hardly be heard. It was very amusing, but the management was enraged.

However, when he learned that Mrs. Homer had not been consulted in the choice of operas he came to her and humbly apologized; he really felt very bad. He was a good fellow at heart and a fine artist, but he was from the Midi and the hot blood of southern France had got the better of him.

It was all over and our trunks were packed when suddenly M. Breton asked my wife to sing one short recital in the small hall for the subscribers. They urgently requested it. This was difficult, but she couldn't refuse. We got out all the songs which had been slumbering for nearly a year and furbished them up. It was a most moving evening. Everyone knew she would never come back and wanted to show the affectionate regard in which she was held. The flowers and wreaths came up after every number, and I am sure my wife never had such a struggle with her tears and emotions.

For thirty years we have thought of that season at Angers as a wonderful experience, sufficient in itself to repay my wife for all the study and hard work she had gone through.

We were back in our little Paris apartment again, and in two weeks must be off to London. My wife had taken a cold after that last Angers recital, the first she had had in years, and was confined to her room. I secured an expert Italian *répétiteur* who taught her Amneris in Italian two or three hours every morning, and a fine German who taught her Ortrud and Fricka every afternoon. She was too hoarse to sing but she could memorize, and, in addition, she had a marvelous ear for diction and the correct pronunciation of languages. It was another fight against time, and she won.

We had almost no money, and I remember borrowing twenty-five dollars from Augustus Saint-Gaudens as an extra precaution. It wouldn't be pleasant to arrive in London with just enough to carry us to the first pay day. We could calculate ahead quite closely what it would cost in a French city and we knew that in France the local management was aware that its artists were entirely dependent on the prompt payment of their salaries. There was never any assumption in a small theatre that an artist was in funds, and a small advance payment could even be requested without loss of dignity. But in London it was different. We felt that a leading artist (Mrs. Homer's contract read "leading artist") would be expected never to refer to anything so mundane as money, and to live and move about with that modest luxury, or, at least, easy refinement, that was the natural atmosphere of Covent Garden. Past successes presupposed funds on hand. Any reference to shortness of cash would be a bore.

Where artistic life is simple, one dares to be poor. You haven't lost caste when the fact creeps out. But in more worldly circles snobbery is the great quicksand of life, and without the glamour of success, admiration may easily change to condescension and awe to patronage.

We put up at a small hotel and started out to find a home. It was discouraging, and we had almost given up when the agent suddenly said one morning: "Mr. Rutledge has not been able to rent his house and will let you have it for three pounds a week. It is a beautiful house facing Regent's Park." Glorious! We moved in that day. It was a palace. Even the piano in the drawing room was lacquered in gold. The library overlooking the park was in red leather, and the house was filled from top to bottom with hunting prints. You would have thought that all Britain wore red coats if you had not had to go through Tottenham Court Road on the way to the bus. Baby Louise had endless adventures in that great house and never tired of exploring. Regent's Park was another great joy to her.

In a few days my mother and sister, and her two lovely little boys, arrived from America, and our happiness was complete. Rehearsals had begun. Artists were arriving from all corners of the earth, and chaos seemed to reign. To get a real rehearsal seemed impossible. So-and-so might rehearse, but who was going to sing at the performance? The various stage managers and orchestral conductors seemed to get in one another's way. Everybody wanted the stage at once. While you rehearsed, groups of people talked in four languages in the wings and all over the theatre. Tall men with silk hats and monocles seemed to have the entrée everywhere. I had never seen auditors at rehearsals before. Rehearsals in France were ceremonies conducted with precision amid silent surroundings.

We were glad to see Mr. Grau again. His office was an oasis of artistic imperturbability in this noisy confusion. He smiled broadly when he saw us. Our minds, and his, went back to that winter afternoon on the Boulevard Haussmann, eighteen months before, when he had advised my wife not to sign any five-year contracts. On that day she had never sung a role; now she had ninety performances of big parts behind her. He seemed very happy about this, almost as if some conviction within himself had come true.

Mr. Grau was a most straightforward man. There was no gush or flattery about him, but you always felt that you had his real respect and utmost consideration. He had that wonderful New York insight into real values and was impervious to "side" or pose. You knew you could trust him. He told my wife she would make her debut as Amneris under Signor Mancinelli's direction, and asked her, as a favor, to learn Lola and sing it, with Mme. Calvé as Santuzza, because the artist whom he had engaged for this part could not arrive in time.

Mancinelli was kindness itself and asked her to sing the Prologue in his opera, *Ero e Leandro*, which would be produced during the season.

Mr. Higgins, the director, and Mrs. Higgins gave a grand concert at their house to introduce some of the new artists, including my wife. On arrival we took convenient seats near the piano. It was a long program in which my wife sang "Mon cœur s'ouvre à ta voix" and several other things, with Landon Ronald at the piano. There was a large and "notable" audience present. Just what a "notable" is I have never been able to discover unless it is a person whose name is mentioned regularly in some column of the newspapers.

Not until the concert was over did we discover that we had innocently taken seats in the section reserved exclusively for dukes and duchesses and others of the higher nobility. Signor Tosti and other musicians present were greatly amused.

The debut was a great success. Amid the éclat of that great audience, with the royal family present, my wife's sincerity and simplicity, her grace and beauty of voice, seemed as something unconventional, almost naïve.

I stood in the wings, a few feet from her, as she sang her last great scene, and at the last, long, high A-natural, with her hands clenched high in the air, she rushed off the stage and fell into my arms, tears streaming down her cheeks! She could hardly take her recalls. It was one of those crucial nights that turn the course of an artist's life one way or another.

It seems cruel that such an atmosphere of exaggeration should be concentrated at a debut. What is a debut? It is but one of hundreds of performances in an artist's career. A number of extraneous things may mar that particular performance—an over-heated house, a draft, unfortunate lighting, some slight indisposition, or a tired and overworked conductor. This is the artist's point of view. But, unfortunately, there is another. At a debut, the emphasis is not on the performance, but on how the audience likes the artist. The cart is placed before the horse, and the greatest artists tremble before this crude, inartistic treatment of a purely artistic thing.

The Covent Garden season went merrily on, and artists came and went. My wife sang *Aida* with three different sopranos in the title role: Mme. Litvinne, Mme. Gadski and Miss MacIntyre. Two or three different tenors sang Rhadames, and at the fourth performance a new Amonasro arrived. He was a young Italian who had been engaged for the Metropolitan Opera House for the following winter. He electrified us with a wonderful performance and then quickly gained the friendship of everyone through his winning personality. His name was Antonio Scotti.

Ero e Leandro had a fair success. Mr. Grau received a command for my wife to sing at Windsor for the Queen on a certain date but had to plead an important performance from which he could not spare her.

Just before the season closed the London agent for B. Schott's Söhne heard some of my songs. He was much interested and wanted Dr. Strecker, the head of the house at Mainz, to hear them. When he learned that we were planning to spend the rest of the summer at Heyst on the coast of Belgium, he was pleased

Photograph Aimé Dupont

AS AMNERIS AT HER DEBUT AT COVENT GARDEN,
MAY, 1899

and said Dr. Strecker would be at a near-by resort and he would ask him to call on us.

In the heat of mid-July the season petered out. Covent Garden had seemed rather strange to me, after my experience in France. There was a pageantry on the stage and in the audience, and much of the self-consciousness of an official or social function. Great artists impressed with their voices and personalities. Sensational climaxes were keenly felt. There seemed to be a deep craving for passionate utterance.

Diction went by the board. Artists from a dozen countries sang in Italian, French, and German, and their diction mattered little. Few in the audience understood them, in any case. Various methods of singing would be jumbled in one performance, but that disturbed no one except, perhaps, the orchestral conductor. What he thought did not count; his job was to manage the orchestra.

In France I had heard two companies sing in perfect French to audiences who hung on every word. The method of singing was homogeneous throughout. The subtlest meanings could be conveyed in quiet passages. The theatres were small and there was perfect intimacy between the stage and the back row. The orchestral conductor took the place of the composer and the poet and strove for the sincerity and truth which they had felt. In France, my wife's diction, which was so much appreciated, had been a great factor in her success. At Covent Garden, it was not needed. (This was in 1899. All may be changed now.)

It became clear to me that operas (as well as symphonies) could be presented in a thousand different ways, and that their value to the public depended on their presentation.

No art can survive unworthy performance. Insincerity and meretriciousness are easily felt in operas, as they are in symphonies or any other form of music.

The protection of music lies in its inherent nature. Under abuse, it quietly disappears. You have the shell of the nut but not the kernel, the appearance of music but not music.

VIII
1899–1900

WE WENT TO HEYST-SUR-MER AND HAD A glorious time. The children revelled in the sand. My mother and sister had entered a new world. They had seen Louise in great parts with great artists in a great opera house and were thrilled beyond measure. One of the rewards in a singer's life is the new, great joy that springs up in the family and among all friends and acquaintances. It is probably the most intimate and touching thing in all her experience. It, alone, seems to justify what might, otherwise, appear to be mere ambition.

We could look back on a first year in opera with its hundred performances in great roles, but we spent little time doing that. With La Monnaie ahead of us we wanted only rest and change.

One day Dr. Strecker sent word that he wished to call. This was exciting! He came early in the morning and stayed all day. My wife sang some thirty or forty of my songs for him, many of them two or three times. He spoke English fluently and entered easily into the spirit of all the poems.

Finally, after a long, hard day, he made me a blanket offer; he would publish all the songs, with both German and English texts, paying a cash price, without royalty. I was surprised. The most I had hoped for was that he might like certain songs. It was a fine offer, and the house of B. Schott's Söhne was internationally famous. Dr. Strecker was the director and must know whereof he spoke. Yet I was uneasy. I thought an American publisher would be in closer contact with the only public I could hope to reach, and I did not like to sell the songs outright. The royalty plan was attractive.

After several days I declined the offer. But the effect of such an offer was not lost. I realized that perhaps I was writing to more purpose than I had thought, and that if I kept on something might come of it all.

It was all most encouraging and kept me from losing myself entirely in the exciting and most absorbing opera life.

In September, completely rested and ready for the fray, we went to Brussels, where we quickly found a house near the park. My mother and sister found one near by, and I found a studio on the noisiest street in town. I had my entire family with me now, and that sense of anxiety which always comes with separation was gone. Baby Louise was almost four years old and talked French with tremendous, almost comical, speed. We couldn't attempt to keep pace with her.

We reported at the opera house, and M. Stumont and M. Calabresi welcomed us royally. We knew we were in the house of our friends, and this was the greatest comfort that could come to us.

There may be vicissitudes in an artist's public life, but they do not count for as much as the friendship, confidence, and loyalty of his director. His responsibility is to his director, and this is always uppermost in his mind.

Stumont and Calabresi watched over their artists as fathers watch over their children, and left nothing undone that could help them. The artists, in turn, knew they were working under two men who had done great, almost impossible things for young singers, and their devotion was complete.

The rehearsals were unique. At nine o'clock every morning, Calabresi, Stumont, Flon, the director of the orchestra, and Almanz, the stage director, would take their seats on a raised platform, built over the orchestra pit. Rehearsals, usually with piano only, would then proceed steadily until one o'clock. During these hours these four men would concentrate on every tone, gesture, step, position, inflection of utterance, and so on, of each singer. It was a university of opera. Not an unkind word was spoken. No matter how awkward or untrained a singer might be, their patience was never exhausted; they took it as a matter of course and went over the difficult points until they were conquered. I had the privilege of seeing them train a young girl, Mlle. Rambly, who was still in the Brussels Ecole Supérieure (High School), for the role of Elsa. The rehearsals extended, irregularly, over a period of four months, and when she appeared she gave a finished performance. It did not surprise me that she afterward became a leading soprano at the Paris Opéra.

These men were working under a small endowment and limited budget and depended on themselves to arrive at an artistic finish, nothing less than which would satisfy them. They persisted and insisted until the performance was a thing of beauty, and then they allowed it to appear before the public.

Aida was the opening performance and was received with enthusiasm. To our great delight Mr. Grau came over from London to see it. He was in high spirits, and I suspect he was, that very night, making plans for the future.

Hamlet and *La Favorite* followed, and then Massenet came up from Paris to produce his new opera, *Cendrillon* (*Cinderella*). My wife had a most difficult part, Mme. de la Haltière, the stepmother. It is one thing for an American girl to sing serious roles on a French stage, but quite another matter to sing a funny part. Humor is a very uncertain and dangerous thing, on the stage, and it was a new experience for my wife. Fortunately, she had Gilibert to help her. He sang the father and shared all her scenes, and took infinite pains to help her all he could. The opera was a great success and was given forty times during the rest of the season, crowding out other operas that the management had hoped to produce. We, of course, were disappointed; but then disappointments of this kind come into every artist's life. After all the success that my wife had as Dalila, at Angers, she did not sing that role again until she sang it with Caruso, nearly twenty years later. It seems a waste that artists have to give up their best parts, but there are many things that enter in, which, apparently, make it necessary.

Lohengrin was a fine performance, and then came *L'Attaque du Moulin*. In this opera, Séguin, who was about to retire from the stage, was superb. This baritone sang with a depth of emotion, a repose and distinction which held one almost breathless. I have rarely heard anything so moving.

The season was moving toward its close when a sad thing happened. M. Stumont, our beloved director, became ill and died. Only those who know the stage can understand what the feelings of the company were. There is something peculiar about the stage. There all work together in a difficult and emotional task. They share great accomplishments, face great tasks, reap a common reward, and understand one another's burdens.

Calabresi announced that he would not continue, and new directors for the following year were appointed. Mr. Bussac came up from Paris, hoping to get the job, and we were very happy to see him again. He rejoiced in my wife's rapid progress. The company grew very nervous. Who, if any, would be reengaged? There was a great deal of assumed indifference, but the green room was very quiet. There was much tension, and it was difficult to sing. Why, after all, should artists, fine artists, have to lead such a precarious existence? It seems unjust. In other walks of life men build secure positions for themselves. Artists build, but another can take away.

We had made no plans for the future and were rather nonplused. Contracts are made far ahead, and it was already late in the season. It might be back to Boston and the good old work. We laughed and were ready for anything. You simply cannot feel discouraged when you have made a lot of progress in your work. Only standing still disheartens one.

In one short week the matter was settled and we couldn't go back to Boston, much as we loved it.

Mr. Higgins came over from London and reengaged my wife

for the Covent Garden spring season. He insisted on the same terms as the first season, which rather surprised us.

Two days later a long cablegram came from Mr. Grau, offering my wife a three-year contract with the Metropolitan Opera House, a five months' season each winter, ten performances each month, four thousand dollars the first season, forty-five hundred the second, and five thousand the third; repertoire, *Aida, Lohengrin,* and so on.

It was great—wonderful! Even if we did not accept it, we were pleased to get it. We had grown hardened by this time and were beyond surprises. We read it again. Ah, I told you so! There was a hitch! It will surprise those who heard my wife during her first two seasons at the Metropolitan to learn what the hitch was. Down at the end of a long repertoire of twenty operas the cablegram read, "Siébel in *Faust,* Urbano in *Les Huguenots.*" Never! Back to Boston first! My wife should never wear tights! We hurried down to Calabresi and showed him the cablegram. We were boiling with indignation!

"My dear," he said, "don't be so excited!" He rang the bell and sent for the costumer and explained the tragedy to her. "Oh, it is nothing! It is nothing! As Siébel you shall wear the long, loose trousers that buckle below the knee. It is the style, the true style. The little soubrettes with their silly tights are wrong, all wrong. They have no style at all. As Urbano you shall wear the long, loose boots that buckle high above the knee! Very high! It is the style. And a coat that comes almost to the top of the boots. It is nothing, my child, nothing. Sign your beautiful contract and tell Mr. Grau I will make your costumes if he wishes."

We cabled Mr. Grau that the conditions were acceptable but that my wife must design her costumes for Siébel and Urbano —they must be long and loose. He cabled back: "Wear anything you like, am sending contract."

The farewell performances took place, and they were real farewells. This company that had worked together like clockwork was dispersing to the four corners. Of the artists that Calabresi had assembled for this season of 1899–1900, Maubourg, Gilibert, Journet, Imbart de la Tour, Decléry, and Flon went to the Metropolitan; Lalla Miranda and Dufranne went, later, to the Manhattan Opera House; Rambly to the Paris Opéra, and Landouzy and Jérôme to the Opéra Comique. Calabresi had a mere pittance to work with, but he had genius. He had to find real artists while they were still young and little known because he could pay but small fees. Most of the great singers of opera in French—Calvé, Melba, Alvarez, Renaud, and so on—made their debuts under his direction.

I should like to emphasize what I have said before: any small city can have fine opera. All that is needed is a great director and not too large a theatre. Very few voices are adapted to large theatres; therefore the larger the theatre, the fewer the available artists. Wagner, at Bayreuth, depended entirely on artistic success to insure the continuation of his performances, and built a small theatre with only twelve hundred seats. The performances have continued for more than fifty years, and this seems to vindicate his judgment. All large halls and theatres militate against artistic success; without artistic success every project falls to the ground. Wagner is the greatest artist who ever designed a theatre; his institution is the most enduring known to modern times. All this deserves the deepest consideration.

We said good-bye to Calabresi; it was a sad farewell. His codirector had died. He had retired from the theatre to which he had dedicated his life. We felt greatly concerned about him. The eighty performances which my wife had sung under his direction had been an experience, the value of which could not be expressed in words. She had grown steadily in artistic power and understanding; her voice was more glorious than ever, and her emotional sincerity ever more apparent. He knew all this and rejoiced. His passion was the making of great artists, and my wife's voice and talent had been an endless joy to him through-

out the winter. We were going to America, and he was old; it
was unlikely that we should ever meet again. Our hearts were
filled with gratitude and sadness.

We hurried to London. The rehearsals were under way, and
there was much excitement. Covent Garden seemed fabulously
rich and able to engage every great artist in the world. It presented a strange contrast to La Monnaie with its little stock
company and quiet order.

We learned that my wife would sing Ortrud under the direction of Felix Mottl, who had just been brought from Munich—
a great role in German, and we realized that German traditions
might vary from those that she had learned in France. We wondered what Mottl would be like, and it was with some trepida-
tion that we went to rehearsal. To our joy we found he was the
easiest-going, pleasantest sort of man, anxious to help in every
way and glad to give my wife all the private rehearsals she
wanted. He became so enthusiastic over her voice that he asked
her to sing some of his own songs at a private musicale. This was
a great compliment, as the company was full of German artists,
any one of whom he could have called on.

The musicale was a grand affair, and all the notables were
there. My wife sang beautifully, and Mottl's accompaniments
were exquisite. It was interesting to meet Henry Irving and Ellen
Terry, Van Rooy, and others, in such an informal way. They
were very impressive in intimate surroundings. Other cities glo-
rify a man's art and leave him in obscurity: London patronizes
his art and magnifies his presence. One has a little of the feeling
of a great zoo with the animals walking loose.

We admire the good taste with which Continental Europe
avoids intrusion into a man's private life. But we are also touched
by London's frank adoration of a great man, even when it cannot give much time to the consideration of his work.

At last *Lohengrin* came, and it was a great night for me. I
loved to hear my wife sing at all times. Romance, beauty, emo-

AS ORTRUD (first performance in German), **COVENT GARDEN,**
MAY, 1900

tion—the whole gamut was fascinating, thrilling to me; but this was holy ground! All my five years in German opera houses came back to me with a rush. There was my wife singing a great German work, in German, with a great cast and a great conductor, and singing wonderfully. She was young, but then perhaps Ortrud wasn't old, after all. The young can sometimes plot, have subtle feelings and deceptive appeal. It was a great night, and everyone was happy. Mottl was enthusiastic, and it meant much to us to have this great man's wholesale, emphatic approval.

Artists value public appreciation of their work, but they value still higher the good opinion of a great musician; and that is one of the compensations in musical life. There is always a court of appeal, a higher one, and a still higher one. Over the heads of indifferent officials they appeal to a great musician, as Walther von Stolzing did to Hans Sachs, the poet, and eventually win with the populace, as Walther did. The apprentices who jeer in the first act, cheer in the last act, and so it goes. Great musicians have always played a great part in musical life, inconspicuous, perhaps, but vital.

We agreed on two things from the start: we would never have a press agent, and we would never have a claque. Public opinion would have to take its course. We were assured on all sides (not by musicians and artists, but by people on the outside fringe) that, if we persisted in this course, success would not be ours. But nothing could swerve us, and we stuck to this plan.

We were conscious, of course, of a world outside the opera house that was deeply interested in the performances, but we had no personal contact with it. We did not meet a critic in either London or Brussels. The world within the opera house was the real world, and the standard of the best musicians was the real objective.

This will, perhaps, sound strange to that part of the public which assumes that an artist's sole object is to please it; but a little thought must convince it that I am right. There is an idealism on the stage, created by the best artists on the stage and in the orchestra; and this, of course, must dominate.

When my wife sang Brangaene for the first time, in San Francisco, Edouard de Reszke said to her: "My child, never change your conception of Brangaene. It is absolutely correct!" This was definite assurance of the kind that an artist must value above all applause.

The season went on at a headlong pace. Every day was exciting. A grand production of the *Nibelungen Ring* was approaching for which Mr. Nielson had been especially engaged as stage manager. Everyone was on the *qui vive*.

At the second or third performance of *Lohengrin* a strange thing happened. The Boer War was going on at this time, and the British public was wrought up over a small garrison of English soldiers which had been besieged for several months in the little town of Mafeking. A British column was making a heroic effort to reach them.

The house was packed, and the royal family was present. The first act was majestic and the enthusiasm at its close was great. The second act, in which my wife had her great scenes, was superb, and you felt Wagner's strange power. The unreal became real. Elsa's danger, Ortrud's triumph, the menace of disaster, all shook the audience. At the close of this act the enthusiasm was unbounded. The curtain went up on the third act, and a curious change took place. In a few minutes the royal family arose and left their boxes; then groups of five or ten got up from their seats in the orchestra and left the house; then the balconies began to empty. A strange noise came in from outside the theatre. The last scene went on in a futile, meaningless droning of musical sounds in an almost empty house. *Lohengrin* became the least important thing in the world, and Wagner just a man who wrote music.

Mafeking was free! The news had come just after the second intermission and opera suddenly became too commonplace to notice. When we came out of the theatre there were a million people in the streets, shouting and parading. It took us two hours to go a few blocks.

One day Lady de Grey came to see Louise with a request from the Queen that she sing at the first state concert. It would be held in Buckingham Palace, and the fee would be forty guineas. Mr. Grau had given his consent. Grand! This would be something new and interesting, profitable, and a real experience. My wife accepted. Great preparations and excitement! The theatre costumer made her a dress of white Liberty satin, of regulation court length. She would sing "Mon cœur s'ouvre à ta voix" as her solo, and quartets with the other artists, who were Suzanne Adams, De Lucia, and Plançon.

The dress cost more trouble than the singing; there were fittings and fittings.

The morning of the great day came: There was a rehearsal at Buckingham Palace, and we drove over there in state at ten in the morning. Several tall footmen conducted us to the great hall, where we met Sir Walter Parrott, music director to the Queen. He was as simple and direct as any musician should be and treated the whole affair as a matter of course. He introduced me to the organist, who invited me to share the organ loft with him in the evening. It was high up and I should have a fine view.

The orchestra and the chorus from the Royal College of Music were in place, and the rehearsal passed off quickly. There was a little talk about court etiquette and curtsies, and we hurried home.

A good rest, a little voice practice, a long tussle building the hair high up on my wife's head; it must be very high; opera wigs were easier; finally it was up, but would it stay? We hoped so. Then the tight dress, so long and clumsy around the feet; she could hardly breathe, she couldn't walk. Then the curtsies. Heavens! The hair would come down! She mustn't bend over, her hands must find the right place on her dress when she curtsied, she mustn't look down. Oh! The voice! How was it? A couple of beautiful notes; the hair—it was time we were off!

From my place in the organ loft, high above the chorus at the end of the hall, I looked on a strange sight. The guests were taking their places. No one below an earl had been invited, except army and navy officers and ambassadors. The noise of animated conversation filled the hall. Friends seemed to be meeting after long absences. Very old ladies with duchesses' crowns and very low, décolleté gowns climbed painfully to their places, with the help of canes. You admired their courage and felt their English stoicism. Younger women came in elaborate gowns, all with tiaras or coronets, men in court dress and officers in brilliant uniforms filled the aisles and chatted gaily. The Indian princes came in, dressed in gorgeous robes and wearing strings of rubies, emeralds, and diamonds that hung down to their feet. There were fourteen hundred guests, and I was told they represented ownership of three-fourths of the land of England, Scotland, and Wales.

One had a tremendous sense of the concentration of power in Great Britain. Sir George White, the hero of the siege of Ladysmith, came in and was immediately surrounded—besieged again, as it were.

The seats were arranged in rising banks along each side of the hall. The guests could not, thus, turn their backs on the artists at our end of the hall nor on the royal family, for whom a dais had been placed at the other end of the hall.

At last the four artists took their places in chairs at the front of the stage. I could look down on my wife's high hair, and I felt she was as calm as could be expected. Plançon looked very nervous; De Lucia seemed far from home, but Suzanne Adams was quite unconcerned, apparently. Women are braver than men in such situations. Suddenly there was a hush; everyone rose. The hall was silent and motionless as the chamberlains appeared at the farther door, walking backward. They were in rows of four, and their bodies were bent level to the waist. It was a nervous moment. There were twenty of them and it seemed inevitable that one would trip over the dais which was raised a few inches from the floor. They were brave lads, and nothing happened. We took another breath. The royal family appeared, led by the Prince and Princess of Wales. The Queen never left Windsor and so was not present. They took their places on the dais, and at that moment the only contretemps occurred. Some one failed to give Sir Walter the proper signal. He waited; there was a pause; the Princess sat down and quickly got up again. Crash! The orchestra and chorus broke out in "God Save the Queen!" We breathed again. The royal family took their seats, the assemblage followed suit, and the concert began. There was no applause; every number closed in absolute silence. Orchestra, chorus, quartet, solo, in measured pace. My wife stood up to sing, and I was proud; proud of her and proud of my country.

She began softly, and instantly I knew her voice was fine and she felt like a queen—a Queen of Song! She grew more and more impassioned, and her voice rang out gloriously. I felt the thrill that was throughout the hall. No one moved. When she finished and quietly took her place I was ready to burst! This silence was a great deal to ask of a man—an American, a musician, a *husband!*

The concert was over, and the royal family rose from their seats. Everyone stood and faced them. As they walked slowly down the broad center aisle, everyone bowed low. They bowed in return. They came nearer and nearer, and then the Princess of Wales came up to my wife and spoke to her. This was the last touch! The Princess had merely nodded to the guests, and here she was talking to Louise! The assemblage, from earls up, looked on in silence—envious, I am sure.

My wife curtsied, the Princess spoke, my wife curtsied. The hair was high, the train was right, the curtsies were superb! I was sure she was having a perfectly grand time. She always did squeeze out all the joy there was in every minute, anyway.

Finally the Princess moved to Suzanne Adams, and the Prince saluted my wife. She curtsied, low and deep. He beamed and saluted all over again. I couldn't blame him. He had seen her often in all her roles, and now he was speaking to her. Lucky man!

All the artists were greeted—it was the royal custom; then the royal family moved out through the door. We breathed again. The hall broke into gay chatter and social confusion, and life seemed normal once more.

We dined with Sir Walter Parrott in one of the rooms of the palace. The plate was gold, the glasses crystal, the footmen resplendent, the champagne excellent—better than any we had in our cellar! (I think we had never owned a bottle of champagne.) We were a large company. The tension was off. We were probably conscious of the superiority of art to all things in the world; most artists feel this way. We feasted and laughed and forgot our decorum, and at three o'clock we went home. We had more than earned our forty guineas. I had earned forty guineas when I held myself in, in the organ loft! Those curtsies were worth forty guineas each! As for the voice—three-quarters of all the land of England, Scotland, and Wales wouldn't pay for— Oh, well! Let's not talk about it—let's go to sleep.

A few more performances, *Aidas* and *Lohengrins*, and the Covent Garden season was over. We were off for France, the coast of Normandy. We had rented a little house at Arromanches overlooking the beach, where the men waded out to the reefs and caught small devilfish. When a man caught one he wrapped its tentacles around his legs and caught another.

My mother and sister had been in our Paris apartment all the spring and now came down to Arromanches to be near us. But one of the boys had had whooping cough, and we couldn't go very near them on account of Baby Louise. The sign language came in handy, and the natives looked on in solemn wonder as mother and I stood on the street, ten feet apart, and talked.

We had our New York contract and our steamship tickets for the *City of New York*, and were as happy as larks. This was vacation time, music was a bore. I had a lot more songs ready, more than I needed. Let's forget them, forget everything but the fun we're having. Won't they be glad to see us at home! And Baby Louise! Won't they be surprised to see how big she has grown, and how beautiful she is!

My mother and sister elected to spend another winter in our apartment in Paris. They had grown quite foreign-minded. My dear mother was perfectly at home anywhere. Her brothers had never budged out of the United States. One beautiful niece was doing great work as a missionary at Madura in India. Otherwise the whole family were home bodies. Mother, who by all right should have been the most confined, was a world traveler. It was surprising!

The blissful summer crept on apace. Life was a symphony, full of great themes and thrilling, dramatic development. We must soon say good-bye to Europe, which had been so generous to us. To the American girl who had come with a beautiful voice and an earnest nature, she had given education, courage, honest praise, and a chance to sing two hundred performances of great roles in two years.

My young American friends with beautiful voices will be amazed as they read this. They will say, "Are such things possible?" Yes, they are possible. Only one thing, one little thing, is needed: a determined and unshakable effort, on the part of those who can, to help the young, to open the door of opportunity.

Music is one of the great defenders of peace, it unites nations in a common art, it has an international language, it reveals the characteristics of races and helps men to understand one another; it is the great enemy of crime, and it builds character. It is created by men of profound insight, sympathy, and genius. Surely, to aid in the development of a fine musical artist is a noble work.

IX

1900–1901

IT WAS TIME TO GO, AND WE SAID GOOD-BYE.
My mother and sister could, with care, live comfortably in Paris,
in our little apartment. My sister was recovering from the terrible shock of her husband's death. New scenes and interests had
had their influence.

My wife and I had enough money to get home on; that is, we
could tip the stewards. Mr. Grau supplied the transportation,
which was according to contract. To be sure, my wife had no
Paris dresses, and we would not trouble the customs officers,
unless they mistook the opera costumes for evening gowns.

The good ship *City of New York* had a frightful passage. It
was the fall when a terrible gale and tidal wave destroyed Gal-
veston. The gale swept up the Mississippi and out the St. Lawrence, and we caught it in full force off the Newfoundland
Banks. My wife and Baby Louise (we had no nurse) were confined to our stateroom, but I managed to get outside with a sailor
behind the deckhouse. It was contrary to rules, but he only
grinned at me. The noise was so great we couldn't talk. The
wind blew eighty miles an hour, and the ocean was completely
white. Every half-hour or so we would pass a fishing schooner,
scudding under bare poles. Our captain would signal, offering
help, and each schooner would decline. It made you exult to
watch them and think of their bravery.

When we sailed into New York harbor, our black funnels
were white to the very top with salt. Some one from the opera
house met us. I think it was Frank Fontenoy, of whom we
later became so fond. Our costume trunks were passed without
trouble.

After a wonderful family reunion at West Chester, we arrived in Boston, good old Boston that we loved so much. Our friends had disapproved of our venture, and even now we knew they would be of the same opinion still. There was yet another battle to fight; the doubting spirit does not die so easily as that. Many Americans have returned with accounts of their successes in Europe, only to meet with polite but cool assent. Europeans may be easily satisfied, but Americans—well, Americans are different.

We went to visit my wife's sister in Newton Center, the same sister who brought her to me to learn "all about music"! Mr. Grau planned to open his season in San Francisco, and we expected to leave Baby Louise with her aunt until we returned to New York for the opening of the Metropolitan.

And then something happened: one of those queer things that we never expect. A few days before the "opera train" was due to leave New York, I came down with rheumatic fever and was taken to a hospital in Newton. I had had two attacks before, just eight years apart, and knew that I should be laid up for three or four weeks. My mind concentrated instantly on that opera contract. We had never been separated since our marriage, and I knew how hard it would be for both of us; harder for my wife than for me, because she would worry about me and yet would have to sing gloriously.

But I was determined that this sickness should not interfere with her prospects, and finally succeeded in inducing her to go to New York. I would follow as soon as I had recovered. It was mean business, but we had to see it through. The opera train was leaving two days later.

I struggled with my sickness. It was not painful; it was simply exhausting and hard to bear. The doctor and nurses knew all about that and worked to get me into comfortable positions. I couldn't move a muscle, except my eyelids. The only real trouble was breathing—that was difficult. One evening I noticed three doctors in the room, one of them a stranger. And then my wife came through the door. I couldn't understand it. The opera train had gone the night before. I could see that she had been crying. What had happened? She made excuses; Mr. Grau had given her tickets on a later train. Everything was all right. I caught a sudden glimpse of my cousin Tom in the corridor. That was strange; what was he doing there? I asked my doctor to relieve my breathing; it was such a nuisance.

That night I had a strange vision. I will risk speaking of it and trust my reader. A most beautiful face appeared. The eyes, so sorrowful and full of deepest sympathy, looked into mine and seemed to yearn to help me, yearn with all the strength that a soul could summon. I felt happy, calm, assured. There was just nothing in the world to be troubled about.

In the morning the three doctors were still there, and my wife was there, in her green street dress. I took matters into my own hands. She must go; her debut in San Francisco would take place in a week; and the trip would take five days. I insisted, the doctors advised and urged, saying the crisis was over. They saw how I felt about it and knew what was best. I said I could not get well unless she went. Finally she went, for my sake, and it was a terrible thing for her and a triumphant and hard thing for me. Telegrams were sent to her train twice a day, but none of them reached her; they were always sent just a little too late. Not until she reached San Francisco did she know that I was improving.

Her debut was a grand success. There is no city in the world more frankly appreciative or more hospitable than San Francisco. She sang Amneris, and I heard much about that evening when we were in San Francisco a year later.

Opera contracts are serious things, and involve moral obligations. If my wife had not gone to San Francisco, Mr. Grau might have been in a serious position. He had placed absolute confidence in her, and it was her duty to fulfill her contract, her promise. And so it happened that her American debut was the most difficult engagement she ever had.

In November Mr. Grau brought his company back to New York, and my wife made her New York debut; again as Amneris. I was still in the hospital but recovering rapidly.

The San Francisco papers with their pictures of my wife and the other members of the company, and their long articles, were a joy in that little hospital room. My wife had secured a large furnished apartment on West Fifty-eighth Street, and I was allowed to go home just in time for Christmas. We had a great celebration and tried to forget the twelve weeks of hardships. Louise said opera meant nothing if I were not there. She has said it on several occasions since then, so it must be true. It takes two to sing an opera performance—one on the stage and one in the audience. The ordeal is shared, and a burden shared may become a pleasure. And when the pleasure does not outweigh the burden, then opera should be abandoned. This is an infallible guide. Good art demands a certain happiness.

In January I heard my wife sing a wonderful performance of *Aida* with Jean de Reszke, and I was the happiest man in New York. This was to be his last season in this country, and this was his only performance of *Aida;* but I did not know that. I was simply filled with joy and pride that my wife should sing with that great artist! Behind the scenes the reverence for a great artist amounts to a religion. It is not a question of popularity and applause but solely of art. Every inch of the opera house is hallowed with art, much of it not apparent to the audience. It may be a musician in the orchestra, it may be that man behind the scenes controlling some detail with the utmost delicacy, or a singer in some minor role. (Gilibert as the Sacristan in *Tosca* and Reiss as the Shepherd in *Tristan* were classic examples.) Or it may be some great artistic personality with his or her unique contribution to musical art. There are no repetitions in music;

each great artist brings something individual which passes with him, and is never heard again.

Thus the public distinction of singing in a great opera house is as nothing compared to the privilege of sharing in the great art which fills it from time to time. All who take part share in the whole; such is the glorious, uplifting nature of music. Opera is no mere makeshift for the exploitation of individual accomplishments. It is a concerted effort toward a well defined objective; namely, good art. Anything less than this is a travesty.

This sense of sharing exists in the audience, also. A work of art is public property. That is why the opera house in every city in the world becomes a sort of public forum in which everyone feels a part ownership. Art is never exclusive, and a man who takes pleasure in seeing a picture or hearing music feels himself part owner in what he enjoys.

The first thing that I noticed as I became familiar with the Metropolitan was that everyone inside and outside the house knew exactly how opera should be produced and made no secret of it. The battle of opinions was delightful, and there was an embryo teacher of singing in every corner. The attention was concentrated on voice emission and technique of acting. All styles known to the world were represented in the opera house, and opinions as to their excellence varied with every individual. The man shifting a scene or placing a chair would say frankly, "I don't like the way he does that place where he . . ." or "She's great when she . . ." and so on.

Across the street in Browne's Chop House the wiseacres were just as positive and outspoken. The old chop house was a meeting place for artists, critics, and music lovers. The conversation was sincere, impartial, and stimulating. The loyalty to Mr. Grau was most apparent, and the interest in everything connected with the opera house very great. The text and inner meaning of operas were not much discussed, but beauty and volume of voice, personal magnetism, and grace in acting were greatly appreciated.

One had the feeling that words and diction counted for little.

In the Metropolitan Opera House certain things were noticeable. The auditorium was so large that only voices with great carrying power were effective. This was not a question of volume but of quality. Soft and *mezza voce* passages were very telling, but fortissimos never swept the house as they did in smaller European houses. Van Rooy, the glorious Hans Sachs and magnificent Wotan, who was said to have one of the greatest baritone voices known to history, complained to me about this. He said: "No fortissimo is really effective at the Metropolitan." He was accustomed to electrifying European audiences by the mere volume of his voice. We used to be amazed, when the Metropolitan company went on tour and sang in smaller houses, to find new and thrilling qualities in the voices of our singers.

Facial expression and certain fine nuances seemed to suffer. Portrayal had to be on broad, plastic lines, and this seemed to affect the sincerity of some of the smaller, more intimate operas. Opera varies with every opera house in the world, and this should be an interesting study for those who are concerned with the future of opera.

Certain things in the audience were distressing. No one in the entire row of parterre boxes which circled the auditorium ever heard the first act at any evening performance. (This was in 1901.) On the other hand, because of the exigencies of the newspapers, some of the critics were never in their seats during the last act. These two things made a tremendous impression on the Europeans. They simply could not and would not understand it. It was barbarism, pure and simple. The empty boxes made the deeper impression, and the comments were filled with righteous indignation. "Who are these people? Let us sell the boxes to people who really love music. What! They own the opera house? Is it possible! What do they want of it? In our country, the aristocracy set an example of courtesy and reverence for art. *Noblesse oblige!*"

Photograph Aimé Dupont

NEW YORK, 1901

About criticism the comment ran: "Why this hurry? In our country, criticism is deliberate and based on the entire performance. It is published on the second day after the performance takes place. Criticism is not news. How can anyone listen with repose and complete absorption, when he has a difficult task to perform before midnight? It is not just to art, and the system will be changed in time."

On the whole, it was evident that the size of the theatre would place the artist at a certain disadvantage, that an intimate relationship with the audience would be hard to achieve, that it would be almost impossible to make the audience feel itself to be part of the picture, which is the ultimate triumph of dramatic art.

On the other hand, the beauty and proportion of the auditorium, its marvelous acoustics, and the evident sympathy and appreciation of the audience would soften these disadvantages in a measure.

The season was brilliant. Mr. Grau was devoted to his artists and very proud of them. He did everything he could to present them in the best possible light and make them famous. He depended on the popularity of his artists to attract the public.

The opera-going public was quite limited and very exacting, and Mr. Grau spent much time devising ways of combining a number of great artists in one grand cast which the public simply could not resist. The opera house was not always full, by any means. We who were indirectly connected with the company rarely asked for seats, but simply walked in and took such seats as were not occupied. I sometimes tried three or four in one evening, in different parts of the house, to get different effects and try out the acoustics.

My wife added Siébel and Urbano to her repertoire, and everyone said she was charming. Her voice was beautiful and filled the great house with ease, and she was rapidly becoming a favorite.

I was the only one who did not thoroughly enjoy having her sing these roles. Only in America are they sung by first dramatic contraltos, and I could not reconcile them with the great dramatic parts that my wife had been singing in Europe. The consolation was in being a member of such tremendous casts and sharing in such brilliant performances. *Aida* was a very different thing; when she sang Amneris I felt she was in her true element, and was filled with pride.

She seemed very, very young that year. Surrounded by older artists with much greater maturity of style, she seemed the very breath of youth, the dawn of spring. Her bright, eager movements and quick gestures, her clear ringing voice and animated spirit all combined to give a beauty to her performance that was most appealing. Even in her dramatic interpretation of Amneris she became just the young, misguided child of Pharaoh, almost justified in her cruelty to Aida by the naïveté of her love for Rhadames. Vindictiveness seemed impossible to such a beautiful princess.

Youth is a wonderful thing in the opera house!

Maturity of art which comes with long experience must of course always have first place. But we must have another theatre where youth can have full sway. We are simply cheating ourselves when we insist always on the finish which comes after long years. It means that we never have the bubbling enthusiasm of the young, the bursting energy and spirit of the creative period. Somewhere in the world they have it. All the mature art that comes to us was once in the period of formation. The young artist is needed everywhere. The whole art of music needs rejuvenation.

A hundred years ago, and before that, young men in the early twenties used to write operas quickly and put them on the stage, where they were sung by young singers. Just now music has passed into the deeply scientific, profoundly metaphysical, psychologically experimental stage where maturity writhes in the laboratory, and youth cannot be trusted with the instruments.

An art that does not provide for the spontaneity of youth is incomplete.

We went to Philadelphia and gave first *Faust*, and then *Aida*. My wife's mother, really my second mother, came to hear her daughter sing. She had never been in a theatre or amusement place of any kind. She didn't need amusement. She lived in a world of such serenity and pure, lofty spirituality, such joy and happiness, that amusement seemed an unnecessary, almost a degrading thing. We hardly knew what to expect and were very anxious. After all, she was the one to be considered above all others. She was the standard that represented all that was best in life; she had those things to which we all aspired. She was, in all our eyes, a perfect spirit on earth whose insight into values must be right. After *Faust* she was broad-minded and tolerant; her daughter's happiness meant much to her, and she was too grand to form judgments hastily. After *Aida* she came behind the scenes, her eyes aglow and her white hair shining. "Louise," she said, "you have converted me to opera."

This simple and spontaneous acknowledgment was a real tribute to art!

With every reason in the world to doubt the sincerity of this showy display she had felt the simplicity and truth of the *master!* He, too, walked in the Elysian fields of joy and idealism that she was accustomed to. It was wonderful!

Everyone in the company loved my wife's voice and admired her talent. Mancinelli, Walter Damrosch, and our old friend Flon, from La Monnaie, were kindness itself. Melba asked her to come and see her, and after a long talk, full of counsel and rare wisdom, told her she had the most beautiful voice in the world. We cherished this quiet, unexpected, but decisive statement.

It took me all winter to get over the effects of my long illness,

At last I began to feel like myself, and one day I said to my wife, "Let's go down to Schirmer's." I bundled up a few songs, and we trotted down to Union Square. The big store was full of music buyers and busy clerks. I sent our names up to the publishers, and very soon we were asked to go up to the editorial department. We were received by a young man with brown hair and very thoughtful eyes, who said he was Mr. Gustave Schirmer. I explained that I had written songs for a number of years (seventeen years in all!), and I wished him to hear some of them. He took us into an inner sanctum, and there we had an impromptu musicale.

My wife sang like an angel; we were both quite moved, and after a while we stopped. Mr. Schirmer said he would like to publish my songs and selected the set of eight Tennyson songs as good ones to begin with. He explained the terms of the contract—10 per cent royalty, etc. He had a quiet, earnest way of talking that inspired confidence. His face was sensitive and artistic, and there was no suggestion that we were discussing a business matter. Music seemed as much an art there as it did in the seclusion of the workroom.

I accepted his offer, and we went away. It seemed too good to be true. In a few minutes I had changed from a composer working in the dark into one with a publisher and a public. It would be foolish to pretend that I had always known this would happen. I had not. Every man who writes knows he may never reach a publisher. A publisher is a man who lives on another planet, two million light years away, with a cold, vast, unknown ether intervening between him and you. So inaccessible is he that you wonder how anyone ever succeeded in reaching him.

Gustave Schirmer and Rudolph Schirmer, who followed him as president of the company, were two of life's noblemen.

We were very happy. This was our first year in New York and already my wife had become a part of its life. We knew hardly anyone outside of the opera house; and many of our comrades there knew no one in the vast city. It is amazing that men and women can occupy conspicuous positions in New York and yet live in utter loneliness.

Our old friend George Stewart of Boston, who had given my wife a symphony concert engagement five years before, came over to New York and asked her to become a member of his company which would give festivals in various parts of the country during the spring. She would sing two or three times a week, and her fee would be two hundred dollars a performance. All our expenses would be paid. He would have a symphony orchestra with Mollenhauer as conductor; and Mr. de Gorgorza would be a member. It sounded very attractive and promised lots of fun and experience, and my wife accepted.

The opera season came to a close in a blaze of glory. Melba and Jean de Reszke were singing there for the last time. Farewells are fraught with sadness. One becomes desperately attached to a great art or a beautiful voice, and when it goes a void is left. The sentiment and devotion behind the scenes regarding these things are sincere and touching. They extend from the great conductor to the smallest chore boy. "Gee, I'm sorry to see her go!" says a stage carpenter as he watches a favorite artist from the wings. She is only twenty feet from him pouring out her glorious tones, and he has been listening to her for ten years. He has often done little favors for her, and she calls him by his first name. He knows when she is in good voice and likes to see her take her curtain calls. He tells his family at home about it: "I like her because she's good to the women," meaning the costumers and dressers. "She always laughs when the curtain goes down, and makes everyone feel good. She's going, and the boys are sorry. She had a good voice." Loyalty is the finest thing in musical life. It is everywhere: in the audience, on the stage, in the director's office, and among the concert managers; both in New York and throughout the country. Much of the supposed jealousy in musical life exists in the popular imagination only. After thirty-five years, my strongest impression is one of loyalty and good sportsmanship.

We went to Boston and had a fine time. The operas were given in the old Boston Theatre with its large stage and wonderful acoustics. My wife sang Siébel, and our friends were proud just to see her on the stage in a great Metropolitan cast. Then she sang Amneris, and the shock was immense! Is this the Louise Homer who used to be the contralto in the choir of Dr. Miner's old church on Columbus Avenue, and who sang in the chorus of Mr. Lang's St. Cecilia Society? Is it possible? We just didn't know what we had in our midst!

Ah, there's the point. Every city in America can say, "What have we in our midst?" They need not say, "Can a prophet come out of Nazareth?" "Can an artist come out of ———?" They need but look in their midst. Art is everywhere. Very little of it reaches fruition, of course. Flowers in a neglected garden are easily choked with weeds. But to look on art as a strange exotic thing, to be surprised, almost incredulous, when a real artist emerges from among us, is the height of folly. We can have all the art that we are willing to cultivate, just as we can have flowers and fruit, when we care for them.

It is not the amount of art it produces, but the amount of art it fails to discover and cherish, that is the amazing phenomenon in America.

As I saw the enthusiasm over my wife's Amneris in Boston, I thought of all the forces in Europe which had labored to make her what she was, and I wished that every true student-artist in America could have the same privileges and care. I wished that America could learn to foster and educate, as it had learned to adore and appreciate. And this was not a vain wish, either! There is nothing that Europe does which we cannot do.

The minute we place art in the hands of artists, as we place finance in the hands of financiers and medicine in the hands of physicians, and give them our whole-hearted support, the results will far exceed our fondest imaginings.

After Boston, my wife sang Urbain in Pittsburgh, her debut in the city where she was born, and in Chicago.

The season came to a close, and the company returned to New York, intact, if a little bruised and scathed. There was exuberance of joy everywhere. Campanari, our great baritone, was the wit of the company, and he kept everybody in an uproar. His practical jokes are historic. We were told that once, at the Metropolitan, as Amonasro in the second act of *Aida* in the most tense moment, with the whole cast and chorus on the stage, he brandished his arms, bound with chains, and sang at the top of his voice in Italian: "Come! All of you! Come! Across the street to Browne's Chop House! And I will treat to beer!" No one in the audience laughed, but the chorus could hardly sing the finale.

In Boston, he sang *Die Zauberflöte* with Fritzi Scheff. In the last act they were dressed like birds, feathers and all. Miss Scheff was perched on a very high stool, where she cooed and sang. When Campanari lifted her down, there on the stool was disclosed a beautiful, large, white egg. Again the company couldn't sing the finale, and poor Mancinelli had to cover it up with the orchestra. The audience saw nothing funny; it was all an allegory anyway.

The last performance was over, the strain was off. Ho for Europe, home, rest and peace! Until next November! Good-bye!

Interlude

LOUISE HOMER (christened Louise Dilworth Beatty) was
born in Pittsburgh, Pennsylvania, on April 30th in the eighteen
seventies. The day and the month are important. Every year I
can feel the shiver of excitement run through our large family
—we are twenty-five—when this magical day comes round. The
year is unimportant; the seventies all sound alike to me. Possibly
the town clerk knows the year, but he doesn't know us. We are
as young as we look, as our voices sound. Who was that who
laughed? Louise? Some laughs never grow old.

Louise Homer's mother, Sarah Colwell Fulton Beatty, was one
of those spirits that hover between heaven and earth. I knew her
only during her widowhood, when she was giving her all for the
education of her children. She gave her utmost, and found ways
and means to carry on. She filled her home with cheer, and she
too had that merry laugh that never grows old. When a woman
becomes a widow at an early age and has eight children to care
for, one quite naturally expects her to have an air of carrying a
heavy burden. But life is so contradictory! Those heavily bur-
dened ones seem so brave and cheery; they seem to love their
burdens. And those who have no burdens but their own natures
often seem so depressed.

Mrs. Beatty's home at West Chester, Pennsylvania, was so full
of happiness that everyone in the family seemed to want to live
there. Her Aunt Sarah and her husband, the Reverend Samuel
Fulton, lived with her; also Aunt Kate and her husband, the
Reverend Martin Schoonmaker. Somewhere in that house there
were rooms for the eight children and Mrs. Beatty. How to give
the children their freedom and, at the same time, preserve the

quiet that was necessary to white-haired, retired clergymen who were living lives of contemplation must have been a problem.

A thrilling, glorious moment came on Sunday morning (I was there in the later years) when we gathered in the living room to go to church. As Mrs. Beatty, in stiff black silk and widow's bonnet, appeared among us, ready to lead her brood to her God, her face shone with an ineffable light, and her voice, always melodious and soft, seemed softer than ever. A church service must needs be of a high order to be worthy of such exaltation. I think her consummate desire was to give her children the burning faith which she and her husband had shared so long. It was a trust, an obligation to him, and I think she felt a desperate need of his help, without which she, perhaps, might not succeed. No worldly success could have any but a secondary place in her eyes.

At the time Louise Homer was born her father, Dr. William Trimble Beatty, had been for several years the first pastor of the Shady Side Presbyterian Church, at the east end of Pittsburgh. He was thirty-three years old when he was called and was to have just fifteen years more of life. This church, founded by men who had shared in the development of Pittsburgh, brought him a tremendous opportunity. Among the members of his congregation were men of power in the community; and when we realize his responsibility, we can admire the vision and wisdom with which he solved part of his problem. Dr. Beatty had no resources beyond the power within himself, and yet he accomplished wonderful things.

Dr. Beatty proposed and urged the building of a college for women on those east-end hills of Pittsburgh, and the Pennsylvania College for Women came into existence. It is a beautiful place, and many thousands of young women have graduated there since that time. It was the first women's college to adopt the academic standard of men's colleges, I am told. When its alumnae made their recent drive for five million dollars the enthusiasm aroused was impressive. I cannot find that Dr. Beatty felt anything more than a humble usefulness in his relation to the college, but a "minute adopted by the session of the Shady Side church emphasizes . . . the beauty of his life, and the love they bore him, recognizing also the fact that in his removal the church loses a wise presbyter, the Pennsylvania Female College, of which he was the originator, a firm supporter, and the community one of its most useful members."

"Originator"—a blessed word. We can never reward our originators—too many of them lie buried in obscurity. We see the finished work and applaud the consummation, but back of that is the conception, the dream, the longing. In music we become more and more aware of the unaffected minds that conceive in humble simplicity, content to discover beauty and pass into oblivion. The Memorial to Dr. Beatty, from which I have quoted, is filled with tributes of the deepest affection and devotion. The church in Pittsburgh and the churches in St. Paul and Minneapolis, where he had gone in search of health, were deeply affected by the death of one so gifted and so beloved, at the very height of his ministry.

There are references to his beautiful and very tender speaking voice. I have often felt in my wife's recitals, and in the hymn-sings which she has conducted at Lake George and Palm Beach for a number of years, that she was, in a way, continuing his interrupted ministry, or at least complementing it.

He must have loved music. My wife tells of the Kinder Symphony in which he took part with the older children. He knew the hymns. My wife was called on so often to play hymns, while she was yet a child, that she determined to learn every hymn in the book so that she would never be surprised. This was the beginning of her study of music. There could be no better. No music is so widely known or so constantly used as the hymns. A great hymn has a place of its own. Men and women who never sing otherwise sing the hymns wonderfully well; they love them and know them by heart.

Mrs. Beatty faced a tremendous responsibility, that of filling the father's as well as the mother's place with her children. I am sure that her mind was still with the ministry. There had been some twenty ministers in her family, and she had been a minister's wife through more than twenty years. These professions grip the heart and soul. The opera singer may stop singing, but she is still the opera singer. The captain may stop sailing ships, but forty years on the sea have made him what he is and always will be—a sea captain. We are at all times the sum total of our lives. Mrs. Beatty's whole life was one long spiritual ministry, and her children and all her friends were intensely conscious of it. Such perfect, unaffected reverence and devotion as that which she inspired is rare indeed.

She wanted to bring her children up in a quiet, unworldly town, where life was simple, and she wished to be near Philadelphia, where her sister and two of her brothers lived. So she decided on West Chester, Pennsylvania.

When I first went to West Chester to be examined by the family—I was an applicant for admittance—I was told that the town was the favored choice of the Quaker farmers of Chester Valley when they retired. It was the most retired retiring town one could imagine. Even the houses seemed to retire behind the massive maple trees. So quiet were the streets that when you walked you walked softly, and if you had to speak you spoke softly.

Mrs. Beatty's relation to music began in her girlhood. Sometimes, in a half-mischievous spirit, she would go to the piano and play some piece she had learned thirty years before, and play it with charm. Two of her daughters, Elizabeth and Louise, had beautiful voices. The oldest daughter, Allie, became organist at her church; Ella studied "elocution"; and the youngest, Daisy, developed a passionate love for all that is great in music. She is the proud mother of the composer Samuel Barber, who, in 1935, was awarded both the Prix de Rome and the Pulitzer Prize for music.

In all the problems that faced her children I never knew Mrs. Beatty to have any but the broadest and most sympathetic point of view. The consciousness that the mother was struggling bravely with economic problems could have but one effect upon the children. It made them long to lighten her burden. Heroic mothers develop energy and ambition in their children. The problems of fathers are less present and clear. Perhaps in the old days when fathers worked at home and took an active part in the education of their children they had more direct influence. As it is, I think the memory of our mothers' efforts to create and maintain happy homes is the most potent influence that remains with us from our youth.

Mrs. Beatty belonged to a family of active builders of democracy. Her great-grandfather, Captain Oliver Brown, had witnessed the Boston Tea Party and had served with distinction in the Revolutionary Army. It was he who led the little troop of American soldiers in that famous escapade when, without orders, they stole through the British lines and pulled down the leaden statue of George III which stood in Bowling Green in the heart of New York City, and carried it off to Connecticut, where it was melted down into bullets. Her uncle, Stephen Colwell, had been prominent in Philadelphia life. He was one of the founders of the Union League of Philadelphia. Her grandfather's cousin was Robert Fulton. I have spoken of all the clergymen who were trying to convert the whole state of Pennsylvania to Presbyterianism. Her brother Samuel had iron mills at Conshohocken. An older brother, Elisha M. Fulton, who lived in New York, was treasurer and director of the National Cordage Company, sometimes known as the Cordage Trust.

It was a family of men and women who did things, endured

necessary hardships, and were apt to succeed in what they undertook. It was quite natural that Mrs. Beatty's children should carry on in the same spirit. Her oldest son, William, became president and later chairman of the board of the Austin-Western Manufacturing Company of Chicago and Aurora, Illinois. A younger son, Fulton, is now president of that company. Howard, the third son, is vice president of the Glidden Company and general manager of the Durkee Famous Foods Company. As her daughter Louise grew up she had exactly the same spirit —nor has she ever lost it.

The opportunities for girls in those days were limited; but there were new ones springing up, in the field of typewriting and stenography among others. As soon as she graduated from high school—she was valedictorian of her class—Louise went to Philadelphia and studied the new technique for which there was such a demand. She hoped that by means of it she would be able to help her mother, and, with a passionate longing that many young people can understand, she hoped to be able to learn to sing.

Yes, she knew she had a fine voice. She had always sung. She had sung in the church choir with her brothers and sisters. When she was fourteen she was asked to sing the contralto part in the cantata *Ruth, the Moabitess,* in West Chester. When the night of the performance came, word was received from Philadelphia that the bass, who was to sing Boaz, would not be able to be present. In the midst of the consternation, Louise Beatty calmly announced that she knew the bass part as well as her own; and so the performance went ahead with this young and fearless girl singing both parts. Afterward the conductor came to Mrs. Beatty and begged her to allow her daughter to study singing.

Singers are like birds; they must sing. If they do not sing, something vital goes out of their lives, something within them is unfulfilled. It is a passion which must not be suppressed. But young singers are faced with problems which, at times, seem cruel. They have voices and a tremendous urge within themselves. But the art of singing is most difficult and subtle. It imposes sacrifices of all kinds, and demands infinite patience. Before they feel they have the right to master this art, they wish to be assured that their voices warrant it. They shrink from what seems to them a display of egotistical vanity. Thus many beautiful voices are lost, and many singing natures deprived of their utterance. There is an attitude toward singing on the part of many which is most discouraging. To them, singing is something abnormal, to be left alone unless one has a prospect, almost a certainty, of becoming a Melba or a Caruso. This absurd and chilling view is confined to the arts. One can study law without expecting to become a judge.

Louise Beatty solved her problems in what seemed to her the only way. She secured stenographic work. Then she presented a letter of introduction to William H. Boner, who had a music store on Chestnut Street in Philadelphia and was himself an organist. With his recommendation she found opportunities to sing in Philadelphia churches. Then she went to Miss Abbie Whinnery, a famous oratorio singer who had retired and was then teaching, and began her lessons.

All very simple if you have the energy and a voice *like that*. Yes—but she could only practice from seven to eight in the morning and after six at night. There were many solos and difficult church works to be learned. The usual leisure of the music student's life was wholly absent. Music was her absorbing passion, yet the entire day was given to something else—something that had to be done superlatively well and which demanded exactness and concentration. All very simple if you have the patience and the character, the quickness and many other things —and the voice.

When she was eighteen she became secretary of the famous William Penn Charter School for boys. At the same time she secured the enviable position of contralto in the quartet of the

Seventeenth and Spruce Street Presbyterian Church. This was one of the big steps upward. The chance to become a fine church singer meant as much to her then as the chance to become an opera singer did at a later time.

Dr. James D. Paxton was the pastor, and he and Mrs. Paxton became her true and lifelong friends. He married us, a few years later. Dr. Paxton wanted his sermons taken down in shorthand, so he engaged Miss Beatty to do it. Those were busy and profitable Sundays, and after the evening service Mrs. Paxton would always entertain at supper. Happy days!

In the next winter Louise established herself in one of her Uncle Samuel's offices and did court stenography—the best-paying and most responsible kind. Her younger brothers were growing up, and she took one of them to live under her charge at her boarding house so that he might have some city training. Responsibility of any kind did not seem to disturb her although she was still only in her teens.

She studied singing with Miss Alice Groff and, when she could afford it, ran over to New York on her free Saturday afternoon for an occasional consultation with some Italian maestro.

In the following September came the great change. All this business success began to take a new aspect. It was flattering and, of course, excited admiration. The sight of a girl with a beautiful voice, a really fine singer, who was willing to give her time to business and the practical side of life with its resulting income (so dear to the American mind), could not but arouse enthusiasm and cause voluble praise.

Fortunately, something rebelled. It must have been that savior of all artists, the little artist-soul, which whispers encouragement when you do right and weeps when you do wrong. It told her perhaps that she should give her whole time to the study of music and resist every other temptation. She made the momentous decision—gave up her office, resigned from the church, and announced that she was going to Boston to study music. It was wonderfully wise of that little artist-soul to suggest Boston, and not some other city. She has often said that, at that time, Boston was considered the really musical city of America, the Mecca of all music students; and when one thinks of Arthur Nikisch, Chadwick, MacDowell, Parker, Carl Baermann and Carl Faelten one can understand this reputation.

So sure was she of making her way and securing a fine church position that she turned her little bank account over to her mother. (Her mother told me of this when, in later years, we talked of the brilliant, if disconcerting, decision to go to Boston.)

When she arrived she told her sister, whom she was visiting at her home in Arlington, a suburb of Boston, that she wished to really understand music and was not satisfied to confine her study to singing. "Why," said her sister (it was Elizabeth of the beautiful voice), "I know just the man. He is the best teacher of Harmony in Boston. He lives here in Arlington with his mother, and has his studio in Boston. I'll take you in there tomorrow." The next day Elizabeth brought her young sister Louise to see me and consult with me in regard to lessons.

X

1901

IT IS AT THIS POINT THAT I INTENDED TO
end my story, and it is with much hesitation and embarrassment
that I continue. I planned to show some of the conditions that
beset the study of music, the barriers and encouragements, doubt-
ings and enthusiasms, fearfulness and warm, helping hands; and
I hoped that my story might contain suggestions for those who
are determined to search out real musical talent, provide for its
development, and, last and most difficult, create opportunities
for its exercise and high expression. We cannot foster artists and
then give them no field in which to work.

The opera house was created by a few composers who wrote
operas that were of great value to human life. The symphony
hall and chamber concert were made inevitable by a few composers who wrote imperishable works, vital to the progress of
humanity. The problem of the layman is to determine how he
can best aid these composers in their irresistible effort to lift man
above himself. Nothing can crush this effort, but many things
can impede it; and, again, many things can aid and abet it. Here
lies a glorious opportunity for all; all can share in artistic progress, and anyone can be a factor in its spreading influence.

It is one thing to describe the events that led us to the Metropolitan, but quite another to write about the steady, artistic
growth that followed. I could fill a volume with vivid and glow-
ing accounts of my wife's performances, but descriptions of past
performances are something like descriptions of lost pictures:
they are never quite adequate, and they make one wistful.

Our first season at the Metropolitan was over, and it had been
a happy one. My wife seemed to fit into the picture, and this

itself was a triumph. It was a difficult and exacting opera house. Personality, individuality, charm, magnetism, and power of characterization were needed, in addition to a voice which would fill the great auditorium and musicianship that could respond to the demands of the most cultured conductors. But, once across the Rubicon, it was a glorious place to be. It was ideal in its opportunities for work and growth.

Mr. Grau was determined that his artists should reach the greatest heights of which they were capable. Opportunity was never lacking. Jean de Reszke passed from Faust and Don José to Siegfried and Tristan, and Lillian Nordica from Marguerite and Philine to Brünnhilde and Isolde. He would support any possibility that he could discover in his artists. His conductors, Damrosch, Mancinelli and Flon, would do their utmost to help him and work tirelessly with his singers. Progress is the soul of an artist's life. When that ceases, thoughts of retirement creep in.

We went to Cornish, in New Hampshire, for the summer and rented a farmhouse next to our cousins, the Augustus Saint-Gaudenses. It was a funny old place. The parlor with its low ceiling was a poor place for singing, so we fixed up a corn-crib as a studio for my wife. The sides were open slats, but the pitched roof was high. Her tones used to float down the road and through the woods. They may have disturbed Augustus in his studio, but I doubt it. He loved to hear her sing.

I worked in the "parlor" and, now that I had a publisher, began to plan larger works. I took up Thomas Hood's "Song of the Shirt." I have always had one conception of life; namely, that of a battlefield. After the Great War came I could express my conception in clearer terms. In France they had the front-line trenches, then the safety zone, and back of that, general headquarters. The sympathy and attention of the world were concentrated on those front-line trenches. So it was with life. The front-line trench was poverty, with its dangers and miseries. The real battles of life were fought there, and the safety zone of protected life was safe only because of the endurance and heroism in that front line.

"The Song of the Shirt" was a good picture of one of those front lines of life, and I tried to give it a musical setting. I thought I had finished it, only to discover at the end of the summer that there was a weak spot. Nine years later I wrote a new theme for this passage and sent the song to my publisher, while my wife placed it on her first program of the approaching season. Then I discovered that my new theme spoiled the homogeneity of the song and ruined it; so I recalled the song from Schirmer's, and Mrs. Homer took it off her program.

The following summer I was able to finish the song in a few minutes, in a very simple way; obvious when I found it, but elusive for a long time. Usually songs make themselves in a very short time. Be they good, bad, or indifferent, they have a defiant air of inevitability and seem to say, "Touch me if you dare!" Tinkering is usually poor business, and a song writer is seldom in the same mood a second time; unless he is, he is apt to introduce extraneous and inconsistent stuff.

"The Song of the Shirt" was one of my few mascots. Like "The Pauper's Drive," "How's My Boy?" and "To Russia"— all songs that dealt with the poor and oppressed on that firing line—it found a place in the repertoire. Frederick Stock made a magnificent setting of it for orchestra, and my wife sang it with the Chicago Symphony Orchestra. I did not hear this concert, but I heard her sing it at the Metropolitan on a Sunday night, with Hageman conducting, and later at a Boston Symphony concert in Boston, with Karl Muck conducting. On this occasion Dr. Muck said to me, "I am glad to meet a man who has something new to say." Every man has a few, sometimes very few, moments of unexpected recognition. This was one of mine. Another was when Toscanini, with the music in his hands, made my wife sing "To Russia" three times running without a pause.

It was a glorious summer. Baby Louise revelled in American

farm life. It was expansive and primitive, after the narrow restrictions of French summer resorts. I think Americans love the primitive. We are descended from men who sought the primitive and deserted the restricted confines of Europe, and it must be in our blood.

Late in the summer we visited our friends the Paxtons, on Lake George. We had a string of beautiful songs which my wife sang for all her friends. We never doubted the beauty of these great works of the masters and loved to do them together. This was before our contact with the large and varied concert-going public and our dismayed consciousness of the ineffectiveness of much of the most beautiful music in the presence of mixed audiences.

Helen Paxton read Browning's "Prospice" to me and asked me to set it to music. Some years later she sent me a copy of Howard Weeden's *Bandanna Ballads*.

The summer was over. To see Augustus Saint-Gaudens every day was enough to make it memorable.

Mr. Grau had planned a grand tour before the opening of the New York season, and the prospect was most exciting. We went to Toronto, where Louise sang Ortrud for the first time in America. Madame Sembrich sang Elsa. To us it was the highest honor one could have to sing in an opera with her.

I always loved the following criticism in the Toronto *Star*, and wish I might have met the writer:

The quality of Madame Homer's voice, which won her such marked applause on Thursday evening, became more apparent in her work as Ortrud. This rich vibrant texture that is noticeable throughout Madame Homer's great range, has a fascination for the ear, a sort of haunting power. When Ortrud pleaded, the round voice had a caressing note. When she hated, the tones broadened with a fearful encompassing reach. When she exulted the notes rang like jubilant bells. . . . It cannot be told how Madame Homer accomplished such a climax. Voice built on gesture, and gesture on voice, the structure growing ever, until the audience, able to resist no longer, burst into applause ere the scene could draw to a close.

At this time the Duke and Duchess of York (afterward King George V and Queen Mary of England) were passing through Toronto, in the course of their world tour, and a state concert was organized. It was a gala affair. Among the artists on the program were Calvé, Fritzi Scheff, and my wife. Toward the end of the concert a resplendent officer appeared at the dressing-room door and requested my wife, the only English-speaking artist, to sing "God Save the Queen." He brought a copy of the music and text with him, as a precaution. My wife consented. After he had gone she suddenly determined to bring Calvé and Fritzi Scheff into this ceremony. They flatly refused. They never could sing the words; it would be terrible! My wife insisted, and then ensued one of the most rapid language lessons ever given. It was wonderful to see my wife solemnly pronouncing the words and the others repeating them. I have never seen her more serious. In fifteen minutes they went out on the stage. My wife stood in the middle with the music raised high in her hands. Calvé and Miss Scheff hung on either arm and peered at the fine print. The orchestra struck up, and it went off gloriously.

From Toronto we went to Syracuse. Madame Calvé went round to the theatre and found, among scores of highly colored vaudeville posters, a small card announcing a three-day season by the Metropolitan Opera company. She was indignant and called a meeting of our French contingent in the hotel lobby. She insisted that they go back with her to New York and report to Mr. Grau. She had heard that the sale of tickets was not large. Of course not! No one knew we were in town. Voices rose, and the lobby was filled with the most picturesque French. Journet and Gilibert, looking very anxious, had difficulty in placating the great prima donna. The traveling men sat in the leather chairs and looked on. It was, perhaps, their first contact with grand opera. If this was a rehearsal, what would the show be like! Too bad all Syracuse couldn't have seen it, they thought. The house would have been filled!

In Syracuse my wife sang in *Lohengrin* again.

Our next city was Buffalo. Here *Aida* was given with, to us, a new cast. Emma Eames sang Aida, probably her greatest part, and our new tenor, De Marchi, sang Rhadames. De Marchi had a very beautiful voice and was a man of refinement and culture. *Aida* took on a high character that it was to maintain for many years, finally becoming the most popular opera at the Metropolitan.

Then we had a long ride to New Orleans, where Louise sang in *Les Huguenots*. We loved the old French city and the wildly enthusiastic audience.

Thence to San Antonio, where my wife did not sing, and then a long, dusty ride on a slow special across Texas. The heat was intense, the windows were open and the dust blew in, in clouds. Coats were off, and homemade fans were going, and the whole company was miserable. They never would be able to sing any more! This dust was ruining their voices! "Listen to me! Oh— Ah— Isn't that horrible?" There was no diner on the train. We had an alcohol stove and a bag of coffee, and my wife cooked potful after potful, the whole morning. We also had a whole roast chicken which disappeared like magic.

A performance of *Les Huguenots* in Los Angeles, and at last we arrived in San Francisco, where we were to stay from November 11 to December 5. It was like getting to a second home. All the friends of the year before crowded around and flooded us with invitations, most of which we could not accept. They told me of what I had missed through my illness; how superb Louise had been at her debut; how they loved her. They talked about each performance as if it had been a world event. Yes, there are people like that in the world, and many of them live in San Francisco. Not all the world is blasé, effete, tired of opera. Think of the audiences of the future! It almost makes one want to begin over again.

There were many reasons why opera in San Francisco was thrilling. In the first place the theatre was not large, and the acoustics were magical. Every nuance could be heard, the quality of the voices was exquisite, there was no temptation to shout. The lighting was fine, and the most subtle changes in face and pose were instantly felt. The intimacy between audience and artist was perfect, and the sensitive response of the listeners led the artists to surpass themselves. Of course, the enthusiasm went beyond all bounds, and was shared behind the scenes.

My wife sang *Aida, Lohengrin, Faust,* and *Les Huguenots.* In the middle of the season a wonderful thing happened. Mr. Grau asked her if she could learn the part of Brangaene in *Tristan und Isolde,* in ten days, and sing it on December 3. He said that Madame Schumann-Heink had concerts in Texas, and he could not give the music drama unless my wife could sing the part. She had never seen it, but promised to look it over and give her answer the next day. Hans Morgenstern, one of the most brilliant *répétiteurs* and teachers I have ever known, came to the hotel and played it for us, and she sang it through. It was most exciting. The part is one of the most intricate in the contralto repertoire—long, exacting, subtle—requiring great musicianship and psychological sensitiveness. How she worked! Morning, afternoon, and evening, except when she was singing at the opera house. Quietly and surely Morgenstern made her letter-perfect in scene after scene. Then Damrosch took hold, and in the most encouraging, masterful way brought her to the point of perfect assurance. Costumes were made, and then there was one orchestral rehearsal. We were in a dream. This glorious work, which she had studied in my classes, and which I had worshipped for many years, was coming within her grasp. It was too wonderful to be true!

At last the evening came. Far from being afraid, my wife was longing for the performance to begin. She always rose to every opportunity, loved to forge ahead, welcomed new experiences, knew she would do her best, which was all she could ask. That's the true story of her life.

Reuss-Belce from Bayreuth was the Isolde; Van Dyke, Tristan; Bispham sang Kurvenal; Edouard de Reszke, King Mark; Muhlmann, Melot; and Reiss sang the steersman and the shepherd. I sat in the audience, entranced. I knew from moment to moment that Louise had found a role that was bringing out something in her that had never existed before. It was a tremendous night for me, such as is rare in any man's life. The very suddenness of the whole thing was overwhelming.

After the performance there was jubilation on the stage. Everyone had had a tremendous task, but no one forgot what my wife had done; and their enthusiasm was unbounded, and without ifs and buts. It was a great night! The newspapers praised and predicted. We were glad we had not said to Mr. Grau: "No, no! Impossible! The time is too short. Why didn't you ask me last summer? I'll do it next year."

The San Francisco season was over, and grateful friends gathered around to see us off. All the artists in the company had friends. San Francisco is the warmest-hearted and the least self-conscious city in the world. The train started, hands and handkerchiefs waving, and we looked with regret at the beautiful city across the bay. When you consider that many of our artists were seven thousand miles from home and in a foreign land, it is easy to understand the meaning to them of such welcome and cordiality.

We had one hard task ahead of us. Mr. Grau had asked my wife to prepare Venus in *Tannhäuser* for this season, and she

AS BRANGAENE, FIRST PERFORMANCE IN
SAN FRANCISCO, DECEMBER, 1901

had relearned it in German during the summer. On account of *Tristan*, there had been no chance for an orchestral rehearsal, but he wanted her to sing it in St. Louis on the way home. Venus is a difficult part, and to sing it without hearing the orchestra even once required courage. It was a tribute to Louise that both Grau and Damrosch thought she could do it. She accepted the situation philosophically, and asked that a piano be placed in her room at Kansas City.

We arrived in Kansas City on the morning of Tuesday December 10. We had celebrated my birthday on the train the day before, and were as happy as larks. Louise was to sing *Aida* in Kansas City that evening, *Tannhäuser* in St. Louis on Thursday afternoon, and *Aida* in the same city on Friday evening. A busy and exciting week. All new cities and all fine roles. When we got to our room we were disappointed to find no piano there. Every minute was precious. After waiting a little while I said I would inquire.

Mr. Grau had gone back to New York. He had engaged, that year, a large, important-looking Englishman to manage his tours. There was also an advance manager who went ahead of the company. I went down to the hotel lobby, and there by the desk I found our new manager. I explained that I was worried about the piano, as Mrs. Homer wanted to rehearse all the morning. "Homer," he said, "I'm sorry, but there was only one piano in Kansas City and I had to give it to Miss Scheff." Bland, debonair, smiling, with that English assurance that we know so well. I felt stunned and did some rapid thinking. "Mr. ——," I said, "if there isn't a piano in our room in half an hour, we take the first train to New York." "What!" "Yes," I said. As I turned away the little advance manager came running up to me with an anxious face. I repeated my remark to him and went upstairs. I told Louise what I had done and suggested that we go out to walk for half an hour. We looked in the shop windows and never spoke of what was in our minds. *Aida* that evening seemed far away, almost in limbo.

In a half-hour we came back, and there were four men placing a piano against the wall of our room. At that moment we heard a commotion on the stairs outside. We looked, and there were six men bringing a piano up the stairs, with our little advance manager waving them on. I said we didn't need two pianos. My wife, whose sense of humor is of the rarest, laughed until I thought there would be no performance that evening!

This was my only experience of this kind in more than thirty years. But we were Americans and at home; it was easy for us. How about those foreigners who were far from home and could not easily break their contracts? Could they protect themselves, or must they submit?

After the performance of *Aida*, this time with Madame Gadski, we took the train for St. Louis. The piano episode had made me suspicious, and as soon as we were settled in our room the next morning I walked around to the theatre. There in the lobby was a large and beautiful frame, filled with photographs of the artists of our company. The only one missing was my wife's. I went back to the hotel and bought the morning papers. There was no mention of her in them. Then I went on the rampage. I put some photographs of my wife in my pocket and went around to the office of the *Republic*. I asked to see the editor and was quickly shown in. He was a little man with keen eyes, over which he wore a large shade. I said I thought the people of St. Louis would like to hear of the new American singer who was in the company. He asked rapid-fire questions and wanted to know where he could get a photograph. I gave him one, and then went around to the *Globe-Democrat*, where I had the same experience over again. These were my only ventures into newspaper offices in my life except when, as a boy, my father took me to see Col. Clapp of the *Boston Journal*. I wish I had had more of them. There is no camouflage in the inner sanctum, and it is refreshing to walk into an atmosphere where nothing counts but the naked facts.

Then came *Tannhäuser*. It was a memory test, pure and simple. There was not time for thought of anything else. Not a note or word must be missed. Mr. Damrosch and Morgenstern carried her through triumphantly. The next morning the newspapers came out with large pictures of Louise.

That night *Aida* was given. De Marchi was unable to sing, but Eames, my wife, and Campanari were in glorious voice, and the audience was most enthusiastic. Some of the papers seemed to mistake the rivalry between Aida and Amneris for rivalry between Emma Eames and my wife. They loved to sing together and were the greatest of comrades. The *Republic* said:

> Perhaps the feature of last night's production of *Aida* by the Grau Opera Company in Music Hall, which will be most vividly remembered by the audience, was the surprising rivalry of Madame Emma Eames in the title role and Madame Louise Homer in that of Amneris. It does not often happen that Amneris imperils the supremacy of Aida, and it is possible, in the case of such an Aida as Eames, only when the part of Amneris is sung and acted by a surpassingly dramatic contralto. This came to pass last night. Nor did the prima donna seem to resent the rivalry in the least. Quite to the contrary. Madame Eames rather appeared to relish it, and she was exceedingly kind to Louise Homer, the daughter of a Presbyterian clergyman in Pittsburgh, and one of the greatest discoveries ever made by Mr. Grau. It struck me that Eames took especial pains to share honors with Homer to the fullest bent of the audience.

One more performance of *Aida,* this time in Cincinnati, and we were off for New York.

When I think of all that this tour meant to us, the opportunities it gave, the fun we had, the friends we made, I can only hope that our young artists, present and future, will have many such experiences. Mr. Grau was a benefactor, both to his artists and to the public.

He believed in the star system. He surrounded his artists with an aura that made them idols of the public. Every city longed for their return, and if it could not have the whole company it would rejoice if just one of the artists returned for a concert or recital.

It was not a sensation-loving public but rather one that loved sentiment, tenderness, humor, simple songs, and, of course, an occasional operatic aria of the simpler type. It was a great public.

XI

1901–1904

AT LAST WE WERE BACK IN NEW YORK WITH our Louise. She had been with "Grandma," three aunts, and a lot of cousins, and she had grown much older and wiser in two months. We had a grand Christmas in our new home—a furnished apartment at 358 West Fifty-seventh Street, near the Y.M.C.A. I had a piano in the dining room, where even the sound of dishes did not disturb me overmuch. Our problem was to get out of earshot of each other, so that we could work in peace. When we rented a home I would go to the farthest corner, with all the doors shut. My wife would raise her voice to the loudest fortissimo. If I couldn't hear her, it was all right; we would consider the apartment or the house, as it might be. We were the despair of every renting agent.

"You can't hear her in this room," the agent would say.

"Yes, I can," I'd say. "She's singing 'Mon cœur.' "

"What?"

" 'Mon cœur,' *Dalila*."

"Oh! Let me show you another house."

We settled down to our simple and concentrated life: rehearsals at the opera house; two or three performances each week; the rest of the time at home. No social engagements or theatres or anything that would endanger the health or the voice in the slightest degree. On the days of performances my wife would save her voice and hardly speak above a whisper. Little Louise understood perfectly, and we three formed a close corporation with but two objectives in view: a happy home and good artistic work. Later I took Louise to matinee performances, and she often went with me to see the dress rehearsals. The art-

145

ists loved to see her there and made much of her. She tells me now that I would not allow her to see anything but Wagner's works and *Hänsel und Gretel*. It sounds narrow-minded, but perhaps I was right. Early impressions are invaluable. I remember asking her piano teacher to give her nothing but Bach, Mozart, Beethoven, Schubert, and Schumann in the early years. Her teacher, Mrs. Tapper, a great artist, was delighted to carry this out. Louise was a musical child. She had a very musical little friend, Katherine Swift, and, together, they learned the entire roles of Hänsel and Gretel and sang and acted them beautifully. Sometimes my wife sang the Witch with them, and we had a wonderful homemade performance.

I went to every rehearsal and every performance. At home we pondered over every passage and every word. I was the ideal singer's husband: no one at the opera house knew that I wrote songs or had any other work to do.

As my reader will perceive from my account of our tour, each performance was an event in itself. The changing casts (I think my wife sang Amneris with six different Aidas in those first two years), changes of conductors involving changes of tempi, the fact that different subscribers heard each performance, all helped to make this so. If the fourth performance was not so good as the second had been, the earlier performance counted for nothing. Each one was judged on its merits as if it were a debut. All this led to a self-consciousness and anxiety which did not make for good art.

Fortunately we had a nucleus who attended many performances of their favorite operas—the young students and music lovers, the Italian crowd, the German crowd. They were in the gallery and behind the rail, and it was among them that one heard intelligent discussions of interpretation. It was not from one performance that they derived their opinion, but from four or five or six. The artists felt their appreciation and friendship, and when an artist raised his hand in their direction, while bowing, it had a real meaning.

The critics also heard many performances, but they had the self-imposed task of reporting exactly what they heard without regard to the past. The artists, to judge by their own accounts, were rarely at their very best. There is the story of the famous Italian basso who said he was in perfect voice just once in his life and on that occasion the critics said he sang too loud. Nevertheless, a great artist is great even if he is not at his very best, and it is this that makes me resent too much emphasis on minor flaws and temporary shortcomings. I have enjoyed many performances in spite of blemishes. The big spirit behind it all is what counts.

My wife added Ortrud and Venus to her Metropolitan repertoire and gained new friends with every performance. She sang in Paderewski's *Manru*, which was produced on February 14, 1902, and was only sorry she did not have more to sing for this great man. She was destined to sing at the grand old institution for nineteen years, but we did not know that then. The future could take care of itself; sufficient unto the day was the task thereof. It was an absorbing and thrilling life.

Warm friendships sprang up with our American fellow artists —Nordica, Eames, Suzanne Adams, Bispham, Blass, and Walter Damrosch, and with some of the other artists. The fact that the operas were all sung in Italian, French, and German gave, inevitably, to all American artists a slight appearance of being interlopers. Italians in Italian opera, Germans in German opera, seemed to the manner born. It is strange that this subtle feeling should be more apparent in America than in Europe. In Germany, a Swede, a Russian, and an American will be in the cast and it will seem perfectly natural. Perhaps it is because they sing in the language of the people over there and, if the pronunciation be good, nationality cannot count. The Americans in our company were naturally drawn to one another, and the advent of a new American singer in the company was hailed with delight.

My wife sang *The Messiah* at Carnegie Hall with Frank Damrosch, and again at the Metropolitan with Walter Damrosch, revealing her deeply religious nature, and new qualities in her beautiful voice. In the spring she again went on a month's concert tour, under the management of our old friend George Stewart of Boston, who had the check for twenty-five dollars which he had given her in 1895 for her first symphony concert hanging in a frame on his wall. I had intended going with her; but just after we took Louise to her grandmother in West Chester she came down with measles, and I gave up the tour to stay with her.

I rented a parlor, with a beautiful Steinway Grand piano in it, in a neighbor's house and wrote songs. West Chester was a grand place in which to work. The little Quaker town seemed to be motionless. All things had come to a standstill, and ideas could germinate. I set Browning's "Prospice," which gained the attention of Francis Rogers and Herbert Witherspoon, and "A Woman's Last Word," which appealed to Nordica and others. These were my first introductions to the concert world. I also wrote another song about the poor, "The Poor Man's Song." "I'll set my right foot to a stone, and 'gainst a rock my back, stretch thus my arms, and sternly say: 'Give me my birthright back!' " This strong, anonymous poem was written by some great man early in the last century. Who was he, and did he fear to sign his name, or was he buried in obscurity? Heinrich Meyn sang this song with feeling, but not many took it up.

The concert tour was a grand success. Those were the days of enthusiasm and gratitude, on the part of the public, for any artistic privileges. Louise sang *Orpheus and Eurydice* in English, in Ann Arbor, foreshadowing the great production of this work at the Metropolitan five years later under Toscanini,

which was the high-water mark of my wife's artistic achievement, and, throughout the tour, Bach's "Erbarme Dich," Schubert's "Die Allmacht," Schumann's "Frühlingsnacht," "Im
Herbst" by Franz, and the Brahms "Sapphische Ode."

The people were hungry for music, and George Stewart had
found one way of satisfying them. With a good conductor, a
small first-class orchestra, a group of young and brilliant singers,
a pianist, a violinist, he toured the country. The point was that
he had been a musician all his life and selected his people with
unerring judgment. Many of our best artists began with him.

We went to Lake Placid for the summer. It was glorious. As
usual we had a little cottage. I had a second piano in the made-
over pump house, outside. I made a setting of Oliver Wendell
Holmes's "The Last Leaf" and Robert Louis Stevenson's "Sing
Me a Song of a Lad That Is Gone." These songs were taken up
by singers. Years later Cecil Fanning wrote me that he had sung
"The Last Leaf" in five hundred concerts. I don't see how he
stood it. My wife sang it in 1929 at the unveiling of the bust of
Holmes at the Hall of Fame. Some fellow composers have told
me that it was not a suitable poem for a song, but I have no
regrets. I may have brought the poem to the attention of some
who had never read it, and that is enough.

My sister had been married again a year earlier, in Paris, to
Jean del Cardayré, a French writer, and was very anxious to return to America. I urged her to come to us, and in August I met
her at the steamer in New York, with mother, her two boys, and
her new husband. I took them all up to our little cottage, and
it was a tight squeeze. It was now necessary to do some careful
planning, because of impending events. I wanted to keep mother
and sister near me; so we decided to rent two houses in West
Chester, Pennsylvania, for the fall months. Early in October we
all migrated in a body to our new homes, two large old houses
just across the street from each other. It was a happy family reunion, and mother flitted back and forth between the houses,

watching over her two daughters. My wife's mother and sisters lived just around the corner and ran in at all times.

Then things began to happen. My sister's little son Sidney was taken sick. On the 15th her third son was born, and to keep the house quiet I took little Sidney to the hospital. Three days later my sister developed fever, and her doctor was anxious. At the same time our little Louise complained and was put to bed. My job was to keep all this from my wife, and support my anxious mother. On the 20th our little Sidney was born. Little Louise, awake and feverish, insisted on seeing him, and the nurse brought him into her room at five in the morning. All the sickness proved to be typhoid of a serious type. I remember that I did not have my clothes off for six days, and counted only eight hours' sleep in all that time. I had three nurses in my house, two at my sister's, and two at the hospital. The doctors felt that our little Louise would not recover, and I got a specialist from Philadelphia. Through all this I had to be jolly when I was with my wife and our precious new baby, and conceal from her the seriousness of the situation. During the second week the doctors insisted that I go to my rented studio two hours every afternoon, and try to take my mind off my anxieties. Music seemed a useless thing, but I tried to do as they said; and it did help. On one of these afternoons I made a setting of Robert Louis Stevenson's "Requiem"; and on another, his "Country of the Camisards" and "Evensong."

All my patients recovered, but it took weeks. In the meantime the opera season was approaching. When little Sidney was two weeks old, we received a telegram from Mr. Grau: Would Madame Homer be able to sing *Carmen* at the end of the first week of the opera season? This was a friendly bombshell! Of course she couldn't do it; the time was too short, but she wanted to, and took a day to think it over. There is a disease in all opera houses which might be called Carmenitis. Nearly every singer, from the highest coloratura to the most sepulchral contralto, thinks she could do wonders with Carmen, and my wife was no exception. Even Covent Garden had asked her to prepare it, and Calabresi had arranged a rehearsal at La Monnaie for his artists who were going to London: Louise, Gilibert (the best Dancaire who ever lived), Journet, and others. She sang this role beautifully, and yet I hoped she would never be called upon to do it. There was a certain nobility which she infused into every part she sang, even distasteful characters like Ortrud, Dalila, and Amneris, and somehow I couldn't associate Carmen with her. At this time Calvé had left the Metropolitan, and it was a grand opportunity; but she had to decline it, because it came too soon. I did not influence her decision, but in my heart I rejoiced. I think she still feels a regret that she never sang this role. She sang it a number of times in concert form, at festivals, but that didn't count.

These were hard days. Louise went to New York and sang once, missed two performances, and was finally restored sufficiently to resume her place in the company.

At last, when little Louise was well enough to be moved, we took a furnished apartment near Carnegie Hall, and set up our lares and penates. Our little girl now had her hair bobbed like a boy, which, in those days, was a strange sight. The fever had made it necessary. The baby boy was a prize baby, husky and big. We spent most of our time taking care of them.

The great event at the opera for us was the addition of Brangaene to my wife's regular repertoire. She made of this character a real human being, filled with tenderness, sympathy, and humility. Her voice was beautiful, and in the second act the warning call was thrilling in its beauty and sense of foreboding. There was something indefinable about it, and every musician in New York felt it. In those days real reputations for musicianship were made principally in Wagnerian roles. She also sang Waltraute in the *Götterdämmerung*.

Schirmer brought out ten of my songs, settings of Browning,

Hood, Longfellow, Holmes, and others. There was some comment on the character of the poems I was using.

In the late winter Mr. Grau announced his retirement. This was a great blow, and caused consternation and sadness. We always felt the impartiality, consideration, and sense of justice at the top of our organization. The company was small and very happy. Each member could always feel sure of Mr. Grau's appreciation and support. His distinguishing qualities were an intense gratitude to his artists for what they did, and a frank, unaffected way of expressing it.

A period of suspense followed. No one knew what would happen. Opera singers are accustomed to moving on. They are often nomads ever seeking new countries, new publics. With a universal language, all countries are open to them. But it was late in the season and contracts are made long in advance.

At last Mr. Heinrich Conried, manager of the German Theatre on Irving Place, was announced as Mr. Grau's successor. Everyone wondered about him. What were his tastes? A new director for such a company as ours should be a director *par excellence*. One day he requested an interview with us. He expatiated on the difficulties he was facing and begged my wife to accept a contract on the same terms as the one she then had, $5,000 for a five months' season. We were disappointed. Mr. Grau had fixed those terms three years earlier, when my wife was unknown in America and had had but a limited experience. He took a speculative chance on her success, and we appreciated that and accepted cheerfully. But Mr. Conried was talking to an artist who had become a favorite in New York and had proved her value to the Metropolitan. Any young artist will accept a probationary contract, but expects recognition at its close if success warrant it.

It was a difficult situation. We loved the Metropolitan, its operas, the artists, and the audience. Our alternative was concert tours, which meant separation from our children. Mr. Con-

Photograph Garo, Boston

AS WALTRAUTE (Götterdämmerung), NEW YORK, 1903

ried had placed the emphasis on the precariousness of his first season; so we accepted his terms for that year, and asked for $7,500 the second year, and $10,000 the third. He agreed, and the contract was signed. We felt that it was unfair, but we chose to cling to the Metropolitan, with its artistic conditions. The concert field with its éclat and large financial returns was always beckoning, but we couldn't yield.

We took a cottage for the summer at Onteora Park in the Catskills. These wonderful summers when we could rest and be human, enter into all kinds of fun, see our friends and forget voice and operas, were our salvation.

John Alexander, that fine artist and great soul, and Heinrich Meyn, my old friend and pupil of the Boston days, were at Onteora. A little boy named Bill Tilden was giving his elders a hard run at tennis. He had long arms and legs and an annoying way of jumping all over the court. It was embarrassing to the graceful, handsome young college men.

During the summer we read in the papers that Mr. Conried had engaged Edyth Walker, leading contralto of the Vienna Royal Opera, for the Metropolitan. This was interesting. Miss Walker had shared the Covent Garden season of 1900 with my wife, and we knew she was a fine artist. Madame Schumann-Heink had retired from the company, and it was quite necessary to have two contraltos for the leading roles.

At this time Mr. Wolfsohn had begun to make concert engagements for my wife. He was a man who loved music, and chose his artists for their great qualities. He was devoted to them, and his whole time and strength were at their service. I think he cared more for artistic success than he did for financial reward. He gloried in the greatness of his artists. We had no contract with him, only a verbal understanding.

Both the Maine Festival and the Worcester Festival wanted my wife for their fall concerts. It seemed necessary to choose as their dates conflicted. But Mr. Wolfsohn would not give up either one and worked out a hair-raising schedule. My wife was to sing in Bangor on September 30th, rush for a train, sing in Worcester on October 1st and 2nd, rush for another train and sing in Portland on October 3rd. Would she do it? Please! They were great festivals! There would be disappointment somewhere if she refused! I have never known my wife to refuse a dare. Her great weakness is her sporting blood, and in this she is a real American. There is no impossible: the word doesn't exist.

Yes, she would accept the contract. When the time came we had great fun. There is a lot of hero worship about music festivals. One can imagine how kings and queens and presidential candidates feel on important occasions. The best part of it is that the tremendous outpouring of feeling is sincere. The American people do not give much time to studying the ideas of their leaders, but they are very sensitive to their personalities. They want to trust some one, wholly and unquestioningly. It is so in music. They long to find some one in whose art they can trust, absolutely, and then settle down to unalloyed enjoyment. Critical or intellectual appreciation is, perhaps, too rare, but its place is taken by an emotional response which is as deep as it is genuine. It is warming to the heart of the artist and repays him a thousandfold for all his study and efforts. An artist loves to be trusted by his listeners, just as a leader loves to be trusted by his people, or a mother by her children.

With a new contract signed, and all this appreciation in concerts, we grew ambitious to have a real home, not just a rented, furnished apartment. We had paid back about half of the money we had borrowed in 1896, and our future seemed secure. We found a fine house at 40 West Ninety-second Street. The tenant, an architect, and a man of most refined taste, wanted to sublet and, also, sell his furniture, much of which he had designed and had had made to order. We also sent for our old Boston furniture! In two days we were in our new home, and how we loved it! The children were up and down stairs, finding new cubbyholes every minute. My wife had room in which to show her genius. She is a good singer, I will admit; but she is a better homemaker! That is where her real talent lies. Singing is all right for an hour or two at a time, but homemaking is a much more important gift in the long run and all the time. But, just as you need large halls in which to sing, so you need room for homemaking. Men must have large offices for business, and factories for work. I wonder how many women need more room for their homemaking? Some day we may be fair, and make homemaking our most important business.

The opera season began, and then the blow fell. Mr. Conried announced Miss Walker in *Aida,* and a little later as Brangaene in *Tristan.* Gone were the two roles in which my wife could best distinguish herself, and in which she had made her reputation! Then we were told by other artists that Miss Walker had complete control, by contract, over all the leading contralto roles. This was something new again! No matter how happy and secure you feel, there is always something which can happen— and always the unforeseen, the very thing for which you had made no preparation, the only thing that could affect you seriously! We looked at each other. We had made what we thought was a sacrifice in order to stay in the Metropolitan and enjoy its opportunities, only to have the opportunities swept away. Just as we thought my wife had graduated from all small parts, she was pushed right back into them again. We had, fondly, felt that in three years she had won a place in the affection of the public, and esteem in the directorate, only to find that our new director seemed to be unaware of it. We did not feel sure that he had ever even heard her sing.

As I look back I am proud of the way we reasoned about the whole matter. This was one time when I was able to be of real service to my wife. We could talk things over calmly, and we had complete confidence in each other's judgment. It was not a problem to be thought out by an artist alone. There are too many lonely artists in the world; but there are others who are not alone and are blessed with moral support, be it husband or wife, father or mother, son or daughter. Morale depends very much on the understanding and strength of another.

Of course we knew that Mr. Conried would gain most of his prestige through the new artists that he introduced. The artists that he inherited from Mr. Grau would add little to his fame. They would always be "Grau's artists." We could not blame him for wanting to give Miss Walker the most brilliant introduction possible. Giving her control, by contract, of the repertoire was another matter. To us this was morally wrong. An artist entrusts his career to his director and expects recognition, impartiality, and justice. A director tied by promises and obligations is no director: he is a mere figurehead, helpless and irresponsible. We did not *know* that Mr. Conried had signed such a clause, or that Miss Walker had asked for it, and we gave them both the benefit of the doubt and assumed that they had not. We decided to wait patiently and let the future shape itself. I had complete faith in my wife and her ultimate triumph, and she had absolute faith in her religion and in ultimate justice. No one at the opera house heard a word of complaint from us. In the meantime we tried to enter into the spirit of what was going on.

Caruso made his debut on the opening night in *Rigoletto*, and my wife sang Maddalena. It was a memorable night and was the beginning of a great change in the spirit of the opera house; change of repertoire, change of audience, particularly behind the rail and in the galleries, change of attitude toward opera. Here was a great personality that everyone could understand, a generous, humanizing influence that everyone felt. He had a glorious voice, but that was not all. Above everything he was a man, a real man, simple, direct, earnest, always giving his utmost, striving for better things, never resting on his laurels, growing in depth and sincerity from day to day. Young singers imitated his voice and copied his methods; but that was not enough.

They might well have cultivated his spirit of determination and his manliness.

In an interview in London, quoted in America, Caruso attributed the thrilling quality of his voice to the fear he felt when he stepped on the stage; he might have gone further: it was his fearlessness in the face of fear that was the ultimate cause of triumph.

Then there were the Wagner music dramas. Alfred Hertz had come to us, and his enthusiasm and passionate insistence on perfection made every performance a memorable event. Fricka, Waltraute, the Erdas, they were all more or less new and thrilling in their beauty. In January my wife sang Brangaene. Ternina was our Isolde, and a grander artist I have never known. Her soul was in the clouds; nothing existed for her but art. Indifferent to all the trimmings of public life, she lost herself completely in her roles—Isolde, Brünnhilde, and the rest. The company was enthralled with her. I noticed a strange thing, and it lasted for years. Whenever she sang one of her great roles, a large part of the company would gather in the wings and watch her. It was an uncommon tribute. And yet she would join my wife and Carrie Bridewell to sing one of the "three ladies" in *Die Zauberflöte*. It was Mozart and great art! No false pride or affected modesty. Only art counted.

Parsifal was produced, and in the first few performances my wife sang the smallest part that exists, the Voice at the end of the first act. It was thrillingly beautiful, and we were surprised at the tributes that came from all directions because of those few seconds.

One day we were having a piano rehearsal of *Ballo in Maschera*, I think, with Eames, Caruso, and Scotti. Conried came in, in the midst of it, anxious and troubled. *Das Rheingold* was to be given that evening, and Madame Fremstad, who was to have sung Fricka, had suddenly been taken ill. Madame Saenger-Bettaque, who had sung that part in Germany, refused to undertake it at such short notice. Would my wife try to learn it? Otherwise he must close the opera house. He pleaded and urged, almost with tears in his eyes. In a foolish moment my wife consented. We went over to the York Hotel with Alfred Hertz and had lunch. None of us spoke. The thing was too enormous, too tragically absurd. We went back to the opera house, and for three hours my wife and Hertz rehearsed and memorized. Over and over again they went through the role, in that dark, dismal, empty opera house. I have never been so depressed in my life. Then we went out for a little supper, and my wife went to her dressing room. The dressers draped her costume, and she stood in a trance. At seven, Hertz came in and sat down at the piano. He struck the first chord, and she could not remember a word! Not a note! The human mind is a strange thing. We waited. Hertz was desperate. I was sullen, indifferent—mad through and through! My wife was in despair. It was the cruelest thing I have ever seen. At seven-thirty the doors opened, and the audience began coming in. My wife tried again, and this time the role began to come back to her. It was a desperate risk, but she determined to go through with it. We left her. Hertz went into the orchestra and began the prelude. I took a seat in the house and cursed the day my wife ever entered an opera house. I felt the cruel injustice of the whole thing. It was the bluest moment I have ever had in my life.

The steam blew away and there stood my wife, a goddess in her white robes, and a goddess in her indomitable spirit. "Erwache dich, Wotan, Gemahl," her voice rang out. I held my breath at every phrase, and rejoiced when it was over. There had been no rehearsal of the *mise en scène*. Very gently Van Rooy led her to her different positions, whispering instructions. At the end of the scene she stood motionless until he gallantly conducted her off the stage.

At the end of the performance I found Conried at her dressing-room door, wildly enthusiastic and waving his arms. He must have seen murder in my eyes; he didn't stay long after I got there. My wife and I felt that this was the worst mistake we had ever made. It was literally weeks before she had fully recovered from this super-fatigue.

Engelbert Humperdinck came to superintend the production of his *Hänsel und Gretel*. My wife sang the Witch, and this was one of the few chances she has ever had of rollicking in a funny part. She made the most of it and enjoyed it hugely. She made herself as ugly as possible, with a long pointed nose and a pointed chin. A few years later the following conversation was overheard in one of the boxes. A lady remarked that Madame Homer had recently become the mother of twins. "Twins!" exclaimed the lady beside her. "Perfect nonsense! She's sixty-five if she's a day. I saw her last week in *Hänsel und Gretel!*"

It was a pleasure to do anything for Humperdinck, and in the bluster and pretensions of the exciting life around us it was both a privilege and a lesson to meet a real poet.

Giacomo Puccini came to assist in producing his *Madama Butterfly*. Geraldine Farrar sang Cio Cio San; Caruso, Pinkerton; Scotti, the Consul; and my wife, Suzuki. Again it was a pleasure to serve a famous composer who was, at the same time, a sincere, deeply sympathetic, unassuming, and most direct man.

Gradually all the big roles came back to my wife, and some new ones, too. *Gioconda* was produced with a great cast: Nordica, Edyth Walker, Caruso, Scotti, and Plançon. My wife sang the part of Laura and endowed it with beauty and charm. Then we had a great production of *Il Trovatore*, with Nordica and my wife, Caruso and Scotti. This role of Azucena proved to be a wonderful part for my wife. She gave it a subtlety and power, tenderness and pathos, far beyond anything that I thought possible. Next to Orfeo, and with Amneris, it was her greatest impersonation. I have seen it under all circumstances, including a performance in 1929 at the Metropolitan, and have never known it to fail to carry its poignant message.

A little opera which brought lots of fun to the artists and some to the public was *Marta*. The cast included Sembrich and Homer, Caruso and Plançon, and the performance was a great success, in spite of the large auditorium and the fact that very few in the audience knew the text.

During these years my wife began to sing in symphony concerts in various cities. These concerts were a source of endless joy because of the contact with great music, fine musicians and a music-loving public.

I wrote whenever I could, and Schirmer brought out my Stevenson songs—six from *Underwoods* and three from *A Child's Garden of Verses*. Of these, "Sing Me a Song of a Lad That Is Gone" and the "Requiem" attracted attention. The latter proved to be a very useful song, both for concerts and for the studio, and has been in use ever since. It is published in London and Australia as well as in New York.

XII

1904–1907

OUR HOME, IN SPITE OF ALL DISTRACTIONS, was our direct concern. It was what one might call the permanent thing in life. Other things might have their ups and downs, but this had only ups. It was built with a determined concentration that nothing could resist. My wife, with the help of that great specialist Dr. Henry D. Chapin, studied and adopted every new discovery in the care of children. We had no social engagements of any kind, and spent more time with our children than most people do. The fact that I had my studio at home brought me into the closest contact with them. Most fathers can envy me. The consequence has been that, to this day, they treat their mother and me as of their own generation—each of us as one of themselves. And a consequence of this is that we feel almost as young as they are.

Another summer at Onteora brought lots of fun of all kinds, and a grand recital of my songs by my wife and Heinrich Meyn. During the next winter Mr. Meyn gave a recital at Mendelssohn Hall, in New York, and introduced six of my songs with the composer at the piano. The critics were severe, and I should have died as a writer, right then and there; but I couldn't. A writer has more lives than a dozen cats, and with a publisher and a few singers behind him he continues. That is the bane of the musical world. If you could only squelch these fellows in the beginning! There should be a musical electric chair, with the self-elect in authority. Then the criminal instinct in music could be controlled.

The next summer we took a house on Cape Cod, at Craigville, near Hyannis, right on the sand. This was to be our playground for four years. New friends, the beach, the simplicity and genuineness made it unforgettable. The eternal problem of two studios arose; so we built a rustic, one-room studio for me out on the dunes. It was a noisy and fascinating place. The wind howled and blew the sand, and the breakers pounded. At times I could hardly hear my piano. Naturally I wrote noisy songs like "How's My Boy?" and "To Russia." These two songs, both about the danger zone of life, were among the fortunate ones.

At the end of his third season Mr. Conried sent his company to San Francisco. There was some grumbling. It was not so easy to travel at the end of a season as at the beginning. Mr. Conried did not go, and his manager—Mr. Goerlitz, a Prussian of great energy and sublime self-confidence—was in charge of the tour. We were comfortably established on the sixth floor of the Palace Hotel. On Wednesday evening we were to give *Lohengrin*, in which my wife was to sing, and in the afternoon, *The Marriage of Figaro*, in which, I remember, Madame Sembrich would make her first appearance. These performances did not take place. At about 5:30 in the morning the tremor came which resulted in the San Francisco fire.

I can see nothing gained in giving a detailed description of this adventure. Certain things stand out in my memory. First, the courage and instant cooperation of my blessed wife. We were the first to leave the hotel. As we stepped into the street it was just light enough to see. Only two people were in sight, a man lying on the sidewalk on the other side of the street, and a woman standing over him, crying. Before we could get to them another man came out of a doorway and ran to their aid. There was an unearthly stillness, after the terrific noise we had had. The street was full of cornices which had fallen from the tops of buildings. I have, ever since, despised ornamental cornices casually fastened on pretentious structures. My plan was to take my wife to St. Francis Square, the only open space I knew of in the neighborhood. Down Market Street was a cloud of smoke from one of the first fires. As a precaution we walked in the middle of the street. The trolley wires were down. I had Miss Bella Alten in my charge, and, as she was quite hysterical, I had difficulty in keeping her from stepping on one of these possibly live wires. We saw no one until we reached the Square. There we found perhaps a hundred people standing around. They were only partially dressed and were cold. No one talked above a low voice. My wife, who had left the hotel in her wrapper, went in the bushes and put on an extra suit of mine which she had picked up as we left our room.

Suddenly a fire engine rattled into the Square and startled the oppressive quiet. There was no fire, but the men went into a tall apartment house and very soon a fireman put his head out of a top story window and called for help. A number of men filed silently into the doorway and all was quiet again. I saw Plançon walking around with his coat buttoned around his neck. He was our Parisian Beau Brummell, but at this moment appearance did not count. Bella Alten found some German comrades and left us. Then a two-horse hack drove into the Square, the second vehicle to appear in an hour and a half. Here was actually a man who wanted to do business or be of some help in this paralyzed city. I told my wife this was our chance; the driver agreed to take us to Mr. George Pope's house at the top of the hill, on Pacific Avenue. The Popes welcomed us, and Mrs. Pope gave my wife some of her clothes, which were much too small and could only be fastened together with safety pins. As we were dressing, the Japanese butler tapped on our door. He apologized for disturbing us, but the house was on fire, he said, and we had better come down. It seemed that the imperturbable Japanese cook had insisted on going ahead with his routine and had started something. The fire was quickly out.

Some one told us that Caruso was in the next block, and we went down to see him. He was glad to see a familiar face, and we were able to reassure him and help restore his confidence. We spent the morning on the Popes' front lawn. The sky, the open were glorious; houses were hateful. I stood beside the president of the Firemans Fund Insurance Company. We had a view of the entire city and, as the conflagration spread, he told me the names of the buildings that were burning and the amount of insurance they were carrying in his company. His was a tragic experience, and I have never seen more acute suffering. He seemed to age perceptibly as the day went on.

Toward noon the exodus began, and the rest of the day a steady stream came up the hill on their way to Golden Gate Park. Every conceivable thing on wheels was used. Pushcarts, trucks, wagons pulled by men, baby carriages, bedsprings on roller skates. The impressive thing was the indomitable, cheerful look on all the faces. Jokes, good cheer, encouragement, helping hands, a spirit of real fellowship. It was a long, high hill, and all day my wife talked with mothers who had struggled up with their children. There was a shortage of water, and therefore, little coffee, but she was able to get some for the most exhausted of them.

By common impulse men had pinned impromptu signs on their trucks: "Cheer up, it might be worse," "Don't be down-hearted!" "Brace up, the worst is over!" Dogs, birdcages, mattresses and bedding, cookstoves, a few treasures like framed pictures and flowering plants in pots, were all they needed with which to face the future.

I wish all men who try to picture to themselves the fundamentals of American character, or even human character generally, could have looked on. Any pessimism they might have had would have undergone revision. That consciousness of human selfishness which weighs so sadly on many minds would have vanished, shamefaced, temporarily at least. The inspiring, exhilarating sight of thousands of men and women cheerful in the face of disaster, grandly courageous before a future of uncertainty, indomitable with a whole city burning behind their backs and every possession, job, connection, and daily habit gone, would have revealed to the most callous mind what man truly is and how superficial his poorer qualities are.

The members of our company were in a precarious situation. Many of them spoke no English and had little money with them. Fortunately they had leaders. Edyth Walker, with fine initiative and resourcefulness, took charge of all the chorus women and the girls who sang small parts, and led them to a safe place where she could care for them. They sang their heartfelt praise of her forever after.

The story told of our manager, Mr. Goerlitz, is a good one. He was in the Palace Hotel. He noticed the tremor, but with true Prussian assurance said it was nothing and asked to be called at seven o'clock. After a nice cup of coffee he went around to the theatre, the dear old California Theatre of marvelous acoustics, where we had given so many glorious performances. It was damaged here and there, but he said we would give our performance just the same, and summoned his staff of stage hands, carpenters, technicians, and so on. While he was giving careful directions about cleaning up, repairing scenic arrangements and other trifling details, the entire rear wall crashed down upon the stage. Even this obstinate, persistent captain had to give in.

As night came, the sky was lit with a brilliant glare. No one wished to be indoors. Mr. and Mrs. Pope arranged cots for their four children in the front hall by the door, with the door wide open. In the yard was their large automobile, an open touring car. I thought my wife would enjoy that and bundled her in with pillows and blankets. She had a fitful night, but got some sleep. I could not think of sleeping. It was all too spectacular. A soldier had been stationed on our corner, and all night long we paced up and down together, watching the progress of the fire. It was the plan of the authorities to check the flames by creating an open space across which they could not leap. For this purpose, they placed dynamite under whole blocks of houses and blew them up. After each terrific blast, with the sky full of burning cinders, I would reassure my startled wife and induce her to go to sleep again. It was an unforgettable night. One was conscious of the heroism and indomitable will which is the soul of San Francisco. It is easy to grow sentimental and speculate on the super-race which may one day develop on the Pacific Coast.

In the morning the Popes started for their country home in their automobile, and we went around the corner to the home of our friends Mr. and Mrs. Bliss, for breakfast. Here all was gaiety and high spirits. Supplies were low, and there was but little water; but they made us feel that nothing mattered save our comfort and good cheer. After breakfast we started for the ferry: five miles away, through the burning district. Our hosts gave us sandwiches, cakes, champagne, blankets—everything we could carry—and sent us to their relatives in Oakland. We walked down the hill and kept on the Bay side, away from the fire. The little open spaces and parks were filled with tents, and men, women, and children, in strange costumes, huddled around little oil stoves trying to get breakfast.

My wife was very tired, and I was desperate. All the vehicles were heavy-laden and were going in the opposite direction. Suddenly I saw a truck going toward the ferry. I stopped it and pleaded with the driver. He said he had been forbidden to take a soul on his truck, on penalty of losing his job. I was eloquent, but it was my wife's lovely face that won the day. He said he would take the chance, and she climbed up onto his seat, while I sat at the back. This was the most important thing that happened to us; I realized that I could never have gotten my wife to the ferry on foot.

There were thousands at the ferryhouse, but we got aboard, and very soon Louise was sitting on the lawn at the house of our new friends, surrounded by lovely ladies all anxious to get her anything she wanted. Toothbrush? "I have a dozen which just came from New York." Shoes? Half a dozen women flew to neighboring houses and came back with arms full of shoes of all descriptions. I went to the station to inquire about transportation, and found that Mr. Goerlitz had arranged everything. He had a special train ready for chorus and orchestra, and drawing rooms on the Overland Limited for his principal singers. All day his messengers kept in touch with the scattered members of the company and instructed them about his plans. When the trains started on the evening of the second day, not one member was missing. It was a fine generalship at a time when some men thought only of themselves and safety.

That night we stood on the pier and took one last look at San Francisco, across the Bay. The fire was raging, and Telegraph Hill, which had thus far escaped, was outlined in flames. One after another the houses quietly disappeared. All aboard! It seemed cruel to leave all these good friends behind, and ride away to safety and peace.

In the morning we compared notes with the artists. They were a disheveled lot of waifs, humbled and subdued. That expansiveness which goes with opera had disappeared, and the gay, harmless arrogance that you get used to was wanting. There were some funny stories. Schindler had run to Golden Gate Park carrying his grip. When he opened it there was one collar inside. Hertz had been taken out there and placed in a comfortable room. In the night a terrible noise woke him and he thought all was over. He was in a keeper's house, right next to the lion's cage.

Bella Alten wanted my beautiful bathrobe, which I had wrapped around her that memorable morning at the Palace Hotel, as a souvenir. No one spoke of his losses except Plançon. For two days he talked of the twelve shirts which he had brought from New York and never worn. Think of it, twelve shirts!

My wife became ill and grew steadily worse. I wired ahead to Des Moines for a doctor, and he came to the train. He did what he could, and I asked him to wire my wife's brother Will to have an ambulance, doctor, and nurse meet us at the train in Chicago. It was an anxious night. In the morning we pulled into Chicago. Will was there, and after everyone had left the train my wife was lifted onto a stretcher and carried to the ambulance. Only Mrs. Goerlitz was in our confidence, and in this way we avoided publicity. Two weeks in a hospital, a very narrow escape, a quick recovery, a terrible longing to be with our children, and at last we were back in our home again.

My sister, who was caring for our children, had suffered terribly; but all was over now. Yes, all was over for us, but not for those people in San Francisco. We had them steadily before our eyes.

A few days later Edyth Walker came to see us. My wife was still in bed, but was strong enough to see her friends. Miss Walker had made up her mind to leave the company. To my wife and me this seemed the height of folly. Here was this beautiful artist, rapidly becoming a great dramatic soprano, leaving the Metropolitan. For two hours we argued with her, trying to make her see the absurdity of such a step. We had a thousand arguments, but they were of no avail. We never saw her again, but we did hear, years later, that she had become the greatest Isolde in Germany, and that all Germany adored her. Perhaps her instincts were right, after all.

At this time our contract with Conried had expired and Mr. Goerlitz approached me on the question of renewing for a year. I finally told him my wife would sing fifty performances at $350 a performance, and could not help seeing the smile of triumph on his face. She was worth much more to the Metropolitan, and he knew it; but we could not dicker with that beloved institution. We could not honestly say we preferred concerts, for which my wife was receiving $1,000 each. It meant leaving our children. We were not in the position of those artists who had left their home cities—Rome, Berlin, Paris—to go to a foreign city, New York, and sing for a strange public. New York was home to us, and the Metropolitan was not a commercial institution but an art center, like the Metropolitan Museum of Art, essential to the culture of the city and a place where a good artist could develop his or her art freely. In this respect American artists who love New York will always be at a disadvantage. The only solution is for the Metropolitan to determine what they are really worth and pay them their full value, not the minimum they will accept.

Vacation at last, and a long rest at good old Cape Cod. A new cottage necessitated carting my studio up the beach to a new location in the scrub oaks. This was the year of the seventeen-year locusts, and their deafening drone was not as inspiring as the wind and waves had been, the year before. I blamed the poverty of my efforts on them. By this time David Bispham, Herbert Witherspoon, and Francis Rogers had begun to use my songs on their programs; and I wanted to give them some new things. Instead, I had lots of fun. The days were not long enough for our little reunited family. The valley of the shadow had disappeared, and the sun, sky, and ocean reigned supreme. There are times when you can give yourself up to the joy of living, and they usually follow some difficult experience.

The fall of 1906 was the beginning of a new period in our lives. It may seem strange to some of my readers that after six years at the Metropolitan any unusual change could take place; but fortunately this is the very nature of art. Changes are always taking place, and if it were not so no artist could continue very long. My wife began to sing with new and greater powers. We can say it was because of our experience in San Francisco; we all thought, at the opera house, that the artists were singing with a deeper note of expression and greater sincerity of feeling. Or we can say it was the unfailing reward of her never-ceasing aspiration for higher things. Whatever the cause, the change took place. Her voice and art stood on firmer ground, and consciousness of this gave her greater freedom and poise and enabled her to concentrate still more on the message of the composers.

In October we went on a concert tour, arranged by the Wolfsohn Bureau. My wife had a group of my songs on her recital programs, and in these I accompanied her. I remember feeling diffident about it, and thinking that the audience could, perhaps justly, resent the presence of her husband's songs, then quite unknown, on her programs. However, she sang them with great effect, ending very dramatically with "How's My Boy?"

Her concerts with the Chicago Symphony Orchestra were thrilling. She gave "Ah, Perfido," the "Sapphische Ode," and the "Lorelei" of Liszt. Here we were among old friends, and they were quick to note the change that had come. One newspaper reported: "Never has the gifted contralto's voice sounded richer, truer, and more beautiful. Never has she sung with finer understanding and greater temperamental warmth. Her work was a joy."

There are certain difficulties which confront singers, and one is the transition from the opera house to the symphony hall. Of course, only real musicians can accomplish it, but even for them it is not easy. It almost seems as if the very effort for excellence in the one place unfits the artist for the other. With my preference for symphonic music it was, naturally, a source of great joy to me that my wife could take part so successfully in symphony concerts.

The whole tour was glorious. As a newspaper in one city said: "After once hearing and feeling Madame Homer's magnificent voice, it seemed hard to realize that the last tones would die away and the last rich cadence come to an end, but the remembrance will not die, nor the sweet memory fade, but ever go on enriching the souls of her listeners."

That's it. Except when she sang my songs, I sat with the audiences, and I was aware that something besides music was present. That steadfast nature, everlasting cheer, eternal humor, and warm heart which my children and I were so accustomed to, around our table and all the time, was reaching out to everyone, and, I felt, doing a world of good. For the next twenty years, I took the ground that every audience that came under my wife's influence was fortunate.

We returned to New York and the opera season began. The repertoire was not exciting. *Hänsel und Gretel, Marta*, with Sembrich, Caruso, and Plançon, *Madama Butterfly* with Geraldine Farrar, Caruso, and Scotti were great fun, but not thrilling for us. In January *Aida* and *Lohengrin* were more interesting, and on February 15th the first *Tristan* of that year was given. During these years Mr. Conried brought over from Europe many famous contraltos: Kirkby Lunn from London, Madame Flahaut from Paris, Meitschik from St. Petersburg.

The Metropolitan was rapidly becoming a Mecca for thousands who had, hitherto, ignored it. Caruso's fame spread throughout the country. His influence on the opera house, particularly in the choice of repertoire, was tremendous. Box-office receipts increased and, indirectly, everyone benefited by this. It is impossible to have success in musical life without, indirectly, helping the whole profession. One successful opera singer enables the management to engage other good artists, enlarge the orchestra, etc. One successful concert artist creates a demand for other artists, for more concerts. It is only the unsuccessful artists who have a depressing effect on musical affairs.

Everyone at the Metropolitan rejoiced in Caruso's success, loved to sing with him, and appreciated his sporting determination to share his success with the rest of the cast. As I have said before, I never saw him take a curtain call alone.

We had a lovely little house at 266 West Eighty-ninth Street. It overlooked a large vacant lot which was used for express wagons. The stableman had a shanty, dogs, pigs, hens, and a cow. The horses and wagons trotted in and out from early morning till dusk. Our children loved to watch them. Louise was now eleven and went to the St. Agatha School near by. She studied piano with the famous Mrs. Tapper, and it was evident that she was very musical. But she was also devoted to her books. Sidney was four—just one of those little New Yorkers that you saw in those days, bright-eyed, red-cheeked, ready to do anything and go anywhere. Dr. Chapin, the great child specialist, used to say that the healthiest children lived in New York, and I believed him. But that was before the days of poison gas and eternal din. It was so quiet then that you could hear a cab turn into Eighty-ninth Street, or a trolley car stop on Broadway. The voices of the teamsters in the vacant lot were clearly audible. At night all was as quiet as a country village.

Our little family was a partnership. Nothing amuses me more than the surprised comments I have heard all these years: how did she do it? Our children knew all the details of their mother's artistic life and loved them. They heard her practice her roles over and over again and knew them all. She was a queen in their eyes, the greatest singer who ever lived, and the best mother. Except for the morning rehearsals and the eight or ten performances a month at the opera, she was with them continuously. Nothing escaped her vigilant eye, and she knew every counter in New York that specialized in children's things. She was that thing which most husbands cannot quite understand, a "fussy" mother, never perfectly satisfied with quality, shape, appearance, warmth, and all those mysteries that go with children's clothes.

The children heard my songs, as soon as they were written. It was always an exciting moment when we gathered around the piano and tried a song I had just finished. Of course, they thought I was the greatest song-writer who had ever lived. We were just a family of boosters; nor was it one-sided. Our children knew we thought them capable of unlimited things.

In the late spring we were back in Craigville on Cape Cod, this time in still another house, which meant another moving of my studio. There was excitement in the air. The children were in our confidence and knew great events were impending. Once when we had a lot of relatives visiting us and were seventeen at the table, little Sidney piped up and called to his sister, who was sitting on the other side of the table: "Lou, do you remember to pray for that baby?" "Yes, Sidney." Anxiously, "Do you pray for a boy?" "No, Sidney, I pray for twins!" All more prophetic than we could dream of then. It was a most happy summer. The peace and unworldly consciousness, the triumphant sense of fulfillment that comes at such times filled our little house. The sea, sky, sun, and sand just echoed our feelings. I cannot imagine a happier world.

I worked in my studio and finished the "Pauper's Drive" and other things. While making a setting of Christina Rossetti's "When Wind-Flowers Blossom on the Sea," I came across her *Sing-song*, children's poems, which Swinburne and other poets admired so much. They were fascinating, exquisite, and spiritual. Imagine my horror when two years later after a recital by Madame Gadski at Carnegie Hall, a famous New York critic spoke of those poems as worthless ditties by an unknown author. I did not have the heart to undeceive him.

I began setting these to music and brought home one every day, at lunch, until I had seventeen of them. The children entered into the fun, and I had a hard time stopping and turning to more serious poems.

Late in September things changed and signs of danger appeared. We returned to New York, and I went through an anxious period. My heroic wife pulled me through. She will tell you that I pulled her through, but she is mistaken.

One morning at seven o'clock—on October 15, 1907, to be exact—I rushed upstairs to the little nursery. "A little girl!" I shouted, as I burst in the door. There they were—Louise, Sidney, and their nurse, all dressed and waiting anxiously. Such joy! They clapped and shouted and laughed and sang. A little girl! A little sister! Ten minutes later I rushed up again. "Another little girl!" This was too much. They all cried; their hearts were too full, and they couldn't bear it! Tears of joy and thanksgiving for a beloved mother who had been very, very ill, and hearts throbbing with love for two little sisters who had just come to them, their very own, two of them! What a welcome for those little souls! If we could only be as wholehearted as children! There is no drop of poison in their ointment. Their devotion is complete, without reserve, glorious in its fullness and purity. They look into our faces for the only response they can understand, feelings just like their own.

Another period of anxiety, but one of action, not of helpless waiting. One of our doctors shook his head over little Anne, who weighed only four and a half pounds. It made me furious—how could he dare even intimate such a thing! Dr. Brodhead, calm, imperturbable, was a tower of strength; he felt as sure as I did. Cotton wool, room up to 90°, in a few days all danger passed, and little Anne was assured of that glorious life she has had ever since. Katharine had never been in danger. She was a big girl of five and a quarter pounds, with large black eyes. My darling wife, out of the valley, happy, dazed at her riches, almost bewildered and overcome. Well, it was all over, and I could look out on the outside world again. There was an outside world, although for a time it had seemed as if all life were concentrated at 266 West Eighty-ninth Street.

It struck the world as unique—twins in an opera singer's home —and they made the most of it. For years the newspapers spoke of the "famous Homer twins"; it became a stock phrase. Fortunately, they were too young to be spoiled by this sudden fame. And yet there was real danger. Nearly everyone who saw them for the first time said, "So these are the famous Homer twins." When they were four years old we took them to the

Metropolitan to see a dress rehearsal. As they sat in the semi-darkness, some one came along and said, "Who are these little girls?" Anne looked up and answered: "Why, don't you know who we are? We are the famous Homer twins." Fortunately, American school life disposes of all such things.

Anne Marie was named for my mother, who was Anna Maria —near enough for me to make the slight concession to the fashion of the day. My mother had died in the previous winter at the age of seventy-nine, after a very full and happy life. Katharine was named for Katharine Hun, the famous beauty of a hundred years ago.

XIII
1907–1908

WE HAD REACHED A NEW POINT IN OUR adventurous life.

We had paid back the loans we had made for our trip to Paris in 1896 (with one exception, which my wife said was a gift). We had replaced some of the things we had lost in the San Francisco fire. We had a fine and flourishing family.

Of course my wife had lost her voice. Everybody knew it, and it was too bad. I never knew a singer who did not lose his or her voice every year or two. Some one always makes this melancholy discovery, even if the singer be quite unaware of it. I used to grow tired of being told of lost voices—told, confidentially, by wise little men who, like stock-market prophets, were the only ones who knew. You really are not anyone in the operatic world until you have "lost your voice" two or three times.

In December, Louise returned to the Metropolitan. Everyone behind the scenes rejoiced—singers, stage men, costumers, callboys, doorboys. We had to describe the twins a hundred times, what they looked like, how we told them apart. "Gee, Madame Homer, you're a wonder!" "You're the greatest woman in the world!" "We're proud of you!" "Wonderful to have you back!" "What can we do for you? Anything!" It was not surprising that my wife cried. These men knew how great a singer she was, yes, great, but a *mother*—

She was to make her reappearance as Ortrud in *Lohengrin* on December 18th, and we celebrated by buying a whole new set of costumes—always a rare thrill in a singer's life. If a new fall dress is exciting, how about new costumes that will last ten years,

176

cost a small fortune and be seen by fifty thousand people? Colors, lines, period styles, crowns, jewels, grace, *weight* (this latter detail very important for Ortrud who stands for a whole hour in the first act and does all her singing in the second).

The 18th came. It was a Wednesday evening, and the house was crowded. I suppose there was pessimism everywhere, except in the seat I occupied. Of course, a singer may own her twins, but the public owns her voice, and its property must not be endangered. The curtain went up, and there she was, regal in her new costume; she looked glorious. After the act various friends met me in the corridors and congratulated me on her appearance. "She looked wonderful!" There was still suspicion in their voices—she had not yet sung. Then the second act began, dark and still. I could feel the suspense. "Ich kann nicht fort!" Out rang the voice, thrilling, ominous, rich, beautiful. On and on it went through the long scene, until it culminated, finally, in the great invocation, "Entweihte Götter." And then the whole house came down in thunderous applause. Bad form in a Wagner music drama, but I did not care. I sat there, monarch of all I surveyed. Let them pound their hands! Why not! She deserved it; nothing was too good for her!

Well, she hadn't lost her voice. The prophets were wrong. In the corridors I heard: "More glorious than ever!" "Superb!" "Magnificent!" and I saw beaming faces filled with genuine joy. The congratulations made any effort seem worth while. I wish all opera artists could know what they mean to the public. Too few of them have any means of getting the first great thrill they create, while it is still warm and excited. Even applause does not tell them, and newspapers come too late. People send telegrams nowadays to the artists they hear over the air. When I build my opera house I shall have a telegraph office on every floor, with no charge for messages. Too many times have I seen artists suffering from the reaction of a tremendous effort and realized how welcome is a single word of cheer.

We went home and peeked at the twins, no longer in cotton wool. It was a happy evening. The newspapers all agreed that Louise had not lost her voice and, if not as important as the fact that the twins had had a fine night, it yet had its value as news.

After a wonderful Christmas tree, to which the twins were joyfully welcomed (I think Sidney was disappointed because they did not clap their hands and shout with glee) came *Tristan*, with Fremstad, Louise, Knote, Van Rooy, and Gustave Mahler conducting. This was a most beautiful performance. I shall never forget its haunting beauty, sublime poetry. The opera house was transformed. Fremstad's expression of Isolde's outraged and wounded heart was the greatest I had ever known. I can still hear the unforgettable beauty and passion of her tones.

"Madame Homer displayed a breadth and richness that seemed new even to the American contralto's admirers."

Progress, the very breath of life to the artist! Those who think that applause and box office are the hypnotic crystal in an artist's life are a million miles from the truth. There is no time for things like that. Art is a merciless mistress and demands all, not a part, and brooks no interference. Lower motives—less art; there is no compromise.

And so the season went on, and the twins grew fat. My wife culled happiness out of the veriest trifles of life as well as the larger things. That was her dominant faculty—finding happiness. Nor did she keep it to herself, but passed it on to all around her.

Various things happened in these years that affected musical life. One day Franz Kneisel asked me to join a small group of musicians who wished to form a society for the purpose of bringing musicians into close personal contact. They would name it the Bohemians. There I met Joseffy. It was he who had first seen the great need of such a society, and felt sure that with patience and persistence it could be created, and that it would become permanent. He was right.

I wish all who try to form some conception of a musical artist's nature could have known Rafael Joseffy. He was a man who did not know that he, himself, existed. So concentrated was his mind on others, and on his wonderful art, that, so far as he was concerned, there was no such person as Joseffy. If you gently reminded him of that fact, he looked uncomfortable. His was a true devotion to, a complete absorption in, others *and* his art. In a world where music and egotism are so cruelly and cheerfully associated, so taken for granted, his whole nature was a denial of the fact. Such men are, of course, exceptions in any rank of society, but their qualities are shared, if in a lesser degree, by many others. As music becomes better understood it is clear that egotism is not its outstanding mark, but rather an uncompromising and unworldly idealism. This idealism may appear fanatical, but it is not egotism. It is more selfless than most human emotions.

We discussed the question of a fund to be used for musicians who had suffered misfortunes. Joseffy was enthusiastic about the idea, and the fund was established. Franz Kneisel, also a self-forgetting idealist, whom everybody loved, and who became our president at Joseffy's death, devoted himself to the building up of this fund, and thus countless musicians have been helped, morally as well as financially. Particularly during the war, when so many in Europe were helpless, did it do untold good. Out of this simple beginning came the most wonderful musicians' club that the world has ever known. It forms, also, the most distinguished audience for which an artist can play or sing.

Some time in 1907 Emilio de Gogorza, an old friend, came to see us. He wanted my wife to sing into a recording machine. He said Caruso and Melba had agreed to do it, and my wife would be paid her concert fee. The company was located in Philadelphia and was called the Victor Company. A little dog listening to a horn was its trade-mark. It seemed a strange thing to sing without an audience—hardly possible. And then, how would it sound? We hesitated. Mr. de Gogorza urged, and said

Heaven Above," from Browning's "Johannes Agricola in Meditation," dedicated to my mother. These poems seemed to me most expressive of some of the grand qualities which they possessed. I hoped some one would sing "Michael Robartes," but the men chose "The Pauper's Drive." The William Blake songs, "The Sick Rose" and "Infant Sorrow," were not taken up. (During recent years, Samuel Barber has sung "The Sick Rose" and "April, April," with text by William Watson, in some of his recitals, very beautifully and with fine effect.)

My wife had now reached a stage of development which most European singers attain before they come to the Metropolitan. She sang expressively and acted eloquently, and had a certain maturity. As I have said, Americans as a whole do not care for the formative period, but love the finished artist. With her new power, all that she needed was opportunity. The season drifted on. Mr. Conried's illness cast a shadow over the company, and it was rumored that this would be his last year as director. There was no prospect of new roles, which was disappointing, but on February 27th *Il Trovatore* was revived with Caruso singing Manrico.

The role of Azucena appealed to Louise tremendously, and she threw herself into its interpretation with heart and soul. She electrified this tattered and triumphant gypsy woman. It was not only her glorious voice that moved, although she acted with her voice—she lost herself in the monomania of this unconquerable spirit. The opera house became something more than a theatre. The result was a great success. With an impending change of management, a genuine success in a popular opera was not to be despised. Julius Rosenwald has said that success in business is largely luck. Something like this runs through the lives of artists. They are really waifs on a stormy sea. The public thinks of popular artists as securely enthroned. But, as we have found since 1914, even thrones are easily swept away.

Photograph Burr McIntosh

AS AZUCENA, NEW YORK, FEBRUARY, 1908

ist's nature could have known Rafael Joseffy. He was a man who did not know that he, himself, existed. So concentrated was his mind on others, and on his wonderful art, that, so far as he was concerned, there was no such person as Joseffy. If you gently reminded him of that fact, he looked uncomfortable. His was a true devotion to, a complete absorption in, others *and* his art. In a world where music and egotism are so cruelly and cheerfully associated, so taken for granted, his whole nature was a denial of the fact. Such men are, of course, exceptions in any rank of society, but their qualities are shared, if in a lesser degree, by many others. As music becomes better understood it is clear that egotism is not its outstanding mark, but rather an uncompromising and unworldly idealism. This idealism may appear fanatical, but it is not egotism. It is more selfless than most human emotions.

We discussed the question of a fund to be used for musicians who had suffered misfortunes. Joseffy was enthusiastic about the idea, and the fund was established. Franz Kneisel, also a self-forgetting idealist, whom everybody loved, and who became our president at Joseffy's death, devoted himself to the building up of this fund, and thus countless musicians have been helped, morally as well as financially. Particularly during the war, when so many in Europe were helpless, did it do untold good. Out of this simple beginning came the most wonderful musicians' club that the world has ever known. It forms, also, the most distinguished audience for which an artist can play or sing.

Some time in 1907 Emilio de Gogorza, an old friend, came to see us. He wanted my wife to sing into a recording machine. He said Caruso and Melba had agreed to do it, and my wife would be paid her concert fee. The company was located in Philadelphia and was called the Victor Company. A little dog listening to a horn was its trade-mark. It seemed a strange thing to sing without an audience—hardly possible. And then, how would it sound? We hesitated. Mr. de Gogorza urged, and said the records would be submitted to my wife for her approval. Finally she consented.

This company gained countless friends for my wife's voice, many of them in remote places; paid her the larger part of what she was able to save, and gave her a sense of security through a number of years that she could not have gained in any other way. But for this unexpected, undreamed-of boon, we should not have dared to build our beautiful home on Lake George. The fact that this income did not continue indefinitely did not affect the happiness it brought us during those fifteen years.

It was all a strange experience. The silent room, the square tin horn that went through the wall, the queer reinforced instruments in the orchestra, the buzzing sound of the recording machine in the next room, the feeling that tempi must be exact, that every tone must be perfectly placed, that the slightest deviation or sound of breathing would be carefully recorded on that truthful master disc, all produced an excitement, an anxiety that no opera house could bring about. I have never seen artists so excited as when they were singing for the recording machine. Broadcasting is not nearly so trying, because your singing is not being recorded. That sense of going on record is something like testifying under oath.

In 1905 my wife sang at Norfolk and Winsted, Connecticut, for the Litchfield County Musical Association. This was the beginning of a beautiful and unique experience. The institution was carried on solely for cultural purposes, and the highest regard was paid to aesthetic values. I think a little description of it will help to convince my readers that idealism is the prime force that runs through musical life.

Choruses were formed in all the larger towns in the county, and a competent conductor was engaged by the year to drill them. Each town had its annual concert, for which younger artists and a small orchestra were brought from New York. In June all the choruses assembled at Norfolk for a grand two-day festival which was held in the "Music Shed" that stood on the grounds of White House, the home of Mr. and Mrs. Carl Stoeckel. For these festivals the most famous artists were engaged, and also the entire Philharmonic Orchestra of New York. Choral works and operas in concert form, symphonic works, and instrumental and vocal solos made up the programs. The acoustics were perfect, and the artistic results often of the highest order. For each festival, some noted composer, such as Chadwick, Parker, Carpenter, Coleridge-Taylor, or Sibelius, was commissioned to write an original work.

For all these concerts throughout the year, no tickets were ever sold, and the entire expense of the whole undertaking was assumed by Mr. and Mrs. Stoeckel. The audience was invited, and of course there were never seats enough to accommodate all those who wished to come. To have a seat was esteemed a rare privilege, not only in Litchfield County, but in New York, Boston, and many other cities. "Oh, if I only had a ticket for the Norfolk Festival!" or, triumphantly, "I have a ticket! I'm going!" was a common exclamation in New York. Thus the spirit was unique. Chorus, orchestra, artists, and audience united in honest, straightforward homage to music, and there was an atmosphere of sincerity rather than display.

Mr. and Mrs. Stoeckel took the attitude that artists were ambassadors. In order to make them perfectly comfortable they placed a large house at their disposition, put the catering in the hands of Delmonico, and gave one of them the keys of the wine cellar. Open carriages were provided for drives through the beautiful country. Nordica and Eames, among others, were there in the first two years, and Alma Gluck and many other famous artists came in subsequent years. All were invariably touched by the consideration and delicate attention which surrounded them.

Schirmer continued to publish my songs. Among them were two which I valued above others: "The Eternal Goodness," to words by Whittier, which I dedicated to my father, and "There's

Heaven Above," from Browning's "Johannes Agricola in Meditation," dedicated to my mother. These poems seemed to me
most expressive of some of the grand qualities which they possessed. I hoped some one would sing "Michael Robartes," but
the men chose "The Pauper's Drive." The William Blake songs,
"The Sick Rose" and "Infant Sorrow," were not taken up. (During recent years, Samuel Barber has sung "The Sick Rose" and
"April, April," with text by William Watson, in some of his
recitals, very beautifully and with fine effect.)

My wife had now reached a stage of development which most
European singers attain before they come to the Metropolitan.
She sang expressively and acted eloquently, and had a certain
maturity. As I have said, Americans as a whole do not care for
the formative period, but love the finished artist. With her new
power, all that she needed was opportunity. The season drifted
on. Mr. Conried's illness cast a shadow over the company, and
it was rumored that this would be his last year as director. There
was no prospect of new roles, which was disappointing, but on
February 27th *Il Trovatore* was revived with Caruso singing
Manrico.

The role of Azucena appealed to Louise tremendously, and
she threw herself into its interpretation with heart and soul. She
electrified this tattered and triumphant gypsy woman. It was not
only her glorious voice that moved, although she acted with her
voice—she lost herself in the monomania of this unconquerable
spirit. The opera house became something more than a theatre.
The result was a great success. With an impending change of
management, a genuine success in a popular opera was not to be
despised. Julius Rosenwald has said that success in business is
largely luck. Something like this runs through the lives of artists. They are really waifs on a stormy sea. The public thinks of
popular artists as securely enthroned. But, as we have found
since 1914, even thrones are easily swept away.

Louise sang *Il Trovatore* in New York and Philadelphia and, during the spring tour, in Boston, Pittsburgh, and Chicago.

I treasured all the newspaper tributes. To me, a critic was just another music lover. The only difference between him and the rest of us was that he had to notice everything that was bad in a performance and refer to it, while we could ignore what was bad and concentrate on what was good and great. I think we had the advantage and kept closer to the composer.

In New York, one paper said:

There are contraltos and there is Louise Homer. Her Azucena is a commanding dramatic figure, intense, powerful and picturesque. As for our countrywoman's singing, I can characterize it with but one word—magnificent.

And after the last performance of the season:

Madame Homer's Azucena was a worthy, artistic companion to Caruso's Manrico. There was splendid dramatic power in her impersonation of the revengeful gypsy, and she sang the music with fullness and richness of tone that compelled enthusiastic expressions of admiration. After the second act, she was repeatedly recalled alone before the curtain.

I remember it well. Over and over again they called her out, and this was a glorious way in which to end a season. The contralto repertoire does not permit many personal ovations, and they make a great impression on a humble and interested listener.

In Philadelphia:

She rose to lofty heights of intense dramatic power, thrilling the house with that indefinable psychical impulse, which only genius can arouse and communicate. For Madame Homer, the performance was a series of ovations by the audience, recalling the brilliant days of the old opera regime, when syndicates were not and stars were passionately worshipped by the populace.

All this was wonderful for my wife, who as a girl had sung in the Presbyterian church at Seventeenth and Spruce streets, just around the corner. Her mother and sisters sat in the audience and wept for joy.

In Boston H. T. Parker wrote:

Here was no operatic contralto assigned to Azucena, but a wild creature of her mountains, caught into the sombre Spanish melodrama that Verdi was clothing with music. And Madame Homer sang, not as one traversing familiar numbers, sure for half a century of their effects, but as a singing actress who has found these hackneyed melodies the thrilling speech of passion and character.

It was most moving to have such appreciation in Boston. Many of our relatives and friends were in the audience, including George Chadwick and Will Whitney, and of course I was in the clouds. We walked up to see our old home at 355 Boylston Street, and the old church on Columbus Avenue where my wife had sung. We are frank sentimentalists and value the memory of every place in which we ever lived, every town in which my wife sang, every comrade, and everyone who has ever sung my songs.

In Pittsburgh: "It was Louise Homer's day of triumph. . . ." "It was a continual glory. . . ." "Madame Homer rose to heights which few latter-day actresses could excel. . . ."

Yes, she was born just around the corner from her father's church, in the East End—of course everyone in Pittsburgh rejoiced.

Whenever an American artist has success, thousands feel it deeply. The only point my record can have is to show what education and opportunity can do, not only for our young artists, but for the vast numbers who are encouraged and exalted by their success. It is not a record of the past, but a hint for the future.

In Chicago:

Madame Homer, who is well known to local audiences on the concert platform, was a magnificent Azucena; her big act was a triumph, and a triumph in the same opera with two other distinct triumphs. A big flexible voice, handled with consummate musicianship, makes Madame Homer's every appearance a joy in prospect as in memory.

Her three brothers, with their families, sat in the audience.

Tristan und Isolde had also been a great success in Boston and Chicago. It was all very thrilling, and we went back to New York in high spirits.

Momentous changes were taking place. Conried had retired, and Andreas Dippel, our old comrade, had been appointed administrative manager of the Metropolitan for the ensuing year. To be associated with him as codirector the head of the great Milan Opera House, La Scala, had been invited to come to New York. He had a very long name, in fact, two names, and we all wondered how we should address him—by one name or both —and also how we should like him and how he would like us. There is nothing so mysterious as a new, unknown director who has never heard you sing. The Americans in our company asked Scotti about him and practiced on his name. Little did we realize that he was destined to guide the fortunes of the Metropolitan Opera House for more than twenty years, and become one of the commanding influences in the musical life of our country.

Mr. Dippel opened negotiations for a new contract; always a disagreeable experience for us. There was the concert field with the Wolfsohn Bureau always trying to raise the fee for my wife's concerts to the highest possible point. Here was the opera, with the directors trying to keep her salary as low as possible. Concerts meant separation from our children. Opera meant a united family. There was no doubt in our minds as to what we would do. We would stay at the Metropolitan, whatever the sacrifice.

It was evident that there should be some increase of salary, and, to offset this, Mr. Dippel devised a plan for sixty perform-ances in the season instead of fifty. The plan was a bad one, and resulted after a few years in Louise asking for a half-season con-tract instead of a full one. Too many performances are worse than too few. The fee was, I believe, $450 a performance (mak-ing $27,000 for the five months), and this increased slowly from year to year until it reached $600, though for a shorter season.

I have seen instances of artists, flushed with success, leaving the Metropolitan, confident that the institution could not get on without them, and that they would be called back at some fabu-lous fee. Nothing could be more foolish. Under normal circum-stances no one is indispensable to the Metropolitan. In foreign cities the public sometimes clamors for a favorite artist. A sort of musical riot takes place. In New York the greatest favorites leave the opera and there is hardly a ripple on the musical waters. Hands off is the American attitude toward all institutions. It is strange that in the most democratic country in the world the voice of the public should be so seldom heard. Apparently the public has no voice.

There was no danger of my wife's head being turned with success. It was not in her character. Always her own severest critic, she looked forward to steady improvement and larger opportunity. Success was great fun, but it made no impression on her. Much more important was how well such and such a scene went, such and such a song. If she could feel that she had done a little better she was happy.

Still more important was the welfare of her family. Here any success really turned her head—and filled it with joy. Her mater-nal pride and happiness was the frankest exhibition imaginable, and was open to any criticism and condemnation that anyone chose to make. She would talk with interviewers about children, but say nothing about singing. If all this militated against her art, as was implied by newspaper accounts of the views of other singers, so be it. It could not be helped. My wife could not more easily change her character than she could the color of her eyes, or the quality of her voice. She had to go ahead as she was, and make the best of it, and her family didn't want her to change, in fact, would not let her change; so there you are.

During the spring Mr. Gatti-Casazza came over from Milan and proved to be a kind and considerate man, easy to talk to and full of understanding of an artist's problems. He quickly stopped all discussion and signed Mrs. Homer's contract. He had never heard her sing, but, somehow, seemed to have perfect confidence in her.

Hurrah! The future assured and the present glorious. Ho for the sandy beach, the sea, the sunshine. We couldn't get our twins down there fast enough, not to speak of Louise and Sidney. Those little babies did not know the joy awaiting them. A whole world of sand! It might fill their hair and get down their necks, but what of that? It was sand, about the only thing as pure and sweet and clean as they were.

The little rustic studio was still there on the shore, a little grayer for wind and weather, but undamaged. (I understand that it still stands there, although I have not seen it for twenty years.) I finished my "Song of the Shirt." I worked at a quintet for piano and strings which I have never shown to my publisher. It seems like old stuff in these days of brilliance and dazzling virtuosity. Twenty years later I heard our daughter Kay and the New York String Quartet play it in three recitals.

The days seemed like minutes, the weeks like days, the months like weeks; all too short. Louise was a beautiful girl of twelve, brimming with life and fun, Sidney a roly-poly of five. I taught him to swim, and he used to jump off the raft into twenty feet of water. He had light hair and blue eyes like his grandfather Homer, and an everlasting, mischievous twinkle in his eye, also like his grandfather. (His wife will tell you today that he has not changed; only grown.) Katharine and Anne held court on the beach every day, and were visited by everyone for miles around. That lady in a linen dress or dark blue bathing suit, the one with the infectious merry laugh that even made strangers smile, was the mother. The tall gink, with queer legs and a crook in his neck, heavy head of hair and drooping mustache, was the father; odd-looking in his bathing suit, but proud and self-satisfied.

American family life is the greatest institution the world has ever known. The undignified playing together of parents and children, the familiar jokes and repartee, the informality and close comradeship, so surprising (and sometimes shocking) to Europeans, is either something new or a reversion to the primitive. In any case, it is glorious.

XIV

1908–1910

IT WAS AN EXCITING FALL; the new direction had taken over the Metropolitan. Mr. Gatti-Casazza of Milan was announced as the general manager. Of course it wasn't *his* opera house; it was ours! It wasn't our place to show him what we could do; it was his place to show us what he could do, what he knew that the Metropolitan didn't know. The shoe was on the other foot, and the complacency and curiosity around the Met was great. Stage hands are not fond of new directors; it disturbs the routine. Those little labor-saving ways of doing things have to be explained all over again. The same is true with artists. All their temperamental peculiarities which have been well understood will now be misunderstood. They will be judged by harmless habits which they acquired in the old days. They will be scrutinized anew—not such great fun for popular and accepted artists.

Of course there was Dippel as administrative manager; he knew how great we were and would protect us from unimportant peccadilloes.

Mr. Toscanini was the new conductor. We had heard how fine he was, and the artists felt sure he would recognize their qualities. Artists feel comfortable and at home with musicians, but not with laymen—and they always regard directors as laymen.

I remember very well our first rehearsal with Toscanini. *Aida* was to be the opening performance, and he wanted to go through the part of Amneris with my wife. As he was from Milan, the home of *Aida*, any traditions he might have would be authoritative. I recall wondering if he would have any suggestions to

189

make. I hoped not. Every tone, every nuance, every gesture in her Amneris was, to me, perfect; had been for ten years.

He greeted us with a cordial smile. No man can put you *en rapport* quicker than Toscanini. Without uttering a word he says, "We are both servants of art, we will do our best." He takes you at your best, expects the best, and never harbors doubts until they are forced upon him. That is a wonderful way to take an artist. You are perfect—until you fail. Quite different from that other way: I wonder—I doubt—I expect little—I hope to be surprised, but—

Artists made wonderful progress under Toscanini; they always began at the top of their ability and *went further*. If he saw possibilities beyond, he made you feel that you could achieve them. Of course, quite naturally, certainly, so, there, now, of course. Nothing astonishing about it. He did it every day.

We had a grand rehearsal; not much change, a little slower tempi, especially in the fourth act, classic dignity, nothing flamboyant or "Italian"—as we used to say *before* Toscanini came!

We went away happy. He smiled on us as if we were children. That look of eternal wisdom made him seem much older than he was.

The orchestral rehearsals began, and before the first performance that feeling of complacency and curiosity I spoke of was gone. The whole opera house knew it was dealing with a new force. Such is genius. As for my wife and me, we were supremely happy. A new world was opening out, and we loved it.

The opening night was one of great excitement. New Yorkers love excitement. With half a chance they will work anything up to a frenzy. With the air charged, the New Yorker is in his element. With calm exterior, bright eye, and throbbing pulse he is his normal self. He never loses his head; he is simply warmed up and comfortable. This ability to respond to a great show, join in an emphatic outburst, pronounce decisive judgment, is one of his greatest charms. No capital city in the world has it to the

AS AMNERIS, FIRST SEASON OF SIG. GATTI-CASAZZA, 1908

same degree. It is not hysteria with a reaction, or morbid craving for the abnormal; it is the joy of bestowing emphatic approval on something great.

Emmy Destinn made her debut: a new and unique voice. Nothing just like it had I ever heard. The medium like some new wood-wind instrument, the high notes pure, yet charged with emotion. A legato like a river of sound, or a Scotch bagpipe. A sort of fatalistic temperament that gave a tragic touch, even in repose. In a world of soprano voices as much alike as peas in a pod, an original voice brings a sigh of relief, a feeling of vast contentment. The average voice is a bore. Why? Is it imitation, or standardization by teachers? And this strange thing: before Caruso came I never heard a voice that even remotely resembled his. Since he came I have heard voice after voice, big and small, high and low, that suggested his, reminded me even forcibly, at times. There was no pleasure in this; it was irritating, if anything.

The art of singing is in its infancy, because the study of individuality is in its infancy. The demands of each age have been met; the execution of the old Italian heyday, the conventionality of the Victorian era, the heroic qualities of the early Wagnerian days. It was remarkable how much alike the great Wagnerian sopranos sounded: Materna, Sucher, Vogl, etc. The two lyric sopranos, Lehmann and Nordica, brought relief as they developed. Ternina was a godsend and brought originality and fresh blood. The demand of our day is for individuality and free personal development. The individuality of Farrar's voice should be a lesson to all. My wife's voice also had an unmistakable originality. The remembrance of Calvé's voice haunts one. Yes, the art of singing, from a modern point of view, is in its infancy and has a great future.

It was a glorious night. Every artist seemed to be at the zenith of his power. The chorus shook the roof. The trio in the third act swept the house. When Caruso gave up his sword the audience stopped breathing. My wife sang the fourth act better than ever, and with greater passion.

It has always seemed to me that from that night a new spirit entered the Metropolitan—more sweeping climaxes, more intense pianissimos, more vivid, tragic atmosphere, more passionate abandon. I used to wonder how the poetic introspection of Jean de Reszke would fit into this new picture, or the art of Victor Maurel. I felt that they would suffer somewhat under these conditions.

The season moved on victoriously. The opera house grew more popular every day.

The children grew strong, and the house grew small—twins take up a lot of room. The Victor Company prospered. I also had my share in this new wave of good fortune. The dramatic songs like "How's My Boy?" and "The Pauper's Drive" seemed to fill a need. I took a studio at the Hotel Belleclaire on upper Broadway, put in a piano, and planned to do better and bigger things.

I scanned the great poets. It is strange how queer great poetry looks to the song writer—angular, stiff, heavy, long-worded, stretched beyond the musical phrase, interrupted with parentheses.

I should be ashamed to tell how many big things I started. I loved them, but they didn't love music. They wouldn't "make themselves"; and unless a song makes itself the game is up. All the king's horses and all the king's men . . . Much of my life has been wasted in vain attempts.

One morning I picked up a little green book that our friend Helen Paxton had sent me two years earlier. It was easy stuff, short lines. I set three of the little poems to music and took them home to show my wife at lunch. I knew she would laugh to see how I had (for the moment, of course) fallen off my high horse. She liked them! And when my wife likes a thing there's no doubting it. I think I was a little crestfallen that she didn't realize I had stepped down from my pedestal.

The three songs were "Mammy's Lullaby," "Uncle Rome," and the "Plantation Hymn" from the *Bandanna Ballads*, by Howard Weeden.

I thought then that I was getting into a bad way, letting down the bars, but now I am glad I wrote those songs.

The high-brow attitude, so natural to musicians who have lived in the atmosphere of the works of the great composers, can be very deceptive. We are lifted to a high plane, but we may not be able to work there. We may have a talent for simpler things.

In trying to form some idea of the future of music, I arrive at certain conclusions. One is that a great amount of simple music of the purest quality is going to be written. The need is great.

The glorious season came to a close. Only one thing disturbed us: we were growing tired of the repertoire. It was all new to Mr. Gatti: new opera house, new public, new artists. But it was old to us: ten years of *Aida*, eight years of *Tristan*, etc. Just before he went back to Milan, Mr. Gatti asked my wife to study Orfeo for the next season; he was sure she would love it, and it would be a great role for her.

Orfeo! The most coveted part in the contralto repertoire! In an opera without a single role for male voices. There must be idealism in these men from Milan. We couldn't understand it, but our delight was boundless. The future suddenly became bright with promise, and a new adventure loomed ahead.

Our little home at 266 West Eighty-ninth Street grew smaller every day. The four children had a way of taking up more room as they grew. We decided on a great change. We would move to the east side, near the park. It was quieter over there, and there were no trolley cars on Fifth Avenue. It would be easy to send the children to the park.

For the first time we began to save money. The Victor Company was largely responsible for this. It was necessary to consider investments, a new experience for us. I knew nothing about speculation, but I had seen its effect on two singers at the Metropolitan. One lost all his money and his voice, the other made a great deal of money and lost his voice. They used to talk stocks up to the moment they stepped out before the audience to sing, and, if they could find listeners, resumed the moment they stepped off. It was rather boresome. What impressed me was the excitement under which they seemed to be laboring and their evident lack of interest in mere singing.

I came to the definite conclusion that speculation, win or lose, meant loss of artistic ability, and decided on long-term trustee bonds.

We found a fine, old-fashioned, four-story brownstone house at 13 East Sixty-fourth Street, and after arranging to have all the inside woodwork done up in white, we packed our trunks and bundled our little family off to our beloved Cape Cod.

Only one thing bothered us. All through the spring, in going back and forth to my studio, I had had little attacks of dizziness. I would stop on a curb and wait for it to pass off. We consulted a stomach specialist. After his pet tests he announced, with bright eyes, that my heart was attached to my ribs. He looked so happy over this discovery that I didn't know whether to be glad or sorry. I have been examined many times since then, and no doctor has mentioned this little novelty; so the heart must have broken loose again. Perhaps (perish the thought) he was mistaken. But something was wrong. During the summer, while walking on Tremont Street in good old Boston, I was suddenly laid out. That passed off, and the summer was as fine as usual. In October we returned to our lovely new home, and on the very first evening I had a return of the trouble. When the boys talk about shell shock I feel that I understand them very well.

As soon as I realized that there was something wrong, my sole

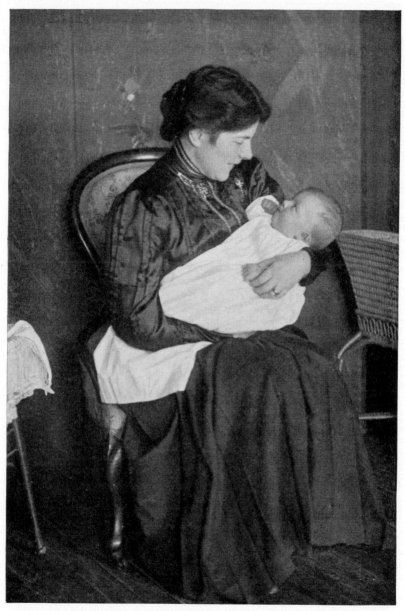

MY WIFE, WITH KAY, NEW YORK, 1909

thought was that it must not interfere with my wife's career. Only those who know can understand how large an opera contract can loom. It is different from anything I can think of. An opera singer is the most difficult person in the world to replace. If she has any equals, they are tied by contracts in other parts of the world, and are not procurable. It is such a highly specialized art, requiring such a rare combination of qualities, that a great opera singer is regarded as a world possession.

There is something most moving in the universal joy at the advent of a great opera singer. It is not a selfish joy but rather a pride in the expression of something inherent in human nature itself. There is a sort of vindication in the culmination of these qualities which all men feel are lurking, to some degree, in their subconscious selves.

My determination to stand by and make the best of it made the whole problem of straightening myself out easier. All people in trouble need an objective, something to steady their efforts. I went to all rehearsals and performances, and no one in the opera house (or among my friends) knew that anything unusual was going on. Sometimes I would see double; there would be two Louise Homers moving about on the stage.

My wife and I worked the whole thing out together, and it took many years. There were ups and downs, but I think we handled them in the best way. Medical science has progressed greatly since then, and disturbances of this kind are regarded in a very different light. I am talking about twenty-five years ago.

We had several exciting events just ahead of us. I will take them in their order. The first was a recital of my songs which Louise had promised to give for the benefit of the Student Fund of the MacDowell Club, on November 1st. Instead of having it in the clubrooms, the club planned it for the Lyceum Theatre, which Daniel Frohman had contributed to the cause. Of course I wanted to play for my wife, but I was not sure that my health would permit it. I might have an attack of dizziness, and it would not be fair to the Club to risk a fiasco. It was quite a dilemma, but I found a happy solution. I asked our friend Richard Hageman to learn the accompaniments, and then turn the pages for me while I played. If I should be unable to continue, have an attack of dizziness, he could slip quietly into my place, and the change would hardly be noticed. Like a fine comrade, he consented.

It was a grand occasion—the only time in our lives that we have given a public recital consisting entirely of my songs. I suffered over the first song, then was able to concentrate, and ended in fine form. Hageman was responsible for this, with his quiet strength.

I will quote an article in the New York *Press* which gives a picture of the afternoon:

Louise Homer, whose steady progress in artistic proficiency and public esteem is a thing to dwell upon with pleasure, sang a program of songs by her husband, Sidney Homer, yesterday afternoon in the Lyceum Theatre, to the delight of a large and representative audience. Her composer husband, himself but recently out of a sickbed, played the accompaniments all too modestly, with Hageman, assistant conductor at the Metropolitan Opera House, beside him to turn the pages.

It was a pretty picture this, husband and wife artistically united in proclaiming a message of musical beauty. In a proscenium box on the right, to add further interest, sat the Homers' eldest child, a smaller Louise, and the sturdy little son, another Sidney, both delighted to add their share of applause to the general expression of approval. The baby twins, not yet trained to listen in respectful silence to their mother, had to be left at home.

Never before has our American contralto looked so beautiful and sung so irresistibly.

There was something immensely appealing in Madame Homer's first appearance, so beautiful and yet so free from self-consciousness. Her husband did not come out with her, as many a man might have done under the circumstances. Quietly, almost

NEW YORK, ABOUT 1910

unnoticed, he took his place at the piano after the first burst of applause was over, and then the concert began.

The first number, "Sing Me a Song of a Lad That Is Gone," which stands out as one of Sidney Homer's best efforts, has been sung in public often, but no one can give it the simple pathos, absolutely without sentimentality or exaggeration, which Mrs. Homer infuses into its measures.

As a composer, Homer is at his best, it seems to us, in words that ask for the simplest treatment,—apparently the simplest, at least. The tender love of a mother, the confiding, ingenuous devotion of a child for its parents are more within his domain than the complicated emotions depicted by so many modern composers. For this reason we count his settings of Christina Rossetti's "Lyrics from Sing-song" among his most delightful contributions.

The New York *Times* said:

He has gained some of his strongest and best effects in the employment of a free declamatory style, or of short or loosely modeled figures for the voice, united to an accompaniment whose independent facture, characteristic expressiveness, and pregnant harmonies, often dissonant and of unconventional progression, is skillfully employed to heighten the emotional coloring given to the poem.

Such verse as that of Browning's "Prospice" and "A Woman's Last Word," Mr. Homer treats in a vividly effective manner. He has done little that is more seizing than his setting of the eight lines of Tennyson, "Thy Voice Is Heard." There is an enhancement of the tense moral of Dobell's "How's My Boy?" through the characteristic and powerful musical expression he has found for it, as has been made known to this public before.

The next event was the opening and dedication, on November 8th, of the new Boston Opera House. The opera was *La Gioconda,* and Nordica and my wife were invited to sing, partly on the ground that they had studied in Boston in their girlhood days. It was a spectacular occasion, but I could not suppress a slight uneasiness. I felt that it would be difficult to create an illusion in that opera house because the audience was so much in evidence. The auditorium dominated the stage, and the listeners were very conscious of one another. The impersonal feeling that one has in a great cathedral makes for concentration. Opera houses should try for something of that kind.

We hurried to Philadelphia that night, after the performance, and on the next evening opened the opera season there with *Aida*, this time with Gadski, Homer, and Caruso. On the next Monday the Metropolitan opened with *La Gioconda*, with Destinn, Homer, and Caruso. Three grand-opening performances in eight days, with three great sopranos!

And now for *Orfeo ed Euridice*, which Mr. Gatti wished to give before Christmas. It was to be a great event. Mr. Gatti was tremendously interested. The scenery had been painted in Paris from sketches by Doré. We had not seen it yet, but we had heard it was very beautiful. John Alexander had designed a wonderful costume for Louise, quite different from what we had expected. It was a tunic to the knees instead of flowing robes. Mr. Toscanini had begun rehearsals with the orchestra, and rehearsals with the artists, with piano, in the foyer. My wife was letter-perfect in the music, and her conception of the character was deepening every day. Musically the role was not difficult to learn, but the artistic possibilities seemed unlimited. We should have loved to give our entire time to it, but no, she had to sing all kinds of operas while she was preparing this: Ortrud, her hardest part, on November 20th, Azucena in *Il Trovatore*, a part she loved, on November 26th, Brangaene, another beautiful role, on November 27th. It was now December, and *Orfeo* was to be given on the 23rd. We longed for a respite, but performances came thick and fast: *Aida* on December 3rd, *Lohengrin* on December 6th, *Tristan* on December 8th, *La Gioconda* on December 9th, *Siegfried* on December 16th, and *Aida* on December 20th.

I admired my wife's pluck and calmness. She did her best in

WASHINGTON, ABOUT 1925

all these operas and, according to the newspaper accounts, was never finer. All her free time she gave to *Orfeo*. Mr. Toscanini appreciated her position and, on one occasion, came to our home to rehearse with her, to save her from the exposure of going to the opera house. At last the rehearsals with orchestra began, and the scenery was placed upon the stage. It was all too beautiful! To hear that music played by the orchestra was a revelation. Toscanini was marvelous; he made the whole thing seem a holy rite. Madame Gadski was Euridice, and Alma Gluck as the Happy Shade, revealed her exquisite voice. My wife was moved to tears again and again as she rehearsed. It was not like anything that she had ever sung. One can understand this when one thinks of the wicked characters she had had to portray. Here was a pure soul and a noble quest. All my wife's life has been a quest: a quest for the true, the beautiful, for duty to be done. To portray the part of Orfeo she had only to be herself.

At last the performance came. She had been so absorbed in the rehearsals that I doubt if the performance was anything more to her than just another rehearsal. I am sure that personal success had no place in her thoughts. Neither she nor I expected such tributes as those which came. We had no idea how her performance would affect the audience. At the end of the first act, after finishing her interpolated "Divinités du Styx," she held her lyre up before her like a cross and strode forth on her quest for her beloved. It was an inspired moment. Toscanini was carried away, the orchestra crashed with eloquence. The audience broke into a sweeping torrent of applause. It came as a complete surprise; applause seemed almost out of place in this opera, and here was the audience moved beyond bounds. It was one of the great moments of my life! I felt grateful to that audience!

In the second act, as she came down that stony path from the top of the theatre to the stage, driving the furies and evil spirits before her by the power of her song, she seemed the incarnation of goodness and truth. Her voice revealed her character. In the

Elysian fields she seemed purer and greater than the spirits who lived there. When she mourned over Euridice, you lost all sense of the fact that she was singing an aria; it had become a scene, as sincere and modern in spirit as anything ever written.

Orfeo was the high point of my wife's career. Nothing she ever did made her so happy. She sang it for five years at the Metropolitan. Of course she must have improved as she went along; but from the beginning it seemed as perfect as it could possibly be. Many have said to me that *Orfeo* seemed to them the most beautiful opera ever given at the Metropolitan.

AS ORFEO, NEW YORK, REVIVAL DECEMBER 23, 1909
(end of first act—starting on her quest for Euridice)

XV

1910

SOON AFTER THE FIRST OF THE NEW YEAR
we began to hear rumors of a trip to Paris. This was startling
news. We had not been in Europe for ten years. We believed
in American summers for American children. In spite of *Orfeo*
and "How's My Boy?" and all the rest, our great happiness lay
in seeing our children grow and flourish. Every day something
new happened in our little house, and the halls and stairs would
ring with laughter. The Metropolitan could grow monotonous
and boresome, but 13 East Sixty-fourth Street was ever a busy
hive of startling events.

We put a piano into the basement for the children to
practice on. Sidney had the American boy's mind, and very soon
we found that he had evolved a new way of reading notes and
was giving lessons to the cook. I have told how little Louise
could sing the part of Gretel, in *Hänsel und Gretel*, from beginning to end without a mistake. She also tried the Wagner music
dramas. *Ho-yo-to-ho*'s, long stretches of Brünnhilde's, Sieglin-
de's, or Elsa's music would peal out. The twins spoke in plurals:
"We fell down," one of them would say, or "We want a drink."
If you gave anything to one of them, the other hand came
right out for sister. They couldn't conceive of having anything
except in twos. All Christmas presents had to be in exact dupli-
cate; a doll in pink and a doll in blue wouldn't do! They might
both prefer pink.

The very thought of taking this precious bunch to Europe
was disturbing. Mr. Gatti consulted us. In addition to the regular engagement fee, all transportation over and back for the
entire family and two governesses would be paid. The Paris

season would begin about May 20th and last for a month, and
then we could come right home if we preferred.

We thought it over and decided that a summer in Switzerland might be a real experience for Louise and Sidney, and perhaps a healthy place for the twins, and we accepted. From that
moment on, the whole family talked Europe. Pictures, guide-
books, French, which Louise was learning all over again in
school in spite of the fact that she had spoken it fluently at the
age of four. Even the twins understood that something was
happening—"Mamma, what's Europe?" "O-oo! Big steamer!"
Their little minds were working hard.

In March we gave our first "Opera in English" at the Metropolitan, *The Pipe of Desire,* by Frederick S. Converse. My wife
gave an interview to Sylvester Rawlings of the New York
Evening World on this subject:

"Upon the public must rest the responsibility for the success
or failure of the initial performance of grand opera in English.
Will it recognize that not only opera in the vernacular but its
own capacity to encourage native art is on trial?" said Louise
Homer last evening.

Promises that season after season have been broken are at last
to be fulfilled. "The Pipe of Desire" by Frederick S. Converse
of Boston is to be produced next Friday night at the Metropolitan Opera House. Madame Homer is to have the leading
woman's part in it and the writer sought her opinion, she being
one of the most distinguished of American singers, upon its
prospects. That was her first answer.

"Mr. Converse's opera has no Indian, no Puritan, no modern
American foundation," Madame Homer continued. "It is based
upon a fairy, fanciful story of Elfland. It is allegorical of life
and points morals; but its appeal primarily is to the imagination.
Will it reach? That is up to the audience.

"If native composers are to be encouraged we must enlarge
our vision and become more lenient in our judgment. Musically,
whatever foreigners think of us, we are a spoiled people. We set
the highest standards of artistic excellence. A composer must be

a Beethoven, or a Mozart, or a Wagner; a singer must be a Patti or a Sembrich. Do you think if such were the attitude of the people of France or of Italy, there would have been founded the new schools represented by Debussy and D'Indy, or by Puccini and Mascagni? Why not give the native genius a chance to find itself in whatever direction it may take?

"In literature we are far more broad. While we may not have developed a Shakespeare, we are producing, because of our larger tolerance, a school of writers, graphic, realistic, distinct and characteristically American. Give our composers a chance to be heard. Let their fancy find flight in any direction. Schools of music are not made by the scores that are never printed.

"I am for English opera unequivocally, but I am not for doing away with opera in the tongues in which the music was composed. That would be a great step backward. True, on the continent of Europe most operas are translated and sung in the vernacular. But we are too big for that. Our Metropolitan Opera House is easily first in its cosmopolitanism. For one thing, we should lose the privilege of hearing some great singers. Foreigners do not find it easy to sing in English. Americans are much better linguists. Yet even many of them fail to achieve the pronunciation that the French, German and Italian public demands. Many American singers, rejected after a season in Italy or Germany or France, have achieved success at Covent Garden, because the English public had not such a delicate appreciation of the pronunciation of Italian, German or French as the natives.

"The demand for opera in the vernacular comes from the public, which insists that it shall understand the text as well as hear the music. Do you think it would be content to listen to broken English, improperly phrased?"

My wife insists that I said a lot of this: we had a way of giving interviews together to newspapermen. But I don't think so; it sounds like Louise to me: clear-cut, emphatic, and full of common sense.

We had a long tour before starting for Europe; first Boston, then a month in Chicago, with short trips to Cleveland, Milwaukee, and Indianapolis, and a week in Atlanta.

The month in Chicago was grand. Whenever we were forced to be away from the children, which was seldom, we made a spree of it. We rented an apartment (with maids and two studios) on the North Shore overlooking the lake, and lived in clover. No bellboys, solemn waiters, tiresome menus, elevators, lobbies and the rest of it.

One morning I was trying to set a Bandanna Ballad, "I Long to See Dat Cotton Field," and it wouldn't go because of an awkward last line; so I turned a page and found another. The time was short as we had a rehearsal at eleven. At the rehearsal I showed it to Morgenstern, and he roared. "You can't write a popular song—look at that!" referring to the sequences on the last page. I was afraid he was right; it was a little cheap and a little dressy. This was "A Banjo Song." I asked Kurt Schindler if he thought it would ruin my reputation. He wanted to spare my feelings, but he had to say he thought it would.

We hurried home from Atlanta and had no time at all to get ready for our trip to Europe. Only a wild opera company would do things in such a way; but who cared? We were all together, never to separate again, and we were all going off on a great lark. Such excitement! Only the twins were composed and calm. All trips looked alike to them: to the zoo in Central Park or to Europe. I have two clippings which describe the departure:

> Surmounting a wagon load of trunks which pulled away yesterday from the Metropolitan Opera House, was a gigantic baby carriage, made large enough to hold two babies.
>
> "It's for the Homer twins," explained the expressman as he drove away.
>
> The Homer twins are to be part of the load of opera singers which the *Kaiser Wilhelm II*, sailing from Hoboken today, is to carry away to Europe.

> The happiest family on board was that of the Homers. Louise Homer, who is perhaps the most popular singer among Americans, will be a "star" of the opening performance in Paris. But

her artistic ambitions do not make her neglect her domestic duties. With her in the big liner yesterday were her husband, Sidney Homer, whose compositions are now much in demand; her tall daughter, Louise, little Sidney, sturdy and stern, and the famous, fascinating twins. After the Paris season the Homers are going to Switzerland for a much needed rest, not to return to New York until October.

It was a glorious passage. No one was sick but the distinguished companion we had engaged to look after Louise and Sidney. It took our united efforts to cheer her up and get her across.

We found a hotel just off the Champs-Elysées. Everyone from the head porter to the smallest bellboy thought it his special duty to take full charge of the children. The governess and companion started right in to practice their French and got nothing but English in return, much to their disappointment. The rooms were large and high-ceilinged, and the furniture gilt. The children felt everything—walls, tapestries, silk spreads; they sat in all the chairs, and were at home in a trice.

There was not a moment to spare. The first performance, an invitation dress rehearsal with all the notables of Paris present, would take place in two days. We hurried to the theatre. Such a place! The cracks between the boards on the stage were so wide that you could look down into blackness. There was no room in the wings. The dressing rooms were miserable and far away. The galleries stretched up forever and looked as if they had never been swept. Things were arriving, and men were struggling with chaos. We have all seen the circus arrive and the tent go up, but that was nothing compared to this. Broadway American and pure French filled the air: choice, short expressions! It was wonderful how the Americans and the French understood one another.

Mr. Gatti had a little way with him and accomplished the impossible. Two nights later at the première the house was brilliant; newspapers said no such assemblage had ever been seen, and I can believe it. "All Paris" was there, by invitation, and the atmosphere was one of the keenest anticipation; you saw intelligence and thought in every face. It was a music-loving, perhaps I should say an opera-loving audience. Only on an occasion like this can you know what a French audience is like—intellect, poise, brilliance, sureness, distinction, directness, sensitiveness; and no pose or pretense. There is reason for the word "French" —no one has ever quite explained it. Many in the audience were acquainted, and there was much visiting and saluting. The President and Cabinet, senators, deputies, intellectuals from the Sorbonne, the French nobility, and many distinguished musicians, painters, and writers were present, and there was joy at being assembled in this festive way. It doesn't often happen.

We hardly realize the intensity of national spirit of the French. Ours is closely bound to our Constitution, but they passed through six kinds of Kingdom, Empire, and Republic in a hundred years, and the spirit never flickered. The glorification and perpetuation of that spirit is their main purpose, and under a unified purpose humanity is at its best. I looked with delight at the men, clear-eyed and filled with an indomitable will; at the women, mobile, assured, full of *esprit*. The French language never sounded more sparkling or full of meaning.

The opera was *Aida*, with Caruso, Amato, De Segurola, Destinn, and my wife in the cast, Toscanini in the chair and the Colonne Orchestra in the pit. The Metropolitan Opera Chorus was there in force.

The performance was fine, the enthusiasm unbounded, warm, sincere, heartfelt. Afterward our old friend Saléza, that great artist of former Metropolitan days, came to my wife's dressing room. He said he had been sent, as a committee of one, by the artists of the Paris Opéra to express their admiration and esteem for my wife. He made a formal address full of that moving sincerity which is French (I wish I could remember every word of it!), and then we talked of the old days when he and my wife sang *Aida* together at the Metropolitan.

This tribute was one of the high moments of my wife's life. There is a special joy in opera which lies behind the scenes; artists understand one another in a way that is possible only to them.

Two days later came the first regular performance open to the public at fabulous prices. "All the world" was there—crowding, scrambling, fussing, complaining, wearing more jewels per woman than Amneris. Twenty languages going at once, lots of glaring at neighbors (the seats were very small), an apparent desire to be *en évidence*, which was difficult as each one seemed determined to notice no one else. So many haggard faces which seemed to say: "When will it be over? When do we go back to our baccarat?"

The disillusioned go to Paris to live, to bask in the Eternal Hope, the everlasting Optimism which is Paris, knowing that hope has gone out of their own hearts forever! From that moment I was filled with disgust at the Paris season of the Metropolitan. It seemed sordid and unworthy of our truly dignified institution. I felt that these peculiar people came out of curiosity, with no love for music, bored from the start, hoping for sensation. They wandered around the lobbies between the acts, silent, like people in the dullest part of a World Exposition. An occasional group of Americans would electrify the air with their cheerful laughter, only to get scornful, glowering looks from this depressing mob.

At this performance a strange thing happened. I will quote from the cabled report in the New York *Evening Sun*, May 24, 1910:

During the first entr'-acte, the gallery started clamoring. When Toscanini took the leader's desk he was received with loud shouting and hissing. He ignored the hostile demonstration and began conducting. The extraordinary row continued, and when the curtain was raised nothing could be heard. Occupants of boxes and stalls applauded, adding to the noise. It was feared the performance would be stopped. The situation was saved by Madame Homer, the American singer, who with the greatest pluck attacked her solo and coolly continued singing until her voice dominated the house. The shouts gradually subsided, and then the audience cheered the American artist.

I sat in a little seat in the fourth row of the orchestra stalls. I measured the distance and planned how I could climb to the stage, if necessary. I watched my wife's face for the first sign of distress, and glanced at the miserable mob for any untoward advance. Louise was superb. She advanced to the footlights with a sure step, looking taller than ever, calm, determined. She threw her arms out in a most eloquent gesture of command and appeal, and sang those high passages with the clarion voice of an angel. Three times it rang out; clamor, hush, clamor, hush, clamor, silence—applause!

Any references to the supposed cause of the disturbance— namely, French resentment at an American company—are misleading; such an assumption was wholly unwarranted, and quite unfair to Paris. The real cause was perfectly clear to me. After the first scene of the first act, in which my wife appeared, and which had passed off gloriously, I had stepped out of the theatre for a breath of air. There in front of an iron grille leading to the entrance to the upper galleries were some two hundred men and women. They were being kept out until after the first act. They were not even admitted after the first scene of the first act! They stood there nearly an hour with their tickets in their hands. No wonder they were boiling with rage! When they finally got into their seats, they just couldn't stop. It was not Mr. Gatti or Mr. Toscanini or the Metropolitan they were mad at, but the Parisian management which was handling all these details in such a high-handed manner. The rest of the performance was one series of ovations, and the newspapers in their accounts of this performance were full of eulogies.

The season continued and was a complete success.

The twins in their big double carriage made a hit on the Champs-Elysées. The French love other people's children and have very few of their own. The bottled-up mother-love in France is one of the strange sights of the world, as is the frugal *économie* that rules all lives there. In France, motherhood is felt to be the supreme privilege and joy of life, and the proud head and shining eyes of a French mother, of whatever class, are something to contemplate.

Our season went on to a spectacular finish, but I never got over a certain sense of humiliation. I longed for the frank dignity of the Metropolitan Opera House and New York City.

At the end of the season, a fine thing happened. The company gave a gala performance at the Paris Opéra, for the benefit of the families of those who had lost their lives in the accidental sinking of the French submarine *Pluviôse*. The program consisted of single acts from different works. Mme. Fremstad, my wife, Burrian, Hinckley, Reiss, and Ananian sang the second act of *Tristan*, with Toscanini conducting. It was grand. This was the first time that German had been sung in this house for many years.

This is a fair illustration of the pacifying influence of great music. Pacifists throughout the world should take notice of this marvelous and effective weapon ready to hand.

Geraldine Farrar sang twice on this occasion. It was an evening of which all Americans could be proud.

The season was over and with a whoop we were off to Divonne-les-Bains, on Lake Geneva, where Dr. Roland would do wonders for me. The children loved the French sleeping car. The companion, book in hand, wanted anxiously to see every French town we went through; I think she sat up all night, not to miss any. I had a grand time all summer pointing out mountain peaks, châteaux, church spires, to her. Map in hand, she could never quite locate them.

Dr. Roland said: heart too weak for a water cure; I must lie two hours in the sun before and after every meal; a sure cure for all ordinary ailments. After three weeks of this, we went to Grindelwald and took Louise and Sidney on little climbs. We spent some time at a quaint pension on the shore of Lake Thun. Then down the Rhine, the children all eyes and ears. We stopped at Cologne for a glimpse of German life, and a quiet time in the cathedral; then on to the steamer and home.

It had been a perfect summer. Only the poor companion had the castles on the Rhine all mixed up; as soon as she learned to pronounce the name of one, another with a harder name would appear. Then she was sadly ill on the trip home; and when we got off the steamer in New York we lost her. After a long search, we found her on the steamer buying postal cards. She was a real traveler.

XVI

1910–1914

THE OPERA SEASON OF 1910–11 OPENED WITH a performance of Gluck's *Armide,* with a powerful cast which included Fremstad and Caruso. My wife had the cheerful part of Hate! Later Humperdinck's *Königskinder* was produced, in which my wife disguised herself as a frightful witch. So pursued was she by these hateful roles that it is amazing that she was able to preserve, unchanged, her own disposition, so full of sunshine and happiness.

Orfeo, Tristan, Aida, La Gioconda, Lohengrin, the *Ring,* etc., made up the rest of the repertory, and it was a glorious season. Of one of her performances of Orfeo, the New York *Times* said:

When Louise Homer sings Orpheus—sings and acts it—she is as one inspired. Her voice assumes a fullness of expression quite beyond its actual emotional thrill; her face is illuminated with a beauty that comes from the soul; her every movement, her every gesture, seems to be the perfect result of irresistible inner impulse. Adamantine, indeed, must have been the man or woman in yesterday's audience not moved deeply by an impersonation which should hold a place among the most perfect operatic portraitures in the Metropolitan Opera Company's gallery.

During the winter, I had the honor of serving as chairman of the music committee of the MacDowell Club of New York. At my request, the club appropriated $50 for each of the weekly concerts and permitted the artists who took part to invite their friends and music lovers who might be interested. As a result, the hall was crowded at every concert, and the enthusiasm was immense. The artists beamed with happiness and felt repaid for their efforts; for music does demand tremendous efforts, a fact which must never be lost sight of. This is the way, I believe, that all music clubs should be conducted. One of their particular concerns is the welfare of the young artists who are beginning their careers. Between the years of study and the time when reputations are finally established, there is a span of most difficult, and often tragic years. In order to attain independence and reputation young artists must, of course, be heard. Their whole future depends upon it. And it is because of this that they are often willing to play and sing for nothing. It is a desperate situation in which the artist is helpless. Should a music club take advantage of this?

This brings up a consideration of the position of the music lover in the world of music. All I can say is that I think his work is to provide paying jobs for real artists. Merely to listen to a musician is to give nothing for something. To buy occasional tickets is not sufficient. As we look back over the very short history of music we feel intense gratitude for every step taken which provided economic independence for the musician. We would not intentionally take away any source of income which has been established. We wish to see the art of music in such an independent position that it can grow naturally, fearlessly, and with that inevitable originality which must follow. Probably the will to help the artists has always been greater than we realize. It has had to wait upon organized methods of reaching him.

It is not appreciation that is lacking; but the organization of appreciation in an effective and enduring way. The question is still with us, and music lovers the world over ask nothing more than that a definite and concrete form may be devised by which their full appreciation may be conveyed to the artist.

One example of the need of such organization is in the relation of the composer to the concert audience. In 1911 three singers returned from concert tours. They had all used a song that had recently been published, and told of their success with it. They compared notes and found that they had, together, sung it to two hundred thousand people in less than three months. "What will the composer get out of this?" one of them asked. Nothing; there was no possible way in which those people could show the composer any tangible appreciation, no matter how much they might wish to. A few hundred, who dared, might buy the song, but this channel was closed to all the rest. It was absurd to buy a song which the purchaser could neither sing nor play, an expensive way of saying "Thank you." Yet there is a very simple way which, if adopted, would enable audiences to express their grateful appreciation. In the case mentioned, a tax of two cents on each concert ticket would have yielded four thousand dollars to be divided among the living composers represented on the program. This is a small way of doing a very large thing; also a very easy way. Something of the kind is in force in France, so far as French composers are concerned. It may obtain here, some day. If it does it should come through the emphatic demand of concert-goers. Composers are more than happy when their works are heard and appreciated, but we all know they need more than that, and we want them to have it. It is our duty to see that they get it.

There was some discussion of this question in 1911. One famous German singer announced that she would never put an American song on her programs if a composers' tax were established. She felt that it would be a tax on singers, and was filled with righteous indignation. She was doing enough for American composers, etc. Her fears were unfounded.

An automatic tax of a few cents on concert tickets would encourage composers to produce broad and effective concert works, too difficult, perhaps, for popular use, but thrilling to listeners when done by fine artists. It would also encourage publishers to bring out such works. And thus the repertoire of all concert singers would be greatly enriched, and music lovers would be happy in the knowledge that they had provided a direct stimulus to greater creative activity.

Suppose a beautiful string quartet is written. The composer would be directly compensated whenever it was performed, and thus have leisure to write another still more beautiful quartet. There is no flaw in the plan. Only in this way shall we discover the richness of the creative powers in our midst.

Private patronage is no adequate substitute. Time to work is needed; but time *earned*, not time given, is what men want. One is a stimulating influence, the other deadening. Let us give the composer an independent place in active life, put him into direct relationship with mankind. Such a course must result in great compositions.

As the use of music in radio broadcasting and moving pictures developed, a remarkable society was formed by a nationally known group of composers and their friends.

The American Society of Composers, Authors and Publishers, known as A.S.C.A.P., protects its members in the use of their copyrighted music; but its authority does not extend to the concert field, and it is here that the public, if it wishes, can create an automatic revenue for living composers.

Some years earlier, at the time of pogroms in Russia, I had set this remarkable poem of Joaquin Miller to music:

> Who tamed your lawless Tartar blood?
> What David bearded in his den
> The Russian bear, in ages when
> You strode your black, unbridled stud,
> A skin-clad savage of your steppes?
> Why, one who now wails out to you,—
> The Jew, the Jew, the homeless Jew!
>
> Who taught you tender Bible tales
> Of honey lands, of milk and wine?
> Of happy, peaceful Palestine?

Of Jordan's holy harvest vales?
Who gave the patient Christ? I say,
Who gave your Christian creed? Yea, yea!
Who gave your very God to you?
Your Jew! Your Jew! Your hated Jew!

In 1911 Mr. Bispham included "To Russia" in his program at his recital at Carnegie Hall. The New York *Times* said:

It was for the fourth group that Mr. Bispham had reserved the bomb of the afternoon, Sidney Homer's "To Russia," which, written to words by Joaquin Miller, had been withheld, it is said, for several years [not by me!] for fear it would give offense in certain quarters. Mr. Bispham sang it yesterday as if he hoped it would, and looked around him defiantly at the end, but all the audience demanded was a repetition. It is a stirring song, the music quite fitting the spirit of the words, although it is perhaps hardly as effective as the same composer's "The Pauper's Drive," which preceded it on the program.

The amazing thing is the answer that time has given to that little song, "To Russia." In 1911, the Jew was in his Ghetto, suspected and menaced. Today he is out on the broad, rolling plains of Russia, by the hundred thousand, driving huge tractors. I am told that the grain he produces is so fine in quality that the macaroni factories of Italy try to secure the entire output. Today my little song is an antiquated curiosity. Nevertheless it was useful for a while. My wife sang it during several years. Mme. Gabrilowitsch sang it.

On December 12, 1911, our Hester was born. The twins were determined to see the angel that brought the baby. One sat on the front stairs, and the other on the back. There were many false alarms and much running back and forth. Somehow the angel slipped by unobserved, and there was much disappointment. But the sight of the baby in the bassinet drove all this away. The twins promptly established joint ownership, and I can testify that it has lasted until this day. A few years ago they had to admit Bob Henry, their new brother, into the partnership, but their sense of partnership still continues.

Hester was named for Hester Makepeace, my wife's earliest American grandmother, who, Mrs. Homer insists, was born in Boston in 1632. This makes her outdate my ancestor, Margery Stevens, also born in Boston, by thirty years.

This was one of the times when my wife had surely lost her voice. It adds a spice of excitement to the return of any artist to dwell on this possibility. Every time that Caruso returned, after an absence, the air was gloomy with pessimism and apprehension. This is only another form of devotion. The public cares, and that is a tribute in itself.

Her first performance was in *Orfeo*, on January 25th. The presence of the Duchess of Connaught and the Princess Patricia gave an especial brilliance to the evening.

The New York *Press*, January 26, said:

> . . . Louise Homer made a triumphal return to the lyric stage last night in the Metropolitan Opera House as Orpheus in Gluck's immortal *Orfeo ed Euridice*. This role has always revealed the American contralto's powers to the very greatest advantage. But lofty as her achievements have been in the past, her achievement last night loomed higher. . . . She has grown to be a far greater singer, a far greater artist.

It was a glorious evening, and I am sure my wife was never happier. The element of uncertainty is always present on such occasions; but, so far as we are concerned, apprehension never played a great part. I had a sublime confidence in my wife; it was a sort of religion with me. I always looked forward with the keenest anticipation to the rising of the curtain or the beginning of a recital. As for my wife, her mind was always concentrated on the artistic objective, and thus external conditions could have little effect. Apprehension should have no place in the heart of an artist or in that of the artist's husband or wife. Of the two, the latter would be the more pernicious. The ordeal is great enough under the most favorable conditions, but an undermining fear converts it into tragedy. Only those who can face the music in the right spirit should undertake it.

On Thursday evening March 14, 1912, the first performance of Horatio Parker's *Mona* was given. Louise had the title role, and I have never known her to throw herself more completely and with greater abandon into the interpretation of a part. It was a most difficult role, and the dramatic possibilities of the music drama seemed to rest largely on her shoulders. Horatio Parker was a dear friend of ours, and our admiration for him, his ideals and musicianship was without bounds. Her passionate desire to make a success of this work was most touching. It occupied her thoughts, almost exclusively, for several months.

Of her performance, the New York *Sun* said:

Madame Homer's impersonation of Mona enriched the brilliancy of her artistic laurel crown. It was superbly dramatic, filled with the dignity which marked her *Orfeo,* but poignant with a pathos greater than that of her classic hero.

The winter of 1913–14 was planned with but one object in view. Our doctor urged that we take a short but complete vacation in the form of a trip to Europe by ourselves. This trip was supposed to be an excellent thing for me in my long fight against ill health. All our vacations had been with the children, and we were rather dubious about this startling suggestion. But we made our plans with it in view and postponed our decision until we could feel sure the trip was justified. We took a house in West Chester, Pennsylvania, near Grandma Beatty and two of Louise's sisters. My sister took charge of the house; and with our daughter Louise at Westover, Sidney and the twins attending the Friends' School, a governess and a nurse, there did not seem to be any good reason why we should not go. But we hesitated, and the days went by. Finally, on December 15th, I said, "Let's go!" And my wife consented—entirely for my sake, I am sure.

On the 18th we broke away, and on the 19th we were sailing down the bay on the *Mauretania*. It was all so sudden that we could hardly realize what was happening. For nearly twenty years the central point of all our thoughts had been, first our child, and then our children. And here we were suddenly cut loose from this safest of all anchorages. The very novelty was good for us. My wife was the gayest person on board, and I was a good second.

Any man who wonders at the monotony of his existence will find the cause in a certain mental fixity. Some one thing is holding his mind prisoner. Not every man can change his environment, but it is always possible to bring new influences to bear upon his machinelike mind. If I did not believe that great music held untold treasures for just this purpose, I could not write this book.

In our case it was not sounds but sights that we needed. We had never traveled for pleasure before. How we reveled in it! A few days in London, searching out the hidden places. We had lived twice before in London when we had simply trod the narrow path from home to Covent Garden and return.

We went to Switzerland, where we had a week of skating and coasting. We shall never forget that three-mile coast where we turned sharp corners on high banks of snow. I steered, and my wife hung on. Once we had a spill: it was great fun.

I wrote ahead to a hotel in Venice for a room with central heat and fireplace. We arrived at Venice at eight in the evening. On the steps of the hotel, on the Grand Canal, we had a great welcome. The manager, head waiter, and four or five others were there to welcome us. We felt important. They took us to a large room up one short flight. The manager rubbed his hands and talked about how warm it was. I felt of the cold radiator and made inquiries about the heating system. "Ah, monsieur, always at this time of year we repair our central heat." I asked for a room with a fireplace, and we all moved into the hall. The manager started up the stairs. I inquired for the elevator. "Ah, monsieur, always at this time of year we repair our—" Then we all had a good laugh.

We started through those little, dark Venetian streets, the staff following with our bags, for a hotel that was really open. We seemed to be almost the only visitors in Venice that winter. We put on galoshes and haunted the unheated picture galleries. My wife fell in love with the early Italians, the primitives. She was something of a primitive, herself, and their naïveté appealed to her. Day after day we went to see the same pictures, and the same corners in St. Mark's. Then we went to Florence, and the same thing happened: Giotto, Fra Angelico, and the later ones. Then on to Rome where we hired a red automobile, with a little revolving devil on the front, and a daredevil driver. Three weeks of Campagna, catacombs, imperial Rome, mighty even in ruins, the Vatican, glorious and proud in isolation, gardens and fountains sad in the desolate winter.

In Naples we found the real bas-relief of Orfeo in his tunic; it made my wife's interpretation seem more real than ever. We were the only visitors in Pompeii on that day, and the lonely roads echoed with our footsteps. The old places look much older when you are alone. You can really people them in your imagination if there are no contemporaries to look at. Sorrento in the winter was a fishing village.

At last we were on the steamship *Adriatic*, fighting our way across the Atlantic through a historic February gale. Our minds were full of Italian art, and our thoughts were on those heroic artists who tried to show humanity what was real in life. In the midst of cynicism and sophistication they saw the truth and expressed it.

One bleak day we pulled into New York. As the boat crept into the dock we saw dear old Richard Copley running alongside of us. "You sing in Wilmington tonight!" he shouted, beaming with smiles. "Sing! I haven't sung a note for two months," called my wife. "Your voice will be better than ever!" More beams. He was trying to make it impossible to say no. "I haven't a note of music with me," yelled my wife. "That's all right. Mrs. Lapham [my wife's accompanist] has the music and is waiting for you at the station. You have just time to make the train!" More beams! Louise loves a stunt; so we went straight to Wilmington and had a surprise concert. Copley was right. My wife was in great voice and exuberant spirits. We were just a few miles from West Chester and the children!

The next morning we were in a hurry, a desperate hurry. A train to Philadelphia and another to West Chester would take too long. We rented a car and piled in our European luggage. The snow was deep and within an hour the car broke down. We went into a farmhouse to warm up. The farmer was slow but good-hearted. Yes, he had an old sleigh at the top of the barn; if we'd wait, he'd get it down and mend it. And so we drove into West Chester in the queer-looking old punt. Such a welcome at the door! "Mamma, Mamma!" "Papa, Papa!"

We had seen Europe at its best. Flourishing, happy, secure in spirit and looking forward to progress and fresh enterprise. In less than six months, war was declared! What evil spirit lurks at the very foundation of civilization? Are we afraid to say? Afraid to know? Do we prefer the false security that comes from voluntary blindness or are we willing to know the truth and grapple with our enemy in a fight to the death?

My wife rejoined the Metropolitan Opera on February 28th, and was given a fine welcome.

ARRIVING FROM EUROPE. ZERO WEATHER—
AND A WARM WELCOME

West Chester, Pennsylvania, February, 1914

XVII

1914–1920

OUR LIVES HAD CHANGED IN THESE YEARS.
We had chosen Lake George as the best place for our summers, and we wished to keep the children in the country through the winter if possible.

Some time after the death of Mr. Wolfsohn, Mr. Adams had bought the Wolfsohn Bureau. He enlarged the concert field, introduced new courses in many cities, created a demand for his artists, and steadily raised their fees. His devotion to his work and to his artists was absolute, and we had the greatest affection for him.

Concert singing became more and more attractive, and we were glad to cut our opera season in half and have more time for these short concert tours. Mr. Adams appreciated my wife's desire not to be away from the children for more than a week or two at a time and arranged her tours accordingly. She declined all tours to the Pacific Coast. Pop (that was his name to all his friends) used to say that she refused more concerts than she accepted.

The Victor Company was having wonderful success. The artists used to marvel at the sums they received for records that were so quickly made. It seemed like an impossible dream come true. That vast record-loving public spread over the entire world was a sort of mystery. My wife used to receive letters from Korea, Japan, and distant points in Europe and South America. They were so full of gratitude and appreciation that one got the impression of a world longing for the beautiful—a world that felt that perhaps the beautiful was the one thing that would make life worth while. Who knows?

In June, our Louise graduated from Westover, and received the medal for music. It was a proud day for us. It was also the beginning of a new happiness, for she was now to be with us all the time, not merely during vacations. These schools and colleges are great disrupters of family life from the parents' point of view. We may find something better some day.

After a summer at Lake George, we took a house at Rye, New York, and on March 28, 1915, Joy was born. Her name was really Helen Joy—Helen for our dear friend Helen Paxton, and Joy because we knew the joy she would bring. For twenty years we have heard the remark: "Well, she was well named!" But then she has had to live up to this name. There's something in a name, after all.

Just to keep the record clear: I had continued to write and publish songs and in the previous fall my wife had introduced a number of new ones. Among them was Southey's "Battle of Blenheim" which I had set soon after the War began. Another was Christina Rossetti's powerful poem, "Babylon the Great." "Sheep and Lambs" and "Sing to Me, Sing" were both new. These two have become better known. Louise also kept "The Song of the Shirt" on her programs.

The New York *Sun*, October 16, 1914, said:

> To quote the poet's own words, "it was a famous victory" that the first of the stars, Louise Homer, won in Brooklyn last night when she daringly made her husband, Sidney Homer, a far from silent partner as composer of a "Battle of Blenheim" fit to set before a king. Old Southey's plain tale of the wars of Marlborough might have been a bedtime story to the opera singer's own children. She acted charmingly its prattle of questions from innocent Peterkin, and its pantomime of wild-eyed Wilhelmine. An Academy audience half in tears and then all in a riot, showed that you can take your war songs quite seriously enough this year by mixing them with a little fun.
>
> Mr. Homer's "Sing, Sing Again," twice over, gave gay con-

FAMILY GROUP, WITH ANNE, HESTER, KAY AND LOUISE, 1914

trast to his sober "Sheep and Lambs," a tender little sacred poem of Mrs. Tynan Hinkson.

We went to Lake George for the summer but, alas, our house suddenly became too small for us. It was quite a large house, too, and belonged, by the way, to Mr. Charles H. Tuttle, famous New York district attorney. It must have been little Joy that crowded us. I never saw a baby take up so much room; the coolest room on hot days, the largest porch on which to sleep, which meant tiptoeing in and out the front door. Then, again, we had a young-lady daughter for the first time, and there was no place for her to receive her large circle of friends. Of course Sidney was no trouble; you can put a boy anywhere; but the twins—ah, they really should have separate rooms; they never woke up at the same time. And as for Hester, to keep her from waking the baby was quite impossible.

All this was the preamble to that ominous rumble which enters into every family—a demand for a home of its own. Big enough, with nice back stairs and side entrance; playroom; place for bicycles; a dignified sitting room for our daughter Louise. Everyone began to plan: bathrooms—an awful question; sleeping porches, a new fad; a place for the little girls' dolls so that they wouldn't be sleeping on all our best chairs. I protested feebly, explained gravely the advantage of bonds, pointed out how free we had been to go to different places in the summer. "But, Daddy, we never want to leave Lake George, never, never!"

We had bought our first automobile, a Stevens-Duryea touring car, with extra seats for the twins which could be set in and taken out, and began cruising up and down the lake, looking for land. No place seemed just right. But the next summer the unexpected happened, and we were lost. Our friend Mr. W. K. Bixby of St. Louis offered us a beautiful piece of land, a hundred acres with a mile of shore front, lovely points, heavily wooded, at one-fourth of its value. He even said he would take it back at the same price, if we didn't build in two years. This was too much. We bought the land and embarked on the great adventure.

This is what I call expansion. The money had been rolling in. The income from the Victor had been mounting up. It would surely go on forever and touch the sky. Everything looked as easy as easy. We had been married twenty years and had never had a home of our own. Why shouldn't we have one?

This was the great event of our lives. No opera house or palace ever seemed so grand to our family as our home on Lake George. It is close to heaven in our eyes, and now the twelve grandchildren are beginning to feel the same way about it. It was our great extravagance, and is our beloved burden.

That summer of 1916 was difficult. An epidemic of infantile paralysis was raging, and parents were frightened. We did not even allow the children to go on the public roads, and lived a secluded life. In the fall we were afraid to take the younger children to New York or allow them to go to school; so we followed an original plan. We rented a heavily built, well heated winter house on the shore of the lake and near the village, and installed our family for the winter. My sister made this possible. Her love for our children and theirs for her was what enabled us to carry on our professional life. She made the rough places smooth and the crooked straight. Her son was five days older than Sidney, and these two boys were like two parts of a Seidlitz powder, quiet enough apart—but together! They were an endless wonder to their devoted followers, the twins, who in turn were the whole world to their sister Hester. I have not yet heard all the marvelous things that happened that winter. All the fairy stories and boys' books ever written came to real life in that three feet of dry snow.

Of course education could not be neglected, and we found a Wellesley graduate, Miss Ziebach, who later became a famous educator, to take charge of this. I always felt, in later years, that it was this experience that taught Sidney how to study. A year with a tutor works magic in a child's mental machinery.

We took Louise and baby Joy with us to New York. Louise was beyond the dangerous age, so far as infantile paralysis was concerned, and Joy we could protect. We rented a furnished house on Riverside Drive. At every available chance, we ran up to see that hilarious family at Lake George and hear all about the new adventures that had taken place. But we were not shown the secret caves, all furnished for housekeeping. They were inviolate, and our presence would have profaned them. It is wonderful what fairy kingdoms children can create when left to themselves.

The War cast a pall over all life. To me, who had lived five years in Germany, three years in France, a year in Belgium, and months in England and Italy, war represented just one thing: the spleen of inefficient leaders. Inefficient leadership is the only trouble with the world at all times. The rank and file of men and women are superior to history. The nature of man is to work, do, and give. Family life proves this. Art, which is a genuine expression of man, is a truer picture of humanity than political history, and it is the intuitive knowledge of his true nature that keeps hope forever alive. Leadership may fail, but human nature knows itself and starts again, willing to forget and forgive but not willing to lose faith in itself.

In April we entered the War, and Joffre and Viviani came over to welcome and inspire us. The unveiling of the Lafayette monument in Brooklyn took place. Viviani, the leading Socialist of France, made an impassioned speech, in French, to fifty thousand Americans; my wife sang "The Star-Spangled Banner" with our flag in hand, Joffre and Viviani facing her with their hands at salute. It was solemn and intensely moving. Thousands of our boys in khaki stood at attention. Where would it end? After stupid leadership into trouble, leadership out of trouble was our only hope. We looked into the grim, determined, yet kindly

faces of these tried and tested Frenchmen and gained new courage. If they could calmly face the future, so could we.

The next night the Metropolitan Opera House welcomed
Joffre. Again Louise sang "The Star-Spangled Banner." She
waved our flag toward the audience and motioned them to join
in the final chorus. Her voice had a quality that I had never
heard before and have never heard since. The audience, deeply
moved, sang in a way that told Joffre once for all what we would
do. He left immediately; I am sure he was too shaken to sit and
see the great tableau the Opera House had prepared.

At this time Horatio Parker made a powerful setting of John
Finley's profoundly moving "Hymn to the Red Cross," and my
wife sang it in Carnegie Hall to a cheering audience.

There were many other incidents of a similar nature, but these
are sufficient for my story.

My wife's contract with the Opera Company had expired and
had not been renewed. The best of friends sometimes differ on
details. In this case it was a question of terms. We notified Mr.
Adams and prepared for a busy concert season in the following
winter.

The plans for our new home were ready, and the contract
with the builders had been signed. We rented the house next to
our property so that we could supervise the building. All the
family, except Joy, supervised. It was most exciting. Every
board, brick, and shingle was scrutinized. The twins would report knotholes in the boards; the house would leak. The carpenters and the children knew one another by their first names and
had great fun working the whole job out together. Every time
anything was finished, a floor laid or a chimney built, there was
great excitement and endless conversation. Finding little spaces
for extra closets was one of the great joys. We felt added responsibility because our architect had been called by the government to plan barracks in Texas. So many architects came up

from New York to superintend the work that my wife called it the house of seven architects.

Late in August I came down with sickness that necessitated an operation. I put it off as long as possible, and Sidney brought me reports every day on the progress of the house, written out in a methodical fashion. There were details to be decided, and he carried our decisions to the builder and made sure they were understood. Finally, on September 1st, the surgeon arrived and urged that I go right back to New York with him. It so happened that Louise had promised to sing for the Presbyterian Church in Lake George that very night. Enough tickets had been sold to pay off the entire debt of the church, some seventeen hundred dollars. She said she simply could not sing if she felt the audience knew what we were going through. So we planned to keep it secret. The doctor and I motored to Albany and took the train, while Louise went bravely ahead, sang her concert, went to a reception, kept a smiling face, and rushed for a train at one-thirty in the morning. A few hours later she was with me in the hospital in New York. She took the room adjoining mine and lived there.

It was a tough time, and I had to stay there six weeks. One day Louise came in full of smiles. "Oh, Sid!" she said, "I have found the loveliest house for the winter, and I got it cheap because the man who has it wants to get rid of his lease. It is absolutely soundproof and you won't hear a thing from your room!" And that was how we happened to live at 30 West Seventy-fourth Street, one of the massive houses built by the Clark estate.

About November 1st we had a great surprise. Mr. Ziegler, controller of the Metropolitan, came up from the Opera House and said my wife simply *must* sing for them. She had very few open dates, but she agreed to sing ten performances at nine hundred dollars a performance. This was much more than she had ever received, but she was firm about it. The next morning Mr.

Gatti came to see us, and after talking nearly two hours about what Italy was going to do in the War, he broached the subject of the contract only to find she was still firm. With a good laugh the matter was settled, and it was arranged that she should receive an advance bonus of one thousand dollars and eight hundred dollars at each performance.

I cannot conceal our enormous pride over this victory for the contralto—the poor contralto who often works harder than the soprano but never receives as high a fee. We knew that it was only a temporary arrangement, and that it was due to the fact that the whole German contingent in the Opera House, including Madame Ober, the great German contralto, had been dismissed, owing to our entrance into the War.

Nothing could exceed our surprise and pride when, at the end of the season, Mr. Gatti expressed a desire to renew the contract for eighteen performances during the following season. The performances were great. Many of them were in *Samson et Dalila* with Caruso. Then she added Fidès in *Le Prophète* to her repertoire and loved it. Thus, the grand air of the fourth act, on which she had worked so hard with Fidèle Koenig twenty years earlier, and which had helped toward her first engagements in France, now became a great and passionate scene, the outpouring of a mother's heart.

There was a certain grandeur about these two seasons which set them apart. Louise was at the height of her power and sang wonderfully.

Everyone's appreciation and understanding of her art was clear and genuine.

Our daughter Louise prepared to go to Europe and sing for the soldiers, but became ill from typhoid preventives at the crucial moment. Our doctor, who had just returned from the front, forbade her going. She was a disappointed child. We even gave a farewell party for her, at which she and her mother sang duets. Mrs. Stires came to this party and brought her son, Ernest, who had just come home after serving in a French ambulance corps. Perhaps he was glad she couldn't go. He knew what the front was really like.

In the spring, we rushed to our new home. There it was, finished! Beautiful, beyond our fondest dreams. Edward Shepard Hewitt was our architect, and we knew then, for the first time, what an artist he was. I had explained to him that we had never owned a home before, and that I hoped it would have the air of an old homestead of indefinite age. It had. We were at home in five minutes, and in no time at all felt that we had always lived there. That's a real home for you! We have never lost that feeling, and every time we go back we breathe a satisfied sigh and in two minutes feel that we have never been away.

It took all summer for us to get over even the first joy of having our new home. There was still much to be done—trees to cut, grading, roads to build; but that made no difference. It took us three or four years to get the place into proper shape, but that was just so much more fun.

I wrote a little poem and set it to music and called it "Homeland." It was published by Harold Flammer. It was a war song, and all the young people of the neighborhood learned it; and we used to sing it in chorus. Perhaps this led to our calling our place "Homeland." At any rate, that is its name.

Our job was to keep the horrors of war out of the lives of the children. We permitted free discussion (our children have always been encouraged to talk freely, at table or elsewhere), but we managed to minimize shocks.

My wife instituted Sunday night hymn-sings. Those were gasolineless Sundays, and the neighbors came in buggies, carryalls, boats and on foot. Professor Auer was teaching at Lake George, and some of his best violinists joined us. We also had a cellist. We would have a hundred and fifty in our house, the children sitting in groups on the floor. My wife led the singing, and I can only say she did it (and does it) as no one else can, so far as I know. There is a spiritual power in the very way in which she approaches a hymn. She would sing an occasional religious number, and sometimes our daughter Louise would sing. We would have the Bach concerto for two violins once in a while. These evenings were a great support and consolation to everyone who was there. My wife still has hymn-sings at Lake George, but the attendance has grown so large that we hold them at the Lake George Country Club.

At some time in these years my wife began her religious studies all over again. It is my impression that this was caused partly by our trip to Italy, where we came into such close contact with the faith of earlier centuries. At all events, since that time she has read hundreds of books by religious writers and still continues to do so. I do not know anyone to whom religion is such a living thing, or who sees more clearly the application of religion to life. Her breadth of view and freedom from intolerance are beyond anything I have ever known, and her resources are unfailing when there is a question of helping others.

At last the day of Armistice, and the unspeakable joy that came to all homes came to ours.

The opening opera of the new season was *Samson et Dalila*, with my wife and Caruso in the name parts. It just had to be a great performance. The air was filled with the exuberance of peace, and this meant an exuberant outpouring of voice and spirits. After the first act a peace demonstration took place.

A New York paper said:

The demonstration took place after the first act. The curtains opened, showing the principals in the foreground surrounded and backed by the chorus. A United States flag was swung at the rear in the middle of the stage and the members of the chorus each waved a small copy of it. Madame Homer held aloft a large national flag. Mr. Rothier held a French flag so that its folds draped Mr. Couzinou's head. Mr. Caruso carried the Italian flag, Mr. Ananian the British and Mr. Reschiglian the Serbian. "The

HOMELAND

Photograph Mattie Edwards Hewitt, courtesy Central Magazine

Star-Spangled Banner" was, of course, sung first, the "Marseillaise" second, the "Garibaldi Hymn" third, and "God Save the King" last.

In January Mr. Burnett, a manager in Detroit, asked our daughter Louise to sing in a joint concert with her mother. She had made her debut in Pittsburgh and had appeared as soloist with the Orpheus Club in Philadelphia. The night she sang this second concert her mother and I went to Philadelphia to hear her. We had not told her we should be there (parents are sometimes a disturbing influence on such occasions), and we sat in one of the upper balconies of the Academy of Music where we were sure she could not see us. It hardly seemed possible that that was our daughter, bowing so sweetly, looking so beautiful. She had been carefully taught by Herbert Witherspoon and had natural musical qualities of a high order. But it is a long step from a studio to a large stage such as this one in the Academy where the Metropolitan Opera Company had given performances for so many years.

That indefinable quality, magnetism, ability to hold and dominate an audience, might or might not be there. We were spellbound as she sang, and hardly breathed. We could scarcely believe our eyes and ears. The poise and dignity, which showed clearly through her modesty, inspired confidence and enabled her listeners to appreciate and enjoy the charm of her voice and singing. The applause sounded sweet to us. After the concert, when we went behind the scenes, she was quite overcome to know that we had been there, but her joy was doubled.

And now she was to sing with her mother, a much more difficult matter. Much would be expected, comparisons would be made. It was quite an ordeal. Then, as so often happens on those momentous occasions in young singers' lives, she developed severe tonsillitis and the doctor said a tonsil operation was imperative. We wired Mr. Burnett explaining why she could not sing, but he wired Louise urging her to defer the operation and sing

if possible; saying how much they wanted her, etc. This aroused
her mettle and she determined to try. She practiced very carefully in that last week, only a little each day, and took the train.
It was a mighty plucky thing to do. I will quote from the account of the concert in the Detroit *Free Press*, January 21, 1918:

We may set down as something altogether charming beyond
former experiences in Detroit concert halls, the appearance of a
daughter singing with a mother universally acknowledged to be
one of the very greatest artists of the time, songs that had been
written by her father. We may make record that the pride of
the mother in the daughter and the spontaneous expressions of
good understanding between the two as they stood together on
the stage were a delight. But the elusive, indefinable fineness of
it all is not translatable into language. We only set down that
these things were so. . . .

As to the young woman's voice, it is the voice of her mother,
as nearly as a soprano may resemble a contralto, just as Miss
Homer herself in many ways is "her mother over again."

This, 1919, was my wife's last season at the Metropolitan as a
regular member of the company, and I am happy it was such a
glorious one. Mr. Gatti offered her a contract for the following
season; but for few performances, to be sung at different times
throughout the season rather than consecutively. One might call
them guest performances. At that time, my wife did not feel that
she could do justice to opera in that way, and declined the offer.
In later years she found she could do it quite easily. Another
thing that influenced her decision was the monotony of the repertoire. Twenty years in the same operas is a long time, and
there was no new role for the contralto voice in sight—not even
one in existence so far as we knew.

We notified Mr. Adams and he immediately began to plan
concert tours for the next season. Because of the success of the
Detroit concert he included Louise in several of the tours. The
Victor Company invited her to make records of duets with her

mother, and so she suddenly found that she was a busy and a very happy girl.

Sidney graduated from the Berkshire School, sharing first honors with another boy.

The twins attended the Veltin School, and, incidentally, distinguished themselves by having their appendixes cut out almost simultaneously. I was afraid that Hester, who copied them in everything, would think that she must have hers out, too. But she had full charge of Joy and did not have time. She had the most impressive way of telling Joy everything she knew, perhaps a few things she didn't know, and Joy looked on her as an oracle. The biggest man would come to the house and tell Joy something; Joy would be polite but would appeal to Hester. "Yes, Joy, I think he is right," she would say gravely.

Joy needed lots of entertaining. I made the awful mistake of inventing an adventurous cat, named Blackie. I had to tell at least a thousand stories about that cat, over a period of years. Hester joined the party, and those kids would wait all day for the hour to come for me to tell them about Blackie. It taxed all my ingenuity. I made him a leader of animals. Those moonlight parties at Lake George when he would assemble all the animals, lone dog, the fox, mink, coon, rabbits, and the bear who had a cave below the vegetable garden on the edge of the marsh, the snakes and, most respected of all, the skunk. And then that great amphibian! He would come to the dock and take them on his back and give them a ride up and down the lake at fifty miles an hour. His name was George. The lake was named for him.

I taught geography with Blackie; took him all over the world, even to Tutankhamen's tomb. Yes, when they opened the tomb there was Blackie. Ah! An Egyptian cat, a mummy! But just then Blackie opened his eyes and stretched, and said, "Where's Tut?"

I placed him in a New York City fire engine house to get a fresh start. What didn't I do? Finally I tried to kill him. Talk

about nine lives! He had ninety-nine. Each time that I had him
nicely buried Joy would say, after a couple of days of mourn-
ing, "Daddy, I saw Blackie today," and I would be off again.
Never invent a black cat! The strange thing is that Joy, who is
twenty-three, remembers those stories to this day.

The season was over, and we were off to Homeland. We
began to build studios and buy pianos. First a studio in the
woods for my wife—a large, high room, with stone fireplace,
bay window, kitchenette for picnics, and a screened porch.
Then one for me on the lake, spacious and beautiful—too beautiful for my simple work. I had to close my eyes to my surroundings in order to do any work at all. I gave my old port-
able studio, which brought me such luck, to Anne, and put it
on a secluded point jutting into the lake where she could study
and write undisturbed. Then Joy began to practice, and we made
a studio out of the end of the new woodshed and called it Joy-
land. And then a new one on the lake for my wife, who turned
over her studio in the woods first to Louise, and then to Kay.
Finally we had five studios and five grand pianos, all out of earshot of one another.

There is one thing I have observed. All children who are going
to practice must have seclusion, and a chance to work undisturbed. Too many children's lives are made difficult through
study in classrooms, in the parlor with grown-ups walking
through, in bedrooms with loud voices in the next room. We
expect a power of concentration in children that we are inca-
pable of ourselves. Seclusion, silence, freedom from disturbance,
these are great things in a child's life. The mind will not allow
itself to be completely absorbed if there is constant fear of interruption.

XVIII

1920–1922

THESE WERE THE DAYS WHEN singing became more and more of a burden and home life more and more absorbing. The children were growing up and becoming our pals. If we had not built Homeland, I believe my wife would have retired at this time. Homeland cost a small fortune, and it has cost as much again to carry it for twenty years; and we can live in it only from May until November.

The dream of a large family is a homestead, large and rambling, with room for everybody—friends, young and old. For years we had from sixteen to twenty-two at our table.

Now we have reunions, with children and grandchildren all over the place. Homeland is an institution. It inspires faith. It is a cure-all for doubts that arise in a sophisticated world. This is because my wife has no doubts. Cheer and happiness fill the place. Her idea is to meet everything as it comes along and allow nothing to undermine your courage or your faith and joy. In forty-three years, I have never known her to have a really unhappy day, except, of course, through her love and sympathy for others.

So much vitality and inspiration were poured out through all these years, for family, friends, and the public, that I often worried lest she suddenly find herself exhausted; but apparently these qualities grow through use. This is a remarkable truth which can only be known when proven.

I was especially anxious about the concerts during the 1920's. It seemed as if a new element had entered the recital world. Managers and committees would create such a state of excited anticipation that when she came on the stage with her quick, unaffected walk the air seemed electrified.

Her task was to bring her listeners close to the composers, not to herself. In an atmosphere of sensation and eager expectation of climax, she had to arouse a spirit of introspection.

She succeeded, but each recital took on such a character of exaggerated importance that I felt there was an unnatural and unnecessary strain on the artist.

I do not know much about the world of music in the 1930's; but with the success of the Mozart operas at Glyndebourne, England, and of the smaller concerts at Salzburg, with the intimate programs of the works of early masters which come over the air, I feel that there is a desire to recover that atmosphere of sincerity and simplicity in which much of our great music was written.

Refinement and good taste will probably dominate the next period in music, and for that artists must prepare themselves now. Our chamber music organizations are leading us more and more into the exalted, inner mysteries of music. When I was young we had only the Kneisel Quartet, and sometimes we had to wait years before we could hear a certain, late Beethoven quartet played; but when it was played it was like a glimpse of heaven, it was so beautiful. Perhaps the rarity of performance had something to do with this. Familiarity with great music is not the only goal. Sensitiveness is more important.

My wife became more and more interested in her religion. She put all the religious numbers on her programs that she thought her listeners could stand: "Die Allmacht," "Dem Unendlichen," "My Heart Ever Faithful," "He Shall Feed His Flock," "Sheep and Lambs," "General William Booth," etc. One year she sang every noon at the religious services at the Palace Theatre in New York during Holy Week. Very soon she began going to Northfield for the religious conferences, often singing there, and one year she had a class there. Our daughter

Louise had organized a delegation to the Northfield girls' conference from Westover School, and introduced us to this great work.

I became interested in the leaders of public opinion in various countries—Sun Yat-sen, Gandhi, the Russian leaders, MacDonald, and others. I was convinced that all these men were sincere, that they held poverty and ignorance to be the real problem of life and the real obstacle to all progress. Theories would adapt themselves if motives were good and remained unchanged.

The relief of the Russian famine interested me tremendously, and I sent telegrams and letters to the committees in Congress and induced my friends in various cities to do the same. It was thrilling when Congress voted to send four million dollars' worth of medical supplies to Russia, and followed this up with twenty million dollars' worth of wheat and a relief expedition.

I continued my work as best I could.

I finished, after a fashion, my quintet for piano and strings, and a sonata for organ in one movement, which was published by Schirmer, together with an introduction and fugue for organ. In New York I wrote a set of thirty-five "Songs from Mother Goose" which was published by the Macmillan Company. I thought then (as I think now) that music should be sold in all bookstores, and I hoped that this venture with Macmillan would help a little to bring this about. They were also published by the John Church Company.

I became interested in some modern English poets, and published a set of songs with poems by James Stephens, Robert Bridges, and Irene Rutherford McLeod. "The Widow in Bye Street" and "The Everlasting Mercy," by John Masefield, fascinated me, and I managed to make three songs out of selected lines of the former, which seemed to tell the story, and one out of lines from the latter. I held these for a few years, but with the encouragement of Oscar Sonneck, then president of G. Schirmer, they were finally published. I also published a setting of Tom Hood's "The Lay of the Laborer," another poor man's song.

Few of my later songs ever really got into the concert repertoire. Charles Clark, that great artist, would use practically all of them, as Charles C. Washburn had done in the earlier days, but most singers preferred the better known songs. Many song writers have this experience. Certain earlier songs will be taken up, but later songs, neglected. Earlier songs are apt to be fresher and more spontaneous, later songs more thoughtful. Songs have different experiences. Some pass to the concert stage, thence to the studio, and then to the home. Others pass directly to the studio, and still others are known only in the home. Some that have the smallest sale make the deepest impression where they are known. Every composer has the delight of having some obscure song mentioned in a remote town where he least expects it.

On Christmas Day, 1920, we had just assembled for our grand family dinner when Pop Adams came in to make a Christmas call. At the same moment a special delivery letter came for me, postmarked "Boston." I opened it and took out a Liberty Bond for $5,000, and a check for $45,000. This was my share of the Sidney Homer Estate which my uncle had left to his relatives, on the strength of which I had borrowed money for our trip to Europe in 1896, twenty-four years earlier. It was a startling if happy moment. I think no one rejoiced more than Pop Adams.

All the past came back to me in a flash. I remembered how my father and mother felt about this $50,000, how far away in the dim, distant, impossible future 1920 had seemed. And here it was! Also how big and almost incredible this amount had seemed then. And then I realized how different, with all our "expansion," it seemed now. I felt a little disturbed and ashamed. There is never perfect satisfaction in "expansion."

In the spring we found that we could not continue to have our house at 30 West Seventy-fourth Street; it was to be sold. With all our little girls practicing piano, and Louise singing, not to speak of the work my wife and I were trying to do, it seemed impossible to find any place that would do. Our agent, in desperation at our plight, asked if I would consider buying an apartment house. I said I would consider anything that promised to solve our problem. He took me to 3 and 5 East Eighty-fourth Street, and the upshot was that we bought the two houses. There were ten apartments in all. The agent rented seven to the old tenants, and we took the three upper floors in No. 3 for ourselves. It was an odd arrangement but it solved the problem of making music. We gave the children the top floor, which was the sunniest, furnished the fourth as living quarters, and took the third floor for ourselves. We had four pianos going at once and could not hear one another.

This was our home for five years, and then, as land went up in value, we were able to sell at an advantage. The old houses are gone now.

These were the years when my wife was in demand everywhere. Pop Adams used to fuss because she wouldn't take longer trips. Each year he urged a tour of the Pacific Coast, but she declined because she would not go so far from the children. Various honors were bestowed upon her. Tufts College conferred the degree of M.A. on her in 1925. The League of Women Voters selected her as one of the "Twelve Most Eminent Women of America." She represented Music.

The joint concerts with our daughter Louise were a great success, and extended, off and on, over a period of nine years. And yet I cannot write of these years with complete enthusiasm. I knew my wife wanted to be at home with our four little girls every moment of the time, and felt anxious when she was away from them. We did everything possible to make home as perfect as we could. My sister lived with us, and this was our greatest support. Her devotion to great literature was an inspiration to the girls. They loved the children's stories she wrote for the *Saint Nicholas Magazine*. They are the most beautiful I have ever read. We had two tutors for the girls, one a college graduate and the other a musician. This enabled us to keep the children at Lake George from May until November without interrupting their studies. But at best it was a makeshift, and we breathed a sigh of relief each time a little tour was over.

On March 12, 1921, my wife and daughter gave their first concert in Carnegie Hall, New York. The house was packed, and all our friends were there. They both sang beautifully, and it was a sort of gala occasion. They sang other concerts there, in later years, but this first one had the charm of novelty.

Less than a month later, April 6th, Louise was married to Ernest Van R. Stires, that young ambulance driver of whom I have spoken. He had managed to break into our united family and win our daughter. Worse than that, he won the whole family!

The wedding was a grand affair. Ernest's father, now Bishop Stires, but at that time rector of St. Thomas', New York, performed the ceremony. The twins were bridesmaids. St. Thomas' was packed to the doors. With a famous father officiating at his son's wedding, and the bride a daughter of a popular opera singer, the occasion was a moving one. Dr. Noble played my organ sonata magnificently (it was the first time I had ever heard it), and this added a touch of sentiment, so far as our family was concerned. The reception was at the Colony Club. As it was in the spring, all our relatives and friends in Pittsburgh, Boston, Atlanta, and other distant points decided to combine this wedding with their annual trip to New York. The result was a great gathering of the clans.

The first great change had come in our family, but we had gained if we had lost. Family life is a strange thing. Bonds are tightly knit, there is a little tearing asunder, then a fresh uniting, and so it goes.

In the meantime our Sidney was very busy. At the end of his first year at Harvard he came to me and said: "Father, I can get through in three years. Lots of boys have done it. All I need to do is to go back to summer school for a few weeks." I consented, with reservations as to health, etc.

During the following Easter vacation, I suggested that he go on one of those short European tours during the summer, in order to get a complete rest from his studies; but a month later he wrote me that he had a chance to go into a Boston bank for two months that summer, and that he wished to learn something about finance before he began his last year at Harvard. I was a little anxious, but needlessly so.

In June, 1923, at the age of twenty, he graduated *magna cum laude,* majoring in Philosophy. Very fine, I thought, after only three years' work. But it's all very easy, apparently, if you have a motive. I discovered that he was deeply interested in a beautiful girl, Marion Symmes of Winchester. It makes all the difference in the world! On July 5, 1924, they were married at Homeland, and again we had a beautiful wedding. The twins were bridesmaids, and Hester was the little flower girl. It was a lovely summer day, and we had an altar built of flowers and pine branches on the lawn. The lake and mountains formed the background. About a hundred guests were there.

XIX

1922–1927

EVERY TIME WE CONSIDERED THE BURNING question of my wife's retiring from public life, something would happen to postpone the day.

At this time it was requests for "guest" performances from the Chicago Civic Opera Company. As these performances were really a part of her concert tours, the company paid her the regular concert fee she was receiving at that time ($1,500), and welcomed her with a courtesy and appreciation that made them among the happiest experiences she had ever had.

She made her debut with the company on November 22, 1922. Perhaps it is pardonable to quote what the Chicago *Tribune* said of these operatic appearances in Chicago:

Never in this generation was there such a marvel of a voice. Twelve and a half years have slipped by since she greeted an operatic audience [in Chicago], and her voice today is young, fresh, beautiful of tone, wide of range, and with the old-time dramatic thrill. The only reason, absolutely the only one whereby one could think of her years, is that she belongs to the old school of singing, the school wherein perfect singing was demanded as a requisite to appearing in opera.

And the Chicago *Daily Journal:*

. . . Homer swept the stage with the magnificence of her ripened powers. Her voice is beautiful, as full as any contralto's that lives, and produced with amazing brilliance. It is smooth from bottom to top, and could teach a lesson to almost any singer now in the public ear. . . . It is seldom that such a finish of acting is combined with such perfection of song. But Homer is a dominating figure because she has mastered the essentials of both fields of her art, and having mastered them, brings out of drama, in fine proportion, all its glitter and power, all those qualities which grip the senses of the hearer and convince him that the theatre houses a tremendous art.

Her return was doubly triumphant because she asked no consideration for the years that have passed since she first sang in opera. We may look in vain for a voice that is fresher than hers. The beauty of her work is unimpaired because it is founded upon the very principles of art, and it is safe to say that as long as Louise Homer sings, she will do so with absolute beauty.

The twins went to Miss Hall's school, at Pittsfield, Massachusetts, in 1922. Hester followed them there two years later, but when they graduated in 1925 she changed to Dana Hall at Wellesley. When the twins graduated a divergence of taste was noticeable. Kay had studied piano carefully with that fine musician Professor Buhler, and played Chopin's Ballade in F Minor at her graduation. She had also learned to paint under Felicie Waldo Howell, the eminent artist. Anne was bent on going to Smith College, and had passed all her examinations. She was one of those rare girls who can study hard and yet never lose their spontaneity. And so it happened that the twins now went different ways—Kay to New York for further study, and Anne to Smith.

These were the years when my wife was at the height of her powers and, also, of her popularity. Every concert brought expressions of esteem and affection. By every process of reasoning and deduction, these should have been our happiest years. But, as in all things which we seek to attain, a certain disillusionment comes with the attaining. I can compare musical life, in the sense of public performance, to a hill; difficult and exciting to climb, but a little flat on the top. The fun of it lies in the climbing. Moreover, with reaching the top comes a new experience. New and higher hills, even mountains, burst into view. It may be safely said that there is no room for complacency in art, and no time when the artist rests on his oars. In these years my wife sought higher technical achievement and deeper expression of feeling. Satisfaction with what she could do was the last thing that entered her mind.

If it had been a mere question of amusing and satisfying the public, she could have dismissed self-criticism from her mind. But she, like every other artist, had something within her that no amount of applause could deaden, something so demanding that anyone seeing her in her studio striving hour after hour for better things would have been amazed—unless by some great fortune he had been an artist himself, in which case he would have understood only too well.

But in the midst of all this the really absorbing and vital thing was the progress of the children. Louise and Sidney were married and could share, more than ever, our solicitude for the four younger girls. Children rediscover their parents when they marry.

Kay was forging ahead with her music and painting, a little undecided, I think, as to which art she preferred, and which she dared neglect.

Anne strove with the abstract and concrete problems of Smith College. In the abstract world, idealism and doubt vied for mastery over her dear soul; and, in the concrete, she fell in love with human nature in all its beauty.

Hester was at Dana Hall, and Joy at Tenacre, the junior school of Dana—both at Wellesley. Teachers, studies, sports, music, school events, school gossip, terrible violations of school rules (in the eyes of the girls), sudden passions for poetry, or books, or clothes—these filled their lives. "You know, Daddy, Dana is the hardest school in the United States," Hester informed me once during each vacation, and I never denied it. It was always the greatest fun to agree with my girls in anything that was possible; and still is. "Daddy, we seem to think just alike." I love that. If I could think like the dear young mind that looks at me through those beautiful eyes, I should be proud.

AT HOMELAND, SUMMER OF 1922

I, Anne, Hester, Sidney, my wife, Joy, Louise, Kay, Ernest Stires

But I can pretend. I can see the world as a dream place of romance, full of exciting adventures, where everything comes out right in the end, and everyone is good at heart. "Aren't they, Daddy, aren't they always good at heart?" Why, of course! Whoever heard of anything else? The whole world is good at heart—if we can only find the heart.

Vacations were grand days of reckoning; one day given entirely to hearing exciting and terrific things about school, teachers, girls, and, after that, weeks given to forgetting there ever was such a place or such people, that there ever was any other place than home, or any people except the family.

I never liked to see them at their schools. It gave me too great a sense of routine and confinement. I longed to have my girls with me so that they could feel free as birds on the wing. I could never understand schools, and I know I never shall. They seem artificial to me. The teachers may be humble enough in the presence of great masters; but before their pupils they may feel that they cannot be humble and maintain their authority. In music we have something different. The teacher may be as humble as he likes, and the pupil will never mistake him. Both teacher and pupil are in the presence of a great master, be it Beethoven or Bach, and both bow before the same shrine in a common spirit.

Our vacations were great reunions in which all ties were tightened up, and all confidences renewed, and all pent-up hearts released. "Oh, Daddy, I just couldn't write you about that! I wanted to tell you!"

People tell me of my wife's eternal youth. If they could have seen her with her girls through all those happy years they wouldn't speak of it in such a tone of wonder. She was a girl with them, and shared their every thought and feeling. They talked to her as one girl talks to another. Nothing was too small to tell her, and they never weighed their words. They poured out everything with a spontaneity that was as precious and heavenly as it was beautiful. And when they all roared with laughter together, my wife laughed like a girl. How could she grow old? She never will. By the same token, even I am not allowed the dignity of my years. These rascals will not have it!

At the moment our little grandson Ernest Stires is exchanging letters with his grandmother; and I'm blessed if he, too, doesn't address her as if she were just a young thing. He calls her "Dear Gumpy"! Barriers of age and generation simply do not exist in our family.

It may be an inheritance from some remote ancestor (Methuselah!) who had a very long youth, or it may be that blessed art of music, which I have always maintained is the real Fountain of Youth.

Those grandchildren began poking their way into our lives. Loulie Stires, born in 1922, is only eight years younger than our daughter Joy, and thus the word "baby" has never quite disappeared from our lives. Louise Homer, third, was born on June 27, 1925, and this precious imitation of a precious mother has quietly made slaves of all those around her.

In the fall of 1925 we took a house at Alexandria, Virginia, where Ernest Stires was finishing his course at the theological seminary, in order to be near our daughter Louise. It was a rare treat to hear the young men, about to graduate, discuss gravely the opportunities for service that might be open to them: West Africa, India, the poorer districts of Georgia, the slums of New York. Not one of them wanted an easy berth.

One behind the scenes knows the idealism and courage that underlie these lives, while he who sees the rector at the church door, in the carved pulpit, in his flowing robes, may hardly guess it. Religion and music are robbed of much of their romance through their conventional absorption by Society; but the real spirit of both goes on undisturbed.

The true picture, in the eyes of these theological students, was that of Albert Schweitzer on the banks of his African river, teaching ethics and self-control to the natives. The fact that

Schweitzer was the greatest organist in Europe, sought for in every capital from London to Moscow, and the greatest living authority on Bach, is but another side of the picture. Idealism burns as fiercely in music as it does in religion, and slowly and with infinite pain the religious world is becoming aware of this fact. There was a certain pleasure in the feeling that idealism was a sort of natural monopoly of religion, but now with idealism revealing itself so unmistakably in art, and then again among atheists, agnostics, honest doubters, followers of discredited faiths, economic students and social theorists, all sorts of fictitious barriers are falling down. Idealism is seeking its kind, as little streams seek one another, and soon a mighty river of disinterestedness will be formed that will sweep all before it. One who does not feel this gathering force of idealism is living in darkness. The young are fully aware of it, it is almost a commonplace with them. There is little use in appealing to their selfish instincts now. They expect a decent purpose behind everything they do, and they expect to play fair. There is slight need to worry about the young. If church attendance has fallen off, it is because men have found idealism in other walks of life, not because their standards have lowered. Purpose was never so high, nor its channels so diverse. To attempt to confine it to a single channel would be but to destroy it. Let us call idealism, idealism, wherever it be found. In this way we can push on to a goal.

When my wife gave a recital in Washington that winter the entire seminary came to hear her. In her program she included my setting of Vachel Lindsay's "General William Booth Enters Heaven," and "The Song of the Shirt," and for a month or two I had quite a reputation at the seminary as a composer. But it is impossible to make a permanent impression on those busy altruists. Ministers are trained to give, not to receive.

On December 17, 1925, Ernest Milmore Stires was born. He was named for his famous grandfather, and I must say that he carries his name easily. I have never known him to be scared but once. For nearly five years he, like Siegfried, knew no fear. On that morning he went into his nurse's room. She was very devout, and was praying. "Come in, Ernest," she said. "Close the door, and be very quiet. God is here." "Oh, boy!" he said, "I'm going!" And in a flash he was gone.

In the winter of 1925 my wife received a letter from Richard Hageman. He wanted her to sing the following September during the San Francisco and Los Angeles opera seasons, for which he had been engaged as conductor. This was something new, and sounded most attractive. Our younger girls would be at school, Anne at Smith, and Kay in New York busy with her music and painting. For the first time in twenty years, it seemed possible to go to the Pacific Coast without the dread of something happening—that bugaboo of all parents, and grandparents.

The upshot was that the Wolfsohn Bureau arranged a fine tour which included concerts up and down the Coast, as well as the opera engagements. The terms were $2,000 for each performance, the highest my wife ever received. This was the second postponement of retirement.

In September, 1926, we went to San Francisco. Everywhere we found the same fascination with life, the same contentment at the sheer privilege of being alive; also a determination to enjoy everything to the utmost. And this extended to the visiting artists, all of whom were warmly welcomed.

Everything about this delightful tour had a little of the air of pageantry. Perhaps this was due to the spectacular and neverending beauty of the country, which inevitably creates and fosters a spirit of enthusiasm. This in turn becomes a habit, and spreads to all affairs of life, including art. Whatever the cause, one felt the unrestrained appreciation and genuine gratitude of the audiences.

My wife was invited to sing at the breaking of the ground for the new San Francisco Civic Opera House. Fifty thousand people, including thousands of veterans in uniform, filled the square. It was Armistice Day, and an air of serious purpose marked the occasion. A city government planned to build an opera house which would cost seven million dollars. We read that the Russian government appropriates five million for an opera house at Kharkov and thinks little of it. But when an American city ventures to do such a thing we realize that something new has happened in our country.

My wife sang "Ring Out, Wild Bells" and "The Battle Hymn of the Republic." The sea of upturned faces inspired her, and she sang with a depth of feeling born of prophetic vision. All minds were on the future. The little spadeful of upturned earth meant opportunity for coming generations, glorious singers who would inspire the people, composers with profound messages.

We left California with regret, and planned to return the following year.

As a special treat, we had our Christmas holidays at Homeland on Lake George—three holy, if noisy, weeks. The ridiculous, romping rabble may have disturbed the winter quiet of the snow, the lake, and the bare trees, but the feeling in all hearts was very deep. "Oh, mother, isn't it lovely!" It brought back the days when the children were small, when they used to sleep in the open playhouse with the thermometer at twenty degrees below zero, each with five blankets and four comforters. Children are as anxious to keep young as we are, and any association with earlier days is precious to them. Toys, nursery books, reminders, should never be thrown away. "Oh, look, Mummie, what I found in the attic! I had that five years ago and loved it!" All the old feelings come back, the forgotten feelings, and with them a little renewing and strengthening of youthful ardor.

That Christmas tree, we cut ourselves! The carols, with five sopranos and one contralto! That turkey! The stories, and school confidences, the grand plans for the future. We were soon to separate, and it was necessary for each girl to assure all the rest that all was well with her, and that she could stand on her own feet.

There were unwritten traditions among our children, most of them based on consideration for their wonderful mother, and for me. From early childhood they were conscious of the courage and the responsibilities attached to her art. She was their heroine, as well as their devoted mother.

The women who wrote articles would usually ask some such question as, "Madame Homer, how were you able to accomplish all that you have?" The right answer would be, "Through the cooperation of the children." It is a joy to any child to share in her mother's life, and my wife had a genius for making each child feel that she (or he) played a large part in everything she did. And there was no fooling about it. They did play a large part. They must have felt, from the beginning, that her happiness depended on theirs, that she had no life apart from them, that they were in her thoughts every moment. And so, always, there was that consideration, that protection which only children can give their parents.

On these bright winter days and long evenings, as we threshed everything out, each one put the best foot forward, told only the happy things, and forgot the boring ones. Family tradition, perhaps, but a good one. We knew we couldn't separate and be happy if there were something wrong, and so happiness became a sort of obligation, a sort of service to the family.

In March, 1927, my wife received a letter from her pianist, Ruth Emerson, saying she was to be married, and would be compelled to resign her position. This was a sad blow. Always the pianists who played for her were her devoted friends, and she became deeply attached to them, and dependent on them—on their friendship as well as on their art. They were all wonderful women, of great character, strong personality, resourcefulness, and charm.

First there was Evadna Lapham, the fine ensemble player; then Florence McMillan, who later became famous as the founder of the Parnassus Club of New York, a residential club for girls where thousands have climbed the mount of idealism under her guidance; then Eleanor Scheib (her real name was "Bucky"), also a fine ensemble player, who always brightened the atmosphere and drove the clouds away; and then Ruth Emerson, who had won the hearts of the entire household. For the California tour we had secured Elizabeth Alexander, of San Francisco.

This group of fine artists represented more than fine playing. Twenty years of travel, hotels, managers, concert halls, committees, telephones: "Yes, this is Madame Homer's accompanist. . . . I'm sorry, she never talks over the phone on the day she sings. . . . I'm sorry, I couldn't possibly disturb her. . . . It's too bad—there's a sign on her door which says, 'Asleep, don't disturb.' . . . Three hundred ladies? She couldn't possibly meet so many people on the day she sings. . . . No, she never leaves her room. . . . No, she isn't sick; she just wants to save her voice. . . . It's too bad. Perhaps if your committee came behind the scenes after the concert she could see them for a moment, although we are catching a train at 11:25 and she will have to hurry right back to the hotel. . . . It's too bad, after all those elaborate preparations. . . . No, I couldn't possibly disturb her. . . . No, there's a sign on her door." And so on.

All sorts of things happened that required quick thinking: cold dressing rooms, draughts, no piano, bad piano, piano tuned too high: "No one will notice it."—"Madame will." "Don't tell her."—"She'll notice it instantly." "The public won't care."— "That isn't the point."—"Oh, well!" And trying to get something hot to eat at the small-town hotel for tired, happy artists. "Very sorry, our cook goes home at eight o'clock."—"Send out for something." "Never tried it."—"Let's try it now." "All right!

We'll fix something. My wife's a pretty good cook; she loves Madame Homer, knows her on the Victor, has a lot of pictures of her and her children which she cut out—"

Snowstorms, missed connections, cross-country motor trips, long waits in way stations, reporters, photographers, old friends: "I knew her twenty years ago. Please!" "I'm related by marriage to her cousin—I know she'll want to see me!" Alas, it is hard to disappoint!

Yes, that lovely pianist you see on the stage is more than a pianist. She is a friend, protector, defender, with no thought for herself.

And so we were to lose Ruth Emerson. We were sad. There were concerts in May—what would we do? Suddenly my wife had a real inspiration. Kay! Could she do it? She played well, but she was only nineteen and had never appeared before the public. It is exciting to do this, and requires a cool head. My wife wired her, and the answer came back, "Mother dear, if you let me do this, I shall be the happiest girl in the world."

And so Kay became her mother's pianist. The first concert was at West Chester, Pennsylvania, the old home town where my wife made her debut at the age of fourteen, in the contralto part of *Ruth the Moabitess*. It seemed quite fitting that Kay should begin, as her mother had, in the dear old Quaker town.

I sat in the audience and knew, almost instantly, that Kay would make a success of her new vocation. Calm, serious, responsive, alert, she seemed to the manner born. My wife sang with a certain grandeur which told clearly how moved she was. On her program were two fine songs by her nephew, Samuel Barber, who played them for her.

We decided to appoint Kay grand pianist to her mother, and, during the summer, they prepared programs for the approaching "coast to coast" tour. In September we started out on our fifteen-thousand-mile trip. What fun it was! Kay was supremely happy to be with us and to have such an important job. She insisted on doing the whole of it. She was very firm, and always got her way. "Mamma must have an easy-chair in her dressing room." "I'm sorry, but we haven't one." "Then will you get one from some place?" She was very conscious of her mother's needs, and was so earnest, in her winning way, that no one could say her nay.

She played the songs beautifully. She had a dramatic sense which enabled her to give a special color to each number. It was a joy to see her on the stage with her mother. There seemed to be an unusually subtle understanding between them which the audiences were quick to see and appreciate.

We went to the University of Oklahoma, where Kay and I saw a fine ball game. In the afternoon she cheered the boys; in the evening they cheered her and her mother. Then to Colorado Springs, where she saw the Garden of the Gods, all new and thrilling to her. She painted a lovely picture of the view from the hotel window, early in the morning.

The concert in Denver was exciting. Then over the plains to Spokane, with its music-loving audience. Kay loved the ride through the mountains to Seattle. Then southern California, whose glories quite took her breath away. We made Pasadena our headquarters and, while there, went to Hollywood, where we had the privilege of seeing Emil Jannings make a thrilling scene in the picture of the Russian Revolution.

This was Kay's trip, and between two concerts we took her to La Jolla for a couple of days. The beauty of the place fascinated her. She was up early, and painted all day. When she painted, we wished she might give up music, but when she played we felt differently.

Again we were loath to leave California. My wife and I felt that we might be seeing it for the last time. Life is much too short, and the world much too big and fascinating. Singing was fascinating, and the thought of retiring became dire. One paper said, "And her voice, rich as cream, sweet and golden as California honey, and vibrant as a plucked violin string, it flowed from her lips in a veritable flood of rich beauty. Undoubtedly, Louise Homer's youthful heart finds its expression in her glorious, youthful voice." It hardly seemed right to stop.

Kay was praised, Sam Barber's song "The Lullaby of the Madonna" (usually repeated) was praised, my songs were praised, and when Louise Stires joined us in Akron for a joint concert, she was praised. There was something for everyone.

We had four concerts in and near Chicago, and stayed at the Blackstone Hotel. It was all new and exciting for Kay. Until this trip, her experience in hotels had been very limited. She tried all the dishes that we do not usually have at home, tried the piano in the drawing room, investigated the lobbies and their shops, met the reporters, who amused her tremendously, had her picture taken, and developed the sang-froid of the experienced traveler. Her sense of humor kept her from being over-impressed. She learned to like people, all kinds of people. I was proud to have her play in Chicago, and my mind went back twenty-six years, when her mother, looking almost as young as Kay, had sung there for the first time. If I seem sentimental, my reader has only to put himself in my place! Be fair!

At last we were back in New York, safe, sound, and happy, and very proud of Kay.

XX

1927–1928

AND NOW IN THE FALL OF 1927 a new experience awaited us. My wife was to return to the Metropolitan Opera House after an absence of eight years. Mr. Gatti had chosen Amneris, one of her best roles, for her reentry, and had selected a date, December 14th, when the children would surely be at home for their Christmas holidays. They must, by all means, hear her! No one associates delicacies of this kind with opera houses.

I was ill at the time of my wife's debut at the Metropolitan as Amneris in November, 1900; but Mary Hartwell, beautiful and beloved, my wife's cousin, had often described it to me. This would be in the nature of a second debut. How would it compare with that of 1900? What had twenty-seven years of singing done to her voice?

My wife had not sung the part for three years, and there would be no orchestral rehearsal. She must plunge directly from her concert singing into one of her greatest operatic roles as if there had been no break in the continuity of her operatic life. It would seem difficult, but the first piano rehearsal with Serafin, the great conductor, made it easy. "The real Amneris," he said simply, with the kind spirit and deep interest that he had for all good American singers.

What fun it was to go backstage again! There they were—Miss Morton, Judels, Philip, Charles, Emma, John; all the old friends, a trifle older, but unchanged. Were they glad to see my wife again? For real devotion, go backstage! Other friends through the house were Frank Garlichs, Aimee Gerber, Earl Lewis, Lionel Mapleson, and William Guard.

At last the afternoon came. We had a box near the stage, and the children were so excited and happy that they could not keep their seats. Hester and Joy had that morning come from Dana Hall at Wellesley. Joy had never seen her mother in an opera, and Hester only once, ten years earlier. The house filled slowly until it was packed. The children, of course, thought everyone had come just to hear their mother. For inflated pride, there is nothing like an artist's family!

The members of the orchestra took their places. They did not seem excited; it might even have been an ordinary performance. The children bounced up and down: "Look, Kay!" "Oh, Anne!" The house darkened, the curtain rose. Martinelli sang "Celeste Aida." It was beautiful! A figure stepped suddenly onto the stage. "Mamma!" And then the audience burst into applause. Serafin stopped the orchestra and laid down his baton. The applause went on and on, and it grew stronger and stronger.

If my readers think I could minimize this, or refer to it modestly, they are mistaken. A whole lifetime was summed up in that moment. My wife stood there with her arm outstretched toward Rhadames, leaning slightly forward on one foot, the old familiar pose which she had practiced so carefully in our little apartment in Paris in 1898. The beautiful costume and long black hair made her look much as she did then. Some of the children wept. I knew she would not bow, and wondered. Suddenly she threw up her other arm in a grand gesture which included the audience and the sun-god, Ra, painted on the scenery. It expressed her gratitude clearly enough.

Then she sang, and her voice pealed forth, and we could literally feel the supreme satisfaction of the audience. Yes—the same voice in all its richness, the voice they had loved so many years. It was not to be an afternoon of toleration, and the recalling of vanished glories. It was to be a great performance, a memorable occasion. The sweeping authority of my wife's voice and acting moved everyone. This afternoon, which might almost have passed unnoticed, drew high tributes from the critics, two of which I shall quote. The whole occasion was far beyond our simple expectations.

The New York *Telegram* said:

There was a real performance of *Aida* at the Metropolitan Opera House yesterday afternoon. This gratifying state of affairs was due in part to the return to Mr. Gatti-Casazza's fold of Madame Louise Homer, an American singer who really adorns the operatic stage. . . . But Amneris was beyond dispute the heroine of the day. Madame Homer sang the role at her Metropolitan debut twenty-seven years ago. And she sang it in particularly memorable circumstances the first night of the Gatti-Casazza regime in November, 1908. . . . The years have dealt kindly with Madame Homer's voice. On this occasion it was in particularly brilliant estate. Its substance and richness were a delight, as were the poise and sweep of Madame Homer's phrasing, the searching authority of her musical interpretation. Although since Madame Homer had been last heard at the Metropolitan, she has frequently appeared in opera in Chicago and on the Pacific Coast, most of her professional activity has been given to concert singing. Whether for that reason or for some other, the finer shades of her art have in the meantime prospered. Her singing today can boast delicacies, finesses, a command of nuance and of innuendo that formerly it lacked. And yet the breadth and vigor were there as of yore. Her entrance in the opening tableau was the signal for the representation to stop while the huge audience greeted her long and vociferously. And there were further ovations later on. This was altogether natural, for the Amneris who, gorgeously appareled, trod the Metropolitan boards yesterday looked a veritable daughter of the Pharaohs, a proud and refulgent princess of many-dynastied Egypt.

The New York *World* said:

Even the callboys at the Metropolitan yesterday could talk of little else—"Louise Homer is back!" It trickled through the wilderness backstage. It swept across the vast orchestra, up through the staid boxes, even unto the family circle, where the gods of music always sit. "Louise Homer is back!" ran the word, and everyone was glad to be there.

Retirement vanished into limbo. Singing took on new charms. Even railroad travel looked easier. We hoped for concerts in towns not far apart, carefully arranged tours, with easy "jumps." We would devote only four months in the year to this; the rest of the year would belong to the children and to our other work and interests. In the search for new fields and conditions we signed a three-year contract with Evans & Salter, the brilliant managers. And now I was at last free to carry out a long-cherished plan! As I have said, my wife had, during the past fifteen years, read innumerable books on the Bible. During some part of every day she had truly lived in the Holy Land. It was no casual interest. Her convictions were such that I am sure she could not understand the attitude of the average man. She had many interests herself, but they all had their relation to the real concern of life. It was not the varied interests of men that troubled her, but their indifference to the thing that mattered most. I longed to take her to the Holy Land, and now, with the future planned, the children busy, there seemed no good reason why I should not do it.

Only once before (in those two months of the winter of 1913–1914) had we been abroad on a pleasure trip; and it was high time that we went again. Of course, my wife knew that I should enjoy seeing the Holy Land as much as she, that I was never happier than when I was seeing new places and new kinds of people, that every trip we took was a spree, that I needed a change as much as she—and all the rest of it.

We evolved an elaborate plan. Kay would go to Paris, where she would continue her studies in music and painting. We would sail on the *Empress of Scotland* on February 4th for the Mediterranean tour, joining Kay in Paris early in April. In June, as soon as the spring terms at Smith College and Dana Hall had ended,

Anne, Hester, and Joy would join us in Paris. A teacher from Dana Hall, who was going over, would look after them. We would then give the girls a summer in Europe, a delight we had looked forward to for several years. It was a wonderful plan.

My wife sang *La Gioconda* at the Metropolitan. Her beautiful and eloquent acting and her moving voice, which had always elevated the unhappy Laura Adorno to a tragic and appealing figure, thrilled the audience.

No one was happier over my wife's success than Antonio Scotti. In this and the following seasons he made a point of hearing every one of her performances, and always came to her dressing room to congratulate her. Mr. Gatti, Mr. Ziegler, and Serafin touched her deeply with their sincere appreciation. In the "front" of the house, our old friend (and the friend of all the subscribers) Tom Bull told me and everyone else that Madame was "Wonderful! Simply wonderful!"

There is no thrill in an opera house to compare with the return of an artist who has been able to retain his or her former powers. Opera folk, before and behind the curtain, are emotional, sensitive, deeply loyal, and they never forget; the memory of performances of the past casts a halo over the present. Their only anxiety is lest powers may wane. They cannot bear to see an artist deteriorate.

The opera world is a strange mixture of devotion and discrimination. Here is one place where appreciation has free and untrammeled expression, where enthusiasm goes beyond the bounds of discreet self-control, where the triumphs of the past still echo through the halls, and the loyalty to artists is given unrestrained emotional power.

The last concert was a joint concert with our daughter Louise, at the Academy of Music in Brooklyn. Mother and daughter made a lovely picture and sang beautifully. We made our last purchases, and hurried to the steamer. Frantic wavings, laughter, tears, cheers, and we were off.

Postlude
1928–1938

"THE BEST LAID SCHEMES O' MICE AND MEN
gang aft a-gley."

It was not, as in the case of Robert Burns' wee, timorous beastie, our home that had been plowed up. No, Homeland was intact and still is. But the plow cut into our plans and compelled my wife to give up her singing, both in concert and at the Metropolitan Opera House.

I remember very well the peculiar feeling I used to have, a sort of sinking at the heart, when some great and beloved artist announced his or her retirement. So it is only fair that I report that my wife and I are quite sure that the ten years that have passed since she gave up public singing have been among the happiest of our lives. Thus no commiseration is in order, although a sense of loss is inevitable. I confess to occasional longings for one of those great performances, for that denunciation of the Egyptian priests, the unheeded warning to Isolde, Azucena's heart-piercing narrative, Waltraute's appeal to Brünnhilde, Orfeo's lament over the body of his beloved.

Nothing can take the place of these, and something has gone —not quite gone! My memory is such that I can live those transcendent moments over again in the silence of my room. Occasionally I meet some one who can also recall the picture, the voice, the emotion and climax, and when I do I see an expression steal into the face which says just what I feel in my heart.

In order to make clear just why our lives took a new channel I must resume my story.

Our tour of the Mediterranean was magnificent. Each place we stopped at seemed a living drama in our eyes. There was a sense of artificial security, of something impending. English authority on the tip of Spain; French on the north coast of Africa and Syria; English again in Palestine, and its shadow in Egypt—all this gave one a sense of fire, smoldering embers hardly concealed, heat without the flame.

Somewhere in Spain I caught a cold, and the dust of Algiers and Damascus, the holy dust of Palestine, and the antique dust of Egypt helped it along, and by the time I was safely in our hotel in Paris it was strong enough to triumphantly lay me low. It was this cold that changed our lives. It was the kind of cold that could do anything it pleased, run rampant over the whole body. The only thing it couldn't do was frighten me. I knew instinctively that this would be fatal. The little French doctor said: "Mr. Homer, you are the drollest patient I ever had. You make the nurses laugh, and you make me laugh." I didn't tell him that that was my way of getting well, but I knew well enough it was my only chance. I insisted that my wife continue practicing with her accompanist in the next room, and to help me she was able to do it for a few days. With her help I was able to convince myself that I was on the sure road to recovery, and could face each new turn with a certain equanimity.

I had double pneumonia and then double pleurisy. (I don't believe I was quite so funny during this phase.) Then the specialist who was called in suspected that I was developing an abscess in the lungs and insisted that I be carried to the American Hospital where he hoped to have the help of the X-ray machine. It was a spooky trip, and the people and taxicabs in the streets looked like playthings, make-believes. My wife took the room next to mine in the hospital, and we were there all summer. She pulled me through with that marvelous will of hers which knows no obstacle and brooks no defeat. Doctors and nurses saw in her a ministering angel who had but one thought and could not fail.

The specialist was right about the abscess, and every time he came, my regular doctor trembled lest he order an operation.

There was no operation, and I had the pleasure of getting well without it. It was a slow process. For one thing, I had to sit up straight, night and day, for a year and a half. Not a great hardship—after a year or so, you get used to it. During that year and a half this book was written—there was nothing else to do; and if, in its pages, there is a smug sense of joy at being alive, of gratitude for everything in the world, including the sun, moon and stars and all the people and some particular individuals, and an easy sureness that everything needful to the triumphant progress of music must surely come to pass, that nothing is difficult if the will be there, then all this must be read in the light of that year and a half. After a real sickness, each day seems a sort of gift, an extra dividend, an encore after the regular program, another glimpse of the artists after the opera is over and the curtain down. Life looks different and quite a bit brighter. Those problems that loomed so big have quite disappeared. Why, where are they?

Anne, Hester, and Joy sailed from New York as planned. Kay, who had been living with a French family in Paris, shared her mother's every moment, so far as it was allowed. The hospital room was a strange place to receive them, and there were tears, but also bright cheering smiles. After they had had time to see "all Paris" my wife established them at Cabourg on the coast of Normandy. As soon as I was able to walk a couple of hundred feet my French doctors packed us off to Gstaad in Switzerland. "Only that particular air will cure your lungs!" they said. It was a bold move, but everything those French doctors did seemed to me drastic, sure and courageous. They believed in air, altitude, and all the help that Nature could give. Also in their native wines. I had a little champagne every hour, burgundy twice a day, and cognac with my coffee. They were very proud of my recovery; said my case was a remarkable one and would be on record for thirty years. Very flattering, I'm sure.

After a month in the life-giving air of Gstaad, during which the four girls made the grand tour of Switzerland (top of the Jungfrau, Lucerne, Andermatt, the Rhône glacier, and Zermatt), we started home, stopping in Montreal to see a great specialist. I was doing wonderfully, but of course I could not live in the north during the winter months; I must be in a warm, tropical climate. The doctor's verdict was a shock, as we had taken an elaborate apartment in New York overlooking the East River, and had planned to spend the winter with three of our girls who were home from school and college for the first time in years. Anne had graduated from Smith *cum laude*, Hester from Dana Hall, and Kay was to play for her mother on her fall concert tour. It was most inconvenient. Were the doctors right? We would see. Yes, the doctors were right, and after the fall concert season, we were off to Palm Beach, where we had spent winter vacations in previous years, and which we had learned to love.

While I sat on the sand and wrote this book, my wife ran up to New York to sing at the Metropolitan and hurried back; up to Boston and some other place—and back again; out to Chicago, and back to Palm Beach. It was clear to both of us that this could not go on, and after struggling a little longer, we canceled my wife's contract with her managers. There were still a couple of performances promised to the Metropolitan, and this led to my wife's name being kept on the Opera's list of artists through several more seasons.

And so this new and very wonderful period of our lives began. No contracts! No keeping in voice, no separation! There was a sense of release, a little bewilderment, a feeling of drifting, a sort of arresting of time. It did not seem quite possible. For several years I had thought of the time when my wife would stop singing and wondered how it would affect her. Thirty years before the public makes the public seem almost a part of one's life. I had felt a little uneasy lest she be not quite happy, lest there be a little sense of emptiness, a looking for something that was not there. All my apprehensions were unfounded. With a family such as ours, life can never have an empty moment.

Soon after her graduation, Anne became dramatic editor of the *Junior League Magazine* and still carries on this fascinating work, in addition to her other literary activities.

Kay lost her job when her mother stopped her concert tours, but immediately took up chamber music and also taught interesting classes at the Neighborhood Music School and at Christodora House.

Louise's voice is more beautiful than ever, and she gives much of her spare time to singing.

On January 1, 1932, Sidney formed Homer & Co., Incorporated, dealers in high-class bonds. Their bulletins are widely read. The Homer Juniors have bought a home in Westport, Connecticut.

Joy graduated from Smith College in 1937 and immediately accepted Muriel Lester's invitation to come to London and be her secretary, assisting her during the preparation of her autobiography, "It Occurred to Me" (published by Harpers). She is now on the high seas on her way to Shanghai where she is to be a special field writer for the China Famine Relief.

It is easy for girls to do things when they see their mother so actively engaged in something worth while.

We announced Hester's engagement to Robert E. Henry, Jr., and they were married in St. James Church, at Lake George, on June 25, 1930. She was eighteen years old and seemed a child. Now, at twenty-six, she is the mother of three beautiful girls. Ernest Stires officiated, and the reception was at Homeland. The fact that the Henry (senior) estate is on Lake George makes it easy to have them with us, or near us, during the summers.

Anne was married to Robert Warner at Homeland on June 2, 1932, by Ernest Stires, and Katharine was married to Douglas Fryer at Homeland on August 25, 1934, by Dr. Paxton, who married us in 1895. These weddings were on the lawn at Homeland again, with the lake and mountains for background.

All the weddings were under bright skies and amid friends from far and near. They were joyous occasions. But they were more than that: they were culminations in our lives, fraught with meaning and promise.

These sons-in-law are sons. Ernest Stires after eight years of service at All Saints, Richmond, has accepted a call to St. Paul's, Waco, Texas. Wherever he goes, he will be the driver of a French ambulance that I knew in 1917. Ambulance means service.

Bob Henry has been with the Seligmans for eight years, and has become an authority on investments. The Henrys have their home in Westport, Connecticut.

Bob Warner is deep in literary activities. The Warners have chosen Dorset, Vermont, as a fine place in which to work.

Douglas Fryer is chairman of the Department of Psychology in New York University (University Heights). He has recently become president of the American Association for Applied Psychology. The Fryers have just bought a house at Scarsdale, New York.

Our family life has flourished like a green bay tree. We have twelve grandchildren. We are a sturdy clan of twenty-five, and frankness is our motto. Any false modesty on my part would be protested. This postlude cannot keep up with the clan, for the picture changes every day.

Yes, public singing may stop, but life goes sweeping on with a greater impetus than ever. The importance of any one thing is swallowed up in the importance of the whole. This growing of the clan makes the years vibrate with excitement.

One of our great joys during these years was watching the artistic growth and success of my wife's nephew, Samuel Barber, and his friend Gian Carlo Menotti. Sam's symphonic and other works have made a deep impression in America and have been played at Rome, Salzburg, and London, and Gian Carlo's opera "Amelia Goes to the Ball" had a brilliant success at the Metropolitan Opera House last winter.

Their visits to Homeland will not be forgotten. They found musical themes all through the woods and worked in some of the studios and were the happiest composers in all the world, I am sure.

The evenings were given up to sheer high spirits. Wherever Sam and Gian Carlo are, there is bound to be fun—may they never change! Sam's sister, Sara, gifted in voice and temperament, is now studying with her Aunt Louise.

After a period of rest, my wife and I grew uneasy. We still had serious responsibilities, including Homeland, with its five sleeping porches, its studios, and its mile of shore front. Besides, we had never enjoyed idleness. We discussed teaching. Would it be practical? We were compelled to live on the southern tip of our country for one-half of the year and on the northern edge, fifteen hundred miles away, during the other half. Could any class travel back and forth? Could pupils leave the large music centers in order to study with Madame Homer?

There were advantages, of course. Florida with its eternal sunshine meant health, no colds, and a chance to work hard in ideal surroundings. Homeland, with the studios scattered throughout our woods, the simple unspoiled life, the fresh beauty on every side, must be inspiring.

We decided to try it. Instantly our dearest friends, Mary and Maurice Hoopes, offered two scholarships covering instruction for two girls with beautiful voices, the girls to be selected by us. We announced a competition for the scholarships in New York, and there were two hundred applicants. We heard voices for four days and finally selected two. It was difficult to let some of the other beautiful voices go. With this beginning, our class grew. I helped my wife as best I could. I organized a symphony class in Palm Beach. It grew to have twenty-five members and ran through four winters. There was also an occasional pupil in Harmony.

As I grew stronger I turned to my composing again, but not to songs. Carl Engel, the new president of G. Schirmer, asked me to write piano pieces for children. I wrote three sets, forty-five in all. I wrote simple sonatas for piano, a string quartet, a sonata for piano and violin, and a trio for piano, violin, and cello.

I have heard the violin sonata beautifully played by Margaret Sittig in several of her recitals, once with Kay and often with her father. She even memorized the work, a fine compliment. The De Blasiis sisters played it with fine effect.

The Stradivarius Quartet played two movements of the string quartet with wonderful artistry at one of their concerts at Palm Beach, and the Curtis String Quartet read it thrillingly for us at our house.

The trio we heard at Fairfield, played by Mrs. Otis and Mr. Patuzzi and his son; a fine performance. It is one thing to write music and quite another to hear it played. I am having a glorious time working in these forms which I hardly dared to touch in other, busier years.

As soon as my wife's pupils sang well enough, she organized invitation musicales at our home in Palm Beach. They were so popular that she soon had to give them in a larger place. Her older scholarship pupils gave public recitals on their own account, with great success. There is no more appreciative audience than that at Palm Beach. Nearly every section of the country is represented in this audience, and it is most cosmopolitan in character.

My wife sent to Lake George for a hundred hymn books and started her Sunday afternoon gatherings at our home for the singing of hymns. Those who have attended these gatherings, either at Palm Beach or at Lake George, know that she conducts them with a simplicity and naturalness which lifts them far above the commonplace and makes them truly inspiring. Her pupils form a choir, and with these beautiful voices to help her she is able to lead the whole roomful to a most thrilling singing from the heart. The pupils sing religious solos and choral numbers. My wife explains the origin and meaning of the hymns and talks of the hymn writers. Our home had room for but a hundred, and she had to move the gathering to larger places, first to the Everglades Club, and then to the Society of the Four Arts.

Thus our life at Palm Beach, always thought of as a playground, became a busy one.

During these years, various honors were bestowed on my wife. In 1925, she received the degree of Master of Arts from Tufts College, as I have said; in 1931, the same degree from Smith College; in 1932, the degree of Doctor of Music from Russell Sage College; in 1933, the degree of Doctor of Letters from Miami University at Oxford, Ohio, the university from which her father had graduated so many years earlier; in 1934, the degree of Doctor of Music from Middlebury College.

A prophet may be without honor in his own country, but an American singer, man or woman, who gains the affection of the American people has gained something which cannot be estimated in conventional terms. Singers from abroad have the same experience in America, although they may not always be aware of how long this gratitude and affection continue after they have left our shores.

Her pupils come to Lake George to study in the summer, and so I can close my story with a short mention of Homeland—our blessed extravagance, and always our source of strength and renewed courage. If the children and grandchildren run all over the place, then this fills out the picture. Homeland began as a free land for six busy and enterprising children (and, incidentally, their parents) and never seems itself without the ring of children's voices.

If, in going through the woods or along the lake shore, one

passes near enough to the studios to hear beautiful voices, one realizes that Homeland has begun to serve a new purpose. Although the students live on the hillside, they pass their days in these studios under the beeches and pines. All around are vistas of mountain and lake, and underfoot are leaves and pine needles. The silence and solitude accentuate the beauty of the music they study.

When one of the girls is singing in my wife's studio, it almost seems as if the master is sitting just outside listening to his work. Yes, Homeland is serving a new purpose. All who come here, even those who come but for an hour or two to hear the informal recitals of the students which my wife arranges from time to time, come under its spell. They, like the students, may come under the spell, too. So much the better! It will do them good. Homeland, with all its associations, its simplicity and naturalness, is but an expression of my wife. It is hard to tell where Nature's influence ends and hers begins.

As for me, it seems to me that with all this beauty around, those yellow maple leaves just fallen, I ought to write better music. That chipmunk sitting on a post of my studio porch looks like a critic. That look in his eyes seems to say that he knows everything. It's a keen look, and he's listening hard. But perhaps he's only a music lover: one of those joyous spirits who see beauty in the sky above and in the earth beneath, and believe in their fellow men and help them on their way, and try their best to discover some beauty (deeply hidden, perhaps!) in their works.

GREGOR

DE LAS
TIERRAS ALTAS

GREGOR

DE LAS
TIERRAS ALTAS

SUZANNE COLLINS

TRADUCCIÓN DE ISABEL GONZÁLEZ-GALLARZA

ALFAGUARA

ALFAGUARA

Título original: GREGOR THE OVERLANDER
Publicado en español con la autorización de Scholastic Inc., 557 Broadway,
Nueva York, NY 10012, Estados Unidos

© Del texto: 2003, Suzanne Collins
© De las ilustraciones de cubierta: 2003, Daniel Craig
© Del diseño de cubierta: Dave Caplan
© De las ilustraciones de interiores: 2004, Juárez
© De la traducción: 2004, Isabel González-Gallarza

© De esta edición:
2007, Santillana USA Publishing Company, Inc.
2105 NW 86th Avenue
Miami, FL 33122, USA
www.santillanausa.com

Edición: Vanesa Pérez-Sauquillo
Dirección técnica: Víctor Benayas
Coordinación de diseño: Beatriz Rodríguez
Maquetación: Cristina Hiraldo
Cuidado de la edición para América: Isabel Mendoza

Alfaguara es un sello editorial del Grupo Santillana. Éstas son sus sedes:
ARGENTINA, BOLIVIA, CHILE, COLOMBIA, COSTA RICA, ECUADOR,
EL SALVADOR, ESPAÑA, ESTADOS UNIDOS, GUATEMALA, MÉXICO,
PANAMÁ, PARAGUAY, PERÚ, PUERTO RICO, REPÚBLICA DOMINICANA, URUGUAY
Y VENEZUELA.

Gregor de las Tierras Altas
ISBN-10: 1-59820-883-7
ISBN-13: 978-1-59820-883-2

Published in the United States of America
Printed by HCI Printing and Publishing, Inc.

10 09 08   1 2 3 4 5 6 7 8 9 10

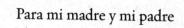Para mi madre y mi padre

ℙ

primera parte

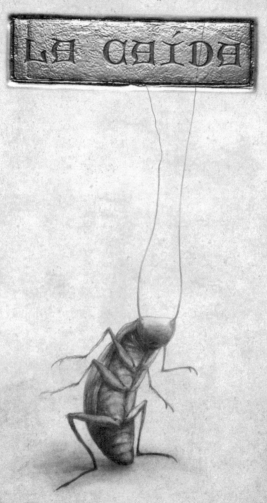

LA CAÍDA

CAPÍTULO PRIMERO

Gregor llevaba tanto tiempo con la cabeza apoyada en la malla del mosquitero que tenía impresa en la frente una multitud de cuadritos. Se tocó los bultitos con los dedos y resistió el impulso de dejar escapar el grito primitivo del hombre de las cavernas. En su pecho crecía por momentos ese largo aullido gutural reservado para las auténticas emergencias, tales como toparse desarmado con un tigre furioso, o que se apagara el fuego en plena Edad del Hielo. Llegó incluso a abrir la boca para respirar hondo, pero se contentó con golpear la cabeza contra el mosquitero con un débil quejido de frustración. «Agghh».

¿De qué servía gritar? No cambiaría nada. Ni el calor, ni el aburrimiento, ni el interminable verano que se extendía ante él.

Pensó en despertar a Boots, su hermanita de dos años, sólo para distraerse un poco, pero la dejó dormir. Por lo menos ella estaba fresquita en la habitación con aire acondicionado que compartía con Lizzie, su hermana de siete años, y con su abuela. Era la única habitación con aire acondicionado del apartamento. En las noches más calurosas, Gregor y su madre extendían colchas en el suelo para dormir, pero con cinco personas en la habitación, la temperatura ya no era fresca, sino apenas tibia.

Gregor sacó un cubito de hielo del congelador y se lo pasó por la cara. Miró al patio, y vio un perro vagabundo olisqueando un cubo de basura lleno hasta rebosar. El animal apoyó las patas en el borde y volcó el contenedor, esparciendo la basura por toda la acera. Gregor alcanzó a ver dos sombras que se alejaban corriendo a toda velocidad junto a la pared, e hizo una mueca. Ratas. Nunca terminaba de acostumbrarse a ellas.

Exceptuando las ratas, el patio estaba desierto. Normalmente se encontraba lleno de niños jugando a la pelota, saltando a la cuerda, o columpiándose. Pero por la mañana había pasado el autobús del campamento, llevándose con él a todos los niños entre los cuatro y los catorce años. Todos, menos uno.

—Lo siento, cariño, pero no puedes ir —le había dicho su madre hacía unas semanas. Y era cierto que lo sentía, Gregor lo había visto en la expresión de su rostro—. Alguien tiene que cuidar de Boots mientras yo estoy trabajando, y los dos sabemos que tu abuela ya no puede hacerlo.

Claro que lo sabía. Durante aquel último año, su abuela había estado entrando y saliendo de la realidad. En un momento estaba tan lúcida como una persona joven y, de repente, de buenas a primeras, se ponía a llamarlo Simón. ¿Quién era ese Simón? Gregor no tenía ni la menor idea.

Hace algunos años todo habría sido diferente. Por aquel entonces su madre sólo trabajaba media jornada; y su padre, que era profesor de ciencias en un instituto, estaba de vacaciones todo el verano. Él se habría ocupado de Boots. Pero desde aquella noche en que su padre desapareció, el papel de Gregor en la familia había cambiado. Era el mayor, por lo que habían recaído sobre él muchas responsabilidades. Cuidar de sus hermanas pequeñas era una de ellas.

De modo que Gregor se había limitado a contestar: «No pasa nada, mamá, de todas maneras, el campamento es para niños pequeños». Se había encogido de hombros para hacer ver que, a sus once años, el campamento ya no le interesaba. Pero sólo había conseguido que su madre se entristeciera más.

«¿Quieres que se quede Lizzie en casa contigo? ¿Para que te haga un poco de compañía?», le había preguntado.

Al oír esto, una expresión de pánico había cruzado el semblante de Lizzie. Probablemente se habría echado a llorar si Gregor no hubiera rechazado la idea. «No, deja que se vaya. Será divertido quedarme con Boots».

De modo que ahí estaba. No era divertido. No era divertido pasarse todo el verano encerrado con una niña de dos años y una abuela que pensaba que él era alguien llamado...

—¡Simón! —oyó a su abuela llamar desde el dormitorio. Gregor sacudió la cabeza, pero no pudo reprimir una sonrisa.

—¡Ya voy, abuela! —contestó, metiéndose en la boca lo que quedaba del cubito de hielo.

Un resplandor dorado invadía la habitación mientras los rayos del sol pugnaban por abrirse paso a través de las persianas. Su abuela estaba tumbada en la cama, cubierta con una fina colcha de retazos de algodón. Cada retazo provenía de algún vestido de los que la abuela se había ido haciendo a lo largo de los años. En sus momentos de mayor lucidez, repasaba los retazos con Gregor.

—Éste de lunarcitos lo llevé en la graduación de mi prima Lucy, cuando yo tenía once años; éste amarillo limón era de un vestido de fiesta, y éste blanco es de mi vestido de novia, no te miento.

Éste, sin embargo, no era un momento de lucidez.

—Simón —dijo, y su rostro mostró una expresión de alivio al verlo—. Pensé que se te había olvidado el almuerzo. Te entrará hambre después de arar la tierra.

Su abuela se había criado en una granja en Virginia, y había venido a Nueva York cuando se casó con su abuelo. Nunca se había acostumbrado del todo a la ciudad. A veces Gregor se alegraba secretamente de que, en su cabeza, la abuela pudiera regresar a su granja. Y le daba un poquito de envidia. No era nada divertido estar encerrado todo el tiempo en casa. A estas horas el autobús ya estaría llegando al campamento, y Lizzie y los demás niños estarían...

—¡Gue-go! —chilló una vocecita. Una cabecita rizada asomó por el borde de la cuna—. ¡Quero salir! —Boots se metió en la boca la punta empapada en saliva del rabo de un perrito de peluche y extendió ambos brazos hacia él. Gregor levantó a su hermanita por los aires y le dio besos ruidosos en la panza. Ella se rió, soltando el peluche. Gregor la dejó en el suelo para recogerlo.

—¡Llévate el sombrero! —le dijo su abuela, que seguía en algún lugar de Virginia.

Gregor le tomó la mano para tratar de atraer su atención al presente.

—¿Quieres beber algo fresquito, abuela? ¿Qué tal una gaseosa?

Ella se echó a reír.

—¿Una gaseosa? ¿Qué es, mi cumpleaños?

¿Qué se podía contestar a una pregunta así?

Gregor le apretó la mano y cogió a Boots en brazos.

—Vuelvo enseguida —dijo en voz alta.

Su abuela seguía riéndose.

—¡Una gaseosa! —repitió, secándose los ojos.

En la cocina, Gregor sirvió gaseosa helada en un vaso, y le preparó a Boots un biberón de leche.

—*Fío* —dijo la niña muy contenta, pasándoselo por la cara.

—Sí, bien fresquito, Boots —le contestó Gregor.

Se sobresaltó al oír el timbre de la puerta. Hacía más de cuarenta años que la mirilla no servía para nada.

—¿Quién es? —preguntó.

—Soy la señora Cormacci, cielo. ¡Le dije a tu madre que me pasaría a las cuatro a hacerle compañía a tu abuela! —le respondió una voz. Entonces Gregor recordó el montón de ropa sucia que tenía que llevar a la lavandería. Era un buen pretexto para salir un rato del apartamento.

Abrió la puerta y en el umbral encontró a la señora Cormacci derretida de calor.

—¡Hola! Qué horror, ¿verdad? ¡Con lo mal que soporto yo el calor! —Entró afanosamente, limpiándose el sudor con un viejo pañuelo—. Oh, eres un amor, ¿es para mí? —dijo, y antes de que Gregor pudiera decir nada, se había bebido la gaseosa de un solo trago, como si llevara varios días perdida en el desierto sin probar una gota de agua.

—Claro —farfulló Gregor, dirigiéndose a la cocina para servirle otra a su abuela. No le caía mal la señora Cormacci, y hoy era casi un alivio verla—. «Fantástico; apenas es el primer día y ya me emociono con la idea de ir a la lavandería», pensó Gregor. «Para cuando llegue septiembre, seguro que doy saltos de alegría sólo porque llega el recibo del teléfono».

La señora Cormacci le devolvió el vaso para que le sirviera otra gaseosa.

—Bueno, jovencito, ¿cuándo me vas a dejar que te eche las cartas? Ya sabes que tengo dotes adivinatorias —dijo. La señora Cormacci ponía anuncios en los buzones ofreciéndose para leer el tarot por diez dólares. «A ti no te cobro nada», solía decirle a Gregor. Él nunca aceptaba porque tenía la sospecha de que la señora Cormacci terminaría haciendo muchas más preguntas que él. Preguntas que no podía contestar. Preguntas sobre su padre.

Farfulló algo sobre que tenía que ir a la lavandería y se fue corriendo a buscar la ropa sucia. Conociendo a la señora Cormacci, probablemente tendría una baraja de cartas en el bolsillo.

Abajo, en la lavandería, Gregor separó la ropa lo mejor que supo, en tres montoncitos distintos: uno para la ropa blanca, otro para la de color y otro para la oscura... ¿Qué se suponía que tenía que hacer con los pantaloncitos a rayas blancas y negras de Boots? Los colocó en el montón de la ropa oscura, con la certeza de que era un error.

De todas maneras la mayor parte de su ropa tenía un colorcillo como tirando a gris, no porque hubiera desteñido al lavarla, sino de puro vieja. Los pantalones cortos de Gregor no eran más que sus viejos pantalones de invierno, cortados a la altura de las rodillas, y sólo tenía unas cuantas camisetas del año pasado, si es que no se le habían quedado pequeñas ya. Pero, ¿qué más daba? Si de todos modos se iba a quedar encerrado en casa todo el verano.

—¡Pelota! —gritó Boots, angustiada—. ¡Pelota!

Gregor extendió el brazo entre las secadoras y sacó la vieja pelota de tenis con la que Boots estaba jugando. La sacudió para desprender las pelusas que se le habían quedado pegadas y se la lanzó a su hermana. Boots corrió como un perrito detrás de ella.

«Qué pinta tienes», pensó Gregor con una risita. «¡Estás hecha un desastre!». Los restos del almuerzo —ensalada de huevo duro y natillas de chocolate— se veían con toda claridad en la carita y la camiseta de la niña. Tenía las manitas pintadas de rotulador violeta, y Gregor pensó que esas manchas no saldrían ni con amoniaco. El pañal le colgaba casi hasta las rodillas. Hacía demasiado calor para ponerle un pantalón corto.

Boots volvió corriendo hacia él blandiendo la pelota, con los rizos llenos de pelusas. Su carita sudorosa lucía una sonrisa de oreja a oreja mientras le tendía la pelota.

—¿Dime por qué estás tan contenta, Boots? —le preguntó.

—¡Pelota! —contestó, y luego chocó a propósito su cabeza contra la rodilla de Gregor, para que espabilara.

Gregor le lanzó la pelota por el pasillo, entre las lavadoras y las secadoras, y Boots salió corriendo tras ella.

Mientras proseguía el juego, Gregor trató de recordar la última vez que se había sentido tan feliz como Boots ahora con su pelota. Había habido momentos bastante buenos en los últimos dos años. La banda de música de la escuela pública había tocado en el Carnegie Hall. Eso había estado genial. Gregor incluso había tocado un solo con su saxofón. Las cosas siempre se veían mejor cuando tocaba; las notas de música parecían llevarlo a un mundo totalmente distinto.

El atletismo también estaba bien. A Gregor le gustaba correr por la pista, esforzar su cuerpo al máximo, hasta expulsar todo pensamiento de su mente.

Pero, si era sincero consigo mismo, Gregor sabía que hacía años que no había conocido la verdadera felicidad. Exactamente dos años, siete meses y trece días, pensó. No necesitaba pararse a contar, los números aparecieron automáticamente en su cabeza. Tenía una calculadora interna que siempre sabía exactamente cuánto tiempo hacía que había desaparecido su padre.

Claro que Boots podía sentirse feliz, ella entonces ni siquiera había nacido, y Lizzie tenía sólo cuatro años. Pero Gregor tenía ocho, y no se había perdido un solo detalle de cuanto había sucedido; por ejemplo, las llamadas desesperadas a la policía, que había reaccionado casi con aburrimiento al hecho de que su padre se hubiera desvanecido sin dejar rastro. Era obvio que pensaban que se había largado. Incluso habían dado a entender que había sido con otra mujer.

Pero eso no podía ser cierto. Si había algo de lo que Gregor estaba seguro, era de que su padre quería a su madre, que los quería a él y a Lizzie, y que habría querido también a Boots.

Pero, entonces... ¿cómo podía haberlos abandonado así, sin una sola palabra?

Gregor no podía creer que su padre fuera capaz de dejar tirada a su familia sin mirar atrás.

—Acéptalo —dijo en voz queda—. Está muerto. —Una oleada de dolor lo recorrió de arriba abajo. No era cierto. No podía ser cierto. Su padre iba a regresar porque... porque... ¿porque qué? ¿Porque lo deseaba tanto que tenía que ser verdad? ¿Porque lo necesitaban?—. «No», pensó Gregor. «Es porque lo presiento. Sé que va a regresar».

El ciclo de lavado llegó a su fin, y Gregor apiló toda la ropa en un par de secadoras.

—¡Y cuando vuelva, será mejor que tenga una buena explicación para justificar dónde ha estado todo este tiempo! —rezongó Gregor cerrando con fuerza la puerta de la secadora—. Por ejemplo, que se dio un golpe en la cabeza y olvidó quién era. O que lo secuestraron unos extraterrestres. —En la tele salía mucha gente que decía que había sido secuestrada por extraterrestres. A lo mejor podía ocurrir de verdad.

En su cabeza solía barajar distintas posibilidades, pero en casa raramente hablaban de su padre. Había un acuerdo tácito de que iba a regresar. Todos los vecinos pensaban que se había largado sin más. Los adultos nunca mencionaban a su padre, ni tampoco la mayoría de los niños; de todas maneras, cerca de la mitad de ellos tampoco tenía padre. Pero los desconocidos sí que preguntaban a veces. Tras cerca de un año de tratar de explicar lo que había pasado, Gregor se inventó la historia de que sus padres estaban divorciados y su padre vivía en California. Era mentira, pero la gente se lo creía, mientras que nadie parecía dispuesto a creerse la verdad, fuera cual fuera.

—Y cuando vuelva a casa me acompañará a... —empezó a decir Gregor en voz alta, y luego se detuvo. Estaba a punto de romper la norma. La norma consistía en que no podía pensar en cosas que ocurrirían cuando volviera su padre. Y como su padre podía volver en cualquier momento, Gregor no se permitía a sí mismo pensar en absoluto en el futuro. Tenía la extraña sensación de que si imaginaba acontecimientos concretos, como tener a su padre de vuelta en casa la próxima Navidad, o que ayudara a entrenar al equipo de atletismo, nunca sucederían. Además, por muy feliz que se sintiera mientras soñaba despierto, la vuelta a la realidad resultaba siempre más dolorosa. De modo que ésa era la norma. Gregor tenía que mantener su mente en el presente, y olvidarse del futuro. Era consciente de que su sistema no era muy bueno, pero era la mejor manera que había encontrado para sobrellevarlo.

Gregor se dio cuenta entonces de que Boots llevaba un tiempo sospechosamente callada. Miró a su alrededor y se asustó al no encontrarla inmediatamente. Entonces descubrió una sandalia rosa que sobresalía de la boca de la última secadora.

—¡Boots! ¡Sal de ahí! —gritó Gregor.

Había que vigilarla cuando había aparatos eléctricos cerca. Le encantaban los enchufes.

Mientras atravesaba corriendo la lavandería, Gregor oyó un sonido metálico y luego una risita de Boots. «Genial, ahora está destrozando la secadora», pensó apretando el paso. Cuando llegó al otro extremo de la habitación, se encontró cara a cara con una extraña escena.

La rejilla metálica que cerraba un viejo conducto de aire y que estaba fijada al marco por dos tornillos oxidados, se encontraba ahora abierta de par en par. Boots miraba por el agujero, de unos sesenta centímetros cuadrados, que se abría en la pared del edificio. Desde donde se encontraba, Gregor sólo veía oscuridad. Después vio una voluta de... ¿qué era aquello? ¿Vapor? ¿Humo? No parecía ni una cosa ni la otra. Un extraño vaho salía del agujero, formando espirales alrededor de Boots. La niña estiró los brazos con curiosidad y se inclinó hacia delante.

—¡No! —gritó Gregor lanzándose hacia ella, pero el conducto de aire pareció aspirar el cuerpecito de Boots. Sin pararse a pensar, Gregor metió la cabeza y los hombros en el agujero. La rejilla metálica se cerró de repente, golpeándole la espalda. Cuando quiso darse cuenta, Gregor estaba cayendo al vacío.

CAPÍTULO SEGUNDO

Gregor giró en el aire, tratando de colocar su cuerpo de manera que no cayera encima de Boots cuando chocaran contra el suelo del sótano, pero el impacto no llegó. Entonces recordó que la lavandería estaba en el sótano del edificio. ¿Adónde llevaba pues el agujero por el que habían caído?

Las volutas de vaho se habían convertido en una densa neblina que generaba una tenue luz. Gregor sólo alcanzaba a ver cerca de un metro en cada dirección. Sus dedos pugnaban desesperadamente por aferrar la neblina blanquecina, tratando de encontrar algún asidero, pero en vano. Estaba cayendo en picado a tanta velocidad que su ropa se inflaba como un globo alrededor del cuerpo.

—¡Boots! —gritó. La voz retumbó con un eco sobrecogedor. Así que pensó que el agujero debía de tener paredes. Volvió a llamar—: ¡Boots!

Oyó una risita alegre unos metros más abajo.

—¡*Gue-go*, yupiiii! —exclamó Boots.

«Debe creer que está en un gran tobogán, o algo así», pensó Gregor. «Bueno, por lo menos no tiene miedo».

Él sí tenía, y mucho. Fuera lo que fuera este extraño agujero por el que habían caído, tenía que tener fondo. Esa caída en picado por el espacio sólo podía terminar de una manera.

El tiempo pasaba. Gregor no sabía exactamente cuánto, pero mucho más de lo normal. La profundidad de un agujero tenía que tener un límite, a la fuerza. Llegado un momento, uno tenía que toparse con agua, o con rocas, o con las placas tectónicas, o algo.

Era como esa pesadilla recurrente suya. Soñaba que estaba en un lugar alto, donde se suponía que no debía estar, como el tejado de su escuela. Mientras caminaba por el borde, la materia sólida bajo sus pies se derrumbaba de repente, y él caía. Todo desaparecía salvo la sensación de estar cayendo al vacío, de que el suelo se acercaba cada vez más, y un terror inmenso lo invadía. Entonces, justo en el momento del impacto, se despertaba sobresaltado, empapado en sudor, con el corazón acelerado.

«¡Un sueño! ¡Me he quedado dormido en la lavandería y ésta es la pesadilla de siempre!», pensó Gregor. ¡Claro! ¿Qué otra cosa podía ser si no?

Tranquilizado por la idea de que estaba dormido, Gregor empezó a calcular el tiempo de su caída. No tenía reloj, pero cualquiera podía contar segundos.

—Uno... dos... tres... —Cuando llegó a setenta dejó de contar y volvió a sentir que lo invadía el pánico. Aunque esto fuera un sueño, tenía que aterrizar en algún momento, ¿no?

Justo entonces Gregor se percató de que la neblina se disipaba ligeramente. Pudo entonces vislumbrar las superficies lisas y oscuras de una pared circular. Al parecer, estaban cayendo por un amplio tubo oscuro. Notó una corriente ascendente que se elevaba por debajo de él. Las últimas volutas de vaho se desvanecieron, y Gregor fue perdiendo velocidad. Su ropa se desinfló.

Por debajo de él oyó un pequeño golpe, y luego el suave tamborileo de las sandalias de Boots. Unos segundos después, sus propios pies tocaron tierra firme. Trató de orientarse, sin atreverse a avanzar en ninguna dirección. Estaba sumido en la más completa oscuridad. Cuando sus ojos se fueron acostumbrando al lugar, distinguió a su izquierda un tenue rayo de luz.

Detrás de éste se oyó un alegre chillido.

—¡Un bicho! ¡Un bicho *gande*!

Gregor corrió hacia la luz que se colaba por una estrecha grieta entre dos paredes rocosas muy lisas. Consiguió a duras penas escurrirse por la apertura. Su zapato tropezó con algo, haciéndole perder el equilibrio, y fue a dar de bruces contra el suelo.

Cuando levantó la cabeza, Gregor se encontró cara a cara con la cucaracha más grande que había visto en toda su vida.

En el edificio donde vivía había insectos bastante grandes. La señora Cormacci aseguraba haber visto uno tan grande como su mano, que había subido por el desagüe de la bañera, y de hecho nadie lo ponía en duda. Pero la criatura que tenía Gregor delante medía por lo menos un metro y medio de altura, y eso que estaba sentada sobre las patas traseras, una postura muy extraña para una cucaracha, por cierto...

—¡Un bicho *gande*! —volvió a exclamar Boots, y Gregor consiguió cerrar la boca. Se irguió sobre las rodillas, pero con todo tuvo que inclinar la cabeza hacia atrás para ver entera a la cucaracha. Ésta llevaba una especie de antorcha. Boots corrió hacia Gregor y le tiró del cuello de la camisa.

—¡Un bicho *gande*! —insistió.

—Sí, ya lo veo, Boots. ¡Un bicho grande! —dijo Gregor en voz baja, rodeándola muy fuerte con los brazos—. Un bicho... muy... grande.

Se esforzó por recordar qué comían las cucarachas. Basura, comida podrida... ¿gente? No, no le parecía que comieran gente. Por lo menos, no las cucarachas pequeñas. A lo mejor sí pretendían comerse a las personas, pero éstas siempre se las arreglaban para pisarlas antes de que les diera tiempo a intentarlo. Fuera como fuere, éste no era el mejor momento para averiguarlo.

Tratando de aparentar naturalidad, Gregor fue retrocediendo despacio hacia la grieta.

—Bueno, señor insecto, nosotros ya nos íbamos, no se mosquee, digo no se moleste, digo...

—¿Huele qué, tan bien, huele qué? —siseó una voz, y Gregor tardó un minuto entero en darse cuenta de que provenía de la cucaracha. Estaba demasiado estupefacto como para acertar a comprender lo que había dicho.

—Eh... ¿qué, perdón? —consiguió articular.

—¿Huele qué, tan bien, huele qué? —volvió a sisear la voz, pero el tono no era amenazador. Tan sólo curioso, y tal vez un poco ilusionado—. ¿Eres pequeño humano, eres?

«Muy bien, estoy hablando con una cucaracha gigante», pensó Gregor. «Sé amable y simpático, y contéstale al insecto. Quiere saber "¿huele qué, tan bien, huele qué?", así que díselo». Con gran esfuerzo, Gregor inspiró una buena cantidad de aire por la nariz, y al segundo se arrepintió de haberlo hecho. Sólo había una cosa que oliera de esa manera.

—¡*Teno* caca! —contestó oportunamente Boots—. ¡*Teno* caca, *Gue-go*!

—Mi hermana necesita un pañal limpio —dijo Gregor, un poquito avergonzado.

Le pareció que su respuesta impresionaba ligeramente a la cucaracha.

—Ah. ¿Ir más cerca podemos, más cerca, podemos? —preguntó la cucaracha, barriendo el suelo delicadamente con una de sus patas.

—¿Quiénes? —preguntó Gregor. Entonces, a su alrededor, vio que otras siluetas emergían de la oscuridad. Los montículos negros y lisos que había tomado por rocas eran en realidad los lomos de alrededor de una docena de enormes cucarachas. Éstas se arremolinaron entusiasmadas alrededor de Boots, agitando al aire sus antenas, y estremeciéndose de placer.

Boots, que adoraba cualquier tipo de piropo, supo instintivamente que la estaban admirando. Extendió sus bracitos regordetes hacia los enormes insectos.

—*Teno* caca —les dijo con un aire enternecedor. Las cucarachas emitieron un siseo apreciativo.

—¿Es ella princesa, Tierras Altas, es ella? ¿Es ella

reina, es ella? —preguntó la cucaracha que parecía el jefe, postrando la cabeza en un gesto de devoción absoluta.

—¿Boots? ¿Una reina? —preguntó Gregor. No pudo contener una carcajada.

Su risa pareció desconcertar a las cucarachas, que se echaron para atrás, algo tensas.

—¿Ríes por qué, Tierras Altas, ríes por qué? —siseó una de ellas, y Gregor comprendió que las había ofendido.

—Pues porque... porque somos pobres, y ella... ella es un poquito desastre y... ¿cómo me estás llamando? ¿Tierras Altas? —concluyó con aire poco convincente.

—¿No eres humano de Tierras Altas, no eres? De Tierras Bajas no eres, no eres —dijo la cucaracha que llevaba la antorcha, mirándolo de cerca—. Aspecto tienes, pero olor no tienes.

Y entonces pareció que el jefe de los insectos caía en la cuenta de algo.

—Rata mala. —Se volvió hacia sus compañeros—. ¿Dejamos aquí a Tierras Altas, dejamos? —Las cucarachas se congregaron para deliberar y se pusieron a hablar todas a la vez.

Gregor oía trozos de conversación, pero no lograba entender nada. Estaban tan enfrascadas en su discusión que pensó en tratar de escapar. Miró a su alrededor. A la tenue luz de la antorcha, le pareció ver que se encontraban en un túnel largo y llano. «Para volver tenemos que ir hacia arriba, no hacia los lados», pensó. Con Boots en brazos nunca podría escalar las paredes del tubo por el que habían caído.

Las cucarachas tomaron una decisión.

—Ven, Tierras Altas, ven. Vamos con humanos —dijo el líder.

—¿Humanos? —preguntó Gregor aliviado—. ¿Hay otros seres humanos aquí abajo?

—¿Montas, Tierras Altas, montas? ¿Corres, Tierras Altas, corres? —preguntó la cucaracha, y Gregor entendió que se estaba ofreciendo para llevarlo a cuestas. No parecía lo suficientemente robusta como para aguantar su peso, aunque Gregor sabía que algunos insectos, como por ejemplo las hormigas, podían soportar varias veces su propio peso. Durante un segundo cruzó por su mente una horrible imagen en la que se veía a sí mismo tratando de subirse a lomos de la cucaracha, y aplastándola con su peso.

—Creo que mejor iré caminando. Bueno, quiero decir corriendo —contestó Gregor.

—¿Monta, la princesa, monta? —preguntó la cucaracha con aire esperanzado, agitando obsequiosamente las antenas y postrándose ante Boots. Gregor iba a decir que no, pero, sin pensárselo dos veces, la pequeñita se subió a lomos del insecto. Debería habérselo imaginado. A Boots le encantaba sentarse sobre las gigantescas tortugas metálicas del zoológico de Central Park.

—Está bien, pero me tiene que dar la mano —exigió Gregor, y Boots se agarró obedientemente de su dedo.

La cucaracha se puso en camino inmediatamente, y Gregor tuvo que correr para no quedarse atrás. Sabía que las cucarachas se movían deprisa; había visto a su madre tratando de matar a muchas. Aparentemente, estas cucarachas gigantes eran capaces de alcanzar una velocidad proporcional a su tamaño. Por fortuna, el suelo del túnel era llano, y Gregor había concluido su entrenamiento de atletismo hacía tan sólo unas semanas. Acompasó su paso al de las cucarachas y pronto encontró un ritmo que le resultaba cómodo.

El túnel empezó a describir curvas y más curvas. Las cucarachas tomaban por caminos laterales, y a veces incluso volvían sobre sus pasos para escoger una nueva ruta. Tras unos minutos, Gregor estaba totalmente perdido, y la imagen mental del camino que había ido formando en su cabeza se parecía a los dibujos llenos de garabatos sin sentido que hacía Boots. Renunció a tratar de recordar el camino y se concentró en mantener el ritmo de los insectos. «Vaya, pensó, ¡estos bichos corren a toda máquina!».

Gregor empezó a jadear, pero las cucarachas no mostraban signos visibles de cansancio. No tenía ni idea de lo lejos que podía quedar su destino. No tendría nada de raro que estuviera a cientos de kilómetros, considerando lo que aguantaban corriendo estos bichos.

Justo cuando estaba a punto de decirles que necesitaba descansar, Gregor percibió un sonido que le resultó familiar. Al principio pensó que era imposible, pero conforme se fueron aproximando, sus dudas se despejaron. Era el clamor de una multitud, y a juzgar por la intensidad, debía de ser muy grande. Pero, ¿dónde había espacio para una multitud en esos túneles?

El suelo empezó a describir una abrupta pendiente, y Gregor tuvo que frenar para no pisar a la cucaracha que iba a la cabeza. Algo suave y ligero le rozó la cara y los brazos. ¿Una tela? ¿Alas? Atravesó frente a él y, de repente, una luz inesperada lo cegó. Instintivamente, Gregor se llevó la mano a los ojos para protegerlos hasta que se acostumbraran a la repentina claridad.

Una muchedumbre dejó escapar un suspiro de sorpresa. Había acertado en lo de la multitud. Después reinó un silencio sobrecogedor, y Gregor se sintió observado por innumerables ojos.

Empezó a comprender dónde se encontraba. En realidad no era tanta la claridad. De hecho, era más bien una luz como la del atardecer, pero Gregor llevaba tanto tiempo sumido en la oscuridad, que por contraste le pareció muy intensa. Lo primero que distinguió fue el suelo, que parecía cubierto de un musgo verde oscuro, pero no irregular, sino liso como pavimento. Lo sentía mullido bajo sus pies. «Es un campo», pensó. «Para algún tipo de deporte. Por eso hay una multitud. Estoy en un estadio».

Gradualmente apareció ante sus ojos una pared muy lisa, de unos quince metros de altura, que rodeaba una amplia cueva ovalada. Toda la parte superior de la pared estaba ocupada por tribunas. Gregor recorrió con la mirada las filas lejanas de espectadores, esperando ver el techo del estadio. En su lugar, sus ojos se toparon con los atletas.

Una docena de murciélagos describían lentas espirales alrededor del campo. El color de su manto iba del amarillo pálido hasta el negro más oscuro. Gregor calculó que el más pequeño tendría una envergadura de unos cinco metros. Seguro que la multitud estaba contemplándolos en el momento en que ellos irrumpieron en el estadio, porque el resto del campo estaba vacío. «Quizá hacen como los romanos, y dan de comer humanos a los murciélagos. Quizá sea ése el motivo por el que nos trajeron aquí las cucarachas», pensó.

Algo cayó de uno de los murciélagos. Golpeó el suelo en el centro del estadio, y rebotó, elevándose como a tres metros en el aire. Gregor pensó: «Pero si es una...».

—¡Pelota! —exclamó Boots, y antes de que Gregor pudiera detenerla, se bajó de la cucaracha, esquivó los cuerpos de los demás insectos, y echó a correr por la superficie de musgo, con sus torpes pasitos de bebé.

—Qué elegante, la princesa, qué elegante —siseó embelesada una cucaracha mientras Gregor se lanzaba tras su hermana. Los insectos se habían echado a un lado gustosos para dejar pasar a Boots, pero ahora se erguían ante Gregor como en una carrera de obstáculos. Una de dos, o trataban de frenarlo intencionalmente, o estaban tan cautivados por la belleza de Boots que se habían olvidado por completo de él.

La pelota rebotó en el suelo por segunda vez y volvió a elevarse por los aires. Boots corrió tras ella, con los bracitos extendidos por encima de su cabeza, siguiendo su trayectoria.

Cuando Gregor logró zafarse de las cucarachas y echó a correr tras su hermana, una sombra pasó por encima de él. Al levantar la mirada vio horrorizado que un murciélago dorado se lanzaba en picado sobre Boots. Gregor no podría alcanzarla a tiempo.

—¡Boots! —gritó, sintiendo que se le contraía el estómago.

Su hermana se dio la vuelta hacia él y vio entonces el murciélago. Se le iluminó por completo el rostro y gritó, señalando...

—*¡Mulcélago!*

«¡Caray!», pensó Gregor. «¿Es que a esta niña no le da miedo nada?».

El murciélago descendió en picado sobre Boots, rozando suavemente con su cuerpo el índice extendido de la niña, y luego volvió a elevarse describiendo una pirueta. En el punto más alto de su trayectoria, el murciélago, que estaba volando cabeza abajo, extendió el cuerpo por completo. Gregor pudo ver entonces por vez primera que había alguien montado encima. El jinete rodeaba con sus piernas el cuello del murciélago. Gregor descubrió entonces que se trataba de una chica.

La muchacha aflojó la presión de las piernas y abandonó su montura. Ejecutó un perfecto doble salto mortal hacia atrás, girando su cuerpo en el último momento para colocarse frente a Gregor, y aterrizó sobre el suelo con la misma delicadeza que un felino, justo delante de Boots. Extendió una mano, sobre la cual cayó la pelota, en lo que a Gregor le pareció una auténtica proeza de sincronización, o la más pura suerte.

Contempló el rostro de la chica. La expresión arrogante que vio reflejada en él le hizo comprender que las acrobacias anteriores no eran, en absoluto, cuestión de suerte.

CAPÍTULO TERCERO

era, por mucho, la persona más extraña que Gregor había visto en su vida. Tenía la piel tan clara que se le transparentaban todas las venas del cuerpo. Gregor se acordó de la sección de anatomía humana de su libro de Ciencias. Pasabas una página y aparecía el esqueleto. Pasabas a la siguiente página, y veías el sistema digestivo. Esta chica era un sistema circulatorio con patas.

A primera vista le pareció que tenía el pelo gris, como su abuela; pero luego vio que era de un color más bien plateado, como rubio con un tono metálico. Lo llevaba recogido en una complicada trenza que le caía por la espalda, y cuyo extremo había remetido por debajo de su cinturón, a la altura de la cadera. Una fina banda de oro rodeaba su cabeza. Podría haber sido algún tipo de diadema, pero Gregor tenía la desagradable sensación de que se trataba de una corona.

No quería que esa chica estuviera al mando. Por su postura altanera, por la media sonrisa que se le escapaba por la comisura izquierda de los labios, por la manera en que se las arreglaba para que pareciera que lo miraba desde arriba, aunque Gregor le sacara un palmo por lo menos, se veía que la chica tenía verdadera presencia. Eso era lo que solía comentar su madre de algunas de las chicas que él conocía. «Esa chica tiene verdadera presencia», decía, sacudiendo la cabeza, pero Gregor se daba cuenta de que su madre lo decía en un tono de aprobación.

Bueno, una cosa era tener presencia, y otra muy distinta ser una auténtica creída.

A Gregor no le cabía duda de que había hecho el numerito del doble salto mortal hacia atrás sólo para impresionarlo. Con una sola voltereta habría sido suficiente. Era su manera de intimidarlo, pero Gregor no tenía intención de dejarse intimidar. La miró directamente a los ojos y entonces vio que sus iris eran de un deslumbrante violeta pálido. Gregor sostuvo su mirada sin pestañear.

No sabía cuánto tiempo habrían permanecido allí de pie, midiéndose mutuamente, si Boots no llega a intervenir. La niña se abalanzó sobre la chica, haciéndole perder el equilibrio. Ésta dio un paso atrás, mirando a Boots como si no diera crédito a lo que acababa de suceder.

Boots esbozó una sonrisa encantadora y extendió una manita regordeta.

—¿Pelota? —preguntó esperanzada.

La chica clavó la rodilla en el suelo y le tendió la pelota, sin soltarla.

—Es tuya si consigues quitármela —dijo con una voz como sus ojos: fría, clara y extraña.

Boots trató de coger la pelota, pero la chica no hacía nada por soltarla. Desconcertada, la niña tiró de los dedos de la muchacha.

—¿Pelota?

La chica negó con la cabeza.

—Si la quieres, tienes que ser más fuerte o más inteligente que yo.

Boots levantó la mirada hacia ella. En ese momento se dio cuenta de algo, y le metió un dedo en el ojo.

—*¡Lioleta!* —exclamó.

La chica se echó bruscamente hacia atrás, soltando la pelota. Boots corrió tras ella y la atrapó. Gregor no pudo evitar decir:

—Me parece que la niña es más inteligente que tú.

—No era un comentario muy amable, pero no le había gustado nada que hiciera rabiar de esa manera a su hermana.

La chica entrecerró los ojos.

—Pero tú, desde luego, no lo eres. De lo contrario, no le hablarías así a una reina.

De modo que había acertado: la chica tenía sangre real. Ahora probablemente le cortaría la cabeza, o algo así. Sin embargo, Gregor tenía la sensación de que sería contraproducente mostrar temor. Se encogió de hombros.

—No, de haber sabido que eras una reina, supongo que te habría dicho algo mucho más chévere.

—¿Chévere? —preguntó la chica, arqueando las cejas con asombro.

—Algo mejor —dijo Gregor, a falta de una palabra más chévere, justamente.

La chica decidió tomárselo como una disculpa.

—Te perdono, pues veo que no obraste a sabiendas. ¿Cómo te llamas?

—Gregor. Y ésta es Boots —contestó, señalando a su hermana—. Bueno, su verdadero nombre no es ése, sino Margaret, pero la llamamos Boots porque en invierno se pone las botas de todos y se lanza a corretear con ellas por toda la casa; y también por un músico que le gusta a mi padre. —Esa explicación le pareció confusa al propio Gregor—. ¿Y tú cómo te llamas?

—Soy la reina Luxa —contestó la chica.

—¿Luc-sa? —pronunció Gregor, tratando de reproducir la extraña entonación.

—¿Qué significa eso, lo que dice la bebé? *¿Líoleta?* —preguntó.

—Violeta. Es su color preferido. Tus ojos son color violeta, y ella nunca había visto antes unos ojos así —explicó Gregor.

Boots oyó la palabra y se acercó mostrando sus manitas manchadas todavía de rotulador violeta.

—*¡Líoleta!*

—Yo nunca había visto unos ojos de color marrón. No en un ser humano —observó Luxa, mirando a Boots a los ojos—. Ni esto. —Tomó a Boots por la muñeca y acarició su suave piel morena—. Ha de necesitar mucha luz.

Boots soltó una risita. Tenía cosquillas por todo el cuerpo. Luxa la acarició a propósito por debajo de la barbilla, para hacerla reír. Durante un segundo, la reina perdió su pose, y Gregor pensó que a lo mejor no era tan creída. Pero acto seguido se irguió y recuperó sus aires altaneros.

—Bien, Gregor de las Tierras Altas, tú y la bebé se tienen que bañar.

Gregor sabía que estaba sudado por la carrera por los túneles, pero aun así le pareció un comentario muy grosero.

— Mejor aún, creo que nos vamos a ir.

—¿Irse? ¿Adónde? —preguntó Luxa sorprendida.

—A casa —contestó Gregor.

—¿Oliendo como huelen? —replicó Luxa—. Estarían muertos antes de alcanzar el Canal, y eso aunque supieran qué camino tomar. —Se dio cuenta de que Gregor no entendía—. Llevan el olor de las Tierras Altas. Eso aquí no es seguro para ustedes. Ni para nosotros.

—Ah —contestó Gregor, sintiéndose un poco tonto—. Bueno, entonces supongo que será mejor que nos enjuaguemos un poco antes de volver a casa.

—No es tan sencillo. Pero dejaré que sea Vikus quien te lo explique —dijo Luxa—. Grande ha sido hoy su ventura, al ser hallados tan pronto.

—¿Cómo sabes que nos han encontrado pronto? —preguntó Gregor.

—Nuestros vigías los detectaron al poco tiempo de tocar tierra. Como han sido los reptantes los primeros en encontrarlos, les hemos permitido que vengan a presentarlos —explicó.

—Ah, entiendo —contestó Gregor. ¿Dónde estaban los vigías? ¿Ocultos en la oscuridad de los túneles? ¿Escondidos en algún lugar entre la neblina que habían atravesado al caer? Hasta llegar al estadio, no había visto a nadie aparte de las cucarachas.

—En cualquier caso, se dirigían hacia aquí —añadió Luxa, señalando con un gesto a los insectos—. ¿Ves?, llevan antorchas. No se molestarían si no tuvieran intención de visitarnos.

—¿Y eso por qué? —quiso saber Gregor.

—Los reptantes no necesitan luz. Pero nos la muestran a nosotros para que sepamos que vienen en son de paz. ¿No les extrañó lo sencillo que les resultó llegar hasta aquí? —preguntó. Sin esperar respuesta, se volvió hacia las cucarachas que aguardaban pacientemente a un lado del campo—. Reptantes, ¿qué quieren a cambio de los de las Tierras Altas?

El líder de las cucarachas avanzó hacia ellos.

—¿Das cinco cestos, das? —siseó.

—Les daremos tres cestos de grano —contestó Luxa.

—Las ratas dan muchos peces —replicó la cucaracha, limpiándose las antenas con parsimonia, como si la cosa no fuera con ella.

—Pues entonces llévenlos con las ratas. Eso *no les dará tiempo* —contestó Luxa.

Gregor no sabía exactamente de qué estaban hablando, pero tenía la desagradable sensación de que lo habían puesto en venta.

El insecto consideró la última oferta de Luxa.

—¿Das cuatro cestos, das? —preguntó.

—Daremos cuatro cestos, y uno más en agradecimiento —dijo una voz detrás de Gregor. Éste se dio la vuelta y vio a un hombre de tez clara y barba que se acercaba a ellos. Su cabello corto era de verdad plateado, no rubio metálico como el de la chica.

Luxa miró enojada al hombre, pero no intentó llevarle la contraria.

La cucaracha sumó trabajosamente cuatro cestos más uno con sus patas.

—¿Das cinco cestos, das? —preguntó, como si la idea le resultara totalmente nueva.

—Daremos cinco cestos —dijo Luxa sin un ápice de amabilidad, haciéndole una seca reverencia al insecto. Éste le devolvió el gesto de cortesía y se marchó corriendo del estadio seguido de los demás bichos.

—Y si de Vikus dependiera, pronto no nos quedaría ninguno —declaró la chica, lanzándole al hombre una mirada cargada de significado. Éste se había volteado para observar a Gregor y Boots.

—Cinco cestos no me parece que sea un alto precio si él es el Esperado —contestó. Sus ojos violetas se posaron sobre a Gregor con atención—. Dime, muchacho, ¿vienes de...? —Hizo un esfuerzo por recordar las palabras—. ¿Nueva York?

CAPÍTULO CUARTO

Omo si le hubieran arrojado una jarra de agua fría, Gregor regresó de pronto a la realidad. Desde que se había caído por el agujero, las cosas habían sucedido tan deprisa, que Gregor apenas había tenido tiempo de asimilarlas. Ahora, en ese momento de calma momentánea, las palabras «Nueva York» lo sacaron de su estupor.

¡Sí! Él era un chico que vivía en Nueva York, tenía que lavar la ropa en la lavandería y volver a casa con su hermanita antes de que su madre... ¡Su madre!

—¡Tengo que volver a casa ahora mismo! —articuló Gregor atropelladamente.

Su madre trabajaba de recepcionista en la consulta de un dentista. Normalmente terminaba su jornada a las cinco y llegaba a casa a las cinco y media. Se preocuparía muchísimo si al volver descubría que él y Boots habían desaparecido. Sobre todo después de lo que le había pasado a su padre. Gregor trató de calcular cuánto tiempo habría transcurrido desde que bajó a la lavandería. «Probablemente tardamos unos cinco minutos en caer, pongamos, y luego calculo que habremos corrido durante unos veinte minutos, y aquí debemos de llevar unos diez», pensó. Treinta y cinco minutos en total.

—¡Muy bien, entonces la ropa ya debe de estar seca! —exclamó en voz alta—. Si volvemos dentro de unos veinte minutos, creo que no habrá problema. —Nadie los buscaría antes, y Gregor podría subir la ropa y doblarla en casa.

—De verdad, necesito volver a mi casa ahora mismo —le dijo a Vikus.

El anciano seguía observándolo atentamente.

—Bajar resulta sencillo, pero subir requiere mucho afán.

—¿Qué quiere decir con eso? —preguntó Gregor, sintiendo un nudo en la garganta.

—Quiere decir que no pueden regresar a casa —contestó Luxa rotundamente—. Deben permanecer con nosotros en las Tierras Bajas.

—¡Huy, no! ¡No, gracias! —exclamó Gregor—. O sea, quiero decir, ustedes son todos muy simpáticos, ¡pero tengo cosas que hacer... arriba! —dijo—. ¡Gracias, otra vez! ¡Ha sido un placer conocerlos! ¡Vamos, Boots!

Gregor alzó a su hermana en brazos y se dirigió al arco por el que habían desaparecido las cucarachas. Con el rabillo del ojo vio que Luxa levantaba la mano. Durante un segundo pensó que le estaba diciendo adiós, pero no podía ser. Luxa no era tan amable como para hacer algo así.

—¡Si no es un gesto de despedida, entonces es una señal! —le murmuró a Boots, e inmediatamente, se precipitó hacia la salida.

Podría haberlo conseguido de no haber tenido que cargar con Boots, pero con ella en brazos le resultaba muy difícil correr. A pocos metros de la salida, el primer murciélago pasó volando a ras del suelo delante de él, haciéndolo caer de espaldas. Su cuerpo amortiguó la caída de Boots, y ésta se le sentó inmediatamente sobre el estómago para disfrutar del espectáculo.

Todos los murciélagos del estadio se habían lanzado en picado y volaban en un círculo estrecho sobre Gregor y Boots, encerrándolos en una cárcel de alas y pelo. Sobre cada uno iba un jinete de tez tan clara y cabello tan plateado como Luxa. Pese a la proximidad y la velocidad de los murciélagos, ninguno de los jinetes tenía dificultad para mantenerse en su montura. De hecho, sólo unos cuantos se molestaban en agarrarse. Un chico con aires de gallito, montado sobre un murciélago de un negro brillante, estaba incluso tumbado sobre el lomo del animal, con la barbilla apoyada en una mano.

Los jinetes no apartaban la mirada de los prisioneros. Mientras pasaban a toda velocidad, Gregor vio que la expresión de sus rostros iba desde la diversión, hasta la más completa hostilidad.

Boots saltó sobre su estómago, aplaudiendo.

—¡Mulcélagos! ¡Mulcélagos! ¡Mulcélagos! ¡Mulcélagos!

«Bueno, por lo menos uno de los dos se está divirtiendo», pensó Gregor.

A Boots le encantaban los murciélagos. En el zoológico, si la dejaban, era capaz de pasarse horas y horas delante del cristal que separaba a los visitantes de la cueva de los murciélagos. En el interior del pequeño habitáculo oscuro, cientos de murciélagos revoloteaban continuamente sin chocar unos con otros. Podían hacerlo gracias a una cosa que se llama ecolocalización. Los murciélagos emiten un sonido que produce un eco al chocar contra algo sólido, y así son capaces de ubicarlo. Gregor había leído el texto que explicaba este fenómeno por lo menos mil veces mientras esperaba a que Boots se cansara de mirar los murciélagos. Se sentía casi un experto en la materia.

—¡*Mulcélagos*! ¡*Mulcélagos*! ¡*Mulcélagos*! —cantaba Boots, utilizando el estómago de su hermano como cama elástica. Mareado, Gregor se incorporó apoyándose sobre los codos, y depositó a su hermana en el suelo. Lo último que le faltaba era vomitar delante de esa gente.

Se puso en pie. Boots le rodeó la rodilla con el brazo y se apoyó en él. El círculo de murciélagos se cerró aún más.

—¿Qué pasa? ¿Acaso creen que quiero ir a alguna parte? —preguntó Gregor fastidiado. Oyó reír a un par de jinetes.

Luxa debió de haber hecho otra señal, porque los murciélagos se elevaron en el aire todos a la vez y se pusieron a describir complicados círculos por encima del campo. Gregor se dio cuenta de que ni ella ni Vikus se habían molestado en moverse de donde se encontraban. Miró hacia la salida y supo que era inútil. Con todo... esta gente era un poquito más arrogante de la cuenta.

Gregor corrió tres pasos hacia la salida antes de girar en redondo para dirigirse hacia Luxa, agarrando de camino la mano de su hermana. Agarrados por sorpresa, los murciélagos rompieron la formación y se lanzaron en picado hacia abajo, pero cuando se quisieron dar cuenta, no había nadie a quien capturar. Volvieron a levantar torpemente el vuelo, y aunque no llegaron a chocar unos con otros, Gregor se alegró de ver que algunos jinetes tuvieron que esforzarse por no caer de sus monturas.

La multitud, que había guardado un silencio sobrecogedor desde su aparición, rompió a reír, apreciando el espectáculo. Gregor se sintió un poco más seguro de sí mismo. Por lo menos no era el único que había quedado como un idiota.

—Se han quedado con dos palmos de narices —le murmuró a Boots.

Luxa le dedicó una mirada helada, pero Gregor vio que Vikus trataba de reprimir una sonrisa mientras se acercaba a él.

—Bueno, ¿habías dicho algo de un baño, no? —le preguntó a Luxa.

—Diríjanse al palacio ahora mismo —dijo ésta enfadada. Chasqueó los dedos, y su murciélago dorado descendió hacia ella. Justo cuando estaba a punto de chocarla, Luxa saltó en el aire. Estiró las piernas hacia los lados, tocándose los dedos de los pies con la punta de las manos, en un movimiento que Gregor recordó haber visto hacer a las porristas del equipo de su escuela. El murciélago se agachó para colocarse por debajo de ella, y ésta aterrizó sin esfuerzo sobre su lomo. El animal se arqueó, levantó el vuelo y pasó rozando el cuerpo de Gregor. Tras enderezarse en el aire, salió zumbando del estadio.

—¡Pierdes el tiempo con esas tonterías! —le gritó Gregor, pero Luxa estaba ya demasiado lejos para oírlo. Estaba enfadado consigo mismo porque no tenía más remedio que reconocer que esa chica lo impresionaba.

Pero Vikus sí lo oyó. Su sonrisa se ensanchó. Gregor lo miró con el ceño fruncido.

—¿Qué pasa?

—¿Les gustaría acompañarnos al palacio? —le preguntó Vikus con mucha educación.

—¿En calidad de qué, de prisionero? —preguntó Gregor sin rodeos.

—En calidad de invitado, espero —contestó Vikus—. Aunque no me cabe duda de que la reina Luxa ha ordenado que les preparen el calabozo. —Sus ojos violetas lanzaron destellos, y Gregor se dio cuenta de que le caía bien ese hombre, a pesar de todo. Tal vez porque estaba bastante seguro de que él le caía bien a Vikus. Sin embargo, resistió la tentación de sonreír.

—Muéstreme el camino —le dijo con aire indiferente.

Vikus asintió con la cabeza y le indicó con un gesto que lo siguiera hacia el otro extremo del campo. Gregor lo siguió a unos pasos, tirando de Boots.

Las gradas estaban empezando a desocuparse. Allá en lo alto, la gente iba saliendo paulatinamente por unas puertas colocadas entre las tribunas. Fuera cual fuera el juego que se había estado desarrollando, había terminado al aparecer Gregor. Algunos murciélagos y sus jinetes seguían volando alrededor del estadio, ejecutando maniobras aerodinámicas. Permanecían allí para vigilarlo.

A pocos metros de la entrada principal del estadio, Vikus se rezagó y dejó que Gregor lo alcanzara.

—Debes de sentirte como atrapado en un sueño.

—Más bien una pesadilla —replicó Gregor tranquilamente. Vikus se rió.

—Nuestros murciélagos y reptantes... no, ¿cómo los llamas tú? ¿Cucamonas?

—Cucarachas —corrigió Gregor.

—Ah, sí, cucarachas —repitió Vikus—. En las Tierras Altas no son sino unas pocas, pero aquí se dan en abundancia.

—¿Cómo lo sabe? ¿Ha estado en las Tierras Altas? —preguntó Gregor. Si Vikus había conseguido llegar hasta allí, entonces también podrían hacerlo él y Boots.

—Oh, no, las visitas de ese tipo son tan escasas como los árboles. Son los habitantes de las Tierras Altas quienes nos visitan a veces. Yo he conocido a seis o siete. Uno llamado Fred Clark, otro llamado Mickey y, más recientemente, una mujer que se hacía llamar Coco. ¿Cuál es tu nombre? —preguntó Vikus.

—Gregor. ¿Están todavía aquí? ¿Están todavía aquí los de las Tierras Altas? —preguntó Gregor muy esperanzado.

—Infortunadamente, no. Éste es un lugar hostil para ellos —contestó Vikus, y su semblante se ensombreció.

Gregor se detuvo, tirando bruscamente de Boots.

—¿Quiere decir que los mataron?

Al instante comprendió que sus palabras habían insultado al anciano.

—¿Nosotros? ¿Nosotros, humanos, matar a los habitantes de las Tierras Altas? Conozco tu mundo, conozco los males que lo asolan. ¡Pero nosotros no matamos por diversión! —declaró Vikus severamente—. Hoy los hemos acogido entre nosotros. ¡Si los hubiéramos rechazado, te aseguro que ahora mismo no estarían respirando!

—No quise decir eso... O sea, es que yo no tengo ni idea de cómo funcionan aquí las cosas —farfulló Gregor. Aunque debería haberse imaginado que no era muy diplomático sugerir que Vikus podía ser un asesino—. Entonces, ¿nos hubieran matado las cucarachas?

—¿Los reptantes? —dijo Vikus—. No, de ningún modo, *eso no les daría tiempo.*

Otra vez esa expresión. ¿Qué significaba eso de «dar tiempo» a las cucarachas?

—Pero si nadie más sabe siquiera que estamos aquí —objetó Gregor.

Vikus lo miró con expresión grave. El enfado había dado paso a la preocupación.

—Créeme, muchacho, ahora ya toda criatura de las Tierras Bajas sabe que están aquí.

Gregor resistió el impulso de mirar a su espalda.

—Y eso no es bueno, ¿verdad?

Vikus negó con la cabeza.

—No. Eso no es bueno en absoluto.

El anciano se volvió hacia la salida del estadio. A cada lado de dos gigantescas puertas de piedra había media docena de guardias de tez clara y ojos violetas. Necesitaron la fuerza de todos para abrir las puertas lo suficiente para que pudiera pasar Vikus.

Gregor cruzó también tirando de Boots, e inmediatamente cerraron las puertas a su espalda. Siguió a

Vikus por un túnel flanqueado de antorchas de piedra hasta un pequeño arco cubierto por algo oscuro que se agitaba. Gregor pensó que tal vez serían más murciélagos, pero observándolo con atención descubrió que se trataba de una nube de diminutas polillas negras. ¿Era esto mismo lo que había atravesado antes, al entrar al estadio?

Vikus penetró suavemente con la mano la cortina de insectos.

—Estas polillas son un sistema de alerta empleado tan sólo en las Tierras Bajas, según tengo entendido. En el preciso instante en que la trayectoria de vuelo de las polillas se ve perturbada por un intruso, todos y cada uno de los murciélagos de la zona lo detectan. Este sistema se me antoja perfecto en su extrema sencillez —explicó antes de desaparecer entre las polillas.

Al otro lado de la cortina de diminutas alas, Gregor le oyó anunciar:

—¡Gregor de las Tierras Altas, bienvenido a la ciudad de Regalia!

Gregor bajó la vista hacia Boots, que lo miraba con una expresión perpleja.

—¿*Mamos* a casa, *Gue-go*? —preguntó.

Él la cogió en brazos y la apretó dulcemente para tranquilizarla.

—Ahora no, linda. Primero tenemos que hacer unas cuantas cosas aquí. Después podremos irnos a casa.

Gregor respiró hondo y atravesó decidido la cortina de polillas.

CAPÍTULO QUINTO

L a cortina de alas aterciopeladas acarició su mejilla. Al dejarla atrás, la ciudad de Regalia apareció
ante sus ojos.

—¡Guau! —exclamó, deteniéndose en seco. Gregor
no sabía muy bien qué se había imaginado. Casas de piedra,
tal vez, o cuevas, algo primitivo, a fin de cuentas. Pero la
grandiosa ciudad que se extendía ante él no tenía nada de
primitiva.

Se encontraban al pie de un valle ocupado por los
edificios más hermosos que había visto en su vida. Nueva
York era famosa por su arquitectura, sus elegantes casas
de piedra rojiza, sus altísimos rascacielos y sus grandiosos
museos. Pero comparada con Regalia, no parecía una urbe
planeada, sino más bien un lugar en el que alguien hubiera
alineado un puñado de cajas de distintas y extrañas formas.

Aquí, los edificios eran todos de un hermoso gris
brumoso que les confería un aspecto onírico. Parecían sur-
gir directamente de la roca, como si fueran parte de ella, y
no un producto de la mano del hombre. Tal vez no fueran
tan altos como los rascacielos cuyos nombres Gregor conocía, pero se elevaban muy por encima de su cabeza. Algunos

tenían hasta treinta pisos, y estaban rematados por artísticos picos y torres. Había cerca de un millar de antorchas dispuestas estratégicamente de manera que una tenue luz iluminara toda la ciudad.

Y los relieves... Gregor había tenido ocasión de ver angelitos y gárgolas en otros edificios, pero los muros de Regalia bullían de vida. Figuras humanas, cucarachas, peces y criaturas cuyos nombres Gregor no conocía luchaban, se divertían y bailaban en cada milímetro de espacio concebible.

—¿Aquí sólo vive gente, o también cucarachas y murciélagos? —preguntó Gregor.

—Ésta es una ciudad de humanos. Las demás criaturas tienen sus propias ciudades, o tal vez «tierras» sea la palabra más adecuada —explicó Vikus—. La mayor parte de nuestro pueblo vive aquí, aunque algunos habitan en la periferia, si así lo exige su trabajo. He ahí nuestro palacio —indicó Vikus, dirigiendo la mirada de Gregor hacia una enorme fortaleza de forma circular que se erguía al otro extremo del valle—. Hacia allí nos encaminamos.

Las luces que brillaban en las numerosas ventanas daban a la ciudad un aire festivo, y Gregor sintió que las sombras de su corazón se disipaban un poco. Nueva York también resplandecía toda la noche... Después de todo, tal vez este lugar no fuera tan extraño.

—Es fantástico —comentó. Le hubiera encantado explorar Regalia, pero tenía que volver urgentemente a su casa.

—Sí, lo es —corroboró Vikus, y sus ojos abarcaron la ciudad con una expresión admirativa—. Mi pueblo tiene en gran estima la piedra. Si tuviéramos tiempo, creo que tal vez podríamos crear una tierra de belleza singular.

—Pues yo creo que ya lo consiguieron —dijo Gregor—. O sea, ésta ciudad es mil veces más bonita que cualquier ciudad de las Tierras Altas.

Vikus parecía contento.

—Ven, el palacio ofrece la mejor vista de la ciudad. Tendrás tiempo de admirarla antes de cenar.

Mientras Gregor seguía sus pasos por la calle, Boots echaba la cabeza hacia atrás, moviéndola de lado a lado.

—¿Qué buscas, Boots?

—¿Luna? —preguntó la niña. Desde su casa rara vez se veían las estrellas, pero si la noche era clara sí se veía la luna—. ¿Luna?

Gregor levantó la vista hacia el cielo de un negro como de tinta china, y entonces cayó en la cuenta de que, por supuesto, no había luna. Se encontraban en una especie de gigantesca cueva subterránea.

—No hay luna, linda, esta noche no —le dijo.

—El sol se la comió —dijo la niña como si se tratara de la cosa más normal del mundo.

—Ajá —convino Gregor. Si las cucarachas hablaban, y los murciélagos jugaban a la pelota, ¿entonces por qué no podría ser verdad eso también? Suspiró al recordar el viejo libro de cuentos guardado en una caja junto a la cuna de Boots.

La gente se quedaba mirándolos desde las ventanas sin ningún disimulo. Vikus saludaba a algunas personas por sus nombres, o con un gesto de cabeza, y éstas le devolvían el saludo con la mano.

Boots se dio cuenta y empezó a saludar a todo el mundo ella también.

—¡Hola! —exclamó—. ¡Hola! —Aunque ningún adulto le devolvió el saludo, Gregor vio que algunos niños agitaban las manitas a su paso.

—Les produces una gran fascinación —explicó Vikus, señalando a la gente en las ventanas—. No recibimos muchas visitas de las Tierras Altas.

—¿Cómo supo que yo era de Nueva York? —preguntó Gregor.

—Que nosotros sepamos, sólo existen cinco puertas de comunicación con las Tierras Bajas —explicó Vikus—. Dos de ellas llevan a la Tierra de la Muerte, pero no hubieras sobrevivido. Otras dos desembocan en el Canal, pero tus ropas están secas. Están vivos, están secos, por lo que conjeturo que cayeron por la quinta puerta, que sé que se halla en Nueva York.

—¡En nuestra lavandería! —exclamó Gregor—. ¡Justo en el edificio en el que vivimos! —De alguna manera, el hecho de que su lavandería conectara con ese extraño lugar hizo que se sintiera como si hubieran invadido su territorio.

—Tu lavandería, sí —dijo Vikus pensativo—. Bueno, la caída de ustedes coincidió con las corrientes de manera muy favorable.

—¿Las corrientes? ¿Se refiere a esa especie de vaho? —preguntó Gregor.

—Sí, les permitieron llegar aquí sanos y salvos. La sincronización lo es todo —dijo Vikus.

—¿Qué pasa si no hay sincronización? —inquirió Gregor, aunque ya se imaginaba la respuesta.

—Entonces, en lugar de un huésped, tenemos un cuerpo que enterrar —contestó Vikus serenamente—. A decir verdad, eso es lo más frecuente. Un habitante de las Tierras Altas que llega vivo como tú, acompañado de una hermana, es francamente algo singular.

Les tomó unos buenos veinte minutos alcanzar el palacio. Gregor sentía cómo le temblaban los brazos de cargar con Boots, pero no quería dejarla en el suelo. No le parecía seguro, con todas esas antorchas alrededor.

Conforme se iban aproximando a la espléndida estructura, Gregor se percató de que en sus paredes no había ningún relieve. La superficie era lisa como el cristal, y la ventana más baja se abría a unos sesenta metros del suelo. Algo no le cuadraba del todo, pero no sabía qué era. Faltaba algo.

—No hay puerta —comentó en voz alta.

—No —confirmó Vikus—. Las puertas son para quienes carecen de enemigos. Ni el mejor escalador podría subir por estos muros.

Gregor acarició el muro de piedra lisa. No había una sola grieta, ni siquiera la más mínima hendidura.

—Y entonces, ¿cómo entran?

—Por lo general, volando; pero si nuestros murciélagos no están disponibles... —Vikus hizo una señal por encima de su cabeza.

Gregor inclinó el cuello hacia atrás y vio que desde una gran ventana rectangular estaban bajando rápidamente una plataforma. Estaba fijada a unas cuerdas, y se inmovilizó a treinta centímetros del suelo. Vikus subió sobre ella.

Gregor subió a su vez con Boots. Su reciente caída a las Tierras Bajas no había hecho sino reforzar su aversión a las alturas. La plataforma se elevó inmediatamente, y Gregor tuvo que agarrarse de una de las cuerdas para no perder el equilibrio. Vikus permanecía tranquilo, con las manos cruzadas sobre el pecho; pero bueno, él no cargaba con una niña pequeña que no paraba de moverse, y probablemente ya habría montado en ese aparato un millón de veces.

El ascenso fue rápido y regular. La plataforma se detuvo a la altura de una ventana, delante de una pequeña escalera de piedra. Gregor y Boots entraron en una espaciosa sala de techos abovedados. Allí esperaba para darles la bienvenida un grupo de tres habitantes de las Tierras Bajas, todos con la misma piel transparente y esos extraños ojos color violeta.

—Buen atardecer —los saludó Vikus, acompañando sus palabras con un gesto de cabeza—. Les presento a los hermanos Gregor y Boots, de las Tierras Altas, que recientemente han caído entre nosotros. Hagan el favor de bañarlos, y a continuación procedan al Gran Salón. —Vikus salió de la habitación sin mirar atrás.

Gregor y los demás se observaron unos a otros, incómodos. Ninguno de ellos mostraba la arrogancia de Luxa, ni la imperiosa presencia natural de Vikus. «Son gente normal», pensó Gregor. «Apuesto a que se sienten tan raros como yo».

—Encantado de conocerlos —dijo, cambiándose a Boots a la otra cadera—. Boots, di hola.

—¡Hola! —obedeció la niña, saludándolos con la mano, con una expresión de total felicidad—. ¡Hola, hola!

El recelo del grupo se fundió como el hielo. Todos se echaron a reír, y sus cuerpos se relajaron. Su risa contagió a Gregor. Su madre solía decir que Boots no sabía lo que era un extraño, lo cual quería decir que pensaba que todo el mundo era su amigo.

A veces, a Gregor le hubiera gustado parecerse un poquito más a su hermana. Tenía un par de buenos amigos en la escuela, pero evitaba formar parte de ningún grupito. Al final, lo importante era con quién te sentabas en el comedor. Podría haberse sentado con los chicos de su equipo de atletismo, o con los de la banda de música. Pero a él le gustaba en cambio estar con Angelina, que siempre andaba metida en la preparación de alguna obra de teatro, y Larry, a quien lo que más le gustaba en el mundo era dibujar. Los que no lo conocían bien pensaban que Gregor era un estirado, pero en realidad más que nada era tímido. Y le resultaba aun más difícil abrirse a la gente desde la desaparición de su padre. Pero incluso antes, nunca había sido tan extrovertido como Boots.

Una chica de unos quince años dio un paso adelante, tendiendo los brazos.

—Mi nombre es Dulcet. ¿Puedo tomarte en brazos, Boots? ¿Deseas tomar un baño? —Boots miró a Gregor como pidiéndole aprobación.

—Está bien. Es la hora del baño. ¿Quieres un bañito, Boots? —le dijo.

—¡Sííí! —exclamó Boots muy contenta—. ¡A bañar! —Tendió los brazos hacia Dulcet, que se hizo cargo de ella inmediatamente.

—Te presento a Mareth y a Perdita —dijo Dulcet, indicando con la mano al hombre y a la mujer que estaban a su lado. Ambos eran altos y musculosos y, pese a no llevar armas, Gregor tuvo la impresión de que eran guardias.

—Hola —les dijo.

Mareth y Perdita lo saludaron con un gesto de cabeza formal, aunque no exento de cordialidad.

Dulcet arrugó la nariz y le dio a Boots una palmadita en la panza.

—Necesitas un paño empapador limpio —dijo.

Gregor se imaginaba lo que podía ser aquello.

—Ah, sí, hay que cambiarle el pañal. —Hacía rato que su hermanita necesitaba un pañal limpio—. Le va a salir un sarpullido.

—¡*Teno* caca! —exclamó Boots sin la menor disculpa, tirándose del pañal.

—Me ocuparé de ello —contestó Dulcet con una sonrisa divertida. Gregor no pudo evitar pensar que era muchísimo más simpática que Luxa—. ¿Quieres proceder a tomar las aguas, Gregor de las Tierras Altas?

—Sí, gracias, procederé a tomar las aguas —contestó. Le llamó la atención lo formales que sonaron sus propias palabras, y temió que pensaran que se estaba burlando de ellos. Recordó lo fácilmente que se habían ofendido las cucarachas—. O sea, quiero decir que sí, gracias.

Dulcet asintió con la cabeza y esperó a que Gregor

la alcanzara. Mareth y Perdita cerraban la marcha, unos pasos detrás. «Sí, son guardias», pensó Gregor.

El grupo abandonó el vestíbulo y caminó por un ancho pasillo. Pasaron por delante de docenas de puertas en forma de arco que se abrían sobre amplias cámaras, escaleras y vestíbulos. Gregor no tardó en darse cuenta de que necesitaría un mapa para orientarse por el palacio. Podía pedir ayuda, pero eso no sería muy inteligente si su intención era escapar. Bien podían llamarlo su huésped, pero eso no cambiaba el hecho de que Boots y él eran prisioneros. Los huéspedes podían marcharse si querían. Los prisioneros tenían que escaparse. Y eso era exactamente lo que pensaba hacer.

Pero, ¿cómo? Aunque lograra encontrar el camino de vuelta a la plataforma, nadie lo dejaría bajar, y no podría saltar al suelo desde esa altura. «Pero tiene que haber otras formas de entrar en el palacio», pensó. «Tiene que haber...».

—Nunca había conocido a nadie de las Tierras Altas —dijo Dulcet, interrumpiendo el hilo de sus pensamientos—. Y si ahora tengo el honor de hacerlo es sólo por la bebé.

—¿Por Boots? —preguntó Gregor.

—Estoy a cargo de los más pequeños —explicó Dulcet—. Normalmente yo nunca llegaría a conocer a alguien tan importante como un habitante de las Tierras Altas —añadió tímidamente.

—Pues es una pena, Dulcet —dijo Gregor—, porque eres la persona más simpática que he conocido desde que estoy aquí.

Dulcet se sonrojó, ¡y caray, cuando esta gente se sonrojaba, se sonrojaba de verdad! Su piel se tornó del color de una sandía madura. Y no sólo la piel de su rostro, sino la de todo su cuerpo, de los pies a la cabeza.

—Oh —balbuceó avergonzada—. Oh, ésa es una gentileza que no puedo aceptar. —Detrás de él, los dos guardias se susurraron algo al oído.

Gregor adivinó que había dicho algo totalmente fuera de lugar, pero no sabía exactamente qué. Tal vez, se suponía que no podías dar a entender que una niñera era más simpática que la propia reina. Aunque fuera verdad. De ahora en adelante, tendría que tener más cuidado con lo que decía.

Afortunadamente, en ese mismo momento se detuvieron en el umbral de una puerta. Gregor oyó agua correr, y unas nubes de vapor se escaparon hasta el pasillo.

«Debe de ser el cuarto de baño», pensó. Miró hacia dentro y vio que una pared dividía la habitación en dos secciones.

—Me llevaré a Boots, y tú te quedarás aquí —dijo Dulcet, indicando una de las secciones.

Gregor se imaginó que las chicas estarían a un lado, y los chicos al otro, como en un vestidor. Pensó que tal vez debía quedarse con Boots, pero algo le decía que podía confiar en Dulcet. Además, no quería volver a disgustarla.

—¿Está bien, Boots? ¿Nos vemos luego?

—¡Adiós, adiós! —dijo Boots agitando la manita por encima del hombro de Dulcet. Estaba claro que la separación no le angustiaba en absoluto.

Gregor se dirigió hacia la derecha. Aquel lugar sí que parecía un vestidor, si es que los vestidores podían ser bonitos y oler bien. En las paredes había relieves de exóticas criaturas marinas, y unas lámparas de aceite iluminaban la sala con un tenue resplandor. «Bueno, sí, pero estos de aquí parecen bancos y casilleros», pensó, abarcando con la mirada los bancos de piedra y la hilera de cubículos que ocupaban uno de los lados de la sala.

Mareth lo había seguido al interior. Se dirigió a Gregor nerviosamente.

—Éste es el cuarto para cambiarse. Aquí están las cámaras de alivio y limpieza. ¿Necesitas algo de mí, Gregor de las Tierras Altas?

—No, gracias, en esto me las arreglo yo solo —le contestó Gregor.

—Estaremos en el pasillo por si nos necesitas — añadió Mareth.

—Muchas gracias —respondió Gregor. Cuando el guardia se agachó para cruzar el umbral, Gregor sintió que los músculos de su cara se relajaban. Se alegraba de estar por fin solo.

Efectuó una rápida inspección del lugar. En la cámara de alivio no había nada más que un sólido asiento de piedra con una abertura en el centro. Gregor miró dentro y vio una corriente de agua que fluía continuamente por debajo. «Ah, esto debe de ser el retrete», pensó.

En la cámara de limpieza había una pequeña piscina llena de agua humeante, con unos escalones de piedra que llevaban al fondo de la cubeta. Una rica fragancia impregnaba el aire. Todo su cuerpo anhelaba sumergirse en el agua.

Gregor volvió rápidamente al cuarto para cambiarse y se deshizo de su ropa sudada. Sintiéndose algo cohibido, orinó en el retrete. Luego se dirigió rápidamente hacia la piscina. Comprobó la temperatura con la punta del pie, y entró despacio en el agua caliente. Le llegaba sólo hasta la cintura, pero entonces descubrió que un banco bordeaba todo el perímetro de la piscina. Cuando se sentó, el agua le llegó hasta las orejas.

Una corriente de agua lo cubrió entonces, deshaciendo los nudos de tensión que agarrotaban los músculos de sus hombros y su espalda. Gregor cortó la superficie de la piscina con la mano, dejando que el agua se escapara entre sus dedos. Como en el retrete, el agua entraba por un extremo, y salía por el otro.

«Debe de tratarse de alguna corriente subterránea, o algo así», pensó.

De repente, cayó en la cuenta de algo importante, y se incorporó rápidamente. ¡El agua entraba y salía por algún sitio!

Si el agua podía entrar y salir del palacio... entonces tal vez él también podría hacerlo.

CAPÍTULO SEXTO

Gregor se frotó el cuerpo con una esponja y una sustancia viscosa que encontró en un cuenco junto a la piscina. Se la untó también en el pelo, y se limpió incluso el interior de las orejas, con el deseo de eliminar hasta el más mínimo rastro de olor de su cuerpo. Si quería escapar, debía pasar lo más desapercibido posible. Colgadas de unos ganchos junto a la piscina había unas toallas blancas. Gregor no podía identificar el grueso tejido con el que estaban fabricadas.

—Algodón no es, seguro —murmuró, pero el paño era suave y absorbía el agua mucho mejor que las toallas delgadas y gastadas que usaban en su casa.

Salió de la cámara de limpieza, secándose el pelo, y descubrió que su ropa había desaparecido. En su lugar encontró montoncito de prendas de un color azul grisáceo dobladas con mucho esmero. Había una camisa, unos pantalones y algo que parecía ropa interior. Eran mucho más delicadas que las toallas, y la tela tenía un tacto sedoso. «¿Qué material será éste?», se preguntó mientras se ponía la camisa.

Se calzó un par de sandalias de esparto trenzado y salió de la habitación. Mareth y Perdita lo estaban esperando.

—¿Dónde está mi ropa? —les preguntó.

—La hemos quemado —dijo Mareth con aprensión. Gregor se dio cuenta entonces de que el guardia temía que él se enfadara por ello.

—Sería muy peligroso conservarla —dijo Perdita, a modo de explicación—. Las cenizas no conservan el olor.

Gregor se encogió de hombros para hacerles ver que no le importaba.

—Está bien —dijo—. Ésta me gusta.

Mareth y Perdita mostraron una expresión de agradecimiento.

—Luego de unos pocos días de consumir nuestra comida, también tú irás perdiendo el olor —dijo Perdita en tono alentador.

—Muy bien —contestó Gregor secamente. Esta gente estaba francamente obsesionada con su olor.

Dulcet emergió de la sección izquierda del cuarto de baño llevando en brazos a una Boots limpia y contenta. Vestía una suave camisa rosa y un pañal limpio fabricado con el mismo material que la toalla de baño de Gregor. La niña extendió la pierna y se señaló orgullosamente las sandalias nuevas.

—Za-pa-to —le dijo a Gregor.

—Yo también —dijo él, estirando la pierna para enseñarle sus sandalias.

Supuso que también habrían quemado la ropa de Boots. Trató de recordar lo que llevaba por si acaso su madre le pedía explicaciones. Un pañal sucio, eso no era ninguna pérdida. Un par de sandalias rosas que de todas maneras ya se le estaban quedando pequeñas, y una camiseta manchada. Suponía que no habría ningún problema.

Gregor no sabía exactamente lo que le diría a su madre sobre las Tierras Bajas... la verdad, le daría un susto de muerte. Ya se inventaría algo cuando estuviera de vuelta en la lavandería; pero cuanto antes regresaran, más sencilla habría de ser la historia.

Boots le tendió los brazos y Gregor la alzó, hundiendo la nariz en sus rizos húmedos. Olía a limpio, y un poco como a mar.

—Ya está bien crecida —comentó Dulcet—. Tus brazos deben estar cansados. —Volvió a entrar en el cuarto para cambiarse y salió con una especie de bolsa. La ajustó a la espalda de Gregor con unas correas, y colocó en ella a Boots, que así sentada podía mirar por encima de su hombro. Gregor había visto en Nueva York gente que llevaba así a sus bebés, en mochilas especialmente diseñadas para ello, pero su familia no tenía dinero para ese tipo de lujos.

—Gracias —dijo como si apenas le diera importancia al regalo, pero por dentro estaba eufórico. Sería mucho más fácil escapar llevando a Boots en una mochila que en brazos.

Dulcet los hizo subir por varias escaleras, atravesando un laberinto de pasillos. Desembocaron por fin en una enorme habitación que se abría sobre una terraza.

—Llamamos a esta habitación el Gran Salón — dijo Dulcet.

—¿Ah, sí?, pues me parece que se les olvidó el techo —comentó Gregor. Las paredes estaban decoradas con sumo gusto, pero por encima de sus cabezas no había nada más que la oscuridad de la cueva.

Dulcet se echó a reír.

—Oh, no, así es como debe ser. A menudo recibimos aquí a nuestros invitados, y pueden llegar muchos murciélagos a la vez. —Gregor se imaginó el atasco que provocaría un centenar de murciélagos tratando de entrar por la puerta. Ahora comprendía las ventajas de una pista de aterrizaje amplia.

Vikus los esperaba en la terraza, acompañado de una mujer mayor. Gregor calculó que tendría más o menos la edad de su abuela, aunque ella estaba encorvada y le costaba moverse por culpa de la artritis. Esta mujer, en cambio, tenía un porte erguido y parecía muy fuerte.

—Gregor y Boots de las Tierras Altas, les presento a Solovet, mi esposa —dijo Vikus.

—Hola —contestó Gregor—, encantado de conocerla.

Pero la mujer dio un paso adelante y le ofreció ambas manos. El gesto no dejó de sorprenderlo. Nadie más había hecho ademán alguno de tocarlo desde su caída.

—Bienvenido, Gregor. Bienvenida, Boots —dijo con una voz cálida y baja—. Es un honor tenerlos entre nosotros.

—Gracias —farfulló Gregor, confundido porque las palabras de la mujer contradecían su estatus de prisionero. Lo hacían sentir verdaderamente especial.

—¡Hola! —dijo Boots. Solovet extendió la mano para acariciarle la mejilla.

—Según me dice Vikus, deseas fervientemente regresar a casa. Me entristece que no podamos ayudarlos inmediatamente, pero buscar esta noche la superficie sería imposible —dijo—. En este momento, las Tierras Bajas son un hervidero de rumores sobre su llegada.

«Me imagino que todos querrán vernos, como si fuéramos animales de feria, o algo así. Pues bien, será mejor que se den prisa en mirar», pensó Gregor. Pero dijo:

—Entonces, tendré tiempo de darme una vuelta por aquí para conocer todo esto.

Vikus le hizo una seña para que se acercara a la barandilla que rodeaba la terraza.

—Ven, ven, hay mucho que ver —le dijo.

Gregor se acercó a la barandilla y sintió que se le formaba un nudo en el estómago. Retrocedió unos pasos involuntariamente. La terraza parecía colgar literalmente de una de las paredes del palacio. Tan sólo lo separaba del vertiginoso abismo la pequeña superficie de piedra.

—No temas, está muy bien construida —dijo Vikus para tranquilizarlo.

Gregor asintió con la cabeza, pero se quedó donde estaba. Si la terraza empezaba a derrumbarse, quería poder refugiarse en el Gran Salón.

—Veo bien desde aquí —dijo, y era verdad.

Desde arriba, Regalia era aún más impresionante. Desde el suelo no podía ver que las calles, cuyos adoquines tenían tonalidades distintas, estaban dispuestas formando complejos motivos geométricos que conferían a la ciudad el aspecto de un gigantesco mosaico. Tampoco se había fijado en lo grande que era. Se extendía varios kilómetros a la redonda.

—¿Cuánta gente vive aquí? —preguntó Gregor.

—Nuestro número asciende aproximadamente a tres mil —contestó Vikus—. Más, si la cosecha es buena.

Tres mil habitantes. Gregor trató de imaginarse cuánto podía ser eso. En su escuela había unos seiscientos estudiantes, así que sería como seis veces su escuela.

—Bueno, y a todo esto, ¿qué están haciendo aquí abajo? —preguntó Gregor.

Vikus se echó a reír.

—Nos sorprende que hayas tardado tanto en preguntar. Pues bien, es una historia maravillosa —dijo Vikus, respirando hondo para empezar a contarla—. Hace muchos años, vivía...

—¡Vikus! —lo interrumpió Solovet—. Tal vez la historia sea un buen acompañamiento para la cena.

Gregor le dio las gracias mentalmente. Estaba muerto de hambre, y algo le decía que Vikus era de los que se enrollan como una persiana.

El comedor se encontraba en una habitación contigua al Gran Salón. La mesa estaba puesta para ocho. Gregor esperaba que Dulcet cenara con ellos, pero después de sentar a Boots en una especie de trono, retrocedió y permaneció de pie a unos pasos de la mesa. Gregor no se sentía cómodo cenando con la muchacha allí de pie, pero pensó que le causaría problemas si decía algo.

Ni Vikus ni Solovet hicieron ademán de sentarse, por lo que él también decidió esperar. Poco después entró Luxa en la habitación, con un atuendo mucho más elegante que el que vestía en el estadio. Llevaba el pelo suelto, y le caía hasta la cintura como una brillante cortina de plata. La acompañaba un chico de unos dieciséis años que se estaba riendo de algo que Luxa acababa de decir. Gregor lo reconoció: lo había visto en el estadio. Era ese jinete tan presumido que se tumbaba tranquilamente sobre el lomo de su murciélago mientras describían círculos por encima de la cabeza de Gregor.

«Otro engreído», pensó. Pero el chico le lanzó una mirada tan simpática que decidió no precipitarse en sus juicios. Luxa era algo desagradable, pero la mayoría de los humanos de las Tierras Bajas eran bastante simpáticos.

—Mi primo, Henry —dijo Luxa lacónicamente, y a Gregor le dieron ganas de reír. Aquí, entre todos esos nombres tan extraños, había un Henry.

Éste se inclinó con una gran reverencia y se acercó a Gregor sonriendo.

—Bienvenido, Gregor —dijo. Luego lo agarró del brazo y le dijo en un susurro teatral—: ¡Cuidado con el pescado, Luxa planea envenenarte esta misma noche!

Vikus y Solovet se rieron, y hasta Dulcet sonrió. Era una broma. Esta gente tenía sentido del humor.

—Cuidado con tu pescado, Henry —replicó Luxa—. Di orden de envenenar a los sinvergüenzas, pero olvidé que tú también cenabas con nosotros esta noche.

Henry le hizo un guiñó a Gregor.

—Cambia tu plato con el de los murciélagos —susurró, y en ese momento dos murciélagos aterrizaron en el Gran Salón y entraron en el comedor—. ¡Ah, los murciélagos!

Gregor reconoció al murciélago dorado que Luxa montaba por la tarde en el estadio. El otro, uno grande y gris, se acomodó sobre una silla junto a Vikus, batiendo las alas, tras de lo cual todos los demás tomaron asiento a su vez.

—Gregor de las Tierras Altas, te presento a Aurora y a Eurípides. Están vinculados a Luxa y a mí mismo —declaró Vikus, extendiendo la mano hacia el murciélago gris sentado a su derecha. Eurípides la rozó con su ala. Luxa y su murciélago dorado esbozaron el mismo gesto.

Gregor se había imaginado que los murciélagos serían como caballos para los humanos, pero ahora veía que eran sus iguales. Se preguntó si también hablarían.

—Yo te saludo, Gregor de las Tierras Altas —dijo Eurípides con un suave susurro.

Pues sí, sí hablaban. Gregor empezó a preguntarse si el pescado que le iban a servir de cena no querría también charlar un poquito antes de que lo cortara en trocitos.

—Encantado de conocerte —dijo Gregor educadamente—. ¿Qué significa eso de que están vinculados unos a otros?

—Al poco tiempo de llegar a las Tierras Bajas, nosotros los humanos creamos una alianza especial con los murciélagos —explicó Solovet—. Ambas partes vieron las ventajas obvias de aunar fuerzas. Pero más allá de esa alianza, individualmente, los humanos y los murciélagos pueden formar sus propias uniones. A eso lo llamamos vincularse.

—¿Y qué hace uno cuando está vinculado a un murciélago? —preguntó Gregor—. Quiero decir, aparte de jugar a la pelota y tal.

Hubo una pausa en la que los comensales intercambiaron miradas. Otra vez había vuelto a meter la pata.

—Mantenernos con vida el uno al otro —dijo Luxa fríamente.

Les había parecido que se burlaba de algo serio.

—Ah, no lo sabía —se disculpó Gregor.

—Por supuesto que no lo sabías —dijo Solovet, lanzándole una ojeada a Luxa—. En tu propia tierra no tienen nada similar.

—¿Y también se vinculan con los reptantes? —quiso saber Gregor.

Henry soltó una carcajada despectiva.

—Antes preferiría vincularme a una piedra. Por lo menos estaría seguro de que no echaría a correr en el momento de la batalla.

Luxa sonrió.

—Y una piedra siempre podría servirnos de arma arrojadiza. Aunque supongo que también se puede lanzar a un reptante...

—¡Pero para eso tendría que tocarlo! —exclamó Henry, y los dos estallaron en sonoras carcajadas.

—Los reptantes no son famosos por sus habilidades guerreras —le dijo Vikus a Gregor a modo de explicación. Ni él ni Solovet reían. Se volvió hacia Luxa y Henry—. Y sin embargo, perduran. Tal vez, cuando logren comprender las razones de su longevidad les tendrán más respeto.

Henry y Luxa trataron de fingir seriedad, pero sus ojos seguían riendo.

—Para los reptantes tiene poca relevancia el que yo los respete o no —dijo Henry displicentemente.

—Tal vez, pero en cambio es de vital importancia para Luxa. O así lo será dentro de cinco años cuando tenga edad de reinar —dijo Vikus—. En ese momento, las bromas necias a expensas de los reptantes tal vez marquen la diferencia entre nuestra existencia o nuestra aniquilación. No necesitan ser guerreros para alterar el equilibrio de poder en las Tierras Bajas.

Estas palabras terminaron de calmar a Luxa, pero apagaron la conversación. La pausa incómoda se alargó hasta convertirse en un silencio violento. Gregor creía comprender lo que Vikus quería dar a entender. Era mejor tener a los reptantes como aliados que como enemigos, y los humanos no debían ir por ahí insultándolos.

Para alivio de Gregor, por fin llegó la comida, y un sirviente dispuso unos pequeños cuencos formando una media luna alrededor de su plato. Por lo menos tres de ellos contenían lo que parecían tres tipos distintos de champiñones. En otro había un cereal parecido al arroz, y el más pequeño albergaba un puñadito de verduras frescas. Lo reducido de la porción daba a entender que esas hojas se consideraban un preciado manjar.

Le colocaron delante una fuente con un pescado entero a la parrilla. Se parecía a los que Gregor estaba acostumbrado, sólo que no tenía ojos. Su padre y él habían visto una vez un documental en la tele sobre unos peces que vivían en lo más profundo de una cueva y tampoco tenían ojos. Lo curioso era que cuando los científicos se trajeron algunos de esos peces para estudiarlos en sus laboratorios, los peces habían percibido la luz, y les habían salido ojos. No inmediatamente, pero sí unas cuantas generaciones después.

A su padre le había encantado el documental, y había llevado a Gregor al Museo de Historia Natural para buscar peces sin ojos. Al final se habían acostumbrado a ir a menudo a ese museo, ellos dos solos. Su padre estaba loco por la ciencia, y parecía que quisiera pasarle a Gregor todos los conocimientos que había en su cerebro. Era un poco peligroso, porque la pregunta más tonta podía generar una explicación de media hora por lo menos. Su abuela siempre solía decir: «A tu padre, si le preguntas qué hora es, te acaba contando cómo se fabrica un reloj». Pero disfrutaba tanto explicando..., y Gregor se sentía feliz de estar con él. Además, le había encantado la exposición sobre la selva tropical, y la cafetería donde vendían papas fritas con forma de dinosaurio. Nunca habían llegado a entender cómo habían conseguido desarrollar ojos los peces. Su padre tenía sus teorías, claro, pero no era capaz de explicar cómo habían podido los peces evolucionar tan deprisa.

Gregor se preguntó cuánto tiempo era necesario para que la piel de alguien se volviera transparente y desarrollar ojos violetas. Se volvió hacia Vikus.

—Bueno, iba a contarme cómo vinieron a parar aquí abajo, ¿recuerda?

Mientras Gregor trataba de no lanzarse como un lobo hambriento sobre su comida, que resultó ser deliciosa, Vikus le fue contando la historia de Regalia.

No lo entendió todo, pero al parecer los habitantes habían llegado desde Inglaterra en el siglo XVII.

—Los condujo hasta aquí un cantero llamado Bartholomew de Sandwich —contó Vikus, y Gregor tuvo que esforzarse por reprimir una carcajada—. Tenía visiones sobre el futuro. Vio las Tierras Bajas en un sueño, y partió en su busca.

Sandwich y un grupo de seguidores se habían embarcado rumbo a Nueva York, donde es sabido que se llevaron muy bien con la tribu local. Los indígenas conocían muy bien las Tierras Bajas. Llevaban siglos realizado viajes periódicos bajo tierra por motivos rituales. No tenían mucho interés en vivir allá abajo, y no les importaba si Sandwich era lo bastante loco como para querer instalarse allí con su gente.

—Por supuesto, estaba totalmente cuerdo —aclaró Vikus—. Sabía que un día la superficie de la Tierra estaría totalmente yerma, y sólo perduraría la vida que se preservaba bajo tierra.

A Gregor no le pareció muy oportuno decirle a Vikus que ahora, en la superficie, vivían millones de personas. En vez de eso, preguntó:

—¿Y entonces todos hicieron las maletas y se mudaron aquí abajo?

—¡Desde luego que no! Pasaron cincuenta años hasta que bajaron las ochocientas personas y se sellaron las puertas que comunicaban con las Tierras Altas. Necesitábamos saber de qué podíamos alimentarnos y edificar muros para defendernos. Roma no se construyó en un día. —Vikus rió—. Así es como lo expresó Fred Clark de las Tierras Altas.

—¿Qué le ocurrió? —preguntó Gregor, pinchando un champiñón con el tenedor. Todos callaron.

—Murió —contestó Solovet con voz suave—. No pudo sobrevivir privado de tu sol.

Gregor dejó el champiñón en el plato. Miró a Boots, que estaba cubierta de los pies a la cabeza con una especie de papilla para bebés. Con un dedo trazaba distraídamente dibujitos en la salsa derramada sobre su mantelito de piedra.

Nuestro sol, pensó Gregor. ¿Se habría puesto ya? ¿Sería ya hora de irse a la cama? ¿Se habrían marchado ya los policías, o seguirían allí, interrogando a su madre? Si ya se habían marchado, Gregor sabía dónde estaría su madre: sentada a la mesa de la cocina, sola en la oscuridad, llorando.

De pronto, Gregor ya no soportaba oír una sola palabra más sobre las Tierras Bajas. Tenía que escapar de allí a toda costa.

CAPÍTULO SÉPTIMO

La oscuridad se abatió sobre los ojos de Gregor con tal intensidad que parecía tener un peso físico, como si fuera una cortina de agua. Nunca antes había estado totalmente sin luz. En su ciudad, el alumbrado de las calles, los faros y, de vez en cuando, los destellos de algún coche de bomberos se colaban por la ventana de su habitación. Aquí, una vez apagada la lámpara de aceite, era como si hubiera perdido por completo el sentido de la vista.

Había tenido la tentación de volver a encender la lámpara. Mareth le había dicho que en el pasillo junto a su habitación había antorchas que ardían toda la noche, y podía volver a encender su lámpara allí. Pero quería conservar el combustible. Sin él, estaría perdido en cuanto saliera de Regalia.

Boots resopló y se acurrucó más cerca de él. Gregor la abrazó con más fuerza. Los sirvientes les habían preparado camas separadas, pero Boots se había metido en la de Gregor.

No había sido difícil conseguir permiso para irse a la cama. Todos veían que Boots apenas podía mantener los ojos abiertos, y él mismo debía verse bastante cansado. Pero no lo estaba. La adrenalina corría por sus venas a tal velocidad que temía que la gente pudiera oír los latidos de su corazón a través de las pesadas cortinas que separaban su habitación del vestíbulo. Lo último que se sentía capaz de hacer era dormir.

Los habían invitado nuevamente a tomar un baño antes de irse a la cama. Para Boots era más que necesario, pues a la papilla se añadió luego una especie de flan con el que se embadurnó el pelo. Gregor tampoco había puesto objeción alguna. Con la excusa del baño podía disfrutar de un lugar tranquilo donde idear su plan de huida.

El baño también le brindó la oportunidad de preguntarle a Dulcet sobre el sistema de aguas del palacio sin levantar sospechas.

—Oye, ¿y ustedes por qué tienen agua corriente caliente y fría? —le preguntó.

La chica le explicó que unas bombas aspiraban el agua desde una serie de corrientes frías y calientes.

—¿Y esa agua luego va a parar otra vez a una de esas corrientes? —preguntó inocentemente.

—Oh, no, eso no sería higiénico —contestó Dulcet—. El agua sucia va a parar al río que discurre bajo el palacio, que a su vez va a parar al Canal.

Era justo la información que necesitaba. El río bajo el palacio era su vía de escape. Y lo mejor de todo era que luego desembocaba en el Canal. No sabía qué era eso exactamente, pero Vikus había mencionado que tenía dos puertas que comunicaban con las Tierras Altas.

Boots volvió a agitarse durante el sueño, y Gregor le dio palmaditas en el costado para tranquilizarla. No parecía haber echado de menos su casa hasta la hora de acostarse, pero se mostró algo inquieta cuando le dijo que era hora de irse a la cama.

—¿Mamá? —preguntó la niña—. ¿Liz-zie?

¿Había sido esa misma mañana cuando Lizzie tomó el autobús para ir al campamento? Parecía que hubiera sido hace miles de años.

—¿Casa? ¿Mamá? —insistió Boots. Aunque estaba agotada, a Gregor le costó mucho dormirla. Ahora se daba cuenta de que estaba nerviosa, a juzgar por su sueño inquieto. «Probablemente lleno de cucarachas y murciélagos gigantes», pensó Gregor.

No tenía forma de calcular cuánto tiempo había transcurrido ya. ¿Una hora, dos, tal vez? Pero los ruidos apagados que le llegaban a través del cortinaje ya habían cesado. Si quería llevar a cabo su plan, tenía que ponerse en movimiento ya.

Gregor se separó con cuidado de Boots y se levantó de la cama. Tanteó en la oscuridad hasta encontrar la mochila que le había dado Dulcet. Colocar dentro a Boots no resultó tarea fácil. Al final optó por cerrar los ojos y dejar que trabajaran los demás sentidos. Así era más fácil. La deslizó dentro de la mochila y se sujetó ésta a la espalda.

Boots murmuró «mamá», y reclinó la cabeza sobre el hombro de su hermano.

—Te llevaré con mamá, linda, te lo prometo —le susurró él a su vez, y buscó a tientas la lámpara. Eso era todo lo que se llevaba consigo: Boots, la mochila y la lámpara. Necesitaría las manos para otras cosas.

Gregor se dirigió a tientas hacia la cortina y descorrió una esquina. Las antorchas iluminaban lo bastante para ver que el pasillo estaba vacío. Vikus y los demás no se habían tomado la molestia de colocar guardias a su puerta ahora que lo conocían mejor. Se estaban esforzando por hacerle sentir como un huésped. Y, además, ¿adónde podría ir?

«Al río», pensó gravemente. «Dondequiera que éste me lleve».

Se deslizó por el pasillo, teniendo cuidado de andar sin hacer el más mínimo ruido. Afortunadamente, Boots seguía durmiendo. Su plan se echaría a perder si se despertaba antes de salir del palacio.

Su habitación estaba convenientemente situada cerca del cuarto de baño, y Gregor se dejó guiar por el sonido del agua. Su plan era sencillo. El río corría por debajo del palacio. Si conseguía llegar hasta la planta baja sin alejarse del sonido del agua, entonces encontraría el lugar por el que ésta iba a parar al río.

El plan era sencillo, pero no así su realización. Gregor tardó varias horas en recorrer todo el palacio hasta la planta baja. Los cuartos de baño no siempre estaban cerca de las escaleras, y más de una vez tuvo que volver sobre sus pasos para no perder el eco del agua. Dos veces tuvo que entrar en las habitaciones y ocultarse para evitar ser descubierto. No encontró a mucha gente levantada, pero había una especie de guardias que efectuaban rondas de vigilancia por el palacio.

Por fin el sonido del agua se amplificó, y Gregor llegó a la planta más baja del edificio. Se dejó guiar por su oído hacia donde el rugido del agua se hacía más potente, y se adentró por un pasillo.

Durante un instante, Gregor estuvo tentado a abandonar su plan. Cuando Dulcet había hablado de un «río», Gregor se había imaginado el que atravesaba la ciudad de Nueva York. Pero este río de las Tierras Bajas parecía sacado de una película de acción. No es que fuera muy ancho, pero la corriente alcanzaba tal velocidad que formaba remolinos llenos de espuma en la superficie del agua. Gregor no podía calcular su profundidad, pero veía que tenía fuerza suficiente para arrastrar grandes rocas a su paso, como si se tratara de latas vacías. Gregor comprendía ahora por qué no se molestaban en situar guardias en el muelle. El río era más peligroso que cualquier ejército que pudieran reunir.

«Pero tiene que ser navegable, porque tienen barcos», pensó Gregor, descubriendo media docena de embarcaciones amarradas por encima del nivel del agua. Estaban hechas con algún tipo de cuero tensado sobre una estructura rígida. Le recordaron las canoas del campamento.

¡El campamento! ¿Por qué no podía él estar en el campamento como un chico común y corriente?

Tratando de no pensar en las rocas azotadas por la corriente, encendió la llama de su lámpara de aceite con una antorcha que ardía junto al muelle. Lo pensó mejor, y cogió también la antorcha. Allí adonde se dirigía, la luz sería tan importante como el aire que respiraba. Apagó la lámpara para ahorrar combustible.

Trepó con cuidado a una de las embarcaciones y la inspeccionó. La antorcha encajaba en una horquilla claramente diseñada para ello.

«¿Cómo harán para bajar esta cosa al agua?», se preguntó. La embarcación estaba suspendida de dos cuerdas atadas a una rueda metálica que estaba fijada al muelle. «Bueno, habrá que probar», pensó Gregor, y le dio un empujón a la rueda. Esta emitió un sonoro crujido, y la nave cayó de golpe al agua, tirando a Gregor al suelo.

La corriente arrastró la embarcación como si de una hoja seca se tratara. Gregor se aferró a los bordes, sin soltarse, mientras se lanzaban a través de la oscuridad. Oyó unas voces, y por espacio de un segundo consiguió mirar hacia atrás, hacia el muelle. Dos hombres le estaban gritando algo. El río describió una curva, y entonces desaparecieron de su vista.

¿Tratarían de perseguirlo? Por supuesto que sí. Pero les llevaba una buena ventaja. ¿En cuánto tiempo llegaría al Canal? ¿Qué era aquello del Canal, y una vez que llegara allí, adónde tendría que ir después?

A Gregor le hubieran preocupado más esas preguntas de no haber estado tan concentrado en permanecer con vida. Además de las rocas, tenía que esquivar los escollos negros que sobresalían del agua. En el fondo de la barca encontró un remo que utilizó para alejar la barca de las rocas.

La temperatura de las Tierras Bajas se le había antojado agradablemente fresca desde su llegada, sobre todo después del intenso calor que hacía en su apartamento. Pero el frío viento que se levantaba del agua le puso la carne de gallina.

—¡Gregor! —le pareció oír que alguien lo llamaba por su nombre.

¿Sería su imaginación, o...? ¡No! Lo había oído otra vez. Sus perseguidores debían de encontrarse ya muy cerca.

El río describió un recodo y de repente Gregor pudo ver un poco mejor. Una larga cueva recubierta de cristales puntiagudos de roca brillaba a ambos lados del río, reflejando la luz de su antorcha.

Gregor distinguió una playa de arena brillante que bordeaba una orilla del río, unos metros más adelante. Un túnel llevaba de la playa a la oscuridad. Siguiendo un impulso, Gregor esquivó una roca y dirigió la canoa hacia la playa. Remó desesperadamente para llegar a la orilla. No tenía sentido permanecer en el río. Los de las Tierras Bajas le estaban pisando los talones. Tal vez le diera tiempo a atracar en la playa y ocultarse en el túnel. Una vez que hubieran pasado de largo, podría aguardar unas horas, y luego volver al río.

La canoa encalló en la arena de la playa. Gregor consiguió por poco no darse de bruces contra el suelo de la embarcación. Boots se medio despertó y lloriqueó un poco, pero Gregor la volvió a dormir arrullándola, pugnando a la vez por arrastrar la canoa sobre la arena con una mano, mientras con la otra sujetaba la antorcha.

—Ea, ea, Boots. Vuelve a dormirte.

—Hola, *mulcélago* —murmuró la niña, y su cabeza volvió a caer sobre el hombro de su hermano.

Gregor oyó su nombre en la distancia y echó a correr. Tan pronto como alcanzó la entrada del túnel, tropezó de bruces con un bulto peludo y cálido. Asustado, retrocedió unos pasos, dejando caer la antorcha. El bulto avanzó hasta colocarse dentro del tenue círculo de luz. Al verlo, las piernas de Gregor se volvieron de mantequilla y cedieron bajo el peso de su cuerpo. El chico cayó lentamente al suelo.

Ante él, el rostro de una rata monstruosa se contrajo en una sonrisa.

CAPÍTULO OCTAVO

Ah, aquí estás por fin —dijo la rata con voz lánguida—. Por tu hedor hace siglos que te esperábamos. Mira, Fangor, trae consigo al cachorro. Un largo hocico asomó por encima del hombro de la rata. Ésta tenía un compañero.

—Pero si es un manjarcito —comentó Fangor con una voz suave y melosa—. Te dejo al chico enterito para ti si me reservas la dulzura del cachorrito, Shed.

—Muy tentador, Fangor, pero el chico tiene más huesos que carne, y ella en cambio parece un bocadito suculento —contestó Shed—. Tu oferta me sume en un profundo dilema. Ponte de pie, chico, y deja que te veamos.

Las cucarachas le habían parecido muy extrañas, y los murciélagos, intimidantes, pero estas ratas, pensó Gregor, eran sencillamente aterradoras. Pese a estar sentadas sobre los cuartos traseros, medían más de un metro ochenta por lo menos, y sus piernas, sus brazos, o como hubiera que llamarlos, revelaban potentes músculos por debajo del pelaje. Pero lo peor de todo eran sus dientes, incisivos de diez centímetros que sobresalían de sus fauces, por debajo de los bigotes.

No, lo peor era que, evidentemente, estaban planeando comerse a Gregor y a Boots. Algunas personas creían que las ratas no se comían a la gente, pero Gregor sabía que se equivocaban. Incluso las de tamaño normal que poblaban las Tierras Altas podían llegar a atacar a una persona si se encontraba indefensa. Las ratas podían atacar a los bebés, los ancianos y los más débiles en general. Se oía cada historia... el vagabundo del callejón... aquel niño que perdió dos dedos... eran demasiado horribles para pensar en ellas.

Gregor se puso en pie despacio, recogiendo la antorcha, pero la mantuvo lejos de su rostro. Empujó a Boots contra la pared de la cueva.

Fangor agitó el hocico para husmear el aire.

—Éste cenó pescado, champiñones, cereales y un poquitín de verdura. Todo un amplio surtido de sabores, tendrás que reconocer, Shed.

—Y el cachorrito se ha atiborrado de puré de ternera con nata —replicó Shed—. Y sobra decir que sigue alimentándose de leche.

En ese momento Gregor comprendió el motivo de tanta insistencia en que se bañaran. Si las ratas podían detectar el puñadito de verdura que había tomado unas horas antes, es que tenían un olfato increíble.

No era pura grosería lo que empujaba a los habitantes de las Tierras Bajas a insistir en que se bañara. ¡Habían estado tratando de mantenerlo con vida!

De tratar de escapar de sus garras, Gregor había pasado a desear fervientemente que lo encontraran. Tenía que mantener a distancia a las ratas: así ganaría tiempo. La expresión lo sorprendió. Vikus había dicho que matándolo, las cucarachas «no ganarían tiempo». Eso de «tiempo», ¿no significaría simplemente más vida para los de las Tierras Bajas?

Se sacudió el polvo de la ropa y trató de imitar la manera de hablar de las ratas.

—¿Tengo yo vela en este entierro? —preguntó.

Para su sorpresa, Fangor y Shed se echaron a reír.

—¡Habla! —exclamó Shed—. ¡Qué regalo! ¡Normalmente sólo cosechamos chillidos y gimoteos! Dinos, muchacho, ¿qué te hace ser tan valiente?

—Oh, no soy valiente —negó Gregor—. Apuesto a que eso ya pueden olerlo.

Las ratas volvieron a reír.

—En efecto, tu sudor apesta a miedo, pero a pesar de todo has conseguido dirigirnos la palabra.

—Bueno, he pensado que tal vez quisieran informarse un poco sobre lo que van a cenar esta noche —les dijo Gregor.

—¡Me cae bien, Shed! —aulló Fangor.

—¡A mí también! —contestó Shed—. Los humanos suelen ser tan aburridos. ¿Qué te parece si nos lo quedamos, Fangor?

—Oh, Shed, ¿cómo podríamos hacer algo así? Habría que dar demasiadas explicaciones. Además, con tanto reír me está entrando hambre —dijo Fangor.

—A mí también. Pero, estarás de acuerdo conmigo en que comerse a una presa tan divertida no deja de ser una lástima.

—Una lástima, en efecto —convino Fangor—. Pero no hay más remedio. ¿Empezamos?

Y con esto, ambas ratas avanzaron hacia él enseñando los dientes. Gregor blandió entonces su antorcha, lanzando por los aires un puñado de chispas. La sostenía ante él, como una espada, iluminando su cara por completo.

Las ratas se detuvieron en seco. Al principio pensó que les daba miedo la llama, pero no se trataba sólo de eso. Parecían estupefactas.

—¿Has visto su rostro, Shed, lo has visto? —dijo Fangor con una voz ahogada.

—Lo he visto, Fangor —dijo Shed en voz baja—. Y no es más que un muchacho. ¿Crees que es...?

—¡No podrá serlo si lo matamos! —rugió Fangor, lanzándose al cuello de Gregor.

El primer murciélago llegó tan silenciosamente que ni Gregor ni las ensimismadas ratas lo vieron. Chocó con Fangor en mitad de su salto, derribándolo.

Fangor se estrelló contra Shed, y ambos cayeron al suelo. Al instante se pusieron en pie y se volvieron hacia sus atacantes.

Gregor vio a Henry, Mareth y Perdita zigzagueando con sus murciélagos por encima de las cabezas de las ratas. Aparte de evitar chocar unos con otros en un espacio reducido, tenían que esquivar las malvadas garras de las ratas. Fangor y Shed podían saltar hasta tres metros sin esfuerzo, y el techo refulgente de la cueva no era mucho más alto.

Los humanos se lanzaron en picado sobre las ratas, blandiendo sus espadas. Fangor y Shed contraatacaron ferozmente con uñas y dientes. La sangre empezó a manchar la playa, pero Gregor no acertaba a distinguir de quién era.

—¡Huye! —le gritó Henry a Gregor mientras pasaba junto a él—. ¡Huye!

Una parte de él deseaba obedecerle, pero otra no podía hacerlo. Para empezar, no tenía ni idea de hacia dónde ir. Su barca estaba encallada en la arena, y el túnel... bueno, si tenía que vérselas con las ratas, prefería hacerlo al aire libre antes que en la oscuridad de un túnel.

Lo más importante era que los habitantes de las Tierras Bajas estaban ahí por su causa, y no podía echar a correr sin más y dejar que se enfrentaran solos con las ratas.

¿Pero qué podía hacer?

En ese momento, Shed alcanzó con los dientes el ala del murciélago de Mareth. El animal se debatió para liberarse, pero la rata no soltaba su presa. Perdita se le acercó por detrás, rebanándole la oreja con su espada. Shed dejó escapar un aullido de dolor, y soltó al murciélago de Mareth. Pero justo cuando Perdita levantaba el vuelo, Fangor saltó sobre su murciélago, arrancándole un pedazo de la piel del cuello y arrastrándola al suelo. Perdita se golpeó la cabeza contra la pared de la cueva y perdió el conocimiento. Fangor se inclinó sobre ella, acercando los dientes hacia su cuello.

Gregor no recordaba si se paró a pensar en su próximo movimiento, sencillamente ocurrió. Un segundo antes estaba apretujado contra la pared de la cueva, y un segundo después había saltado hacia delante, lanzando su antorcha a la cara de Fangor. La rata chilló y cayó hacia atrás, empalándose en la espada de Henry. El cuerpo sin vida de Fangor cayó al suelo, arrastrando consigo la espada.

El aullido de dolor de la rata terminó por despertar a Boots, que echó una ojeada por encima del hombro de Gregor, y acto seguido rompió a llorar a gritos. Su llanto retumbaba sobre las paredes de la cueva, poniendo histérico a Shed y desorientando a los murciélagos.

—¿Qué tal vuelas, Mareth? —gritó Henry.

—¡Podemos hacerlo! —contestó el hombre, aunque su murciélago sangraba abundantemente del ala herida.

La situación no tenía buen aspecto. El murciélago de Mareth estaba desorientado, Henry había perdido su arma, Perdita estaba inconsciente, su murciélago yacía en el suelo tratando de recuperar el aliento, Boots daba alaridos y Shed estaba loco de dolor y de miedo. Aunque sangraba a borbotones, no había perdido un ápice de su velocidad ni de su fuerza.

Mareth trataba desesperadamente de alejar a la rata de Perdita, pero él solo no daba abasto. Henry trataba de ayudarlo, pero sin espada no podía acercarse demasiado. Gregor se acuclilló junto a Perdita, antorcha en mano. Parecía una frágil defensa contra la rata enloquecida, pero tenía que hacer algo.

Entonces Shed saltó, agarrando de las patas al murciélago de Mareth. El animal se estrelló contra la pared, arrastrando consigo a su jinete. La rata se volvió hacia Gregor.

—¡Eres hombre muerto! —gritó Shed. Boots chilló a su vez, presa del pánico, mientras Shed se lanzaba sobre ellos. Gregor se preparó para el ataque, pero éste no llegó. En vez de eso, Shed exhaló un suspiro y con la pata tocó la espada que se había clavado sobre su garganta.

Gregor acertó a ver a Aurora, el murciélago de Luxa, que se elevaba como una flecha hacia lo alto. No tenía ni idea de cuándo había llegado. Luxa estaba volando cabeza abajo cuando atravesó a Shed con su espada. Aunque ella se había tumbado por completo sobre el lomo del murciélago, Aurora apenas consiguió concluir la maniobra sin arañar el cuerpo de la muchacha contra el techo.

Shed se desplomó contra la pared de la cueva. Ya no le quedaban fuerzas para luchar. Sus ojos lanzaban chispas cuando los dirigió sobre Gregor.

—Tú, el de las Tierras Altas —articuló—, no pararemos hasta darte caza. —Y tras estas palabras, murió.

Gregor tuvo apenas un segundo para recuperar el aliento antes de que Henry aterrizara a su lado. Empujándolo hacia la playa, tomó a Perdita entre sus brazos y se elevó con ella en el aire, gritando:

—¡Quemen la tierra!

Aunque la sangre manaba a chorros por su rostro, Mareth logró extraer sendas espadas de los cuerpos de Shed y de Fangor. Arrastró a las ratas hasta el río, y la corriente se llevó los cadáveres rápidamente. Su murciélago batió tembloroso las alas, y él consiguió subirse con esfuerzo sobre su lomo. Luego subió a Gregor y a Boots en su murciélago.

Gregor vio que Aurora aferraba entre sus garras el pelaje del murciélago herido de Perdita. Luxa había recuperado la lámpara de aceite del fondo de la embarcación. Cuando se elevaron por los aires, la dejó caer sobre el suelo.

—¡Suelta la antorcha! —gritó Mareth, y Gregor extendió los dedos, dejándola caer al suelo.

Lo último que vio mientras se alejaban de la cueva a toda velocidad fue la playa estallando en llamas.

CAPÍTULO NOVENO

Gregor contempló el agua del río, devorada ahora por las llamas, mientras se agarraba con todas sus fuerzas al murciélago. Durante un segundo, sintió alivio por haber escapado de las ratas. Pero entonces el miedo de estar volando a toda velocidad sobre un murciélago herido se apoderó de él por completo. Boots se aferraba a su cuello con tanta fuerza que apenas lo dejaba respirar, y mucho menos hablar. Y de todas maneras, ¿qué podía decirle a Mareth? «Huy, siento mucho todo lo que ha pasado en la playa», ¿por ejemplo?

Por supuesto, él no sabía nada de las ratas. ¿Pero acaso no habían tratado todos de prevenirlo? No, habían hablado de peligro, pero nadie había mencionado concretamente a las ratas, salvo las cucarachas. «Rata mala», había dicho una de ellas. Y después habían hablado de cuánto pagarían las ratas mientras Luxa regateaba. Podían haberlos vendido a las ratas, y entonces, ¿qué habría sido de ellos?

Sintió náuseas y cerró los ojos para no ver los remolinos que se formaban en la superficie del agua. Las imágenes de la lucha en la playa llenaban su cabeza, y decidió que era mejor el panorama del agua. Ésta se sumió en las tinieblas cuando se extinguió la luz de las llamas. Cuando de nuevo vieron antorchas reflejadas sobre las olas, supo que se estaban aproximando a Regalia.

Un grupo de ciudadanos esperaba junto al embarcadero. Se llevaron de allí a Perdita y a su murciélago herido. Trataron de acomodar también a Mareth sobre una camilla, pero él los apartó con un gesto e insistió en ayudar a cargar con su murciélago hasta el palacio.

Gregor se sentó en el muelle, allí donde lo había empujado Mareth al aterrizar, y deseó que se lo tragara la tierra. Boots ya no lloraba, pero Gregor notaba que sus pequeños músculos estaban rígidos de miedo. Quince, tal vez veinte minutos transcurrieron así. Gregor no acertaba a calcular cuántos exactamente.

—¡Arriba! —gruñó una voz, y vio que Mareth lo estaba mirando furioso. Le habían vendado el corte en la frente, y el lado derecho de su cara estaba hinchado y magullado—. ¡Muévete! —le gritó el guardia. ¿De verdad le había parecido, hacía tan sólo unas horas, que ese hombre era tímido y amable?

Gregor estiró lentamente sus piernas engarrotadas y se puso de pie. Mareth le ató bien fuerte las manos a la espalda. Esta vez ya no había duda. Era decididamente un prisionero. Otro guardia se unió a Mareth, y empujaron a Gregor por delante de ellos. Sus piernas estaban como dormidas. ¿Qué pensaban hacer con él ahora?

No se fijó en el camino que tomaban. Se limitó a avanzar hacia donde le indicaron a empujones. Fue vagamente consciente de subir muchas escaleras antes de entrar en una amplia sala en forma de diamante. En el centro había una mesa. Mareth lo sentó de un empujón sobre un taburete que había junto a una chimenea en la que ardía ferozmente un fuego. Los dos guardias retrocedieron un par de pasos, vigilándolo como aves de presa.

«Tan peligroso soy», pensó como en una nube.

Boots empezó a agitarse dentro de la mochila. Le jaló una oreja.

—¿Casa? —suplicó—. ¿*Mamo* a casa, *Gue-go*? —Gregor no tenía respuesta para ella.

La gente pasaba deprisa por delante de la puerta, hablando animadamente. Algunos se quedaban mirándolos, pero nadie entró en la habitación.

Al calor del fuego sintió, de pronto, que estaba helado. Se encontraba empapado hasta la cintura, y temblaba de frío y de horror por lo que había presenciado. No sólo lo había presenciado, sino que también había tomado parte en ello.

Boots estaba mejor que él. Su mochila parecía impermeable, y estaba acurrucada contra él. Con todo, notó que los deditos de sus pies estaban fríos como el hielo cuando rozaron su brazo.

El cansancio se apoderó de Gregor, y deseó poder acostarse, relajarse y dormir, para despertar después en su cama, desde donde veía los faros de los coches reflejados en la pared de su habitación. Pero ya había renunciado a pensar que todo aquello era un sueño.

¿Qué había sido de los demás? ¿Cómo estaban

Perdita y su murciélago herido? ¿Y el de Mareth? Si morían, sería culpa suya. Ni siquiera trataría de sostener lo contrario.

Justo en ese momento apareció Luxa. Temblando de ira, atravesó la habitación y lo golpeó en la cara. La cabeza de Gregor se inclinó con violencia hacia un lado y Boots dejó escapar un grito.

—¡No se pega! —chilló—. ¡No, no, no se pega! —Miraba a Luxa agitando su dedito índice. Pegar estaba absolutamente prohibido en casa de Gregor, y Boots no había tardado mucho en aprenderlo.

Al parecer tampoco era algo aceptable entre los habitantes de las Tierras Bajas porque Gregor oyó a Vikus exclamar severamente desde el umbral: «¡Luxa!».

Con una expresión como si estuviera deseando volver a pegarle otra bofetada, Luxa se dirigió hacia la chimenea y contempló indignada el fuego.

—Debería darte vergüenza, Luxa —la reprendió Vikus, acercándose a ella.

Ella se volvió hacia él, furiosa.

—¡Han caído dos voladores, y no podemos despertar a Perdita, sólo porque el de las Tierras Altas tenía que escapar! ¿Pegarle? ¡Yo propongo que lo arrojemos a la Tierra de la Muerte y dejemos que se las arregle! —gritó Luxa encolerizada.

—Sea como fuere, Luxa esto no es lo correcto —contestó Vikus, pero Gregor se dio cuenta de que las noticias lo habían disgustado—. ¿Están las dos ratas muertas? —preguntó.

—Muertas y en el río —dijo Luxa—. Hemos quemado la tierra.

—Ya hablaremos tú y yo de eso de «hemos» —dijo Vikus severamente—. Esto no complace al Consejo.

—Poco me importa lo que complace al Consejo —masculló Luxa, pero eludió la mirada de Vikus.

«De modo que se suponía que ella no tenía que estar ahí», pensó Gregor. «Ella también se ha metido en un lío». Deseó poder saborear mejor el momento, pero estaba demasiado atormentado por la preocupación, el sentimiento de culpa y el agotamiento como para que pudiera importarle. Además, Luxa le había salvado la vida al matar a Shed. Gregor suponía que le debía una, pero todavía le ardía la cara por la bofetada, así que no sacó el tema.

—No se pega —repitió Boots, y Vikus se volvió hacia ellos.

Como Luxa, Gregor era incapaz de sostener la mirada del anciano.

—¿Qué hizo el muchacho, Luxa? ¿Luchar o huir? —preguntó Vikus.

—Henry dice que luchó —reconoció Luxa a regañadientes—. Pero sin destreza ni conocimiento de las armas.

A Gregor le dieron ganas de decir: «¡Eh, sólo tenía una estúpida antorcha!». ¿Pero para qué molestarse?

—Entonces tiene mucho valor —concluyó Vikus.

—El valor sin prudencia acorta la vida, o al menos, eso es lo que me dices tú todos los días —objetó Luxa.

—Te lo digo, sí, ¿y me escuchas, acaso? —preguntó Vikus, arqueando las cejas—. No escuchas, como tampoco él escucha. Son ambos muy jóvenes aún para padecer sordera. Desátenlo y déjennos solos —ordenó a los guardias.

Gregor sintió que la hoja de un cuchillo cortaba las ligaduras de sus muñecas. Se frotó las cicatrices, tratando de restablecer la circulación de la sangre. Le dolía la mejilla, pero no tenía intención de darle a Luxa la satisfacción de comprobarlo.

Boots alargó el brazo por encima de su hombro y le tocó las marcas de las muñecas.

—Aya-yai —lloriqueó—. Aya-yai.

—Estoy bien, Boots —dijo, pero la pequeña negó con la cabeza.

—Acérquense —dijo Vikus, sentándose a la mesa. Ni Gregor ni Luxa se movieron—. ¡Acérquense, vamos a hablar! —exclamó Vikus, golpeando con la mano la superficie de piedra. Esta vez ambos obedecieron, pero se sentaron lo más lejos posible el uno del otro.

Gregor sacó a Boots de la mochila levantándola por encima de su cabeza. La niña se acomodó en su regazo, estrechando con fuerza los brazos de Gregor alrededor de su cuerpo, y mirando a Vikus y a Luxa con unos grandes ojos solemnes.

«Creo que después de esta noche, Boots ya no volverá a pensar que todo el mundo es su amigo», pensó Gregor. Sabía que tenía que descubrirlo tarde o temprano, pero no pudo evitar sentirse triste por ella.

Vikus empezó a hablar.

—Gregor de las Tierras Altas, es mucho lo que no aciertas a comprender. No hablas, pero tu rostro habla por ti. Estás preocupado. Estás enojado. Crees que tenías derecho a huir de quienes te retenían en contra de tu voluntad, pero te duele que hayamos sufrido por salvarlos. Nunca te hablamos de las ratas, y no obstante Luxa te culpa de nuestras pérdidas. Parecemos tus enemigos, y sin embargo te hemos dado tiempo.

Gregor no contestó. Le parecía que eso lo resumía todo bastante bien, excepto el hecho de que Luxa le hubiera pegado. Vikus le leyó el pensamiento.

—Luxa no debería haberte golpeado, pero tu huida ha puesto en peligro de muerte, y de una muerte horrible, a aquellos a quienes ella ama. Eso le duele profundamente, pues tanto su padre como su madre murieron a manos de las ratas.

Luxa dejó escapar un grito.

—¡Eso no le concierne!

Parecía tan consternada que Gregor estuvo a punto de protestar también. Daba igual lo que le hubiera hecho; ése no era asunto suyo.

—Yo creo que sí le concierne, Luxa, pues tengo motivos para pensar que tal vez el propio Gregor haya perdido también a su padre —prosiguió Vikus.

Ahora le tocaba a Gregor asombrarse.

—¿Y usted cómo lo sabe?

—No tengo certeza, es tan sólo una suposición. Dime, Gregor de las Tierras Altas, ¿reconoces esto? —Vikus se llevó la mano al bolsillo y extrajo un objeto.

Era un aro metálico del que colgaban varias llaves. Pero fueron las tiras de cuero rojo, negro y azul, torpemente trenzadas, lo que dejó a Gregor sin respiración. Las había trenzado él mismo en el taller de artesanía del mismo campamento en el que estaba ahora Lizzie. Se podía elegir entre hacer tres cosas: una pulsera, un señalador para libros o un llavero. Gregor había elegido el llavero.

Su padre nunca iba a ningún sitio sin él.

segunda parte

LA BÚSQUEDA

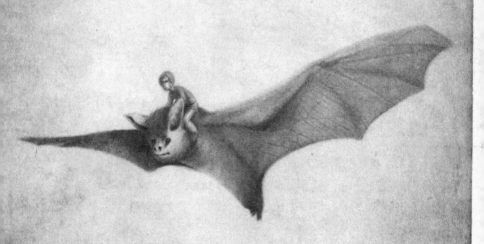

CAPÍTULO DÉCIMO

Cuando el corazón de Gregor volvió a latir, lo hizo con tal fuerza, que pensó que le iba a estallar el pecho. Su mano se movió sola y sus dedos buscaron asir el llavero.

—¿De dónde ha sacado esto?

—Te dije que ya habían caído aquí otros habitantes de las Tierras Altas. Hará algunos años rescatamos a uno de facciones y porte muy similares a los tuyos. No recuerdo la fecha exacta —dijo Vikus, poniendo el llavero en la mano de Gregor.

«Hace dos años, siete meses y trece días», pensó éste y, en voz alta, dijo:

—Es de mi padre.

Oleadas de felicidad recorrieron su cuerpo mientras acariciaba la trenza de cuero gastado y el aro metálico para enganchar el llavero en la trabilla del pantalón. Su mente se llenó de recuerdos. Su padre, extendiendo las llaves para dar con la que abría la puerta de casa. Su padre, agitando el llavero delante de la carita de Lizzie, sentada en su carriola de bebé. Su padre, de picnic en Central Park, utilizando una de las llaves para abrir un recipiente de ensalada de papa.

—¿Tu padre? —Luxa abrió los ojos como platos, y una extraña expresión cruzó su semblante—. Vikus, no pensarás que es...

—No lo sé, Luxa, pero las señales son poderosas —dijo Vikus—. No he podido pensar en otra cosa desde que llegó.

Luxa se volvió hacia Gregor, con una expresión burlona en los ojos.

Bueno, ¿y ahora qué? ¿Qué mosca le picaba ahora?

—Tu padre, como tú, estaba desesperado por volver a casa —explicó Vikus—. Con gran esfuerzo lo persuadimos para que permaneciera aquí algunas semanas, pero la tensión era demasiada para él y, una noche, como tú también, se escapó. Las ratas lo alcanzaron antes que nosotros.

Gregor se dio de bruces con la realidad, y toda la alegría se esfumó de su cuerpo. Por supuesto, no había más habitantes de las Tierras Altas vivos en Regalia. Vikus se lo había dicho en el estadio. Su padre había tratado de volver a casa, y había encontrado el mismo destino que Gregor. Pero los de las Tierras Bajas no habían estado ahí para salvarlo. Hizo esfuerzos por tragarse el nudo que le apretaba la garganta.

—Entonces está muerto.

—Eso asumimos nosotros. Pero después nos llegaron rumores de que las ratas lo habían mantenido con vida —anunció Vikus—. Nuestros espías nos confirman este hecho regularmente.

—¿Está vivo? —preguntó Gregor, sintiendo que la

esperanza volvía a apoderarse de todo su ser—. Pero, ¿por qué? ¿Por qué no lo mataron?

—No sabemos con certeza el motivo, pero tengo varias hipótesis. Tu padre era un hombre de ciencia, ¿no es así? —preguntó Vikus.

—Sí, es profesor de Ciencias —contestó Gregor. No entendía adónde quería llegar Vikus. ¿Querían las ratas que su padre les diera clases de química?

—En nuestras conversaciones, se hizo evidente que entendía el funcionamiento de la Madre Naturaleza —dijo Vikus—. Del rayo cautivo, del fuego y de los polvos que explotan.

Gregor estaba empezando a captar la onda.

—Mire, si piensa que mi padre está fabricando armas o bombas para las ratas, olvídelo. Él nunca haría una cosa así.

—Resulta difícil imaginar lo que haría cualquiera de nosotros en manos de las ratas —dijo Vikus con dulzura—. Conservar la cordura debe de ser una lucha constante, conservar el honor, una tarea hercúlea. Yo no juzgo a tu padre, sólo trato de explicarme las razones de su larga supervivencia.

—Las ratas luchan bien en las distancias cortas —intervino Luxa—. Pero si las atacamos desde lejos, no tienen más recurso que huir. Lo que desean por encima de todo es hallar la manera de matarnos a distancia.

Luxa tampoco parecía acusar a su padre. Y ya no parecía enfadada con él. Gregor sólo deseaba que dejara de mirarlo tan fijamente.

—Mi esposa, Solovet, tiene una teoría distinta —dijo Vikus, y su semblante se iluminó un poco—. ¡Ella cree que las ratas quieren que tu padre les fabrique un pulgar!

—¿Un pulgar? —preguntó Gregor. Boots blandió su dedo para enseñárselo—. Sí, linda, ya sé lo que es un pulgar —le dijo sonriendo.

—Las ratas no tienen pulgar, y por eso no pueden hacer muchas de las cosas que hacemos nosotros. No pueden construir herramientas o armas. Son los amos de la destrucción, pero la creación se les escapa —explicó Vikus.

—Alégrate de que piensen que tu padre puede serles útil. Es lo único que le está dando tiempo —dijo Luxa apesadumbrada.

—¿Tú también conociste a mi padre? —le preguntó.

—No —contestó ella—. Yo era demasiado pequeña.

—Por aquel entonces Luxa aún jugaba con muñecas —dijo Vikus. Gregor se esforzó por imaginarse a Luxa con una muñeca, pero no lo consiguió.

—Mis padres sí lo conocieron, y hablaban bien de él —añadió Luxa.

Sus padres. Entonces todavía tenía padres. Gregor tenía curiosidad por saber cómo los habrían matado las ratas, pero sabía que nunca se lo preguntaría.

—Luxa dice la verdad. En el presente, las ratas son nuestros peores enemigos. Si te topas con una fuera de las murallas de Regalia, tienes dos opciones: luchar o morir. Tan sólo la esperanza de obtener una gran ventaja mantendría con vida a un humano entre sus garras. Especialmente si proviene de las Tierras Altas —explicó Vikus.

—No entiendo por qué nos odian tanto —protestó Gregor. Pensó en los brillantes ojos de Shed, y en sus últimas palabras: «No pararemos hasta darte caza». Tal vez saben que en las Tierras Altas la gente trataba de exterminar a todas las ratas, ya fuera con trampas o con veneno. Salvo las que se usan en los laboratorios para hacer experimentos.

Vikus y Luxa intercambiaron una mirada.

—Tenemos que decírselo, Luxa. Debe saber a lo que se enfrenta —dijo Vikus.

—¿Piensas de verdad que es él? —preguntó ella.

—¿Quién? ¿Que si soy quién? —dijo Gregor. Esa conversación no le daba muy buena espina.

Vikus se levantó de la mesa.

—Ven —lo invitó, saliendo de la habitación.

Gregor se levantó. Con gran esfuerzo, sus brazos cansados cargaron de nuevo a Boots. Luxa y él llegaron al mismo tiempo al umbral de la puerta.

—Tú, primero —le dijo Gregor.

Ella lo miró de soslayo y siguió a Vikus.

Las paredes estaban flanqueadas de ciudadanos que los miraban pasar en silencio, para después romper a hablar en susurros. No tuvieron que andar mucho antes de que Vikus se detuviera frente a una puerta de madera pulida. Gregor cayó en la cuenta entonces de que era la primera cosa de madera que veía en las Tierras Bajas. ¿No había dicho Vikus que algo era «tan escaso como los árboles»? Los árboles necesitaban mucha luz, ¿entonces cómo podían crecer aquí?

Vikus sacó una llave y abrió la puerta. Tomó una antorcha del pasillo y entró de primero, indicándoles que lo siguieran.

Gregor penetró en una sala que parecía un cubo de piedra vacío. En cada una de las superficies había inscripciones grabadas. No sólo en las paredes, sino también en el suelo y en el techo. No se trataba de los animalitos retozando que había visto en Regalia, sino de palabras. Diminutas palabras que alguien debía de haber tardado siglos en grabar sobre la piedra.

—A, B, C —dijo Boots, que era lo que siempre decía cuando veía letras—. A, B, C, D —añadió luego para dar énfasis.

—Éstas son las profecías de Bartholomew de Sandwich —declaró Vikus—. Una vez que sellamos las puertas de las Tierras Bajas, dedicó el resto de su vida a grabarlas sobre piedra.

«Y tanto como el resto de su vida», pensó Gregor. Al loco de Sandwich le alegraba mucho hacer una cosa así. Arrastrar a una pandilla de gente bajo tierra, y luego encerrarse en una habitación a grabar más disparates en las paredes.

—¿Qué quiere decir con eso de profecías? —preguntó Gregor, aunque sabía muy bien lo que era una profecía. Eran predicciones de lo que iba a ocurrir en el futuro. La mayoría de las religiones tenían las suyas, y a su abuela le encantaba un libro de profecías que había escrito un tal Nostradamus, o algo así. A juzgar por lo que decía el libro, el futuro era bastante deprimente.

—Sandwich era un vidente —explicó Vikus—. Predijo numerosas cosas que ya le han sucedido a nuestro pueblo.

—¿Y otras cuantas que no? —preguntó Gregor, tratando de poner un tono inocente. No es que descartara de plano las profecías, pero era bastante escéptico respecto a todo lo que pudiera venir de Sandwich. Además, aunque alguien te dijera algo que iba a pasar en el futuro, ¿qué podías hacer al respecto?

—Algunas todavía no las hemos descifrado —reconoció Vikus.

—Predijo la muerte de mis padres —dijo Luxa con tristeza, acariciando una parte de la pared—. En eso no había ningún misterio.

Vikus la abrazó, mirando la pared.

—No —convino—. Eso era tan claro como el agua.

Gregor se sintió fatal por décima vez aquella noche, por lo menos. De ahora en adelante, fuera cual fuera su opinión, trataría de hablar con respeto de las profecías.

—Pero hay una que nos causa una gran preocupación. Se llama la Profecía del Gris, porque no sabemos si predice el bien o el mal —explicó Vikus—. Lo que sí sabemos es que era para Sandwich la más sagrada y desesperante de sus visiones, pues nunca podía ver el desenlace, aunque le rondara la cabeza una y otra vez.

Vikus señaló con un gesto una pequeña lámpara de aceite que iluminaba un panel de la pared. Era la única fuente de luz de la habitación, aparte de la antorcha. Al parecer, mantenían viva la llama constantemente.

—¿Quieres leer? —preguntó Vikus, y Gregor se acercó a la pared.

La profecía estaba escrita a modo de poema, en cuatro estrofas. La letra era un poco extraña, pero consiguió entenderla.

—A, B, C —dijo Boots, tocando las letras. Gregor empezó a leer.

Cuidado, Tierras Bajas, se acerca nuestro final.
Los cazadores cazados serán,
el agua blanca de rojo se teñirá.
Los roedores atacarán y a todos aniquilar querrán.
Los desesperados sólo en una búsqueda
la esperanza hallar podrán.

Un guerrero de las Tierras Altas, un hijo del sol,
podría devolvernos la luz, o tal vez no.
Congregad a vuestros vecinos
y responded a su llamada
o las ratas de nosotros no dejarán nada.

Dos de arriba, dos de abajo de real ascendencia,
dos voladores, dos reptantes,
dos tejedores dan su aquiescencia.
Un roedor al lado y uno perdido antes.
Tras contar a los muertos
ocho vivos serán los restantes.

El último en morir su bando elegirá.
El destino de los ocho en su mano estará.
Rogadle, pues, prudencia cuando con cautela salte,
pues la vida puede ser muerte
y la muerte, vida, en un instante.

Cuando Gregor terminó de leer no sabía qué decir.

—¿Qué significa? —preguntó.

Vikus hizo un gesto negativo con la cabeza.

—Nadie lo sabe con certeza. Habla de unos tiempos oscuros en los que el futuro de nuestro pueblo habrá de decidirse. Es un llamamiento a emprender una búsqueda, no sólo nosotros, los humanos, sino también numerosas criaturas. Ésta nos llevará a la salvación, o a la aniquilación. La búsqueda la dirigirá un habitante de las Tierras Altas.

—Sí, ya eso lo entendí. Un guerrero —dijo Gregor.

—Habías preguntado por qué las ratas sienten un odio tan profundo por los de las Tierras Altas. Es porque saben que uno de ellos será el guerrero de la profecía —explicó Vikus.

—Ah, ya lo entiendo —dijo Gregor—. Bueno, ¿y cuándo va a venir ese guerrero?

Vikus miró fijamente a Gregor.

—Creo que ya está aquí.

CAPÍTULO UNDÉCIMO

Gregor despertó de un sueño agitado. Imágenes de ríos teñidos de sangre, su padre rodeado de ratas y Boots cayendo en abismos sin fondo habían poblado sus sueños durante toda la noche.

Ah, y también estaba aquello del guerrero.

Había tratado de decírselo. Cuando Vikus había dado a entender que él era el guerrero de la Profecía del Gris, Gregor se había echado a reír. Pero el anciano no hablaba en broma.

—Se ha equivocado usted de persona —le había dicho Gregor—. De verdad, se lo juro, yo no soy un guerrero.

¿De qué servía fingir que sí y que se hicieran ilusiones? Guerreros samurai, apaches, africanos, medievales. Gregor había visto películas y había leído libros sobre todos ellos. Él no se parecía en nada a un guerrero. Para empezar, los guerreros eran adultos, y solían tener un montón de armas especiales. Gregor tenía once años y, a menos que una hermana de dos años contara como arma, había llegado con las manos vacías.

Además, a Gregor no le gustaba pelear. Devolvía el golpe si alguien lo atacaba en la escuela, pero eso no ocurría a menudo. No es que fuera muy fuerte, pero era rápido, y a la gente no le gustaba meterse con él. Alguna que otra vez se había interpuesto en una pelea si veía que un grupo de muchachos estaba abusando de uno más pequeño; eso no le gustaba nada. Pero nunca andaba buscando pelea, ¿y no era pelearse lo que hacían normalmente los guerreros?

Vikus y Luxa habían escuchado sus protestas. Le pareció que podría haber convencido a Luxa —de todas maneras, ella no lo tenía en gran estima—, pero Vikus era más insistente.

—¿Cuántos habitantes de las Tierras Altas supones que sobreviven a su caída a las Tierras Bajas? Yo diría que una décima parte. Y después de eso, ¿cuántos sobreviven a las ratas? Tal vez otra décima parte. De modo que de mil habitantes de las Tierras Altas, digamos que tan sólo diez sobreviven. Es muy extraño que no sólo tu padre, sino también tú y tu hermana llegaran con vida ante nosotros —dijo Vikus.

—Bueno, supongo que es bastante extraño —admitió Gregor—. Pero no entiendo por qué eso me convierte en el guerrero éste.

—Lo entenderás cuando comprendas mejor la profecía —contestó Vikus—. Cada persona tiene su propio destino. Estas paredes hablan del nuestro. Y el tuyo, Gregor, requiere que desempeñes un papel en él.

—Yo no sé nada de destinos —objetó Gregor—. Vamos a ver, mi padre, Boots y yo... todos tenemos la misma lavandería y aterrizamos cerca de donde viven ustedes, así que a mí me parece que es más una coincidencia que otra cosa. A mí me gustaría ayudarlos, pero me parece que van a tener que esperar un poco más a su guerrero.

Vikus se limitó a sonreír y dijo que por la mañana someterían la cuestión a la opinión del Consejo. Esa mañana. Ahora.

Pese a todas sus preocupaciones, que eran muchas, Gregor no podía evitar una sensación de felicidad embriagadora que lo invadía de vez en cuando. ¡Su padre estaba vivo! Casi al instante, lo asaltaba una oleada de angustia. Sí, estaba vivo, ¡pero era prisionero de las ratas! Sin embargo, su abuela siempre decía: «Donde hay vida, hay esperanza».

Seguro que su abuela se pondría contenta si supiera que hablaban de él en una profecía. Pero claro, no era de él de quien se hablaba. Era de un guerrero que Gregor deseaba que apareciese muy pronto para ayudarlo a liberar a su padre.

Ése era ahora su principal objetivo. ¿Cómo podría rescatar a su padre?

La cortina se descorrió, y la luz obligó a Gregor a entrecerrar los ojos. De pie, en el umbral, estaba Mareth. La hinchazón de su rostro había bajado, pero los moratones tardarían más en desaparecer.

Gregor se preguntó si el guardia seguiría enfadado con él, pero su voz le pareció serena.

—Gregor de las Tierras Altas, el Consejo reclama tu presencia —anunció—. Si te apresuras, tal vez puedas bañarte y comer algo antes.

—Está bien —contestó Gregor. Al incorporarse, se dio cuenta de que Boots había apoyado la cabeza en su brazo. Se levantó sin despertarla—. ¿Y qué hago con Boots?

—Puede seguir durmiendo —dijo Mareth—. Dulcet cuidará de ella.

Gregor se bañó rápidamente y se puso ropa limpia. Mareth lo condujo a una pequeña habitación donde habían dispuesto un desayuno, y se quedó haciendo guardia en la puerta.

—Eh, Mareth —dijo Gregor, atrayendo la atención del guardia—. ¿Cómo están los demás? Me refiero a Perdita y a los murciélagos. ¿Están bien?

—Perdita ha despertado por fin. Los murciélagos se curarán —dijo Mareth con tono neutro.

—¡Eso es fantástico! —exclamó Gregor, muy aliviado. Después de la situación de su padre, lo que más lo preocupaba en esos momentos era el bienestar de los habitantes de las Tierras Bajas.

Gregor se comió ávidamente el pan con mantequilla y la tortilla de champiñones. Se bebió una infusión caliente hecha a base de alguna clase de hierba, y le pareció que la energía empezaba a correr por sus venas.

—¿Estás preparado para comparecer ante el Consejo? —preguntó Mareth, al ver su plato vacío.

—¡Listo! —exclamó Gregor, levantándose de un salto. No se había sentido mejor desde su caída a las Tierras Bajas. Las noticias sobre su padre, la recuperación de sus salvadores, el descanso y la comida lo habían hecho revivir.

El Consejo, un grupo de unos doce ancianos de las Tierras Bajas, se había reunido en torno a una mesa redonda junto al Gran Salón. Gregor vio a Vikus y a Solovet, y ésta le sonrió para darle ánimos.

Luxa también estaba ahí, con una expresión cansada y desafiante a la vez. Gregor se imaginaba que la habrían regañado por haberse unido al equipo de rescate la noche anterior. Estaba seguro de que Luxa no había mostrado ni el más mínimo arrepentimiento.

Vikus le presentó a los miembros del Consejo. Todos tenían nombres extraños que Gregor olvidó inmediatamente. Entonces empezaron a hacerle preguntas de todo tipo, como cuándo había nacido, si sabía nadar y lo que solía hacer en las Tierras Altas. Gregor no acertaba a comprender por qué eran importantes esas cosas. ¿Era de verdad relevante que su color preferido fuera el verde? Pero un par de miembros del Consejo estaba tomando apuntes de todo lo que decía, como si su vida dependiera de ello.

Transcurrido un tiempo, los miembros del Consejo parecieron olvidarse de su presencia, y se pusieron a deliberar entre ellos. Gregor captó frases como «un hijo del sol» y «el agua blanca de rojo se teñirá» y comprendió que estaban hablando de la profecía.

—Discúlpenme —intervino por fin—. Me figuro que Vikus no se los habrá dicho, pero yo no soy el guerrero. Miren, yo lo que de verdad necesito es que me ayuden a encontrar a mi padre para llevarlo de vuelta a casa.

Todos se quedaron mirándolo un momento, y luego se pusieron a hablar a la vez, muy animados. Ahora

Gregor oía una y otra vez las palabras «responded a su llamada».

Al cabo de un tiempo, Vikus dio unas palmaditas sobre la mesa para llamarlos al orden.

—Miembros del Consejo, hemos de tomar una decisión. He aquí a Gregor de las Tierras Altas. ¿Quién lo considera el guerrero de la Profecía del Gris?

Diez de los doce miembros alzaron la mano. Luxa mantuvo las suyas sobre la mesa. O no pensaba que fuera el guerrero, o no le estaba permitido votar. Ambas cosas, probablemente.

—Creemos que eres el guerrero —dijo Vikus—. Si pides nuestra ayuda para recuperar a tu padre, entonces nosotros responderemos a tu llamada.

¡Iban a ayudarlo! ¿Qué importaba el motivo?

—¡Está bien, genial! —exclamó Gregor—. ¡Me da igual lo que haya que hacer! O sea, quiero decir que pueden creer lo que quieran. Por mí no hay problema.

—Hemos de emprender el viaje cuanto antes —apremió Vikus.

—¡Estoy preparado! —declaró Gregor con entusiasmo—. Déjenme que recoja a Boots y podemos irnos.

—Ah, sí, la bebé —dijo Solovet. Esto originó otra ronda de deliberaciones.

—¡Esperen! —gritó Vikus—. Esto nos cuesta mucho tiempo. Gregor, no sabemos si la profecía incluye a tu hermana.

—¿Qué? —preguntó Gregor. No recordaba bien la profecía. Tenía que preguntarle a Vikus si podía entrar en la habitación para volverla a leer.

—La profecía menciona doce seres. Sólo dos provienen de las Tierras Altas. Tú y tu padre completan el cupo —explicó Solovet.

—La profecía también habla de uno perdido. Ése podría ser tu padre, en cuyo caso Boots sería el segundo habitante de las Tierras Altas. Pero también podría ser una rata —dijo Vikus—. El viaje será difícil. La profecía advierte que cuatro de los doce perderán la vida. Tal vez lo más prudente sea dejar a Boots aquí.

Un murmullo general de aprobación puntuó sus palabras.

A Gregor empezó a darle vueltas la cabeza.

¿Dejar a Boots? ¿Dejarla aquí, en Regalia, con los de las Tierras Bajas? ¡No podía hacerlo! No porque pensara que la fueran a tratar mal. Pero, se sentiría tan sola. ¿Y qué pasaría si él y su padre no regresaban? Entonces, ella nunca podría volver a casa. Con todo, sabía lo malvadas que eran las ratas. Y que no pararían hasta darle caza.

No sabía qué hacer. Miró los semblantes resueltos y pensó que los miembros del Consejo ya habían decidido separarlos.

«¡No se separen!». ¿No era eso lo que siempre le decía su madre cuando se llevaba a sus hermanas de paseo? «¡No se separen!».

Entonces se dio cuenta de que Luxa eludía su mirada. Había entrelazado los dedos sobre la mesa y los miraba fijamente, con una expresión tensa.

—¿Qué harías tú si se tratara de tu hermana, Luxa? —preguntó. Un silencio absoluto cayó sobre la habitación.

Era obvio que el Consejo no quería escuchar su opinión.

—Yo no tengo hermanas —dijo Luxa.

Gregor se quedó muy decepcionado. Algunos miembros del Consejo emitieron un murmullo de aprobación. Luxa barrió la habitación con unos ojos que echaban chispas y frunció el ceño.

—Pero si tuviera, y me hallara ahora en tu lugar —dijo con vehemencia— ¡nunca me separaría de ella ni un instante!

—Gracias —le dijo Gregor, pero no le pareció que ella pudiera oírlo en medio del griterío de protesta que se elevó entre los miembros del Consejo. Entonces, dijo, levantando la voz—: ¡Si Boots no va, yo tampoco!

El alboroto era grande cuando un murciélago entró por la puerta y se estrelló sobre la mesa, haciéndolos callar a todos. Una mujer fantasmagórica se desplomó sobre el lomo del murciélago, llevándose las manos al pecho para contener la sangre que manaba de él. El animal replegó una de las alas, pero la otra quedó extendida formando un ángulo extraño, claramente rota.

—Anchel ha muerto. Daphne ha muerto. Las ratas encontraron a Shed y a Fangor. El rey Gorger ha lanzado a sus ejércitos. Vienen por nosotros —dijo la mujer con un hilo de voz.

Vikus la recogió en sus brazos justo cuando iba a derrumbarse.

—¿Cuántas son, Keeda? —le preguntó.

—Muchas —susurró esta—. Muchas ratas. —Y dicho esto, se desmayó.

CAPÍTULO DUODÉCIMO

Den la alarma! —gritó Vikus, y el palacio estalló en una frenética actividad. Sonaban cuernos por doquier, la gente entraba y salía corriendo, los murciélagos bajaban para recibir órdenes y volvían a levantar el vuelo sin tiempo para aterrizar.

Nadie se fijaba en Gregor, todos estaban muy ocupados en sus quehaceres de emergencia. Gregor quería preguntarle a Vikus qué estaba pasando, pero el hombre estaba en el Gran Salón, rodeado de murciélagos, dando órdenes a diestra y siniestra.

Gregor salió a la terraza y vio a Regalia convertida en un hervidero de actividad. Muchas ratas estaban en camino. Los habitantes de las Tierras Bajas se aprestaban para defenderse. De repente, cayó en la cuenta de que estaban en guerra.

Esa aterradora idea (y el vértigo de la altura) lo marearon. Cuando volvía tambaleándose al interior de la habitación, una mano lo agarró del brazo con fuerza.

—Gregor de las Tierras Altas, prepárate, partimos enseguida —dijo Vikus.

—¿Adónde? ¿Adónde vamos? —preguntó Gregor.

—A rescatar a tu padre —contestó Vikus.

—¿Ahora? ¿Podemos ir, aunque nos ataquen las ratas? —dijo Gregor—. Porque está empezando una guerra, ¿no es así?

—No es una guerra cualquiera. Creemos que es la guerra a la que se refiere la Profecía del Gris. La que puede traer consigo la aniquilación total de nuestro pueblo —explicó Vikus—. Emprender la búsqueda de tu padre es nuestra mayor esperanza de sobrevivir a esta guerra —prosiguió Vikus.

—¿Puedo llevarme a Boots, verdad? —preguntó Gregor—. Lo que quiero decir es que me la voy a llevar —se corrigió a sí mismo.

—Sí, Boots te acompañará —confirmó Vikus.

—¿Qué tengo que hacer? Usted dijo que debía prepararme —preguntó Gregor.

Vikus reflexionó un segundo y luego hizo llamar a Mareth.

—Llévalo al museo, y que escoja lo que piense que puede ayudarlo en el viaje. ¡Ah, he aquí la Delegación de Troya! —anunció Vikus. Una vez más, volvió a rodearlo un tropel de murciélagos.

Gregor corrió detrás de Mareth, que se había precipitado hacia la puerta. Tres escaleras y varios pasillos más adelante, llegaron a una espaciosa habitación cubierta de estantes abarrotados de objetos.

—Esto es cuanto ha caído de las Tierras Altas. Recuerda que tienes que llevar tú mismo todo aquello que elijas —explicó Mareth, entregándole una bolsa de cuero que se cerraba tirando de un cordón.

En los estantes había desde pelotas de béisbol hasta neumáticos. A Gregor le hubiese gustado disponer de más tiempo para inspeccionar los estantes cuidadosamente; algunos de los objetos debían de tener más de cien años. Pero el tiempo era un lujo que no tenía. Trató de concentrarse.

¿Qué podía llevarse que lo ayudara en su viaje? ¿Qué era lo que más necesitaba en las Tierras Bajas? ¡Luz!

Encontró una linterna que funcionaba y fue sacando pilas de todos los aparatos eléctricos que había en el museo.

Otro objeto llamó su atención. Era un casco como los que suelen llevar los mineros y los obreros de la construcción. Tenía una bombilla incorporada, para que pudieran ver en los oscuros túneles que se extendían por debajo de Nueva York. Cogió el casco y se lo caló en la cabeza.

—¡Tenemos que irnos! —ordenó Mareth—. ¡Tenemos que recoger a tu hermana y levantar el vuelo!

Gregor dio media vuelta para seguirlo y entonces la vio. ¡Una gaseosa! Una lata de gaseosa de las de toda la vida, sin abrir, y apenas un poquito abollada. Parecía casi nueva. Sabía que era un capricho, que sólo debía llevarse lo esencial, pero se le antojaba mucho. Era su refresco preferido, y además le recordaba su casa. Metió la lata en la bolsa.

La guardería estaba cerca del museo. Gregor entró corriendo y descubrió a Boots sentada muy contenta con otros tres niños de las Tierras Bajas, jugando a la cocinita. Durante un segundo, estuvo a punto de cambiar de idea y dejarla ahí. ¿No estaría más segura en el palacio? Pero entonces recordó que el lugar pronto estaría bajo el asedio de las ratas. Gregor sabía que no podía dejarla sola frente a un peligro así. Pasara lo que pasara, no se separarían.

Dulcet lo ayudó rápidamente a ponerse una mochila a la espalda y a meter en ella a Boots. Luego, Dulcet ató un paquetito a la base de la mochila.

—Paños empapadores —dijo—. Unos juguetes y algo rico de comer.

—Gracias —dijo Gregor muy contento de que alguien hubiera pensado en los aspectos prácticos de tener que viajar con un bebé.

—Que tengas buen viaje, dulce Boots —dijo Dulcet, besando la mejilla de la niña.

—Adiós, *Du-ce* —contestó Boots—. ¡Hasta *ponto*!

Así era como siempre se despedían unos de otros en casa de Gregor. No te preocupes. Volveré. Hasta pronto.

—Sí, hasta pronto —dijo Dulcet, pero sus ojos se llenaron de lágrimas.

—Cuídate, Dulcet —le dijo Gregor, dándole un torpe apretón de manos.

—Vuela alto, Gregor de las Tierras Altas —contestó ella.

En el Gran Salón, la expedición se preparaba para la partida. Algunos murciélagos habían aterrizado, y los estaban cargando con provisiones y materiales.

Gregor vio a Henry dándole un abrazo de despedida a una adolescente extremadamente delgada. Ésta lloraba incontroladamente, pese a los esfuerzos de Henry por consolarla.

—Las pesadillas, hermano —dijo la chica entre sollozos—, son cada vez peores. Un terrible mal te aguarda.

—No te aflijas, Nerissa, no tengo intención de morir —dijo Henry para tranquilizarla.

—Hay males peores que la muerte —contestó ella—. Vuela alto, Henry. Vuela alto. —Se abrazaron, y Henry subió a lomos de su murciélago negro.

Gregor miraba nervioso a la chica mientras ésta se acercaba a él. Nunca sabía qué decir cuando alguien lloraba. Pero ya se había serenado cuando llegó a su altura. Ella le entregó un pequeño rollo de papel.

—Para ti —le dijo—. Vuela alto. —Y, antes de que Gregor tuviera tiempo de contestar, la chica ya se había alejado, apoyándose en la pared para no caerse.

Gregor desenrolló el papel, que no era tal, sino algún tipo de piel curtida de animal, y vio que en ella alguien había copiado cuidadosamente la Profecía del Gris. «Qué extraño», pensó Gregor. Justamente quería volver a leerla para tratar de comprenderla un poco mejor. Había pensado en pedirle permiso a Vikus, pero luego con las prisas se le había olvidado.

—¿Cómo sabía ella que yo quería la profecía? —le murmuró a Boots.

—Nerissa sabe muchas cosas. Tiene el don —dijo un muchacho junto a él, montado a lomos de un murciélago dorado. Cuando Gregor lo volvió a mirar, descubrió que se trataba de Luxa, pero ahora llevaba el cabello muy corto.

—¿Y tu pelo? —preguntó Gregor, metiéndose la profecía en el bolsillo.

—Los rizos largos son peligrosos para luchar — dijo Luxa despreocupadamente.

—Ah, qué pena, bueno, quiero decir que... también te queda bien corto —se apresuró a añadir Gregor.

Luxa soltó una carcajada.

—Gregor de las Tierras Altas, ¿acaso piensas que en tiempos como éstos mi belleza tiene relevancia alguna?

Gregor sintió que le ardía todo el cuerpo de pura vergüenza.

—No era eso lo que quería decir.

Luxa miró a Henry sacudiendo la cabeza de lado a lado, y éste le contestó con una amplia sonrisa.

—El de las Tierras Altas dice la verdad, prima, pareces una oveja esquilada.

—Tanto mejor —replicó Luxa—, pues, ¿quién atacaría a una oveja?

—*Beee* —dijo Boots—. *Beeeee.* —A Henry le entró tanta risa que estuvo a punto de caerse del murciélago—. Las ovejas hacen *beee* —dijo Boots a la defensiva, lo cual le dio más risa todavía.

Poco faltó para que Gregor se riera también. Durante un momento, se había sentido como entre amigos. Pero la verdad era que estas personas estaban muy lejos de ser sus amigos. Para disimular ese momento de debilidad, se concentró en dar con una manera cómoda de llevar la bolsa de cuero, de forma que le dejara las dos manos libres. Al final, optó por atarla a una de las correas de la mochila.

Cuando levantó la vista, descubrió que Luxa lo estaba mirando con curiosidad.

—¿Qué llevas en la cabeza? —le preguntó.

—Es un casco con luz —explicó Gregor. Apagó y encendió la bombilla para que lo viera. Gregor se dio cuenta de que Luxa se moría por probarse el casco, pero no quería pedírselo. Rápidamente, Gregor sopesó en su cabeza las opciones que tenía. No eran amigos... pero era mejor llevarse bien con ella, a ser posible. La necesitaba para recuperar a su padre. Gregor le tendió el casco—. Toma, échale un vistazo.

Luxa trató de aparentar indiferencia, pero sus manos, ávidas por encender y apagar la bombilla, la traicionaban.

—¿Cómo haces para conservar la luz encendida sin aire? ¿No te quema la cabeza? —preguntó.

—Funciona con pilas. Es electricidad. Y hay una capa de plástico entre la bombilla y tu cabeza. Puedes probártelo si quieres —le ofreció.

Sin dudarlo un momento, Luxa se puso el casco en la cabeza.

—Vikus me ha hablado de la electricidad —dijo. Paseó el haz de luz por la habitación antes de devolverle el casco de mala gana—. Toma, no debes malgastar el combustible.

—Vas a imponer una nueva moda —dijo Henry alegremente. Cogió una de las pequeñas antorchas que había en la pared y se la colocó encima de la cabeza. Las llamas parecían salir directamente de su frente—. ¿Qué me dices, Luxa? —preguntó, mostrándole su perfil con una arrogancia exagerada.

—¡Tu cabello está en llamas! —exclamó de pronto Luxa, señalándolo con el dedo. Henry soltó la antorcha, dándose palmetazos en el pelo, mientras Luxa se destornillaba de risa.

Al comprender que se trataba de una broma, Henry la cogió por el cuello y se puso a darle coscorrones, mientras ella seguía riéndose sin parar. Por un momento Gregor pensó que parecían un par de chicos normales de las Tierras Altas. Unos hermanos, como Gregor y Lizzie, que jugaban a echar luchitas.

Vikus entró en la habitación.

—Están de muy buen humor, considerando que estamos en guerra —dijo frunciendo el ceño mientras montaba a lomos de su murciélago.

—No es más que exceso de brío, Vikus —dijo Henry, soltando a Luxa.

—Conserven su brío, lo necesitarán allí donde vamos. Monta conmigo, Gregor —dijo Vikus, extendiendo la mano. De un salto Gregor se colocó detrás de él, a lomos de su gran murciélago gris.

Boots le dio paraditas al murciélago en los costados muy animada.

—Yo *tamén* monto. Yo *tamén* —gorjeó.

—¡A sus monturas! —dijo Vikus, y Luxa y Henry saltaron a lomos de sus murciélagos. Gregor vio a lo lejos a Solovet y a Mareth, preparándose también para partir. Mareth montaba un murciélago que Gregor nunca había visto antes. Probablemente el otro animal aún estaría recuperándose.

—¡Al aire! —ordenó Solovet, y los cinco murciélagos levantaron el vuelo formando una "v" en el aire.

Mientras se elevaban, Gregor se sentía a punto de estallar de emoción y felicidad. ¡Iban en busca de su padre! Lo rescatarían y regresarían a casa, y su madre volvería a sonreír otra vez, a sonreír de verdad, y vivirían las vacaciones como ocasiones de celebración y no de angustia, y habría música y... y estaba anticipando demasiado. Estaba incumpliendo su norma totalmente, así que dentro de un minuto dejaría de hacerlo, pero mientras tanto, Gregor estaba decidido a seguir imaginando todo cuanto se le antojara.

Mientras volaban por encima de la ciudad de Regalia, la actividad frenética que veía a sus pies le recordó a Gregor la gravedad de su misión. Estaban fortificando las puertas del estadio con enormes losas de piedra. Carromatos de comida obstruían las carreteras. Por todas partes se veían adultos corriendo, con niños en brazos. En todos los barrios se encendían antorchas adicionales, con lo que la ciudad casi parecía bañada por la luz del sol.

—Si los van a atacar, ¿no sería mejor que hubiera más oscuridad? —preguntó Gregor.

—Nosotros no, pero las ratas sí lo preferirían. Necesitamos ver para luchar; ellas, no —contestó Vikus—. La mayoría de las criaturas de las Tierras Bajas, los reptantes, los murciélagos, los peces, no necesitan luz. Nosotros, los humanos, estamos perdidos sin ella.

Gregor almacenó esa información en un rinconcito de su cerebro. Había sido una gran idea llevarse la linterna del museo, después de todo.

Rápidamente, las calles de la ciudad dejaron paso a tierras de cultivo, y Gregor pudo ver así, por vez primera, de qué se alimentaban los de las Tierras Bajas. Una especie de cereal crecía en grandes campos, gracias a hileras e hileras de lámparas blancas colgantes.

—¿Con qué funcionan esas lámparas? —preguntó.

—Con gas que extraemos de la tierra. Tu padre quedó muy impresionado por nuestros campos. Propuso un proyecto para iluminar también nuestra ciudad pero, por el momento, toda la luz ha de reservarse para la agricultura —dijo Vikus.

—¿Ese sistema se lo enseñó alguien de las Tierras Altas? —le preguntó Gregor.

—Gregor, no dejamos el cerebro en las Tierras Altas cuando bajamos aquí. Entre nosotros también hay inventores, y la luz es nuestro bien más preciado. ¿Acaso piensas que a nosotros, pobrecitos, no se nos podía ocurrir alguna manera de aprovecharla? —le dijo Vikus sin un asomo de descortesía.

Gregor se sintió avergonzado. Había pensado que los de las Tierras Bajas estaban un poco atrasados. Todavía utilizaban espadas y vestían de una forma muy rara. Pero no eran tontos. Su padre decía que hasta entre los hombres de las cavernas había genios. Al fin y al cabo, uno de ellos había inventando la rueda.

Solovet volaba en paralelo a ellos, pero estaba enfrascada en una conversación con un par de murciélagos que se habían unido al grupo. Desenrolló un gran mapa sobre el lomo de su murciélago y se puso a escrutarlo.

—¿Está tratando de encontrar dónde está mi padre? —le preguntó Gregor a Vikus.

—Está trazando un plan de ataque —contestó—. Mi esposa dirige a nuestros guerreros. No nos acompaña para encauzar la búsqueda, sino para calibrar el grado de apoyo que podemos esperar de nuestros aliados.

—¿En serio? Pensé que era usted el que estaba al mando. Bueno, usted y Luxa —añadió, porque en realidad no tenía ni idea de cómo estaba organizado todo. Luxa parecía tener derecho a dar órdenes a la gente; sin embargo Gregor tenía la impresión de que había cosas que no le estaba permitido hacer.

—Luxa subirá al trono cuando cumpla dieciséis años. Hasta entonces, Regalia está gobernada por el Consejo. Yo no soy sino un humilde diplomático que dedica su tiempo libre a tratar de enseñar prudencia a la juventud de sangre real. Tú mismo ves el éxito de mi empresa —comentó Vikus irónicamente. Miró a Luxa y a Henry, que surcaban el cielo a gran velocidad, tratando de derribarse el uno al otro—. No te dejes engañar por la delicadeza de Solovet. En la planificación de la batalla, es más astuta y artera que una rata.

—Caray —exclamó Gregor. La delicadeza de Solovet sí que le había llevado a engaño.

Gregor cambió de postura sobre su montura y notó que algo le molestaba en la pierna. Se sacó del bolsillo la copia de la profecía que le había dado Nerissa y la desenrolló. Tal vez, ése era un buen momento para hacerle a Vikus unas cuantas preguntas.

—Bueno, ¿y cree usted que podría explicarme esto de la Profecía Gris?

—La Profecía del Gris —lo corrigió Vikus—. ¿Qué parte de ella te deja perplejo?

«Toda ella entera», pensó Gregor, pero dijo:

—Tal vez podríamos repasarla verso a verso.

Entonces, estudió el poema.

Cuidado, Tierras Bajas, se acerca nuestro final.

Bueno, eso estaba bastante claro. Era una advertencia.

**Los cazadores cazados serán,
el agua blanca de rojo se teñirá.**

Gregor pidió a Vikus que le descifrara el segundo verso de la profesía.

—Tradicionalmente, los cazadores de las Tierras Bajas son las ratas, pues mucho les complacería darnos caza y matarnos a todos. Anoche, les dimos caza nosotros a ellas para salvarte a ti y a tu hermana. De modo que los cazadores cazados fueron. El agua blanca de rojo se tiñó cuando arrojamos sus cuerpos al río.

—Ah —dijo Gregor. Había algo que le causaba una cierta desazón, pero no sabía exactamente qué.

Los roedores atacarán y a todos aniquilar querrán.

—¿Los roedores son las ratas? —preguntó Gregor.

—Exactamente —contestó Vikus.

Los desesperados sólo en una búsqueda
la esperanza hallar podrán.

Esta búsqueda para encontrar a su padre. Recapitulando, él se había escapado, los de las Tierras Bajas lo habían salvado, y ahora estaban en guerra y habían emprendido la búsqueda. Gregor supo de pronto qué era lo que lo inquietaba.

—Entonces... ¡todo esto es mi culpa! —exclamó—. ¡Nada de esto habría ocurrido si yo no hubiera intentado escapar! —Pensó en el ejército de ratas que se aproximaba. ¿Qué había hecho?

—No, Gregor, aparta ese pensamiento de tu mente —dijo Vikus con firmeza—. No eres sino un personaje más dentro de una larga y difícil historia. La Profecía del Gris te ha atrapado, como nos atrapó a todos nosotros hace mucho tiempo.

Gregor guardó silencio. Esas palabras no le ayudaban a sentirse mejor.

—Sigue leyendo —lo apremió Vikus, y Gregor acercó la cabeza lo más posible a la página. Las luces de Regalia se habían alejado en la distancia, y tuvo que hacer un esfuerzo para poder distinguir las letras a la tenue luz de la antorcha.

Un guerrero de las Tierras Altas, un hijo del sol,
podría devolvernos la luz, o tal vez no.

Congregad a vuestros vecinos
y responded a su llamada
o las ratas de nosotros no dejarán nada.

—Así que, según usted, esta parte habla de mí —dijo Gregor lúgubremente.

—Sí, tú eres el «guerrero de las Tierras Altas» por motivos del todo obvios —dijo Vikus, aunque a Gregor esos motivos no le parecían tan obvios—. Como habitante de las Tierras Altas, eres un «hijo del sol», pero también eres el hijo que busca a su padre. Ésta es la clase de juego de palabras jocoso que tanto gustaba a Sandwich.

—Sí, era un tipo muy divertido —dijo Gregor con desánimo. Sí, jajá, divertidísimo.

—Los versos que siguen son muy grises —prosiguió Vikus—. Sandwich nunca acertó a ver claramente si conseguías traer la luz, o si fracasabas en tu empeño. Pero insistió categóricamente en que habíamos de probar suerte, o moriríamos a manos de las ratas.

—Pues no es muy prometedor, ¿no? —dijo. Pero, por primera vez, Gregor no se sentía tan alejado de Sandwich. La posibilidad de que el guerrero pudiera fracasar hacía la profecía más plausible.

—¿Qué luz se supone que tengo que traer? —preguntó—. ¿Es que hay una antorcha sagrada, o algo así?

—Eso es una metáfora. Cuando dice «luz», Sandwich se refiere a «vida». Si las ratas logran extinguir nuestra luz, entonces también extinguen nuestra vida —explicó Vikus.

¿Una metáfora? Gregor había pensado que una antorcha de verdad sería más fácil de traer. Pero, ¿cómo podía traer algo que era una metáfora que ni siquiera entendía bien?

—Eso puede resultar difícil —comentó, antes de proseguir con su lectura.

Dos de arriba, dos de abajo de real ascendencia,
dos voladores, dos reptantes,
dos tejedores dan su aquiescencia.

—¿Quiénes son todos estos que van de dos en dos? —quiso saber Gregor.

—Estos versos nos dicen a quién debemos persuadir de que nos acompañe en la búsqueda. Lo hemos entendido como que los «dos de arriba» son tú y tu hermana. Los «dos de abajo de real ascendencia» son Luxa y Henry. La hermana de Henry, Nerissa, como puedes imaginar, no era una opción válida. Los voladores son murciélagos; los reptantes, cucarachas; y los tejedores, arañas. Ahora vamos a convocar a nuestros vecinos en el orden que dicta la profecía. Primero, los murciélagos.

El número de murciélagos había ido aumentando conforme avanzaba el viaje. Henry llevó al grupo hasta una amplia cueva. Gregor se llevó un pequeño susto al descubrir que el techo estaba cubierto de bultos, que no eran sino cientos y cientos de murciélagos que colgaban cabeza abajo.

—¿Pero es que no tenemos ya murciélagos? —preguntó Gregor.

—Necesitamos permiso oficial para que nos acompañen en la búsqueda —dijo Vikus—. Además, hay aspectos de la guerra que se han de discutir.

En el centro de la cueva se erguía un alto cilindro de piedra. Sus lados eran tan lisos como los muros del palacio. Sobre su cima redonda y plana aguardaba un grupo de murciélagos.

Vikus se volvió hacia Gregor y le susurró:

—Nosotros los humanos sabemos que tú eres el guerrero, pero tal vez otras criaturas tengan sus dudas. Pienses lo que pienses, es esencial que nuestros vecinos crean que eres el guerrero.

Gregor estaba tratando de encontrar sentido en las palabras de Vikus cuando aterrizaron junto a los murciélagos en la cima de la enorme columna de piedra. Todos los humanos bajaron de sus monturas. Ambos grupos intercambiaron profundas reverencias y saludos.

Había un murciélago de pelaje blanco plateado, especialmente imponente, que era a todas luces el jefe.

—Reina Athena —dijo Vikus—, te presento a Gregor de las Tierras Altas.

—¿Eres tú el guerrero, eres tú el que llama? —preguntó el murciélago en un suave susurro.

—Bueno, el caso es que... —Gregor vio que Vikus fruncía el ceño y calló inmediatamente. Había estado a punto de soltar su rollo de que él no era el guerrero, pero de haberlo hecho, ¿qué habría ocurrido? Vikus le había dicho que los demás creían que él era el guerrero. Había estallado una guerra. Lo más seguro era que los murciélagos no quisieran mandar a los suyos a una aventura sin sentido. Si ahora negaba ser él el guerrero, la búsqueda se cancelaría y ya no habría forma de salvar la vida de su padre. Eso hizo que Gregor se decidiera.

Se irguió y trató de dominar el temblor que se colaba en su voz.

—Yo soy el guerrero. Yo soy el que llama.

El murciélago permaneció inmóvil por un momento, y después asintió con la cabeza.

—Es él.

La reina habló con tanta certeza que, durante un segundo, Gregor consiguió verse a sí mismo como un guerrero. Un guerrero audaz, valiente y poderoso cuyas gestas serían cantadas durante siglos y siglos en las leyendas de las Tierras Bajas. Casi podía verse a sí mismo llevando un escuadrón de murciélagos a la batalla, imponiéndose sobre las ratas, salvando a las Tierras Bajas de...

—*¡Gue-go, teno pipí!* —dijo Boots.

Y ahí estaba él, un muchacho con un ridículo casco, una linterna del año del caldo y un puñado de pilas que ni siquiera sabía si aún servían.

El poderoso guerrero se disculpó y le cambió los pañales a su hermana.

CAPÍTULO DECIMOTERCERO

Vikus y Solovet realizaron las gestiones necesarias con el objetivo de concertar un encuentro privado con los murciélagos para hablar sobre el tema de la guerra.

—¿Es necesario que yo también asista? —preguntó Gregor. No tanto porque pensara que podía aportar algo a la reunión, sino porque se sentía más seguro cuando Vikus estaba cerca. Quedarse abandonado a su suerte en la cima de una alta columna, rodeado de cientos de murciélagos, le hacía sentir un poquito incómodo.

¿Y quién se quedaría a cargo de todo si ocurría algo? ¿Luxa? A Gregor no le gustaba nada esa idea.

—No, gracias, Gregor. Discutiremos cuestiones de estrategia bélica, no los pormenores de la búsqueda. No nos ausentaremos por mucho tiempo —dijo Vikus.

—Está bien, no hay problema —contestó Gregor, pero en su fuero interno no estaba tan tranquilo.

Antes de que se marcharan, el gran murciélago de Vikus susurró algo al oído de Luxa. Ésta sonrió, miró a Gregor, y asintió con la cabeza.

«Seguro que se están riendo de que yo sea el guerrero», pensó Gregor. Pero no se trataba de eso.

—Eurípides dice que le haces daño en los costados —dijo Luxa—. Quiere que te enseñe a montar.

Ese comentario molestó a Gregor. Él pensaba que lo había estado haciendo bastante bien para ser ésta su primera vez.

—¿Qué quiere decir con eso de que le estoy haciendo daño en los costados?

—Te agarras demasiado fuerte con las piernas. Debes confiar en los murciélagos. No te dejarán caer —dijo Luxa—. Es la primera lección que enseñamos a los niños pequeños.

—Muy bien —contestó Gregor. Luxa tenía el don de humillarlo, aunque no lo hiciera a propósito.

—A los niños pequeños les resulta más fácil —intervino Mareth apresuradamente—. Como tu hermana, aún no han aprendido a sentir temor. Aquí abajo tenemos un dicho: «El valor sólo cuenta cuando uno sabe contar». ¿Sabes contar, Boots? —Mareth extendió los dedos delante de Boots, que estaba muy ocupada tratando de desabrochar la sandalia de su hermano—. ¡Uno... dos... tres!

Boots sonrió de oreja a oreja y levantó sus gordos deditos, imitándolo.

—¡No, yo! ¡Uno... dos... *tes... cuato...* siete... diez! —exclamó, y levantó las dos manitas para celebrar su proeza.

Henry tomó a Boots en brazos, sin acercársela, como se suele agarrar a un cachorro mojado.

—Boots no tiene temor, ni lo tendrá tampoco cuando aprenda a contar. ¿Te gusta volar, verdad, Boots?

¿Qué opinas de un paseíto a lomos del murciélago? —preguntó con picardía.

—¡Yo monto! —exclamó Boots, y se revolvió para tratar de zafarse de los brazos de Henry.

—¡Pues monta, entonces! —contestó Henry, y la lanzó al vacío desde la cima de la columna.

Gregor dejó escapar un grito al ver a Boots, como en cámara lenta, dejar las manos de Henry y desaparecer en la oscuridad.

—¡Henry! —exclamó Mareth escandalizado. Pero Luxa se destornillaba de risa.

Gregor avanzó tambaleándose hasta el borde de la columna y escrutó la oscuridad. La tenue luz de la antorcha que les habían dado los murciélagos apenas iluminaba unos metros. ¿De verdad había tirado Henry a Boots al vacío, a una muerte segura? Gregor no podía creerlo. No podía...

En eso, un alegre chillido retumbó por encima de su cabeza.

—¡Más!

¡Era Boots! ¿Pero qué estaba haciendo allí arriba? Gregor apuntó con su linterna. El haz era potente, y abrió un amplio pasillo de luz a través de la oscuridad.

Veinte murciélagos daban vueltas alrededor de la cueva, jugando con Boots. Uno volaba muy alto con la niña montada en su lomo, y de repente se ponía cabeza abajo en pleno vuelo, dejando caer a Boots al abismo. Pero mucho antes de que la niña diera contra el suelo, otro murciélago la recogía en el aire, para volver a elevarla y repetir otra vez la misma operación. Boots reía extasiada. «¡Más, más!», ordenaba a los murciélagos cada vez que aterrizaba sobre ellos. Y cada vez que la volvían a lanzar al vacío, a Gregor se le subía el estómago a la garganta.

—¡Basta! —gritó. Henry y Luxa adoptaron una expresión de sorpresa. Una de dos, o nunca nadie había gritado a esos idiotas de sangre real, o todavía no habían visto a Gregor perder la paciencia. Éste agarró a Henry por el cuello de la camisa—. ¡Tráela aquí, ya mismo! —Seguramente Henry podía hacerlo picadillo, pero no le importaba.

Henry levantó las manos, haciendo que se rendía.

—Tranquilízate. No corre peligro —dijo con una gran sonrisa.

—A decir verdad, Gregor, está más segura con los murciélagos que en manos de los humanos —dijo Luxa—. Y, además, no siente temor.

—¡Tiene dos años! —gritó Gregor, volviéndose hacia Luxa—. ¡Va a pensar que puede saltar desde cualquier parte y que alguien la recogerá!

—¡Puede pensarlo! —exclamó Luxa, que no veía cuál era el problema.

—¡No donde vivimos nosotros, Luxa! ¡No en las Tierras Altas! —contestó Gregor—. ¡Y no tengo intención de quedarme para siempre en este sitio que me pone los pelos de punta!

Tal vez no entendieran exactamente qué significaba «poner los pelos de punta», pero les quedó bastante claro que era algo ofensivo.

Luxa levantó la mano, y entonces un murciélago se acercó despacio y dejó caer suavemente a Boots en brazos de su hermano. Éste la tomó y la abrazó muy fuerte. Ya nadie reía.

—¿Qué significa eso que mencionaste de «los pelos de punta»? —preguntó Luxa fríamente.

—Olvídalo —dijo Gregor—. No es más que algo que decimos en las Tierras Altas cuando vemos a unos murciélagos lanzando por los aires a nuestras hermanas pequeñas. A nosotros eso nos «pone los pelos de punta», ¿entiendes lo que quiero decir?

—Se supone que esto era una diversión —intervino Henry.

—Oh, sí, claro, una diversión, por supuesto. Deberías montar un parque de atracciones. Las colas de gente llegarían hasta la superficie —contestó Gregor.

Ahora sí que no sabían de qué estaba hablando, pero a nadie se le pasó por alto su tono sarcástico.

Boots se zafó de su abrazo y corrió hasta el borde de la columna.

—¡Más, *Gue-go*! —rogó.

—¡No, Boots! ¡No, no! ¡No saltes! —exclamó Gregor, atrapándola justo a tiempo—. ¿Lo ves? ¡Esto es justo lo que te decía! —le dijo a Luxa.

Acto seguido, metió a la niña en la mochila y se la puso a la espalda.

Todos estaban desconcertados por su enojo y molestos por su tono, aunque no hubieran entendido el significado de sus palabras.

—Bueno, de todos modos, no era Boots quien necesitaba unas cuantas lecciones, sino tú —comentó Luxa.

—Oh, olvida esa idea, Luxa —rió Henry con desprecio—. El de las Tierras Altas no se entregaría jamás a los murciélagos. ¡Pero cuando regrese a casa, tal vez olvide que ya no está en esta tierra que «le pone los pelos de punta», y se tire desde su propio tejado!

Luxa y Henry soltaron una carcajada hostil. Mareth, en cambio, parecía incómodo. Gregor sabía que lo estaban desafiando, y una parte de él se moría por aceptar el reto. Correr y lanzarse al vacío, y dejarle el resto a los murciélagos. Otra parte de él, no quería entrar en ese jueguito. Luxa y Henry querían que saltara para poder burlarse de él al verlo dar vueltas en el aire como un pelele. Pero se imaginaba que a los dos les sentaría fatal que los ignorara por completo. De modo que los miró con desdén y les dio la espalda.

Gregor notó claramente que Luxa estaba furiosa.

—¡Podía haberte tirado al vacío, y no habría tenido que responder ante nadie! —exclamó.

—¡Pues, hazlo! —exclamó Gregor, extendiendo los brazos. Sabía que era mentira. Habría tenido que responder ante Vikus.

Luxa se mordió el labio, irritada.

—Oh, deja al guerrero tranquilo, Luxa —dijo Henry—. Muerto no nos es de ninguna utilidad... por ahora... y tal vez ni siquiera los murciélagos pudieran compensar su torpeza. Vamos, te echo una carrera hasta el borde. —Luxa vaciló un segundo, y luego se lanzó a correr. Ella y Henry se tiraron al vacío como dos preciosos pájaros y desaparecieron, probablemente a lomos de sus murciélagos.

Gregor permaneció allí de pie, odiándolos con toda su alma. Había olvidado que Mareth estaba justo detrás de él.

—No debes tomarte a pecho lo que te digan —

le dijo con voz suave. Gregor se volvió y vio el rostro de Mareth, que reflejaba el conflicto que había en su mente—. Ambos eran más amables de niños, pero cuando las ratas se llevaron a sus padres, cambiaron.

—¿Las ratas también mataron a los padres de Henry? —preguntó Gregor.

—Unos años antes que a los de Luxa. El padre de Henry era el hermano menor del rey. Después de los habitantes de las Tierras Altas, a quienes más complacería ver muertos a las ratas es a todos los miembros de la familia real —explicó Mareth—. Cuando los mataron, Nerissa se volvió frágil como el cristal y Henry, duro como la piedra.

Gregor asintió con la cabeza. Nunca conseguía odiar a nadie demasiado tiempo porque siempre acababa descubriendo algo triste de esa persona que lo hacía recapacitar. Como aquel niño de su escuela que le caía mal a todo el mundo porque siempre se estaba metiendo con los más pequeños, y luego un día se enteraron de que una vez su padre le había pegado tanto que lo había mandado al hospital. Con cosas como ésa, Gregor no podía evitar sentir pena, y no odio.

Vikus llegó unos minutos después y Gregor montó a lomos de su murciélago sin decir palabra. Cuando levantaron el vuelo cayó en la cuenta de la fuerza con que sus piernas se agarraban a los flancos del murciélago, y trató de relajarse. Vikus montaba con las piernas colgando, sin aferrarse al animal. Gregor lo imitó y entonces se dio cuenta de que, de hecho, así era más fácil montar. Mantenía mejor el equilibrio.

—Ahora hemos de ir a visitar a los reptantes —anunció Vikus—. ¿Quieres seguir analizando la profecía?

—Tal vez más tarde —contestó Gregor.

Vikus no insistió. Probablemente tenía ya suficientes preocupaciones en la cabeza con todo aquel asunto de la guerra.

Había otra cosa que angustiaba a Gregor, ahora que volvía a sentirse calmado. Sabía que no se había negado a saltar al vacío sólo para molestar a Henry y Luxa. Y tampoco era sólo porque no quería que se burlaran de él. No era ninguna casualidad que hubiera hablado de parques de atracciones. Gregor odiaba las montañas rusas, las caídas libres, los saltos con paracaídas y todo eso. A veces se montaba en ese tipo de atracciones porque si no lo hacía, todos pensarían que era un cobarde, pero no se divertía en absoluto. ¿Qué tenía de divertido sentir que el suelo desaparecía bajo tus pies? Y eso que esas atracciones por lo menos tenían cinturones de seguridad.

Gregor no había saltado porque, en lo más profundo de su ser, le daba miedo hacerlo, y todo el mundo lo sabía.

CAPÍTULO DECIMOCUARTO

Recorrieron oscuros túneles durante horas. Gregor sintió que Boots apoyaba la cabecita sobre su hombro, pero no se lo impidió. En casa, no se le podía dejar que durmiera demasiado durante el día, porque si no luego se despertaba en mitad de la noche, queriendo jugar. Pero, ¿cómo podía mantenerla despierta cuando todo estaba oscuro a su alrededor y no podía moverse? Más tarde ya vería cómo arreglárselas.

La oscuridad le volvió a traer todos sus pensamientos negativos. Su padre, prisionero de las ratas; su madre, llorando; los peligros de llevar a Boots en ese viaje a lo desconocido; y su propio temor en lo alto de la columna.

Cuando notó que el murciélago descendía para aterrizar, sintió alivio de poder por fin distraer su mente de todas esas ideas, aunque no le agradaba nada volver a encontrarse con Henry y con Luxa. Estaba seguro de que estarían más arrogantes y creídos que nunca.

Penetraron en una cueva tan baja que las alas de los murciélagos rozaban tanto el suelo como el techo. Cuando aterrizaron, Gregor desmontó, pero no podía incorporarse sin golpear el casco contra la roca. El lugar le recordaba una tortilla, porque era grande, redondo y plano. Entendía por qué lo habían elegido las cucarachas. Los murciélagos no podían volar bien, y los humanos y las ratas no podían luchar cómodamente con techos tan bajos.

Despertó a Boots, que parecía contenta de estar en la cueva. Correteó por ahí, poniéndose de puntillas para tocar el techo con los dedos. Los demás se sentaron en el suelo a esperar. Los murciélagos se encorvaron, alertas a lo que Gregor suponía que serían sonidos que su oído ni siquiera alcanzaba a percibir.

Entonces apareció una delegación de cucarachas que se postró ante ellos para saludarlos. Los humanos se arrodillaron y les devolvieron la reverencia, de modo que Gregor los imitó. Boots, que no conocía mucho de protocolos, corrió a su encuentro, extendiendo los brazos en un gesto de saludo.

—¡Bichos! ¡Bichos *gandes!* —exclamó.

Un alegre murmullo recorrió el grupo de cucarachas.

—¿Es ella la princesa, es ella? ¿Es ella, Temp, es ella?

Boots dirigió su atención hacia una cucaracha en particular, y le acarició la cabeza entre las dos antenas.

—¡Hola! ¿Me llevas? ¿*Mamos* de paseo?

—¿Me conoce, la princesa, me conoce? —preguntó la cucaracha sobrecogida, y todas las demás dejaron escapar un suspiro de asombro. Incluso los humanos y los murciélagos intercambiaron miradas de sorpresa.

—¿*Mamos* de paseo? ¿Más paseo? —preguntó

Boots—. ¡Bicho *gande* lleva a Boots de paseo! —dijo, dándole unas palmaditas más fuertes en la cabeza.

—Suavecito, Boots —dijo Gregor, corriendo a sujetarle la mano. La colocó con suavidad sobre la cabeza del insecto—. Tócala suavecito, como si fuera un cachorrito.

—Oh, sua-ve-ci-to-sua-ve-ci-to, —dijo Boots, dándole suaves palmaditas a la cucaracha. Ésta se estremecía de alegría.

—¿Me conoce, la princesa, me conoce? —susurró—. ¿Recuerda el paseo, lo recuerda?

Gregor observó con atención a la cucaracha.

—¿Eres tú quien la llevó hasta el estadio? —preguntó.

La cucaracha asintió con la cabeza.

—Soy yo Temp, soy yo —dijo.

Ahora Gregor entendía a qué venía tanto revuelo. A sus ojos, Temp era exactamente igual que las otras veinte cucarachas sentadas a su alrededor. ¿Cómo diablos había podido Boots distinguirla entre todas las demás? Vikus lo miró arqueando las cejas, como pidiéndole una explicación, pero Gregor sólo acertó a encogerse de hombros. Para él también era muy extraño.

—¿Más paseo? —suplicó Boots. Temp postró la cabeza reverencialmente, y la niña se subió a su lomo.

Durante un minuto, todos se quedaron mirándolas mientras daban vueltas y vueltas por la habitación. Luego Vikus carraspeó y dijo:

—Reptantes, tenemos asuntos graves que tratar. ¿Nos conducen donde su rey, nos conducen?

A regañadientes, las cucarachas desviaron su atención de Boots y se alejaron, seguidas de Vikus y Solovet.

«Oh, genial, otra vez solo con esta gente», pensó Gregor. Se sentía aún más incómodo que la primera vez que se había marchado Vikus, de pensar en lo que podían hacer ahora Luxa y Henry. Además, por los insectos gigantes. No se sentía especialmente seguro en la tierra de las cucarachas. Ayer, sin ir más lejos, habían barajado la posibilidad de venderlos a Boots y a él a las ratas. Bueno, por lo menos estaba Mareth, que parecía un buen tipo. Y los murciélagos también parecían simpáticos.

Temp y otra cucaracha llamada Tick se habían quedado allí con ellos. Se turnaban para llevar a la niña de paseo por la cueva, y no hacían caso a nada más.

Los cinco murciélagos se acurrucaron juntos y se quedaron dormidos, exhaustos tras la dura jornada de vuelo.

Mareth reunió todas las antorchas para hacer una especie de hoguera, sobre la que puso a calentar algo de comida. Henry y Luxa se sentaron un poco alejados, y se pusieron a hablar en voz baja, pero a Gregor no le importaba, porque Mareth era el único con el que le daban ganas de hablar.

—Oye, Mareth, ¿tú puedes distinguir unos reptantes de otros? —preguntó Gregor mientras colocaba en el suelo todas las pilas. Se disponía a separar las gastadas de las buenas mientras hablaban.

—No, es muy extraño que tu hermana pueda. Entre nosotros son pocos los que pueden hacer distinciones así. Vikus es el más dotado para eso. Pero distinguir a uno entre tantos... Es muy extraño —dijo Mareth—. ¿Tal vez sea un don que sólo existe en las Tierras Altas? —sugirió.

—No, a mí me parecen todos idénticos —dijo Gregor. Boots era muy buena para esos juegos en que había que descubrir una pequeña diferencia entre cuatro dibujos que parecían exactos. Por ejemplo, cuatro gorritos de fiesta con seis rayas, salvo uno que tenía siete. Y si todos bebían de vasos de papel, siempre sabía cuál era de cada cual, aunque todos se mezclaran en la mesa. Tal vez para ella cada cucaracha fuera sensiblemente diferente de las demás.

Gregor abrió la linterna. Funcionaba con dos pilas medianas. Empezó a probarlas todas, para ver cuáles no estaban aún gastadas. Enfrascado en su tarea, sin darse cuenta, apuntó con el haz de luz a los rostros de Luxa y Henry. Éstos dieron un respingo, pues no estaban acostumbrados a luces repentinas. Lo volvió a hacer un par de veces más, a propósito, aun sabiendo que era una chiquillada, porque le gustaba ver cómo se estremecían. «Éstos no durarían ni cinco segundos en las calles de Nueva York», pensó. Esa idea hizo que se sintiera un poquito mejor.

De diez pilas, sólo había dos gastadas. Gregor abrió el compartimiento de su casco y vio que funcionaba con una pila rectangular especial. Como no tenía ninguna de repuesto, la tendría que utilizar con moderación. «Tal vez debería reservar esta luz. Si pierdo las otras pilas, o si se gastan, todavía me quedará esta», pensó. Así que apagó la bombilla del casco.

Gregor se guardó las pilas buenas en el bolsillo, y apartó las dos gastadas.

—Éstas no sirven —le dijo a Mareth—. No funcionan.

—¿Quieres que las queme? —preguntó éste, extendiendo la mano para tomar las pilas.

Gregor lo sujetó por la muñeca antes de que tuviera tiempo de tirarlas al fuego.

—¡No, podrían explotar! —No sabía exactamente lo que pasaría si se tirase al fuego una pila, pero recordaba vagamente haber oído a su padre decir que era peligroso. De reojo, vio que Luxa y Henry intercambiaban miradas inquietas—. Te podrías quedar ciego —añadió, sólo para impresionarlos.

Bueno, al fin y al cabo, eso perfectamente podría pasar si explotaban.

Mareth asintió con la cabeza y volvió a dejar las pilas con sumo cuidado junto a Gregor. Éste las pisó y las hizo rodar sobre el suelo con el pie, poniendo nerviosos a Henry y Luxa. Pero cuando vio que Mareth también parecía inquieto, se metió las pilas en el bolsillo.

Vikus y Solovet regresaron justo cuando Mareth terminó de preparar la comida. Parecían preocupados.

El círculo se estrechó mientras Mareth repartía pescado, pan y algo que a Gregor le recordaba un camote, pero que no era eso exactamente.

—¡Boots! ¡A cenar! —llamó Gregor, y la niña se acercó corriendo.

Cuando se percató de que no la seguían, volvió la cabeza e hizo un gesto impaciente a las cucarachas.

—¡Temp! ¡Tick! ¡A cenar!

Durante un momento, nadie supo muy bien cómo reaccionar. A nadie más se le había ocurrido invitar a las cucarachas. Mareth no había preparado comida suficiente. Era obvio que no era habitual cenar con cucarachas. Afortunadamente, éstas declinaron la invitación con un gesto de cabeza.

—No, princesa, no comemos ahora, no comemos —contestaron alejándose.

—¡Quédense aquí! —exclamó Boots, señalándolas con el dedo—. Quédense aquí, bichos *gandes.* —Las cucarachas se sentaron obedientemente.

—¡Boots! —la reprendió Gregor avergonzado—. No tienen por qué quedarse, es que Boots es una mandona —les dijo—. Lo que le pasa es que quiere seguir jugando con ustedes, pero primero tiene que comer.

—Nos sentaremos —dijo una de ellas fríamente, y a Gregor le dio la impresión de que la cucaracha lo estaba mandando a que se metiera en sus propios asuntos.

Todos comieron con apetito salvo Vikus, que parecía distraído.

—¿Cuándo partimos, pues? —preguntó Henry con la boca llena de pescado.

—No partimos —dijo Solovet—. Los reptantes se han negado a acompañarnos.

Luxa levantó la cabeza indignada.

—¿Se han negado? ¿Y por qué motivo?

—No desean suscitar la ira del rey Gorger uniéndose a nuestra búsqueda —explicó Vikus—. Ahora están en paz tanto con los humanos como con las ratas. No quieren alterar ese equilibrio.

«¿Y ahora qué?», pensó Gregor. Necesitaban dos cucarachas. Así lo decía en la Profecía del Gris. Si las cucarachas no venían, ¿podrían todavía ir a rescatar a su padre?

—Les hemos rogado que reconsideren su decisión —dijo Solovet—. Saben que las ratas están en camino. Este hecho tal vez incline la balanza a nuestro favor.

—O a favor de las ratas —dijo Luxa entre dientes.

Gregor pensaba lo mismo. Las cucarachas habían considerado venderlos a él y a Boots a las ratas aun sabiendo que estas se los comerían. Y eso era ayer, cuando aún no había guerra. Si Boots no les hubiera resultado tan cautivadora, no cabe duda de que ahora estarían muertos. Las cucarachas no estaban hechas para luchar. Gregor pensó que harían lo que fuera mejor para su especie, y probablemente las ratas eran el aliado más fuerte. Bueno, si es que podían confiar en ellas.

—¿Qué hace pensar a las cucarachas que pueden confiar en las ratas? —preguntó Gregor.

—Los reptantes no piensan de la misma manera que nosotros —contestó Vikus.

—¿Cómo piensan? —siguió preguntando Gregor.

—Sin lógica ni razón —dijo Henry furioso—. ¡Son las criaturas más estúpidas de las Tierras Bajas! ¡A duras penas saben hablar!

—¡Silencio, Henry! —le espetó Vikus con gran severidad.

Gregor volvió la vista hacia Temp y Tick, pero las cucarachas no dieron ninguna muestra de haber oído esas palabras. Pero por supuesto que las habían oído.

Las cucarachas no parecían muy inteligentes, pero era una falta de educación decírselo así a la cara. Además, eso no iba a ayudar a convencerlas de que los acompañaran.

—Recuerda, Henry, que cuando Sandwich llegó a las Tierras Bajas los reptantes ya llevaban viviendo aquí desde innumerables generaciones. No te quepa duda de que perdurarán cuando se haya desvanecido todo recuerdo de lo que era la sangre caliente —declaró Vikus.

—Eso son rumores —dijo Henry con desprecio.

—No, no lo son. Las cucarachas llevan en la tierra como unos trescientos cincuenta millones de años, y los humanos en cambio no llevan ni seis —dijo Gregor. Su padre le había enseñado una cronología de la evolución de distintas especies animales. Recordaba cuánto le había impresionado ver lo viejas que eran las cucarachas.

—¿Y tú cómo sabes todo eso? —preguntó Luxa bruscamente, pero Gregor veía que el tema le interesaba de verdad.

—Es ciencia. Los arqueólogos desentierran fósiles y cosas así, y pueden calcular la edad de lo que hallan. Las cucarachas —o sea, quiero decir los reptantes— son antiquísimos y nunca han evolucionado demasiado —explicó Gregor. Ahí ya se estaba metiendo en terreno desconocido, pero le parecía que era cierto lo que estaba diciendo—. Son unas criaturas increíbles. —Esperaba que Temp y Tick lo estuvieran escuchando.

Vikus le sonrió.

—Para sobrevivir tanto tiempo, no cabe duda de que son todo lo inteligentes que necesitan ser.

—Yo no creo en tu ciencia —objetó Henry—. Los reptantes son débiles, no pueden luchar, no perdurarán. Así es como lo quiso la Madre Naturaleza.

Gregor pensó entonces en su abuela, que era vieja y dependía ahora de la bondad de las personas más fuertes que ella. Pensó en Boots, que era pequeña y todavía no era capaz de abrir una puerta. Y luego estaba su amigo Larry, que había tenido que ingresar tres veces en urgencias el año anterior porque con sus crisis de asma no le llegaba el aire a los pulmones.

—¿Tú piensas lo mismo, Luxa? —preguntó Gregor—. ¿Piensas que los seres que no son fuertes merecen morir?

—Lo que yo piense carece de importancia, si ésa es la verdad —dijo Luxa evasivamente.

—¿Pero es esa la verdad? Es una excelente pregunta para que la futura reina de Regalia reflexione —dijo Vikus.

Comieron rápidamente y Vikus propuso que todos trataran de dormir un poco. Gregor no tenía ni idea si era de noche o de día, pero se sentía cansado, por lo que aceptó la propuesta sin rechistar.

Mientras él extendía una fina manta sobre el suelo, en un extremo de la habitación, Boots intentaba enseñar a las cucarachas a jugar a "pito, pito, colorito". Las cucarachas agitaban confundidas las patas delanteras, sin saber muy bien lo que se esperaba de ellas.

—Pito, pito, *coloíto*; pito, pito, mi bichito, *onde* vas tú tan bonito, a la era *veldadela*, pimpampún, ¡fuera! —canturreó Boots, dando palmaditas en las patas de las cucarachas.

Los insectos estaban totalmente desconcertados.

—¿Qué canta la princesa, qué canta? —preguntó Temp. O tal vez fuera Tick.

—Es una canción que se canta a los niños pequeños en las Tierras Altas, para jugar —explicó Gregor—. Te ha incluido en la canción. Eso es un gran honor —añadió—. Boots sólo incluye en una canción a quien le gusta mucho de verdad.

—Me gusta bicho *gande* —declaró Boots con satisfacción, y volvió a cantar la cancioncilla con las cucarachas.

—Lo siento, chicos, ahora se tiene que ir a la cama —dijo Gregor—. Vamos Boots, a dormir. Dales las buenas noches a tus amigos.

Boots abrazó espontáneamente a las cucarachas.

—*Menas* noches, bichos *gandes*. Sueñen con los angelitos.

Gregor se acurrucó junto a ella bajo la manta, sobre el duro suelo de piedra. Tras su larga siesta, la niña no tenía mucho sueño. La dejó que jugara un ratito con la linterna, encendiéndola y apagándola, pero le daba miedo que gastara las pilas, y la luz intermitente estaba poniendo nerviosos a los demás. Por fin consiguió dormirla. Justo cuando él estaba también a punto de conciliar el sueño, le pareció oír a Temp, o tal vez a Tick, susurrar:

—¿Nos honra la princesa, nos honra?

Gregor no sabía qué lo había hecho despertar. Por la rigidez que sentía en el cuello supo que llevaba horas tumbado sobre el duro suelo. Somnoliento, extendió el brazo para acercar más hacia sí el cuerpo calentito de Boots, pero no encontró nada más que la fría piedra. Abrió los ojos de golpe y se incorporó. Su boca se entreabrió para gritar su nombre mientras sus ojos se iban acostumbrando a la oscuridad. No fue capaz de pronunciar palabra.

Boots estaba en el centro de la gran sala redonda, balanceándose de un pie a otro mientras describía lentamente un círculo. La linterna que sostenía en la mano iba iluminando secciones de la habitación. Gregor distinguió siluetas que se movían en perfectos círculos concéntricos. Giraban a la vez, algunas a la izquierda, y otras a la derecha, con movimientos lentos e hipnóticos.

En el silencio más total, cientos de cucarachas bailaban alrededor de Boots.

CAPÍTULO DECIMOQUINTO

Oh, no, se la van a comer!», pensó Gregor, y al ponerse en pie de un salto se golpeó la cabeza contra el techo. «¡Ay!». Había sido un error quitarse el casco para dormir.

Una mano lo agarró del hombro para tranquilizarlo, y en la oscuridad pudo distinguir a Vikus, que con un gesto le indicaba que guardara silencio.

—¡Shhh! ¡No los interrumpas! —susurró con apremio.

—¡Pero le van a hacer daño! —contestó Gregor también en un susurro. Se acuclilló y se llevó la mano a la cabeza. Notó que le estaba empezando a salir un chichón.

—No, Gregor, la están honrando. Honran a Boots de una manera sagrada. Es muy poco frecuente —susurró Solovet desde algún rincón de la habitación.

Gregor volvió la mirada hacia las cucarachas, tratando de comprender su comportamiento. Boots no parecía estar corriendo ningún peligro inmediato. En realidad, ninguno de los insectos la tocaba siquiera. Lo único que hacían era balancear sus cuerpos, girar e inclinar la cabeza, siguiendo el compás de su lento y rítmico baile. Se quedó sobrecogido ante la solemnidad de la escena, el silencio absoluto, la concentración. Gregor entendió entonces lo que estaba pasando: las cucarachas no estaban sólo honrando a Boots, ¡la estaban venerando!

—¿Qué están haciendo? —preguntó Gregor.

—Es la Danza del Anillo. Cuentan que los reptantes la ejecutan sólo en el mayor secreto, para aquellos a quienes consideran los elegidos —contestó Vikus—. En nuestra historia, sólo la han ejecutado para otro humano, y ése fue Sandwich.

—¿Elegidos para qué? —susurró Gregor preocupado. Esperaba que las cucarachas no pensaran que podían quedarse con Boots sólo porque habían decidido bailar a su alrededor.

—Elegidos para darles tiempo —dijo Vikus sin más, como si eso lo explicara todo. Gregor tradujo esas palabras en su cabeza, dándoles este significado: «Elegidos para darles vida».

Tal vez fuera algo aún más sencillo. Desde el momento en que habían aterrizado en las Tierras Bajas, las cucarachas habían sentido una conexión especial con Boots. Si sólo lo hubieran encontrado a él, habría conseguido un billete de ida a la tierra de las ratas, y ése hubiera sido el fin de la historia. Pero Boots se había hecho amiga de ellas inmediatamente. No le habían dado asco, ni miedo, ni se había sentido superior. Gregor pensó que el hecho de que le hubieran gustado tanto las cucarachas había impresionado mucho a los insectos. La mayoría de los humanos las tenían en muy baja estima.

Y luego estaba aquello tan extraño de que hubiera reconocido a Temp entre todas las demás... Gregor todavía no encontraba explicación para ello.

Las cucarachas describieron unos cuantos círculos, y luego se postraron ante Boots. Después, círculo a círculo, se desvanecieron en la oscuridad. Boots las contempló desaparecer sin decir nada. Cuando la habitación quedó vacía, soltó un enorme bostezo y se acercó hasta Gregor sin hacer ruido.

—*Teno* sueño —dijo. Luego se acurrucó contra él y se quedó dormida al instante.

Gregor le quitó la linterna de la mano, y a la luz de la bombilla vio que todos los demás estaban despiertos y los miraban fijamente.

—Tiene sueño —dijo, como si no hubiera pasado nada extraño, y apagó la linterna.

Al despertar, las cucarachas anunciaron que Temp y Tick se unían a la búsqueda. A nadie le cabía ninguna duda de que lo hacían por Boots.

Gregor se debatía entre un profundo orgullo y unas ganas irresistibles de echarse a reír a carcajadas. Al final resultaba que Boots sí que constituía un arma especial.

El grupo se preparó rápidamente para la partida. Temp y Tick se negaron categóricamente a montar en ningún murciélago sin Boots. Esto provocó una breve discusión porque Boots tenía que montar con Gregor, lo cual significaba que un solo murciélago tendría que cargar con ambos humanos y con las dos cucarachas. Los murciélagos podían soportar ese peso, pero el problema consistía entonces en que habría cuatro jinetes sin experiencia en un solo murciélago.

Vikus le encargó la responsabilidad a Ares, el gran murciélago negro de Henry, pues era a la vez fuerte y ágil, y Henry compartió montura con Luxa. Ares recibió instrucciones de volar por encima de los demás. De esta manera, si alguna de las cucarachas perdía el equilibrio, los demás murciélagos podrían recogerla antes de que se estrellara contra el suelo.

Estos conciliábulos no tranquilizaron en nada a Temp y a Tick, a los que la idea de cruzar volando el espacio abierto a muchos metros por encima del suelo aterrorizaba claramente. Gregor trató de infundirles seguridad, lo cual no dejaba de ser irónico, pues a él mismo tampoco le hacía mucha gracia volar. Además, hubiera preferido montar cualquier murciélago. Probablemente Ares lo apreciaba tan poco como su dueño.

No había tiempo para desayunar, así que Mareth repartió pedazos de pan y carne seca para comer durante el camino. Vikus le dijo a Gregor que volarían durante varias horas sin descanso, así que éste le puso a Boots un pañal doble. También la colocó en la mochila de manera que mirara hacia atrás, y no por encima de su hombro, para que así pudiera charlar con Temp y Tick, y tal vez distraerlas un poco de su miedo.

Gregor subió con cuidado a lomos de Ares, y dejó colgando las piernas a ambos lados del cuello del animal. Temp y Tick montaron detrás, agarrándose desesperadamente al pelaje del murciélago. A Gregor le pareció ver que Ares se estremecía ligeramente, pero el animal no dijo nada. Los murciélagos casi nunca se expresaban en voz alta.

Parecía costarles mucho esfuerzo. Probablemente se comunicaban entre ellos con sonidos que el oído humano no era capaz de percibir.

—Ahora hemos de dirigirnos a la tierra de los tejedores —dijo Vikus—. Tengan presente con cuánta frecuencia patrullan las ratas esta zona.

—Volemos bien juntos. Podemos necesitar protección unos de otros —aconsejó Solovet—. ¡Al aire!

Los murciélagos levantaron el vuelo. Boots estaba feliz como una lombriz con sus nuevos compañeros de viaje. Cantó todo su repertorio de canciones, que incluía «estrellita, ¿dónde estás?», «Arre, borriquito», «La bonita arañita», «La canción del alfabeto» y, por supuesto, «Pito, pito, colorito». Cuando terminó, las volvió a cantar todas otra vez. Y otra vez. Y otra más. Cuando ya las había cantado unas veinte veces, Gregor decidió enseñarle «Aserrín, aserrán», sólo para variar un poquito. Boots se la aprendió enseguida, y trató de enseñársela a las cucarachas. No parecía importarle que desafinaran, aunque Gregor sentía que los músculos del cuello de Ares se iban tensando más con cada verso de la canción.

Gregor observó que el territorio de las cucarachas era mucho más grande que Regalia y que las cuevas de los murciélagos. Éstos y los humanos tenían pocas tierras muy densamente pobladas que se podían proteger fácilmente. Las cucarachas, en cambio, se extendían a lo largo de kilómetros y kilómetros por todas las Tierras Bajas.

¿Cómo podían resguardarse de un ataque con tanto territorio que defender?

Le llegó la respuesta cuando sobrevolaron un valle en el que había miles de cucarachas. Los reptantes tenían muchos, muchísimos efectivos, comparados con los humanos. Si sufrían un ataque, podían permitirse el lujo de perder más guerreros. Y, con tanto territorio, podían escabullirse, obligando a las ratas a perseguirlos. Gregor pensó en las cucarachas que había en la cocina de su casa en Nueva York. No luchaban. Huían. Su madre las exterminaba, pero siempre volvían.

Tras lo que le pareció una eternidad, Gregor sintió que Ares aminoraba la marcha y se preparaba para aterrizar. Tocaron tierra en la orilla de un río perezoso y de escaso caudal. Gregor saltó del murciélago y cayó sobre algo blando y esponjoso. Se agachó para investigar lo que era y su mano encontró unas hierbas de un verde grisáceo. ¡Plantas! Aquí crecían plantas sin la ayuda de la luz de gas que había visto en los campos a las afueras de Regalia.

—¿Cómo puede crecer sin luz esta planta? —preguntó a Vikus, mostrándole un puñado de hojas.

—Tiene luz —contestó Vikus, señalándole el río—. Sale fuego de la tierra. —Gregor miró el agua con atención y vio minúsculos haces de luz que surgían del lecho del río. Los peces se escabullían entre múltiples especies de plantas. Los largos tallos de algunas de ellas se extendían hasta las márgenes del río.

«Son como volcanes en miniatura», pensó Gregor.

—Este río también pasa por Regalia. Nuestro ganado se alimenta de estas plantas, pero no son aptas para el consumo humano —explicó Solovet.

Gregor llevaba toda la mañana comiendo carne seca sin preguntarse ni un momento siquiera de qué se alimentaban las vacas. Podría estar años en las Tierras Bajas antes de comprender cómo funcionaban las cosas allí. Pero no tenía ganas de quedarse más tiempo del estrictamente necesario.

Unas cucarachas que pescaban desde la orilla intercambiaron unas palabras con Temp y Tick y extrajeron del agua varios peces grandes con ayuda de sus bocas. Mareth los limpió y los dispuso sobre antorchas para asarlos.

Gregor sacó a Boots de la mochila para que pudiera estirar las piernas y encargó a las cucarachas que la vigilaran. Se pusieron a corretear junto al río, manteniendo a la niña alejada en todo momento del agua, y permitiéndole que se les subiera encima. Pronto se corrió la voz de su llegada y al poco aparecieron docenas de insectos. Se sentaron para contemplar a «la princesa».

Cuando el pescado estuvo listo, Vikus insistió en invitar a Temp y a Tick a comer con ellos.

—Ha llegado la hora —dijo como respuesta a la mueca de Henry—. Ha llegado la hora de que los personajes de la profecía compartan un mismo camino, un mismo objetivo y unas mismas ideas. Somos todos iguales aquí. —Temp y Tick permanecieron un poco al margen, detrás de Boots, pero comieron con todos los demás.

—Ya no queda lejos —dijo Vikus, señalando un pequeño túnel—. Incluso a pie llegaríamos enseguida.

—¿Adonde está mi padre? —preguntó Gregor.

—No, adonde están los tejedores. Hemos de persuadir a dos de ellos para que se unan a la búsqueda —contestó Vikus.

—Ah, sí, los tejedores —dijo Gregor. Esperaba que mostraran más entusiasmo por el viaje que las cucarachas.

Justo estaban terminando de comer cuando los cinco murciélagos levantaron bruscamente la cabeza. «¡Ratas!», siseó Ares. Inmediatamente, todos se pusieron en movimiento.

A excepción de Temp y Tick, todas las demás cucarachas desaparecieron por los túneles que se abrían cerca de las orillas del río.

Vikus metió a Boots en la mochila de Gregor y los empujó a ambos hacia la boca del túnel que les había enseñado antes.

—¡Corre! —ordenó. Gregor trató de protestar, pero Vikus no lo dejó hablar—. ¡Corre, Gregor! Todos nosotros somos prescindibles; ¡tú, no!

El anciano saltó sobre su murciélago y se reunió con los demás en el aire justo cuando un escuadrón de seis ratas apareció corriendo en la orilla del río. El jefe, una rata retorcida de color gris con una cicatriz que le cruzaba la cara en diagonal, señaló a Gregor y ordenó: «¡Mátenlo!».

Abandonado en la orilla sin armas, Gregor no tenía otra alternativa que correr hacia la boca del túnel. Temp y Tick se lanzaron tras él. Gregor miró un segundo atrás y vio que Vikus derribaba con la empuñadura de su espada a la rata retorcida. Los demás, blandiendo sus armas, atacaron al resto del escuadrón.

—¡Corre, Gregor! —ordenó Solovet con una voz ronca que en nada recordaba a la voz suave a la que el chico estaba acostumbrado.

—¡Deprisa, Gregor, deprisa! —lo apremiaron Temp y Tick.

Apuntando con su linterna, Gregor se adentró en la boca del túnel. El techo era lo suficientemente alto para que pudiera correr erguido. Se dio cuenta entonces de que había perdido a Temp y Tick, y cuando se volvió para buscarlos vio que el túnel entero, desde el suelo hasta el techo, se estaba llenando de cucarachas. Estaban empleando sus cuerpos para formar una barricada que resultara casi imposible de penetrar.

«¡Oh, no, van a dejarse matar!», pensó Gregor. Se dio la vuelta para ayudarlas, pero las cucarachas que estaban más cerca de él insistieron:

—¡Corre! ¡Corre con la princesa!

Tenían razón: tenía que escapar. Tenía que sacar a Boots de ahí. Tenía que salvar a su padre. ¿Quién sabe?, tal vez incluso tuviera que salvar de las ratas a las Tierras Bajas. Pero en ese momento, ni él podía atravesar la barricada de cucarachas para enfrentarse a las ratas, ni podían éstas hacerlo para acabar con él.

Echó a correr por el túnel, adoptando un ritmo que le pareció que podría mantener durante media hora.

Veinte minutos después, dobló una esquina y se topó de bruces con una enorme telaraña.

CAPÍTULO DECIMOSEXTO

Al despegarse de la cara los hilos pegajosos de la telaraña, Gregor sintió como si alguien le hubiera arrancado pedazos de cinta adhesiva de la piel. «¡Ay!», exclamó. Liberó el brazo que sostenía la linterna, pero el otro quedó enredado en la tela. Por suerte, Boots estaba encaramada a su espalda, por lo que había quedado fuera de la telaraña.

—¡Eh! —llamó—. ¿Hay alguien ahí? ¡Eh! —Paseó el haz de luz a su alrededor, pero no se veía más que telaraña.

—Soy Gregor de las Tierras Altas. Vengo en son de paz —dijo. «Vengo en son de paz». ¿De dónde se había sacado eso? De alguna película vieja probablemente—. ¿Hay alguien en casa?

Sintió que alguien tiraba suavemente de sus sandalias y miró hacia abajo. Una gigantesca araña estaba atándole los pies con un largo hilo de seda.

—¡Eh! —gritó Gregor, tratando de liberar sus pies. Pero en tan sólo unos segundos, la araña lo había rodeado con el hilo hasta las rodillas—. ¡No lo entiendes! ¡Yo... yo soy el guerrero! ¡El de la profecía! ¡Yo soy el que llama!

La araña seguía rodeando su cuerpo afanosamente con el hilo. «Madre mía», pensó Gregor. «¡Nos va a cubrir por completo!». Sintió que el brazo que tenía atrapado en la telaraña se aplastaba cada vez más contra su cuerpo.

—¡Gue-go! —gritó Boots. Los hilos de seda la empujaban contra su espalda mientras se enrollaban alrededor de su pecho.

—¡Me manda Vikus! —gritó Gregor, y por primera vez, la araña se detuvo. Gregor se apresuró a añadir—: ¡Sí, me manda Vikus, y él llegará enseguida, y cuando se entere de que me están atrapando en esta red se va a enfadar muchísimo!

Agitó el brazo que tenía libre, el de la linterna, para subrayar sus palabras, y el haz de luz se posó de lleno sobre el rostro de la araña. Ésta retrocedió unos metros, y Gregor pudo ver por primera vez al arácnido con todo lujo de detalles. Tenía seis ojos negros y redondos, ocho patas peludas, y unas enormes mandíbulas que terminaban en colmillos curvos y muy puntiagudos. Apartó rápidamente la linterna. Mejor no poner furioso a un bicho así.

—Bueno, ¿sabes quién es Vikus? —preguntó Gregor—. Llegará aquí de un momento a otro para sostener una reunión oficial con tu rey. O reina. ¿Tienes un rey, o una reina? Bueno, a lo mejor es otra cosa. Nosotros tenemos presidente, pero eso es distinto, porque los presidentes se eligen por votación. —Calló un momento—. ¿Bueno, no te parece que ya nos puedes liberar?

La araña se inclinó hacia adelante y cortó uno de los hilos con los dientes. Gregor y Boots salieron despedidos varios metros hacia arriba, y empezaron a subir y bajar, como un yoyó, como si colgaran de una gran goma elástica.

—¡Eh! —gritó Gregor—. ¡Eh! —Su almuerzo empezó a dar vueltas y vueltas en su estómago. Por fin, al cabo de un rato, cesaron los rebotes.

Gregor alumbró a su alrededor con la linterna. Había arañas por todas partes. Algunas se ocupaban afanosamente en distintos quehaceres; otras parecían dormidas. Ninguna le prestaba la más mínima atención. Eso era nuevo. Las cucarachas y los murciélagos lo habían recibido con bastante educación, toda una multitud en un estadio se había callado al verlo aparecer, y las ratas se habían enfurecido al reconocer sus rasgos... pero, ¿y las arañas? No les importaba un rábano.

Les estuvo gritando durante un buen rato. Cosas agradables primero; luego, disparates; y al final, insultos. No reaccionaron. Le dijo a Boots que cantara un par de estrofas de «La bonita arañita», ya que se llevaba tan bien con los insectos. No hubo respuesta. Entonces, tiró la toalla y se dedicó a observarlas.

Un desdichado insecto cayó en la telaraña. Una araña acudió corriendo y le clavó sus malvados colmillos. El insecto se quedó rígido. «Veneno», pensó Gregor. La araña rodeó rápidamente al insecto con hilos de seda, lo despedazó y le lanzó una especie de líquido. Gregor apartó la vista cuando la araña empezó a sorber las vísceras licuadas del insecto. «Buaj, ese insecto podríamos haber sido nosotros. ¡Todavía podríamos serlo!», pensó. Deseó que vinieran Vikus y los demás.

Pero, ¿vendrían? ¡Qué habría pasado en la orilla del río? ¿Habrían conseguido derrotar a las ratas? ¿Habría resultado alguien herido, o peor aún, muerto?

Recordó que Vikus le había ordenado que corriera. «¡Los demás somos prescindibles; tú, no!». Probablemente hablaba de la profecía. Siempre podían encontrar más reptantes, voladores, y tejedores. Tal vez pudiera Nerissa participar en caso de que les pasara algo a Luxa o a Henry. O tal vez nombrarían a otro rey o a otra reina. Pero Gregor y Boots, dos habitantes de las Tierras Altas cuyo padre era prisionero de las ratas, ellos eran irremplazables.

Gregor pensó con tristeza en las personas que habían sacrificado sus vidas allá en las orillas del río. Debería haberse quedado allí para luchar, aunque su probabilidad de vencer era baja. Estaban arriesgando sus vidas porque pensaban que él era el guerrero. Pero él no lo era. Gregor suponía que, a esas alturas, ya se tenían que haber enterado.

Los minutos pasaban despacio. Tal vez murieron todos, y Boots y él estaban ahora solos. Tal vez las arañas lo supieran, y los estuvieran dejando vivir por el momento para que estuvieran frescos y sabrosos cuando decidieran comérselos.

—¿*Gue-go?* —dijo Boots.

—Sí, Boots —le contestó.

—¿*Mamos* a casa? —preguntó suplicante—. ¿A ver a mamá y a Lizzie?

—Bueno, primero tenemos que ir a buscar a papá —dijo, tratando de parecer optimista aunque estuvieran colgando de un hilo, impotentes, en la guarida de una araña.

—¿Pa-pá? —preguntó Boots con curiosidad. Conocía a su padre por fotos, aunque nunca lo había visto en persona—. ¿A ver a pa-pá?

—Primero recogemos a papá, y luego vamos a casa —dijo Gregor.

—¿A ver a mamá? —insistió Boots. Gregor empezó a recordar a su madre, y la tristeza le encogió el corazón—. ¿A ver a mamá?

Una araña que estaba cerca de ellos empezó a emitir un sonido rítmico y pronto todas las demás la imitaron. Era una melodía suave y tranquilizadora. Gregor trató de recordar la música para luego poder tocársela a su padre con su saxofón. Su padre también tocaba, sobre todo jazz. Cuando Gregor tenía siete años, le había comprado su primer saxofón, de segunda mano, en la casa de empeños, y había empezado a enseñarle a tocarlo. Gregor justo había comenzado a tomar clases en la escuela cuando su padre desapareció y cayó prisionero de las ratas, que seguramente odiaban la música.

Por cierto, ¿qué le estarían haciendo las malvadas ratas a su padre?

Trató de pensar en cosas más positivas, pero, dadas las circunstancias, no lo consiguió.

Cuando Henry en persona apareció en el suelo de piedra a varios metros por debajo de él, Gregor sintió ganas de llorar de alivio.

—¡Está vivo! —exclamó Henry, que se alegraba sinceramente de verlo.

Desde algún rincón en la oscuridad, Gregor oyó a Vikus preguntar:

—¿Liberas al de las Tierras Altas, lo liberas?

Gregor sintió que lo bajaban hasta el suelo. Cuando sus pies tocaron la piedra, cayó de bruces, incapaz de sostenerse con las piernas atadas.

Todos lo rodearon al instante, cortando los hilos de seda con sus espadas. Incluso Henry y Luxa se pusieron a ello. Tick y Temp royeron las cuerdas que atrapaban la mochila de Boots. Gregor contó los murciélagos, uno, dos, tres, cuatro, cinco. Veía varios heridos, pero por suerte todos estaban vivos.

—Te creíamos perdido —comentó Mareth, que sangraba abundantemente de una herida en la cadera.

—No, no podía perderme. El túnel llevaba directamente hasta aquí —contestó Gregor, liberando alegremente las piernas de las ataduras.

—No perdido en el camino —dijo Luxa—. Perdido para siempre. —Gregor comprendió entonces que quería decir «muerto».

—¿Qué ha pasado con las ratas? —preguntó.

—Las hemos matado a todas —contestó Vikus—. No temas, pues no te han visto.

—¿Es peor si me ven? —quiso saber Gregor—. ¿Por qué? Pueden oler a kilómetros de distancia que vengo de las Tierras Altas. Saben que estoy aquí.

—Pero sólo las ratas muertas saben que te pareces a tu padre. Que eres «un hijo del sol» —puntualizó Vikus.

Gregor recordó entonces cómo habían reaccionado Shed y Fangor al ver su rostro a la luz de la antorcha: «¿Has visto su rostro, Shed, lo has visto?». Si habían querido matarlo no era sólo porque venía de las Tierras Altas.

¡Sino porque también ellos habían pensado que era el guerrero! Quiso decírselo a Vikus, pero entonces vio que una veintena de arañas bajaba de las alturas para colgarse en unas telarañas, muy cerca de ellos.

Una grandiosa criatura con hermosas patas rayadas bajó a su vez y se colocó justo delante de Vikus. Éste hizo una reverencia hasta casi tocar el suelo con la frente.

—Yo te saludo, reina Wevox.

La araña se acarició el torso con las patas delanteras, como si estuviera tocando el arpa. Una extraña voz salió de ella, aunque su boca no se movió en absoluto.

—Yo te saludo, lord Vikus.

—Te presento a Gregor de las Tierras Altas —dijo Vikus señalando a Gregor.

—Hace mucho ruido —dijo la araña con desagrado, volviéndose a acariciar el torso con las patas delanteras.

Gregor comprendió entonces que era así como hablaba la araña, haciendo vibrar su cuerpo. Sonaba un poco como el señor Johnson, el vecino del apartamento 4Q, a quien le habían hecho una operación y hablaba por un agujero en el cuello. Sólo que la araña daba miedo.

—Las costumbres de las Tierras Altas son extrañas —dijo Vikus, lanzándole a Gregor una mirada que significaba que no debía objetar nada.

—¿A qué vienen? —vibró la voz de la reina Wevox.

Vikus contó toda la historia en diez frases, empleando una voz dulce. Así que, al parecer, a las arañas había que hablarles rápida y suavemente. Gritarles sin parar había sido contraproducente.

La reina reflexionó un momento.

—Por tratarse de Vikus, no nos los beberemos. Envuélvanlos.

Una horda de arañas los rodeó. Gregor contempló cómo una especie de hermoso embudo de seda iba creciendo a su alrededor como por arte de magia. El grupo quedó completamente aislado del resto. Las arañas dejaron de tejer cuando llegaron a una altura de unos tres metros. Dos se colocaron en lo alto del embudo, como centinelas. Todo ocurrió en menos de un minuto.

Todos miraron a Vikus, que dejó escapar un largo suspiro.

—Sabías que no habría de ser fácil —dijo Solovet con dulzura.

—Sí, pero había esperado que con el reciente acuerdo comercial... —Vikus se interrumpió—. Mis esperanzas eran desproporcionadas.

—Todavía respiramos —dijo Mareth para animarlo—. Que no es poco con los tejedores.

—¿Qué está pasando aquí? —preguntó Gregor—. ¿Es que no van a venir con nosotros?

—No, Gregor, no —dijo Solovet—. Somos sus prisioneros.

CAPÍTULO DECIMOSÉPTIMO

¡Prisioneros! —exclamó Gregor—. ¿Es que también están en guerra con los tejedores?

—Oh, no —dijo Mareth—. Estamos en paz con los tejedores, no nos invadimos mutuamente... pero sería una exageración considerarlos nuestros amigos.

—Y tanto —corroboró Gregor—. O sea que todo el mundo sabía que nos iban a encerrar menos yo, ¿es eso? —le resultaba muy difícil disimular la irritación que sentía. Se estaba cansando de ser siempre el último en enterarse de las cosas.

—Lo lamento, Gregor —dijo Vikus—. Llevo mucho tiempo pugnando por construir puentes entre nosotros y los tejedores. Pensé que tal vez se mostrarían más razonables, pero sobrestimé mi influencia sobre ellos.

Vikus parecía cansado y viejo. No había sido intención de Gregor hacerlo sentir aún peor.

—No, lo respetan de verdad. O sea, quiero decir que creo que estaban pensando en comerme hasta que les mencioné su nombre.

Vikus se animó un poquito.

—¿De verdad? Bueno, eso ya es algo. Donde hay vida hay esperanza.

—Qué extraño. ¡Eso es lo que dice siempre mi abuela! —exclamó Gregor. Se rió y, de alguna manera, eso sirvió para relajar la tensión.

—¡*Gue-go, oto* pañal! —exigió Boots con una pizca de mal humor, dándose tironcitos de los pantalones.

—Sí, Boots, otro pañal —dijo Gregor. Hacía siglos que no le cambiaba el pañal. Hurgó en la bolsa que le había dado Dulcet y comprobó que sólo le quedaban dos—. Vaya —se lamentó—. Ya casi no me quedan paños empapadores.

—Pues bien, no podrías estar en un mejor lugar. Los tejedores fabrican todos nuestros paños empapadores —dijo Solovet.

—¿Y cómo es que no son pegajosos? —preguntó Gregor, tocándose la cara.

—Los tejedores pueden fabricar seis tipos distintos de seda, algunas son pegajosas, y otras son tan suaves como la piel de Boots. También tejen nuestras ropas.

—¿En serio? —preguntó Gregor—. ¿Y cree usted que querrán hacernos más paños empapadores? ¿Aunque seamos prisioneros?

—No lo dudo. Los tejedores no tienen por objetivo enfrentarse a nosotros —explicó Solovet—. Tan sólo retenernos hasta que decidan qué hacer con nosotros. —Llamó a uno de los centinelas, y unos minutos después, dos docenas de pañales llegaron hasta ellos atados a un hilo de seda. La araña también les hizo llegar tres recipientes llenos de agua clara.

Solovet empezó a ocuparse de todos, uno por uno, limpiando heridas y colocando vendajes. Luxa, Henry y Mareth la observaban con atención, como si estuviera dándoles una clase. Gregor comprendió entonces que la capacidad de curar heridas de guerra era probablemente muy importante en las Tierras Bajas.

Solovet comenzó por limpiar el corte en la cadera de Mareth, y luego lo cosió con aguja e hilo. Gregor se estremeció pensando en el dolor de Mareth, pero el rostro de éste, si bien se veía algo pálido, no mostró emoción alguna. Hubo que coser también las alas de un par de murciélagos y, aunque hacían un gran esfuerzo por no moverse mientras Solovet les perforaba una y otra vez la piel con su aguja, era obvio que sufrían enormemente.

Una vez atajadas todas las hemorragias, Solovet se volvió hacia Gregor.

—Ocupémonos ahora de tu rostro.

Gregor se tocó la cara y comprobó que allí donde se había arrancado las telarañas se le habían formado unas ampollas. Solovet mojó en agua uno de los paños empapadores y se lo aplicó sobre la cara. Gregor tuvo que apretar los dientes para no gritar.

—Sé que quema —dijo Solovet—, pero debes quitarte el pegamento de la piel, o las llagas se volverán purulentas.

—¿Purulentas? —repitió Gregor como un eco. Eso sonaba fatal.

—Si resistieras echarte agua en la cara, el proceso sería más doloroso, pero también más rápido —indicó Solovet.

Gregor respiró bien hondo y metió la cabeza entera en uno de los cubos de agua. «¡Aaaayyy!», gritó en silencio, y sacó la cabeza jadeando. Tras cinco o seis zambullidas, el dolor desapareció.

Solovet asintió con la cabeza, complacida, y le dio un frasquito de arcilla con un ungüento para que se lo aplicara en la cara. Mientras Gregor se extendía cuidadosamente la medicina, Solovet limpió y vendó una serie de heridas de menor consideración, y obligó a un Vikus muy reticente a que le dejara vendarle la muñeca.

Por fin se volvió hacia Temp y Tick.

—Reptantes, ¿necesitan mi ayuda?

Boots señaló a una de las cucarachas, que tenía una antena doblada.

—Temp *tene* una heridita—dijo.

—No, princesa, nosotros nos curamos solos —dijo Temp. Gregor lamentaba que Temp estuviera herido, pero lo bueno de ello era que ahora podía distinguir mejor a la una de la otra.

—¡Curita! —insistió Boots, y alargó la mano para coger la antena herida.

—¡No, Boots! —dijo Gregor, bloqueándole la mano—. Temp no se pone curita.

—¡Curita! —Boots hizo una mueca a Gregor y lo apartó de un empujón.

«Vaya, genial», pensó éste. «Estamos en problemas». Por lo general Boots era una niña muy buena. Pero sólo tenía dos años, y de vez en cuando todavía le daba alguna rabieta que dejaba agotada a toda la familia. Solía ocurrir cuando estaba cansada o tenía hambre.

Gregor metió la mano en la bolsa. ¿No había mencionado Dulcet algo de que había cositas ricas de comer? Sacó una galleta.

—¿Una galleta, Boots? —la niña tomó la galleta a regañadientes y se sentó para comérsela. Al parecer, ya todo estaba bajo control.

—¿Nos odia, la princesa, nos odia? —preguntó Tick con gran preocupación.

—Huy, no —contestó Gregor—. Es sólo que a veces se pone así. Mi madre dice que son caprichos de la edad. A veces le da una rabieta sin motivo.

Boots los miró a todos frunciendo el ceño y empezó a golpear el suelo con los pies.

—¿Nos odia, la princesa, nos odia? —murmuró Temp con tristeza.

Probablemente las crías de las cucarachas no tenían rabietas.

—No, de verdad, le siguen cayendo bien —les aseguró Gregor—. Sólo necesita un poco de espacio. — Esperaba que el comportamiento de Boots no hiriera tanto a las cucarachas como para que les entraran ganas de marcharse. Bueno, ahora mismo nadie podía irse a ningún sitio, de todas formas.

Vikus le indicó con un gesto que se reuniera con ellos. Le susurró:

—Gregor, mi esposa teme que los tejedores puedan informar a las ratas de nuestro paradero. Aconseja que escapemos sin demora.

—¡Estoy con ella! —aprobó Gregor—. Pero, ¿cómo

vamos a hacerlo? —Boots se acercó a él por detrás y le dio un pellizco en el brazo sin motivo alguno—. ¡No, Boots! —exclamó—. ¡No se pellizca!

—¡*Ota* galleta! —le dijo, tirándole del brazo.

—No, para las niñas que pellizcan no hay galletas —dijo Gregor con firmeza. El labio inferior de Boots empezó a temblar. Dio media vuelta, se alejó de él, se tiró al suelo, y empezó a darle patadas a la bolsa.

—Perdón, ¿cuál es entonces el plan? —preguntó Gregor, volviendo a unirse al grupo—. ¿Podemos abrirnos camino a través de la telaraña y echar a correr sin más?

—No, al otro lado del embudo de seda hay veintenas de tejedores preparados para zurcir cualquier agujero y atacarnos con el veneno de sus colmillos. Si huimos hacia arriba, seguramente saltarán sobre nosotros desde las alturas —susurró Solovet.

—¿Y qué nos queda entonces? —preguntó Gregor.

—Sólo nos queda una única alternativa. Tenemos que dañar la telaraña tanto y tan rápidamente que no puedan repararla, y que no aguante tampoco su peso —indicó Solovet. Se quedó callada un momento—. Alguien deberá ejecutar la Maniobra en Espiral.

Todos miraron a Luxa, de modo que Gregor los imitó. Su murciélago dorado, que estaba detrás de ella, inclinó la cabeza y le tocó el cuello.

—Podemos hacerlo nosotros —dijo Luxa despacio.

—No insistimos, Luxa. El peligro, especialmente arriba de todo, es muy grande. Pero a decir verdad, eres nuestra mayor esperanza —dijo Vikus con tristeza.

Henry la rodeó con el brazo.

—Pueden hacerlo. Las he visto entrenar. Ambas son veloces y precisas.

Luxa asintió con la cabeza con expresión resuelta.

—Podemos hacerlo. No perdamos más tiempo.

—Gregor, monta el murciélago de Vikus. Vikus, tú, conmigo. Henry y Mareth, ocúpense de un reptante cada uno —ordenó Solovet.

—Necesitamos una distracción para cubrir a Luxa —dijo Mareth—. Yo podría ir por un lado.

—No con una herida en la pierna —dijo Solovet, dirigiendo la mirada en derredor—. Y nadie se aventura por un lado. Significa una muerte segura.

—Los tejedores son muy sensibles al ruido —comentó Vikus—. Lástima que no tengamos cuernos.

Gregor sintió un par de piececitos que golpeaban furiosos su pierna. Se dio la vuelta y vio a Boots en el suelo, dándole patadas.

—¡Basta! —le dijo severamente—. ¿Quieres que te castigue?

—¡Castigar no! ¡Tú castigado! ¡Tú castigado! ¡Galleta! ¡Galleta! —gimoteó Boots. Estaba a punto de estallar de un momento a otro.

—¿Necesitamos ruido? —preguntó Gregor con gran frustración—. Pues aquí lo tienen. —Cogió a Boots en brazos y la metió a la fuerza en la mochila.

—¡No! ¡No! ¡No! —gritó Boots, con una voz cada vez más fuerte y aguda.

—¿Todos preparados? —preguntó Gregor, sacando una galleta de la bolsa de Dulcet.

Los demás no estaban muy seguros de lo que estaba haciendo, pero unos segundos después estaban todos listos para levantar el vuelo. Solovet asintió con la cabeza.

—Estamos preparados.

Gregor blandió la galleta.

—¡Eh, Boots! —dijo—. ¿Quieres una galleta?

—¡No *quero* galleta! ¡No, no, no, no! —contestó Boots, para quien ya no existía galleta que pudiera quitarle el enfado.

—Está bien —dijo Gregor—. Pues entonces, me la como yo. —Y, asegurándose de que Boots pudiera verlo, se comió la galleta de un solo bocado.

—¡Es mía! —chilló Boots—. ¡Es mía! ¡Es mía! ¡Míiiiiiiaaaaa! —Era un chillido tan fuerte como para romperle el tímpano a cualquiera, y Gregor sintió que le iba a estallar el cerebro.

—¡Adelante, Luxa! —exclamó Solovet. La chica levantó el vuelo con su murciélago. Ahora entendía Gregor por qué era tan difícil la Maniobra en Espiral. Luxa se elevaba describiendo círculos por dentro de la tela a una velocidad de vértigo, blandiendo la espada por encima de su cabeza. Con ésta iba cortando el embudo, dejándolo hecho jirones. Sólo un extraordinario jinete, increíblemente flexible, podría realizar una maniobra así.

—¡Caray! —exclamó Gregor con admiración. Subió de un salto al gran murciélago de Vikus.

—¡Míiiiaaa! —seguía chillando Boots—. ¡Míiiaaa!

Por encima de su cabeza veía a Luxa dando vueltas y cortando la tela con su espada. Los demás la seguían, cortando a su vez las paredes del embudo de seda. Gregor cerraba la marcha con Boots y sus ensordecedores chillidos.

En lo alto del embudo, el murciélago estaba suspendido en el aire, ejecutando cabeza abajo una complicada figura en forma de ocho. Bajo el amparo de la espada de Luxa, los de las Tierras Bajas se escabulleron hacia la libertad.

Gregor era el único que seguía en el embudo cuando todo ocurrió. Desde arriba cayó con fuerza sobre Luxa un chorro de seda, que rodeó el brazo que sostenía la espada, y derribó a la chica de su montura. Un par de patas rayadas tiraron de ella como si fuera un pez atrapado en una caña de pescar.

Los colmillos de la reina Wevox se abrieron para recibir el cuello de su presa.

CAPÍTULO DECIMOCTAVO

Gregor se quedó boquiabierto de horror. Luxa estaba a unos segundos de morir. Ella también lo sabía. Se debatía, aterrorizada, tratando de romper con los dientes el hilo que aprisionaba su muñeca, pero era demasiado grueso.

Gregor buscó un arma desesperadamente. ¿Qué tenía él? ¿Pañales? ¿Galletas? ¿Por qué no le habrían dado una espada? El guerrero estúpido, ése era él. Metió la mano en su bolsa de cuero y encontró la lata de gaseosa. ¡Gaseosa! Sacó la lata, agitándola con todas sus fuerzas.

—¡Al ataque! ¡Al ataque! —gritó.

Justo cuando los colmillos estaban a punto de hincarse sobre la garganta de Luxa, Gregor levantó el vuelo y abrió la lata. El chorro de gaseosa salió disparado, golpeando a la araña en plena cara. Ésta soltó a Luxa, y se llevó las patas a los ojos.

Luxa cayó y su murciélago la recogió. Se unieron a los demás, que ya regresaban para ayudarla.

—¡Sierra circular! —ordenó Solovet, y los murciélagos se congregaron para formar el mismo círculo estrecho que había rodeado a Gregor la vez que había tratado de escapar del estadio. Los humanos blandieron sus espadas, apuntando a los lados del embudo, y la formación empezó a moverse por el aire, describiendo círculos cerrados, como una sierra eléctrica.

Los espantosos gritos de Boots obligaban a las arañas a protegerse asustadas, acurrucándose como ovillos. Gregor no sabía si era por el ruido, por la sierra circular, o por miedo a la gaseosa. Lo único que sabía era que, unos minutos después volaban libres, lejos de las arañas.

Gregor relajó las piernas cuando se dio cuenta de que debía de estar asfixiando a su murciélago. Todavía sostenía en la mano la lata de gaseosa medio vacía. De haber sido capaz de tragar, se la habría bebido.

Los gritos de Boots pronto se fueron convirtiendo en gemidos. Apoyó la cabeza en el hombro de Gregor y se quedó dormida. Estaba tan alterada que aún seguía gimiendo en sueños. Gregor se dio la vuelta y le besó la cabecita llena de rizos.

Luxa estaba tumbada sobre su murciélago, viva pero exhausta. Vio que Solovet y Vikus se le acercaban volando para hablar con ella. Luxa asintió, pero no se incorporó. Ambos se pusieron a la cabeza de la formación, y los murciélagos se alejaron de allí, surcando la oscuridad a la velocidad del rayo.

Sobrevolaron túneles desiertos por un largo rato. Gregor no vio señal alguna de vida, ya fuera animal o vegetal. Por fin, Solovet y Vikus les indicaron que descendieran, y el grupo aterrizó en una amplia cueva que se abría en la boca de un túnel.

Todos se dejaron caer prácticamente al suelo desde sus monturas, y no se movieron. Temp y Tick parecían casi inconscientes de puro miedo. Los murciélagos se acercaron unos a otros, formando un grupito cerrado y tembloroso.

Poco después, Gregor se oyó a sí mismo decir:

—Bueno, ¿no piensan que ya va siendo hora de que yo también tenga una espada?

Hubo un momento de silencio, y luego todos estallaron en sonoras carcajadas. No podían parar de reír. Gregor no veía dónde estaba el chiste, pero se rió con ellos, sintiendo que las tinieblas iban abandonando su cuerpo poco a poco.

La risa despertó a Boots, que se frotó los ojos y preguntó alegremente:

—¿*Onde* está la araña?

Por algún motivo, esa pregunta volvió a provocar las carcajadas de todos. Encantada con la reacción, Boots repetía una y otra vez «¿*Onde* está la araña?», ante las risas complacientes de los demás.

—La araña se ha ido, adiós, adiós —le dijo Gregor por fin—. ¿Quieres una galleta?

—¡Síiii! —exclamó Boots, sin la menor sombra de enfado por el incidente anterior. Ésa era una de sus grandes virtudes. Una vez que se calmaba y se dormía, al despertar volvía a ser la niña dulce de siempre.

Cuando se dieron cuenta de que la princesa no los odiaba, Temp y Tick se unieron a ellos, y se pusieron a corretear por allí, jugando al lobo con Boots.

Mareth empezó a preparar la comida, pero Solovet le ordenó que se tumbara y pusiera la pierna en alto. Ella y

Vikus prepararon la cena mientras Henry y Mareth se enfrascaban en algo que parecía un juego de naipes.

Gregor se acercó a Luxa, que estaba sentada sobre un saliente de roca. Se acomodó junto a ella, y comprobó que la chica aún temblaba.

—¿Qué tal estás? —le preguntó.

—Estoy bien —contestó con voz tensa.

—Me gustó un montón esa espiral que hiciste —le dijo Gregor.

—Era la primera vez que estaba en una telaraña de verdad —le confesó ella.

—Yo también. Aunque, claro, en las Tierras Altas los tejedores son pequeños, y no los consideramos nuestros vecinos —explicó Gregor. Luxa hizo una mueca.

—Nosotros no tratamos mucho con ellos.

—Pues tanto mejor, me parece a mí. O sea, quiero decir, ¿quién querría tratar con alguien que se pasa el rato pensando en cómo beberte las entrañas? —dijo Gregor.

Luxa parecía escandalizada.

—¡No te burlarías de esa manera si la reina te hubiera atrapado a ti!

—Eh, oye, un momento, que yo estuve una hora ahí colgado, gritando, hasta que a ustedes se les ocurrió aparecer, ¿eh? —protestó Gregor—. Y las arañas me odiaban a muerte.

Luxa se rió.

—Ya me he dado cuenta, sí. Por lo que ha dicho la reina Wevox. —Luxa calló unos instantes. Le costó mucho pronunciar la siguiente palabra—: Gracias.

—¿Por qué? —preguntó Gregor.

—Por salvarme con... ¿Qué arma es ésa? —señaló la lata de gaseosa.

—No es un arma. Es una gaseosa —explicó Gregor. Bebió un sorbito.

Luxa parecía asustada.

—¿No es peligroso beberla? —preguntó.

—Qué va, pruébala —dijo Gregor, ofreciéndole la lata con presteza.

Luxa bebió un sorbo cautelosamente, y abrió los ojos como platos.

—Siento como un extraño cosquilleo en toda la lengua —comentó.

—Sí, ya, por eso explotó. La agité para que hubiera muchas burbujas. Pero ahora no es peligrosa. Es como beber agua. Anda, termínatela si quieres —dijo, y Luxa siguió bebiendo sorbitos, con mucha curiosidad.

—Bueno, de todas maneras te debía una —dijo Gregor—. Tú me salvaste de la rata la primera noche. Así que estamos en paz.

Luxa asintió con la cabeza, pero se veía muy preocupada.

—Hay una cosa más. No debí haberte pegado por tratar de escapar. Lo siento.

—Y yo siento haber dicho que tu tierra me ponía los pelos de punta. No es del todo verdad. Hay partes que están genial —dijo.

—¿Yo también «te pongo los pelos de punta»? —preguntó Luxa.

—No, qué va. Lo que me pone los pelos de punta son cosas como las ratas, ya sabes, cosas que te dan escalofríos. Tú eres simplemente... difícil —dijo Gregor, tratando de expresar sus sentimientos con sinceridad pero sin mala educación.

—Tú también lo eres. Resulta difícil persuadirte de que... de que hagas ciertas cosas —explicó Luxa.

Gregor asintió con la cabeza, pero hizo una mueca de impaciencia cuando ella no lo miraba. Luxa era la persona más terca que había conocido en su vida.

Vikus los llamó a todos a cenar, y hasta las cucarachas se sintieron lo suficientemente cómodas como para unirse a ellos.

—Estoy bebiéndome el arma que usó Gregor contra los tejedores —anunció Luxa, blandiendo la lata de gaseosa. Gregor tuvo que volver a explicar otra vez lo de las burbujas, y luego todos quisieron probar un sorbito.

Cuando la lata llegó hasta Boots, Gregor dijo:

—Bueno, ya casi no queda nada. —Pensaba que la niña se bebería de un trago el poquito que quedaba. Pero, en vez de eso, Boots vertió la gaseosa en el suelo formando dos charquitos.

—Bichos *gandes* —dijo, señalando el primer charco—. *Mulcélagos* —dijo, indicando el segundo. Ambos grupos de animales obedecieron diligentemente y se acercaron para probar la gaseosa.

—Boots es una embajadora nata —dijo Vikus sonriendo—. Trata a todos con una igualdad a la que yo mismo aspiro. Y ahora, a comer.

Todos se lanzaron sobre sus platos como si nunca antes hubieran visto comida. Una vez que hubo engullido la suficiente cantidad para empezar a detenerse a saborear-la, Gregor formuló la pregunta que lo había estado preocupando desde que habían escapado de las arañas.

—¿Podemos seguir con nuestra búsqueda aunque no nos acompañe ningún tejedor?

—Ésa es la cuestión —contestó Vikus—. Ésa es la cuestión que todos hemos de considerar. Es obvio que no podemos esperar que ningún tejedor se una a nosotros por voluntad propia.

—Deberíamos haber atrapado a dos de ellos cuando tuvimos oportunidad —dijo Henry sombríamente.

—La profecía dicta que los tejedores han de mostrar su aquiescencia, es decir, aceptar —objetó Vikus—. Sin embargo, sabemos que las ratas han hecho prisioneros a muchos tejedores. Tal vez podamos liberar a unos cuantos y persuadirlos de que se unan a nosotros. He tenido buenos resultados con ellos en múltiples ocasiones.

—Pero tú no estarás allí, Vikus —dijo Solovet con voz serena.

—¿Qué quiere decir? —preguntó Gregor, y sintió que se le aceleraba la sangre en las venas.

Vikus calló un momento, observando a todo el grupo con mucha atención.

—Ha llegado la hora de que quienes no aparecemos en la profecía regresemos a casa. Mareth, Solovet y yo nos marcharemos cuando hayamos descansado.

Gregor vio su propia sorpresa reflejada en los rostros de Luxa y de Henry.

—Nada en la profecía te prohíbe venir, Vikus —objetó Luxa.

—No hay razón para que estemos aquí. Y además, tenemos una guerra que ganar —dijo Solovet.

La idea de dar un solo paso sin Vikus y Solovet llenó de pánico a Gregor.

—Pero no pueden abandonarnos. Si ni siquiera sabemos adónde vamos —protestó Gregor—. ¿Saben ustedes acaso adónde hay que ir? —preguntó a Luxa y a Henry. Ambos negaron con la cabeza—. ¿Lo ven?

—Ya se las arreglarán. Henry y Luxa están bien preparados, y tú has dado muestras de una gran inventiva —dijo Solovet. Habló con sencillez y determinación. Estaba pensando en la guerra, en asuntos mucho más importantes, no en ellos.

Gregor supo instintivamente que no conseguiría hacerle cambiar de opinión. Se volvió hacia Vikus.

—No pueden irse. Los necesitamos. Necesitamos a alguien... ¡alguien que sepa lo que hay que hacer!

Miró a Luxa y a Henry para ver si se habían ofendido con este comentario, pero ambos aguardaban ansiosos la respuesta de Vikus. «Lo saben», pensó Gregor. «Se hacen los duros, pero saben perfectamente que no podemos arreglárnoslas solos».

—No es mi intención abandonarlos en la Tierra de la Muerte —dijo Vikus.

—Vaya, fantástico, encima estamos en la Tierra de la Muerte —dijo Gregor—. Entonces, ¿qué piensan hacer...? ¿Dibujarnos un mapa?

—No, les he previsto un guía —contestó Vikus.

—¿Un guía? —preguntó Henry.

—¿Un guía? —repitió Luxa como un eco.

Vikus respiró hondo, como si estuviera a punto de lanzarse a una larga explicación. Pero entonces alguien lo interrumpió.

—Bueno, yo, la verdad, prefiero considerarme una leyenda, pero supongo que tendré que conformarme con ser un guía —pronunció una voz profunda y lánguida que emergió de algún lugar entre las sombras.

Gregor apuntó con su linterna en la dirección en que provenía la voz.

Apoyada en la entrada del túnel había una rata con una cicatriz que le cruzaba la cara en diagonal. Gregor apenas tardó unos segundos en reconocer al animal que Vikus había derribado y empujado a las aguas del río.

tercera parte

LA RATA

CAPÍTULO DECIMONOVENO

Q uietos! —exclamó Vikus al ver que Luxa, Henry y Mareth se ponían en pie de un salto, espada en mano—. ¡Quietos!

La rata miró divertida a los tres humanos armados.

—Sí, quietos, no vaya a tener que moverme yo, y eso siempre me pone de pésimo humor —dijo lánguidamente.

Luxa y Mareth se detuvieron, sin saber muy bien cómo reaccionar, pero Henry hizo caso omiso de la orden de Vikus y se lanzó sobre la rata. Sin mover ningún otro músculo, esta chasqueó la cola. El apéndice salió disparado, como un látigo, sobre la mano de Henry, haciéndole soltar la espada. El arma rebotó sobre el suelo de piedra y chocó contra la pared de la cueva. Henry se sujetó la muñeca, dolorido.

—La lección más difícil que ha de aprender un soldado es obedecer órdenes que estima equivocadas —dijo la rata filosóficamente—. Ten cuidado, muchacho, o terminarás como yo, desposeído de toda respetabilidad y calentando tu triste trasero a la lumbre de tus enemigos. —La rata hizo un gesto con la cabeza al anciano—. Vikus.

—Ripred —dijo Vikus con una sonrisa—. Acabamos de empezar a cenar. ¿Quieres unirte a nosotros?

—Pensaba que nunca me lo ibas a preguntar —dijo Ripred, abandonando la pared donde seguía apoyado, y acercándose al fuego arrastrando los pies. Se sentó sobre las patas traseras, junto a Solovet—. Mi querida Solovet, qué amable de tu parte salir a recibirme. Estando además en guerra.

—Por nada del mundo me hubiera perdido la oportunidad de compartir el pan contigo, Ripred —dijo Solovet.

—Vamos, vamos, sabes perfectamente que sólo me has seguido para sonsacarme información —dijo Ripred—. Y para regocijarte con tu victoria.

—Te destruí —dijo Solovet con júbilo—. Tu ejército dio media vuelta y se metió aullando en las aguas del río.

—Ejército —se burló Ripred—. Si eso es un ejército yo soy una mariposa. Habría tenido más oportunidades si hubiera luchado con un grupo de reptantes. —La rata miró a Temp y Tick, que se refugiaban asustados contra la pared de la cueva, y suspiró—. Exceptuando a los presentes, por supuesto.

Boots frunció el ceño y gateó hasta Ripred. Lo señaló con su dedo regordete.

—¿Tú *latón*?

—Sí, soy un ratón. Mira cómo chillo: hiiii, hiiii. Y ahora, largo de aquí y vuelve con tus amiguitos los bichos —dijo Ripred, cogiendo un pedazo de carne seca. Arrancó un trozo con los dientes, y entonces vio que Boots no se había movido de su sitio. Estiró los labios, revelando así una hilera de dientes puntiagudos y le lanzó un siseo amenazador.

—¡Huy! —exclamó Boots, corriendo hacia las cucarachas—. ¡Huy!

—No hagas eso —dijo Gregor. La rata volvió hacia él sus ojos brillantes, y Gregor se quedó atónito ante lo que vio en ellos: inteligencia, un destello letal y, lo más sorprendente de todo, dolor. Esta rata no era como Shed o Fangor. Era mucho más compleja y mucho más peligrosa. Por primera vez, desde que estaba en las Tierras Bajas, Gregor sintió que la situación lo superaba por completo. Si tenía que luchar contra esta rata, no tendría ni la más mínima posibilidad de salir vencedor. Perdería. Moriría.

—Ah, éste debe de ser nuestro guerrero —dijo Ripred suavemente—. Pero cuánto te pareces a tu papaíto.

—No asustes a mi hermana —dijo Gregor, tratando de que no le temblara la voz—. No es más que un bebé.

—Según me han dicho, tiene más agallas que todos ustedes juntos —dijo Ripred—. Por supuesto, el valor sólo cuenta cuando sabes contar. Supongo que todos los demás saben contar, así que ya están armándose de valor para venir a sentarse aquí conmigo, muy bien.

La rata lanzó una mirada en derredor a Luxa, Mareth y Henry, que se mantenían a distancia. Los murciélagos extendían y replegaban las alas, sin saber muy bien qué hacer.

—Bueno, ¿qué pasa, es que nadie más tiene hambre? Odio comer solo. Me hace sentir tan poco querido...

—No los había preparado, Ripred —dijo Vikus.

—Salta a la vista —contestó la rata—. Resulta obvio que mi llegada es un placer inesperado. —Se puso a roer el hueso de carne, haciendo un espantoso ruido con los dientes.

—Les presento a Ripred, el roedor —dijo Vikus al resto del grupo—. Se unirá a la búsqueda en calidad de guía de la expedición.

Se oyó una especie de suspiro, pues la mitad de los presentes tragó aire con dificultad. Siguió una larga pausa, en la que nadie se atrevió a respirar. Gregor trató de asimilar lo que Vikus había anunciado con tanta tranquilidad. Una rata. Los abandonaba en las garras de una rata. Quiso protestar, pero se le había petrificado la garganta.

Por fin Luxa habló con una voz ronca de odio.

—No, no lo hará. Nosotros no viajamos con ratas.

—La Profecía del Gris así lo exige, Luxa —dijo Solovet—. «Un roedor al lado».

—«Al lado» podría significar cualquier cosa —gruñó Henry—. Tal vez signifique que lo dejamos «de lado», que lo matamos y no viene con nosotros.

—Tal vez sí. Pero habiendo sido testigo de tu último ataque, lo dudo mucho —dijo Ripred, concentrándose en un pedazo de queso.

—Hemos matado a cinco ratas desde el mediodía —dijo Luxa.

—¿Te refieres a los imbéciles que escogí cuidadosamente por su cobardía y su ineptitud? Oh, sí, bravo, majestad. Todo un ejemplo de maestría en el combate —dijo Ripred, con una voz cargada de sarcasmo—. No cantes victoria, todavía no te has enfrentado a una rata de verdad.

—Ellos mismos fueron quienes mataron a Shed y a Fangor —intervino Mareth con valentía.

—Bien, entonces permíteme que me corrija. Fangor y Shed eran excelentes guerreros, en las escasas ocasiones en que estaban sobrios —dijo Ripred—. Sin embargo, me imagino que los superabas en número, y que estaban algo aturdidos por la llegada de nuestro guerrero. ¿Qué dices tú, guerrero? ¿Tú también te niegas a ir conmigo?

Gregor observó los ojos burlones y atormentados de Ripred. Quería negarse, pero si lo hacía, ¿encontraría alguna vez a su padre?

Como si le hubiera leído el pensamiento, Vikus se le adelantó:

—Necesitarás a Ripred para que te guíe hasta tu padre. Los humanos no tenemos mapas de estos túneles. Sin él nunca encontrarás el camino.

Pese a todo, no dejaba de ser una rata. Gregor sólo llevaba unos pocos días en las Tierras Bajas y ya despreciaba a las ratas. Habían matado a los padres de Luxa y de Henry, habían hecho prisionero a su padre, y casi se los habían comido a él y a Boots. Sintió que una especie de oleada de poder recorría todo su cuerpo cuando pensó en lo mucho que las odiaba. Pero si todas las ratas eran malvadas, ¿quién era esa extraña criatura que lo miraba desde el otro lado de la hoguera, y que se ofrecía a servirles de guía?

—¿Y qué ganas tú con esto? —le preguntó Gregor a Ripred sin vacilar.

—Una pregunta de lo más justa —contestó la rata—. Pues bien, guerrero, estoy planeando derrocar al rey Gorger y necesito que me ayudes.

—¿Que te ayude, cómo? —quiso saber Gregor.

—No lo sé —reconoció Ripred—. Ninguno de nosotros lo sabe.

Gregor se levantó y cogió a Vikus del brazo.

—Tengo que hablarle a solas —dijo. Él mismo se sorprendió de la rabia que afloraba en su voz. ¡Pues sí, estaba furioso! La rata no formaba parte del trato. Esto no era en lo que él había aceptado embarcarse.

Vikus se tomó su enfado con calma. Tal vez se había imaginado que reaccionaría así. Se alejaron unos metros del resto del grupo.

—Bueno, ¿cuánto tiempo hace que tiene este plan con la rata? —preguntó Gregor.

Vikus reflexionó un momento.

—No sabría decirte con exactitud. Tal vez unos dos años. Por supuesto, todo dependía de tu llegada.

—¿Y cómo es que no me ha dicho nada hasta ahora? —quiso saber Gregor.

—No soy partidario de dar a la gente más información de la que puede asimilar —contestó Vikus.

—¿Quién dice que no puedo asimilarla? ¡Sí puedo asimilarla! —dijo Gregor, dejando más que patente que en realidad no podía.

—Tal vez puedas, por lo menos mejor que Luxa y Henry. Es posible que te lo hubiera contado si hubiéramos terminado nuestra charla sobre la Profecía del Gris —añadió Vikus—. No cabe duda de que me habrías preguntado, y sí, es muy posible que te lo hubiera contado.

Gregor se sacó la profecía del bolsillo y dijo:

—Vamos a terminarla ahora. —Buscó la parte en la que se habían quedado la última vez.

Un roedor al lado y uno perdido antes.

—Así que Ripred es el «roedor», y mi padre es el «otro perdido antes» —dijo Gregor. Prosiguió su lectura.

*Tras contar a los muertos
ocho vivos serán los restantes.*

—¿Qué significa esto? —preguntó Gregor, señalando el verso con el dedo.

—Si sumas todos los participantes de la profecía, dos de arriba, dos de abajo, dos voladores, dos reptantes, los dos tejedores, un roedor y uno perdido, son doce en total —dijo Vikus con gravedad—. Al final de la búsqueda, sólo quedarán ocho con vida. Cuatro habrán muerto. Pero nadie sabe quiénes serán esos cuatro.

—Ah —dijo Gregor, anonadado. Había oído antes esas palabras, pero sólo ahora empezaba a asimilarlas—. Cuatro de nosotros, muertos.

—Pero ocho vivos, Gregor —dijo Vikus con dulzura—. Y tal vez un mundo entero salvado.

Gregor no podía pensar en eso ahora, no podía dejar de preguntarse una y otra vez quién seguiría con vida al final de la prueba. Pasó a la estrofa final de la profecía.

El último en morir su bando elegirá.

El destino de los ocho en su mano estará.
Rogadle, pues, prudencia cuando con cautela salte,
pues la vida puede ser muerte
y la muerte, vida, en un instante.

—No entiendo esta última parte —declaró Gregor.

—Yo tampoco, ni nadie. Es muy enigmática. Creo que nadie la entenderá completamente hasta que llegue el momento final —dijo Vikus—. Gregor, lo que te pido que hagas no es agradable ni fácil, pero es esencial. Esencial para ti, si quieres encontrar a tu padre. Esencial para mi pueblo, si queremos sobrevivir.

Gregor sintió que la rabia lo iba abandonando y el miedo iba ocupando todos los resquicios de su ser. Adoptó una táctica distinta.

—No quiero ir con esa rata —dijo Gregor, con voz casi suplicante—. Nos matará.

—No, no puedes juzgar a Ripred por lo que sabes de otras ratas. Tiene una sabiduría a la que ninguna otra criatura podría siquiera aspirar. Las cosas no siempre estuvieron tan mal entre los humanos y las ratas. Cuando Solovet, Ripred y yo mismo éramos más jóvenes, vivíamos en una paz relativa. A Ripred le gustaría restaurar esa paz, pero el rey Gorger desea ver muertos a todos los humanos —explicó Vikus.

—Así que está usted diciendo que Ripred es una rata buena —dijo Gregor, atragantándose con las palabras.

—Si no lo fuera, ¿crees que le confiaría a mi nieta? —le preguntó Vikus.

—¿Su nieta? —dijo Gregor, atónito.

—La madre de Luxa, Judith, era mi hija —le explicó Vikus.

—¿Es usted su abuelo? ¿Y por qué lo llama Vikus? —preguntó Gregor. Esta gente era tan extraña y tan ceremoniosa. ¿Por qué nadie le había dicho nada?

—Son nuestras costumbres —dijo Vikus—. Cuida de ella. Si esto es duro para ti, para Luxa es una tortura.

—¡Todavía no he dicho que acepto! —exclamó Gregor. Miró al anciano a los ojos—. Está bien, de acuerdo, acepto. ¿Hay alguna otra cosa más que necesite saber y que todavía no me haya dicho?

—Sólo una: a pesar de lo que te dije, desde el primer momento en que te vi supe que eras el guerrero de la Profecía —confesó Vikus.

—Gracias. Fantástico. Eso me ayuda mucho —dijo Gregor, y ambos volvieron junto al resto del grupo—. Bien, Boots y yo nos vamos con la rata. ¿Quién más se apunta?

Durante un momento, nadie dijo nada.

—Adonde va la princesa, vamos nosotros —dijo Temp con decisión.

—¿Qué dices tú, Luxa? —preguntó Vikus.

—¿Qué puedo decir, Vikus? ¿Puedo volver a mi pueblo y decirle que abandoné la búsqueda cuando nuestra supervivencia pende de un hilo? —dijo Luxa amargamente.

—Por supuesto que no puedes, Luxa. Por eso ha calculado tan bien su maniobra —dijo Henry.

—Podrías optar por... —empezó diciendo Vikus.

—¡Podría optar! ¡Podría optar! —replicó Luxa—. ¡No me ofrezcas opciones cuando sabes que no existe ninguna! —ella y Henry le dieron la espalda al anciano.

—¿Voladores? —inquirió Solovet, al ver que Vikus parecía haber perdido la habilidad de hablar.

—Aurora y yo vamos allá adonde vayan nuestros vínculos —dijo Ares entre dientes.

—Entonces, está decidido. Ven, Mareth, nos necesitan en Regalia —dijo Solovet.

Mareth, muy apesadumbrado, se puso a preparar rápidamente paquetes de comida para los miembros de la búsqueda.

—Vuelen alto —dijo con voz ahogada, y montó a lomos de su murciélago.

Solovet subió al suyo y desenrolló su mapa. Mientras Ripred la ayudaba a trazar el camino más seguro de vuelta a Regalia, Vikus se dirigió a Henry y Luxa. Ninguno de los dos se volvió para mirarlo.

—No quisiera despedirme así, pero comprendo sus corazones. Tal vez algún día puedan perdonarme este momento. Vuela alto, Henry. Vuela alto, Luxa —dijo Vikus. Aguardó una respuesta, pero no obtuvo ninguna. Se dio la vuelta y se dejó caer pesadamente sobre su murciélago.

Por muy desgraciado que se sintiera Gregor de que lo abandonaran en manos de una rata, sentía más tristeza aún por Vikus. Quería gritarle a Luxa: «¡Di algo! ¡No dejes que tu abuelo se marche así! ¡Cuatro de nosotros no volveremos!». Pero las palabras quedaron atrapadas en su garganta. Y además, una parte de él tampoco estaba dispuesta a perdonar a Vikus por abandonarlos así.

—Vuela alto, Gregor de las Tierras Altas —se despidió Vikus.

Gregor se debatía internamente sobre cómo reaccionar. ¿Debía hacer caso omiso de Vikus? ¿Hacerle ver que ninguno de ellos, ni siquiera uno de las Tierras Altas, podía perdonarlo? Justo cuando había decidido no contestarle, Gregor pensó en los dos años, siete meses y, ¿cuántos días sumaban ya, quince? Había tantas cosas que deseaba haberle dicho a su padre cuando aún era posible... Cosas como lo genial que era cuando subían al tejado por la noche para ver las estrellas. O cuánto le gustaba cuando tomaban el metro hasta el estadio para ver un partido de béisbol. O decirle simplemente que se sentía afortunado de que, entre todas las personas que había en el mundo, él fuera su padre.

Ya no cabían en su corazón más palabras no pronunciadas. Los murciélagos estaban levantando el vuelo. Sólo tenía un segundo.

—¡Vuela alto, Vikus! —gritó—. ¡Vuela alto!

Vikus se volvió, y Gregor vio lágrimas brillando en sus mejillas. El anciano levantó la mano hacia Gregor, en un gesto de agradecimiento.

Hecho esto, desaparecieron.

CAPÍTULO VIGÉSIMO

De modo que ahí se quedaron los nueve, completamente solos. Gregor se sentía como si todos los adultos se hubieran marchado, dejando a los niños con una rata de niñera. En su interior se sentía mareado, vacío, y muy vulnerable. Miró a su alrededor y cayó en la cuenta de que no había nadie a quien pudiera recurrir en busca de protección.

—Bueno, será mejor que descansemos un poco —declaró Ripred con un gran bostezo—. Así recuperaremos fuerzas y podremos marcharnos dentro de unas horas. —Se sacudió de encima unas migas de queso, se agazapó, y menos de un minuto después ya estaba roncando.

Ninguno sabía qué decir. Gregor extendió su manta en el suelo y llamó a Boots.

—¿Se van adiós-adiós? —preguntó la niña, señalando en la dirección en que había visto desaparecer a Vikus y a los otros.

—Sí, Boots, se fueron adiós-adiós. Vamos a dormir aquí. Es hora de irse a la cama. —Gregor se tumbó sobre la manta, y Boots se acurrucó a su lado sin protestar. Temp y

Tick se colocaron uno a cada lado de ellos. ¿Estarían montando guardia? ¿De verdad pensaban que podrían hacer algo en caso de que Ripred decidiera atacarlos? Con todo, de alguna manera era reconfortante tenerlos ahí.

Luxa no quiso tumbarse. Aurora vino y la envolvió entre sus alas doradas. Ares apoyó su suave espalda negra contra la de Aurora, y Henry se tumbó a los pies de su murciélago.

Por muchas precauciones que tomaran, Gregor estaba seguro de que Ripred podía matarlos a los ocho en un abrir y cerrar de ojos. «Primero, dejará fuera de combate a Henry y a Luxa, ya que son los únicos que van armados; y luego ya no tendrá más que ocuparse de los demás, uno por uno», pensó Gregor. Tal vez Ares o Aurora pudieran escapar, pero los demás eran presas fáciles. Ésa era la verdad, más le valía aceptarla.

Por extraño que parezca, una vez que la aceptó, Gregor se sintió más relajado. No tenía más opción que fiarse de Ripred. Si podía confiar en la rata, entonces lograría quedarse dormido. Así que dejó que lo fuera invadiendo el sueño, tratando de eliminar de su cabeza imágenes de patas peludas de arañas y puntiagudos dientes de rata. Francamente, había sido un día de perros.

Se despertó sobresaltado al oír un fuerte chasquido. Instintivamente, se inclinó sobre Boots para protegerla con su cuerpo, hasta que cayó en la cuenta de que el ruido lo había hecho Ripred golpeando el suelo con su cola.

—Vamos, vamos —gruñó—. Es hora de levantarse. Coman algo y luego nos vamos.

Gregor emergió de debajo de su manta y esperó a que Mareth le trajera la comida. Entonces recordó que Mareth se había marchado.

—¿Cómo quieres que nos organicemos para la comida y eso? —le preguntó a Henry.

—Luxa y yo no servimos comida, somos de sangre real —contestó él muy altanero.

—¿Ah, sí? Pues yo soy el guerrero, y Boots es una princesa. Y ustedes dos van a pasar mucha, pero mucha hambre si esperan a que yo les sirva la comida —dijo Gregor. La verdad es que a él le importaba un pepino esa tontería de la sangre real.

Ripred se echó a reír.

—Díselo, chico. Dile que tu país combatió una guerra para que no tuvieras que someterte a ningún rey, ni a ninguna reina.

Gregor miró a Ripred, sorprendido.

—¿Cómo sabes tú eso?

—Oh, yo sé muchas cosas de las Tierras Altas que nuestros amigos ni se imaginan. He pasado mucho tiempo enfrascado en sus libros y papeles —explicó Ripred.

—¿Pero tú sabes leer? —preguntó Gregor.

—La mayoría de las ratas sabe leer. Nuestra frustración es que no podemos sostener una pluma para escribir. Y ahora, muévete, chico. Come, no comas, me da igual, pero en marcha —ordenó Ripred.

Gregor inspeccionó los paquetes de comida para comprobar de qué provisiones disponían. Había sobre todo carne seca, pan y esa especie de camotes. Calculó que bastaría para tres días, si tenían cuidado. Aunque claro, Ripred comía como un cerdo, y probablemente contaría con que le dieran de comer a él también. Así que bueno, más bien dos días.

Luxa se acercó y se sentó a su lado. Parecía estar muy incómoda.

—¿Qué pasa? —le dijo Gregor.

—¿Qué hay que hacer para... preparar la comida? —preguntó por fin.

—¿Qué quieres decir?

—Henry y yo nunca antes hemos preparado comida —reconoció.

Desde donde estaba, Gregor vio que Henry miraba a Luxa con el ceño fruncido, pero ésta hacía caso omiso de su actitud.

—¿Me estás diciendo que ni siquiera te habías hecho nunca un sándwich? —preguntó Gregor. Él no tenía mucha idea de cocinar, pero si su madre tenía que quedarse hasta tarde trabajando, a veces hacía él la cena. Sólo se atrevía con cosas fáciles, como huevos revueltos, o macarrones con queso, pero era capaz de arreglárselas.

—¿Un sándwich? ¿Es eso un plato llamado así en honor de Bartholomew de Sandwich? —preguntó perpleja. Gregor le contestó:

—Pues la verdad es que no lo sé. Son dos rebanadas de pan con carne dentro, o queso, o mantequilla de cacahuate, o lo que se te ocurra.

—No he preparado nunca un sándwich —dijo Luxa con humildad.

—No es difícil. Mira, corta rodajas de carne. No muy gruesas —le dijo, tendiéndole un cuchillo. Gregor se ocupó del pan, y consiguió sacar 18 rebanadas de una sola barra. Luxa cortó muy bien la carne; claro, estaba acostumbrada a manejar cuchillos. Gregor le enseñó entonces cómo preparar los sándwiches. Luxa parecía bastante orgullosa de lo bien que se las había arreglado. Cogió cuatro para ella, su primo y los dos murciélagos. Gregor se ocupó de los otros cinco. Esperar que sirviera también a Ripred y a las cucarachas obviamente era pedirle demasiado.

Luego despertó a Boots, y ésta atacó inmediatamente su sándwich. Temp y Tick agradecieron los suyos con corteses gestos de cabeza. Después Gregor se acercó a Ripred, que estaba apoyado contra la pared del túnel, con cara de mal humor. Le tendió su comida.

—Toma —le dijo.

—¿Para mí? —preguntó Ripred, con exagerada sorpresa—. Pero qué detalle de tu parte. Estoy seguro de que el resto del grupo se alegraría de matarme de hambre.

—Si te mueres de hambre, nunca encontraré a mi padre —dijo Gregor.

—Muy cierto —replicó la rata, metiéndose el sándwich entero en la boca—. Me alegro de que tengamos este acuerdo. La necesidad mutua constituye un vínculo muy fuerte. Más fuerte que la amistad; incluso, más fuerte que el amor.

—¿Es que acaso pueden las ratas sentir amor? —preguntó Gregor secamente.

—Oh, sí —contestó Ripred con una sonrisita—. Sentimos mucho amor por nosotras mismas.

«Sí, eso salta a la vista», pensó Gregor. Se alejó y fue a sentarse junto a Boots, que se estaba comiendo hasta la última miga de su sándwich.

—Más —dijo la niña, señalando el de su hermano.

Gregor estaba muerto de hambre, pero no podía dejar a su hermanita así. Justo cuando iba a partir su sándwich por la mitad, Temp empujó el suyo delicadamente con la pata hasta dejarlo delante de Boots.

—La princesa puede comerse el mío —dijo.

—Pero, tú también necesitas comer, Temp —objetó Gregor.

—No mucho —contestó el insecto—. Tick estará encantada de compartir su comida conmigo.

Encantada. Así que Tick era entonces una cucaracha hembra.

—Yo comparto con él —dijo Tick.

Y Temp era un macho. Tampoco es que eso cambiara mucho las cosas para Gregor; pero así por lo menos ya sabía algo más para evitar ofender a los insectos.

Como Boots ya se había comido la mitad del sándwich de Temp, Gregor aceptó el ofrecimiento. En la próxima ocasión ya intentaría él darles parte de su comida.

Terminaron de desayunar en dos minutos, y recogieron sus cosas. Estaban a punto de montar sobre sus murciélagos cuando Ripred los hizo detenerse.

—No vale la pena. Allí adonde vamos no podrán volar —dijo, señalando el túnel. Apenas medía un metro ochenta de alto y uno y medio de ancho.

—¿Tenemos que meternos ahí? ¿No hay ningún otro camino para llegar hasta mi padre? —preguntó Gregor.

No quería avanzar por un espacio tan estrecho y oscuro con Ripred, por mucho que se necesitaran mutuamente.

—Hay otro camino, pero no es mejor que éste. A no ser que ustedes sepan de alguno—contestó Ripred.

Gregor vio que los murciélagos se agitaban, presas de la angustia.

—¿Y qué hay de los murciélagos?

—Estoy seguro de que sabrás cómo arreglarlo —dijo Ripred con un tono de profundo hastío.

—¿Puedes andar? —le preguntó Gregor a Ares.

—No mucho. No muy lejos —contestó éste.

—Entonces, tendremos que llevarte a cuestas —concluyó Gregor.

—¿Montas, voladores, montas? —preguntó Temp amablemente.

—Los voladores no montan a lomos de reptantes —dijo Aurora muy tensa.

—¿Y por qué no? Ellos sí montaron sobre ustedes —dijo Gregor. Ya estaba harto de que todos despreciaran tanto a las cucarachas. Ellas nunca se quejaban de nada, arrimaban el hombro y cuidaban de Boots. En general, los bichos eran los mejores compañeros de viaje de todo el grupo.

Los murciélagos aletearon con reserva, pero guardaron silencio.

—Pues bien, yo no pienso cargar con ustedes. Ya tengo a Boots, y una bolsa con comida. Y Luxa y Henry no pueden cargar ellos solos con los dos. De modo que si son demasiado buenos como para montar a lomos de un reptante, supongo que no les queda más opción que pedirle a Ripred que los lleve él.

—No les hables en ese tono —le espetó Luxa—. No es que desprecien a los reptantes. El problema es la estrechez del túnel. A los voladores no les gusta estar en un lugar donde no pueden extender las alas.

—Sí, bueno, está bien, pero te recuerdo que la mitad de nosotros tampoco la ha pasado muy bien que digamos teniendo que volar por los aires, a cientos de metros del suelo —le replicó Gregor. Se dio cuenta entonces de que estaba empezando a comportarse como un completo idiota. Ares y Aurora no se habían mostrado impacientes ni desagradables cuando a las cucarachas y a él les había dado miedo volar—. Miren, sé que no va a ser fácil, pero estoy seguro de que el viaje entero no será por túneles tan estrechos. ¿Verdad, Ripred?

—Pues claro que el viaje «entero» no —contestó él, a quien esta discusión aburría mortalmente—. ¿Podemos marcharnos ya, por favor? Para cuando nos hayamos puesto de acuerdo sobre los planes de viaje la guerra ya habrá terminado.

—Montaremos sobre los reptantes —dijo Ares para atajar la discusión.

Gregor ayudó a Luxa y a Henry a instalar a los murciélagos a lomos de las cucarachas. Tenían que tumbarse boca abajo, aferrándose al caparazón con sus garras. Gregor tuvo que reconocer que no parecía una manera muy cómoda de viajar. Luego metió a Boots en la mochila, y cargó con la parte de comida que le correspondía.

—Está bien, muéstranos el camino —le pidió Gregor a Ripred.

—Por fin, ya iba siendo hora —contestó éste, y se adentró por la boca oscura del túnel. Detrás lo seguía Henry, con una antorcha y blandiendo su espada. Gregor se imaginó que lo hacía para tratar de infundir algo de seguridad a los murciélagos. Éstos lo seguían, en fila india, a lomos de las cucarachas. Gregor esperó para dejar pasar primero a Luxa, pero ésta negó con la cabeza.

—No, Gregor, creo que es mejor que yo les cubra a todos las espaldas.

—Supongo que sí —dijo Gregor, y entonces se dio cuenta de que seguía sin tener una espada. Se adentró por fin en el túnel, y le dio a Boots la linterna para que la sostuviera. Luxa cerraba la marcha.

El túnel era horroroso: estrechísimo, sin aire y con un líquido asqueroso con olor a huevos podridos que goteaba del techo. Los murciélagos estaban muy tensos por las condiciones del viaje, pero las cucarachas se sentían como en su casa.

—¡Guácala! —dijo Boots cuando una gota del líquido cayó sobre el casco de su hermano—. ¡Qué *aco*!

—Sí, guácala, qué asco —corroboró Gregor. Esperaba que el túnel no fuera muy largo; uno se podía volver loco en poco tiempo dentro un agujero como ése. Se volvió para ver qué tal estaba Luxa. No parecía muy contenta, pero se las arreglaba.

—¿Qué significa eso de «guácala»? —le preguntó llena de curiosidad.

—Pues... asco, lo que te da algo repugnante... inmundo —explicó Gregor.

—Sí, todo eso describe bien la tierra de las ratas —dijo Luxa con un resoplido.

—Oye, Luxa, por cierto —dijo Gregor—, ¿cómo es que te sorprendió ver aparecer a Ripred? O sea, yo no conozco muy bien la profecía, pero tú sí. ¿No sabías que habría también una rata?

—No. Pensaba que «un roedor al lado» significaba que nos seguiría una rata, que tal vez incluso nos daría caza. Nunca imaginé que formaría parte de la búsqueda —explicó.

—Vikus ha dicho que podíamos confiar en él —dijo Gregor.

—Vikus habla demasiado —contestó Luxa. Parecía tan furiosa que Gregor decidió dejar el tema.

Siguieron avanzando trabajosamente y en silencio durante un rato. Por las gotas que caían periódicamente sobre su cara, Gregor sabía que también Boots se estaba mojando. Trató de ponerle su casco, pero se le caía a cada rato. Al final, decidió cubrirle la cabeza con unos paños empapadores. Lo último que necesitaban era que se resfriara.

Tras varias horas de camino en esas horribles condiciones, todo el mundo estaba empapado y deprimido. Ripred los llevó hasta una pequeña cueva. El agua maloliente resbalaba sobre las paredes como si fuera lluvia. Los murciélagos estaban tan rígidos que Luxa y Henry tuvieron que bajarlos en brazos de las cucarachas, y ayudarlos a extender las alas.

En tanto, Ripred levantó el hocico y husmeó profundamente.

—Bien. Con esto hemos conseguido disfrazar bastante su olor —dijo con satisfacción.

—¿Quieres decir que nos has llevado por ese camino sólo para que oliéramos a huevos podridos? —se indignó Gregor.

—Bien necesario que era. Eran una pandilla de lo más repugnante —declaró Ripred.

Gregor estaba demasiado agotado como para discutir con él. Luxa y él abrieron los paquetes y se pusieron a repartir comida. Nadie tenía ganas de hablar. Ripred se zampó su almuerzo de un bocado, y se quedó montando guardia en la entrada del túnel.

Estaban terminando de comer cuando los murciélagos dieron la voz de alarma.

—Tejedores —advirtió Aurora.

—Sí, sí, han estado siguiéndonos la pista casi desde que empezamos el viaje. Mi olfato no me puede decir cuántos son, con tanta agua como hay aquí. Me pregunto qué querrán —Ripred golpeó el suelo con la cola y ordenó a Luxa y a Henry—: eh, ustedes dos, arco de tres puntos.

Luxa y Henry intercambiaron una mirada pero no se movieron.

—¡Arco de tres puntos, y éste no es momento de poner a prueba mi autoridad, chicos! —rugió Ripred, descubriendo sus terribles dientes. De muy mala gana, Henry y Luxa se colocaron cada uno a un flanco de Ripred, pero unos pasos atrás. Los tres formaban así un pequeño arco interpuesto entre el resto del grupo y la boca del túnel. Los murciélagos tomaron posición detrás de ellos.

Gregor aguzó el oído, pero no oía más que el ruido del agua que caía. ¿Los perseguía entonces un ejército de arañas? Una vez más se sintió desarmado e indefenso. Esta vez ni siquiera tenía una lata de gaseosa.

Todos se quedaron inmóviles. Gregor se dio cuenta de que ahora también Temp y Tick habían descubierto a los invasores. Boots chupeteaba solemnemente una galleta, pero sin hacer el más mínimo ruido.

Conforme se iban acercando los tejedores, Gregor vio tensarse los músculos de la ancha espalda gris de Ripred. Gregor se preparó para recibir una avalancha de arañas sedientas de sangre, pero nunca llegó.

Una gran araña naranja que llevaba a la espalda a otra más pequeña de color marrón entró tambaleándose y se derrumbó sobre el suelo. Del cuerpo de la araña marrón manaba un extraño líquido azul. Con gran esfuerzo, consiguió incorporarse un poco. Sus patas delanteras acariciaron su torso mientras hablaba.

—Nos envía Vikus. Los roedores han atacado las telarañas. Hemos perdido muchos tejedores. Nosotros dos... nos unimos... a la búsqueda.

Y habiendo dicho esto, la araña marrón cayó al suelo, sin vida.

CAPÍTULO VIGESIMOPRIMERO

Gregor miró a la araña horrorizado. En su agonía final, el animal se había tumbado boca arriba, encogiendo las patas. Un líquido azul manaba de una herida que tenía en el abdomen, manchando el suelo de piedra.

—Ya estamos todos —dijo Gregor en voz baja.

—¿Qué quieres decir? —preguntó Henry.

Gregor se sacó la profecía del bolsillo.

—Sandwich tenía razón. Ya estamos todos reunidos. O por lo menos lo hemos estado, por espacio de unos segundos. —Leyó en voz alta:

> Dos de arriba, dos de abajo de real ascendencia,
> dos voladores, dos reptantes,
> dos tejedores dan su aquiescencia.
> Un roedor al lado y uno perdido antes.

Gregor no fue capaz de leer el verso siguiente, así que Ripred tuvo que hacerlo por él:

—«Tras contar a los muertos ocho vivos serán los

restantes». Bien, uno ha muerto ya, así que sólo quedan tres —comentó, dándole un empujón a la araña muerta con la punta de la cola.

—¡No hagas eso! —exclamó Gregor.

—Vamos, ¿qué pasa? Ninguno de nosotros puede fingir que sintiera mucho aprecio por este tejedor. Ni siquiera sabemos cómo se llamaba. Bueno, tú sí, tal vez —le dijo Ripred a la araña naranja.

—Se llamaba Treflex —contestó la araña—. Y yo me llamo Gox.

—Bien, Gox, supongo que tendrás hambre después del viaje, pero nuestras provisiones son reducidas. Ninguno de nosotros se escandalizará si optas por cenarte a Treflex —dijo Ripred.

Inmediatamente, Gox empezó a cubrir de líquido el cuerpo de Treflex.

—No irá a... ¡oh, madre mía! —exclamó Gregor.

—Las arañas no son ni tiquismiquis, ni sentimentales —explicó Ripred—. Afortunadamente.

Gregor se dio la vuelta para que ni Boots ni él tuvieran que presenciar la escena de canibalismo. Se alegró de ver que también Henry y Luxa parecían impresionados.

—Eh, si algo me pasara a mí o a Boots, no dejen que esa araña nos beba así. Nos tiran por un precipicio, a un río, lo que sea, ¿está bien?

Ambos asintieron con la cabeza.

—¿Nos devolverás ese mismo favor? —preguntó Luxa con voz lánguida—. ¿Y a nuestros murciélagos también?

—Y a Tick y a Temp, prometido —aseguró Gregor. Oía los lentos sorbidos de Gox mientras se bebía las entrañas de Treflex—. ¡Qué espanto! —añadió.

Afortunadamente, Gox no tardó mucho en terminar su cena. Ripred empezó a interrogarla sobre el ataque de las ratas. Gox le contó que un ejército entero —por lo menos varios centenares de ratas— había invadido la tierra de las arañas. Éstas habían logrado contener el ataque, pero las bajas habían sido numerosas en ambos bandos. Por fin las ratas se habían batido en retirada. Vikus había llegado después de la matanza y había enviado a Gox y a Treflex hasta la entrada del túnel a lomos de su murciélago.

—¿Por qué? —preguntó Gox—. ¿Por qué nos matan los roedores?

—No lo sé. Tal vez el rey Gorger haya decidido lanzar un ataque indiscriminado en las Tierras Bajas. O puede ser también que las ratas se enteraran de que dos habitantes de las Tierras Altas se dirigen a su territorio. ¿Mencionaron al guerrero de la Profecía del Gris? —preguntó Ripred.

—No hubo palabras, sólo muerte —dijo Gox.

—Es una suerte que nos encontraran. Nos habría llevado mucho tiempo liberar a dos tejedores de las prisiones del rey Gorger sin dar la alarma, y no tenemos tiempo que perder —le dijo Ripred. Luego se volvió hacia Gregor—. Este ataque sobre los tejedores no augura nada bueno para tu padre.

—¿Por qué? ¿Qué quieres decir? ¿Por qué no? —preguntó Gregor, sintiendo que se le helaban las entrañas.

—Vikus ha hecho una magnífica labor para ocultarte. Ninguna rata aparte de mí que te haya visto ha vivido para contarlo. Las ratas no saben que ha llegado el guerrero. Pero el hecho de que los humanos hayan llevado a habitantes de las Tierras Altas ante los tejedores levantará sospechas entre las ratas —explicó Ripred. Mientras hablaba, iba sacando conclusiones en su cabeza—. Afortunadamente, la guerra provoca mucha confusión y, por el momento, ninguna rata te ha identificado. ¡Y ahora en marcha!

Nadie protestó. Recogieron los bártulos y atravesaron la cueva en dirección a un túnel más espacioso y seco. Aurora y Ares ya podían volar, aunque el lugar era peligroso para los jinetes.

—Iremos a pie —le dijo Luxa a su murciélago—. Aunque ustedes pudieran llevarnos, ¿qué haríamos con el roedor? —Entonces, los murciélagos levantaron el vuelo, cargados con todos los bultos.

Gregor los contempló con envidia.

—Menos mal que no soy un murciélago. A lo mejor me daba por huir de aquí volando, sin mirar atrás.

—Aurora y Ares no harían nunca una cosa así. Están vinculados a Henry y a mí —dijo Luxa.

—¿Y cómo es que funciona eso exactamente? —preguntó Gregor.

—Cuando un murciélago y un humano se vinculan el uno al otro, juran luchar hasta la muerte el uno por el otro —explicó Luxa—. Aurora nunca me dejaría en peligro, ni yo a ella.

—¿Y todo el mundo tiene un murciélago? —preguntó Gregor, pensando que sería bonito saber que alguien iba a estar cerca de él, defendiéndolo, en un lugar como ése.

—Oh, no. Algunos nunca encuentran un murciélago al que vincularse. Aurora y yo nos convertimos en uno cuando yo era muy pequeña, pero eso no es frecuente —dijo Luxa.

—¿Y cómo te vinculaste tan pronto? —quiso saber Gregor lleno de curiosidad.

—Después de que asesinaron a mis padres, pasé un tiempo en el que nunca me sentía a salvo en el suelo. Me pasaba las horas en el aire con Aurora. Por eso volamos tan bien juntas —explicó—. Vikus convenció al Consejo de que nos permitiera vincularnos antes de lo normal. Después de eso, dejé de sentir tanto miedo.

—¿Tienes miedo ahora? —le preguntó Gregor.

—A veces —reconoció Luxa—. Pero no más que cuando estaba en Regalia. ¿Sabes?, me cansé de sentir miedo constantemente, de modo que tomé una decisión. Cada día, cuando me despierto, me digo a mí misma que éste será mi último día. Si uno no trata de aferrarse al tiempo, no le da tanto miedo perderlo.

Gregor pensó entonces que ésta era la cosa más triste que le había dicho nadie nunca. No tenía respuesta.

—Y luego, si uno llega vivo a la noche, siente el gozo de haberle ganado un día más a la muerte —dijo ella—. ¿Entiendes?

—Creo que sí —contestó Gregor, como atontado. Acababa de ocurrírsele una idea espantosa. ¿No era acaso la estrategia de Luxa una forma extrema de su propia norma? Bueno, no es que él pensara todos los días que se iba a morir, pero se negaba a sí mismo el lujo de pensar en el futuro, con o sin su padre. Si no se hubiera caído por el conducto de ventilación de su lavandería y no hubiera descubierto así que su padre estaba aún vivo, si su padre nunca hubiera regresado a casa, ¿cuánto tiempo habría seguido él negándose el derecho a ser feliz? ¿Toda su vida? «Tal vez. Tal vez toda mi vida», pensó. Se apresuró a seguir su conversación con Luxa.

—Bueno, ¿y cómo se hace eso de vincularse con un murciélago? —le preguntó.

—Es una ceremonia sencilla. Se congregan numerosos humanos y murciélagos. Uno se coloca frente a su murciélago, y recita una promesa. De esta manera —dijo Luxa, extendiendo la mano:

> *«Aurora, yo me vínculo a tí,*
> *nuestra vida y nuestra muerte una son,*
> *nosotras, dos.*
> *En las tinieblas, en la luz, en la guerra, en la huida,*
> *yo te salvaré a tí como a mi propia vida».*

—Y luego tu murciélago la recita a su vez, pero incluyendo tu nombre. A continuación hay un banquete de celebración —concluyó Luxa.

—¿Y qué pasa si uno de los dos rompe la promesa? ¿Qué pasaría, por ejemplo, si Aurora se marchara volando y te dejara en peligro? —quiso saber Gregor.

—Aurora no haría algo así, si bien es cierto que algunas promesas se han roto. El castigo es severo. El culpable es desterrado y obligado a vivir solo en las Tierras Bajas

—dijo Luxa—. Y aquí nadie consigue sobrevivir solo por mucho tiempo.

—Sus rituales nativos son fascinantes, ¿pero les parece que podríamos tratar de avanzar en silencio? Dado que hasta la última rata nos está buscando, tal vez sería lo más prudente —dijo Ripred.

Luxa y Gregor cerraron el pico. Gregor hubiera deseado poder seguir hablando. Luxa se comportaba de otra manera cuando no estaba con Henry. Más simpática, y menos arrogante. Pero Ripred tenía razón en lo de no hacer ruido.

Por fortuna, Boots se quedó dormida. Durante horas, lo único que oyeron fue el tenue sonido de sus pasos sobre el suelo y el ruido que hacían los dientes de Ripred mientras roía un hueso que se había guardado del almuerzo.

Gregor volvía a consumirse de angustia por las nuevas preocupaciones que le habían surgido sobre su padre. Por lo que le había dicho Ripred, parecía probable que las ratas lo mataran para impedir que Gregor diera con él. Pero, ¿por qué? ¿Acaso podría eso cambiar la profecía? Suponía que nadie lo sabía a ciencia cierta. ¿Y qué significado tenía la última estrofa? Desenrolló la profecía y la leyó tantas veces que al final se la aprendió de memoria sin proponérselo.

El último en morir su bando elegirá.
El destino de los ocho en su mano estará.
Rogadle, pues, prudencia cuando con cautela salte,

pues la vida puede ser muerte
y la muerte, vida, en un instante.

Para Gregor, eso no tenía pies ni cabeza. Lo único que lograba entender era que quienquiera que fuera el cuarto en morir, tenía una responsabilidad enorme para con los demás. Pero, ¿cómo?, ¿dónde?, ¿cuándo? La última estrofa de la Profecía del Gris no mencionaba ninguno de los detalles que más útiles habrían resultado para entenderla.

Ripred los obligó a seguir caminando hasta que todos tropezaban de puro agotamiento. Dio la orden de detenerse en una cueva que al menos tenía un suelo seco y una fuente de agua potable.

Gregor y Luxa repartieron sus cada vez más escasos víveres, que se iban consumiendo mucho más rápido de lo que Gregor había calculado. Trató de protestar cuando las cucarachas le dieron su parte de comida a Boots, pues ya había pensado antes en compartir la suya con su hermana.

—Deja que le den su comida —dijo Ripred—. Un reptante puede sobrevivir un mes sin comer si tiene agua suficiente. Y no te molestes en alimentar a Gox. Treflex le durará más que nuestro viaje.

Hacía frío en la cueva. Gregor le quitó a Boots la ropa mojada y la vistió con prendas secas. Pero la niña no parecía encontrarse bien; estaba demasiado callada, y tenía la piel sudorosa y fría. Se tumbó junto a ella bajo la manta, abrazándola, para tratar de calentarla con su propio cuerpo. ¿Qué haría él si Boots se enfermaba? Necesitaba estar de vuelta en casa con su madre, que siempre sabía la dosis exacta de medicinas, zumos y mantas para curar lo que fuera. Trató de consolarse con la idea de que su padre los ayudaría en cuanto lo encontraran.

Todos estaban tan cansados a causa de la larga caminata que se quedaron dormidos inmediatamente.

Algo despertó a Gregor de un profundo sueño. ¿Un ruido? ¿Un movimiento? No estaba seguro. Lo único que sabía era que, en el momento en que abrió los ojos, Henry estaba inclinado sobre Ripred, a punto de hundir su espada en el cuerpo dormido de la rata.

CAPÍTULO VIGESIMOSEGUNDO

Gregor abrió la boca para gritar «¡No!» en el mismo momento en que Ripred entreabrió los ojos. Henry se encontraba detrás de la rata. Todo lo que debió de acertar a ver ésta fue la expresión en el rostro de Gregor, pero no le hizo falta más.

En la décima de segundo que tardó Henry en asestarle una estocada con su espada, Ripred se dio la vuelta y le lanzó un zarpazo con sus terribles garras. La hoja de la espada abrió un corte en el pecho del animal, pero éste acertó a propinarle a Henry una profunda herida en el brazo.

Para entonces el «¡No!» ya había salido de la boca de Gregor, y su grito despertó al resto del grupo. Ripred, sangrando a chorros, se irguió furioso sobre las patas traseras, aterrorizándolos a todos. En comparación, Henry parecía pequeño y débil; apenas podía blandir la espada con el brazo herido. Al instante, Luxa y Aurora levantaron el vuelo, y Ares se lanzó en picado sobre la rata.

Pero Gregor la alcanzó primero. Se interpuso entre ésta y Henry, con los brazos extendidos.

—¡Quietos! —gritó—. ¡Quietos!

Por increíble que parezca, todos obedecieron. Gregor suponía que ésta debía de ser para todos la primera vez que veían a alguien interponerse en una pelea entre una rata y un humano. Su segundo de vacilación le dio el tiempo justo de hablar:

—¡Todo el que quiera matar a alguien, antes tendrá que pasar por encima de mi cadáver!

Su exclamación no fue especialmente poética, pero logró el efecto deseado. Nadie quería que Gregor muriera. Todos sabían que el guerrero era esencial para la búsqueda.

—¡Apártate, Gregor; la rata nos matará a todos! —ordenó Luxa, preparándose para atacar a Ripred.

—La rata sólo estaba durmiendo. Créeme, cachorrito, si mi intención hubiese sido matarlos, ahora mismo no estaríamos manteniendo esta conversación —declaró con ironía Ripred.

—¡No malgastes tus mentiras con nosotros, roedor! —dijo Luxa—. ¿Acaso piensas que creeríamos en tu palabra por encima de la de uno de los nuestros?

—¡Es la verdad! ¡Dice la verdad! ¡Él no empezó la pelea! ¡Fue Henry! —gritó Gregor—. ¡Ha intentado matar a Ripred mientras dormía!

Todos se volvieron hacia Henry. Éste escupió:

—¡Sí, y ahora estaría muerto si no hubiera sido por Gregor!

A estas palabras siguió un momento de confusión. Por la expresión de Luxa, Gregor adivinaba que no estaba al corriente de los planes de Henry. Luxa había dado por hecho que la rata había sido la primera en atacar. Ya no sabía qué hacer.

—¡Quieta, Luxa! ¡Por favor! —le rogó Gregor—. ¡No podemos permitirnos el lujo de perder a ningún buscador más! ¡Tenemos que mantenernos todos juntos! —Se le había ocurrido la palabra «buscador» sobre la marcha, y le pareció que quedaba muy bien.

Luxa bajó despacio al suelo, pero permaneció sobre su murciélago. Ares siguió en el aire, sin saber muy bien qué hacer. Gregor se preguntó entonces si el murciélago estaba al corriente de las intenciones de su jinete. Pero si lo estaba, ¿por qué no habían atacado juntos desde el aire? Era tan difícil adivinar los pensamientos de los murciélagos...

Gregor se percató entonces, por primera vez, de que las dos cucarachas estaban de pie delante de Boots, protegiéndola con sus cuerpos. Gox seguía colgada de la telaraña improvisada que había tejido para dormir.

—Se acabó —dijo Gregor con una autoridad que hasta entonces no sabía que tuviera—. Envaina tu espada, Henry. Y tú, Ripred... ¡siéntate! ¡Se acabó!

Gregor no sabía si lo obedecerían, pero estaba decidido a mantenerse firme. Fue un momento muy largo, de mucha tensión. Entonces Ripred bajó el labio inferior para cubrir sus colmillos y estalló en una carcajada.

—Tengo que reconocer, guerrero, que no te falta audacia —dijo.

Henry dejó caer su espada, lo cual no era una gran concesión, pues Gregor vio que apenas podía sostenerla.

—O traición —dijo Henry en voz baja.

Gregor lo miró fijamente:

—¿Sabes una cosa? En las Tierras Altas no

tenemos en gran estima a los que se levantan por la noche sin hacer ruido y apuñalan a una persona mientras duerme.

—No es una persona, es una rata —dijo Henry—. Si no sabes hacer esa distinción, pronto te contarás entre los muertos.

Gregor sostuvo la mirada fría de Henry. Sabía que después se le ocurrirían un par de respuestas cortantes para hacerlo callar, pero en ese momento no le venía ninguna a la cabeza. En lugar de eso, se volvió hacia Luxa y le dijo ásperamente:

—Será mejor que los curemos.

Para curar heridas no eran mucho más expertos que para cocinar, pero al menos Luxa sabía qué ungüento utilizar. Gox resultó ser la criatura más útil del grupo. Tejió una telaraña especial, y les dijo que aplicaran puñados de aquellos hilos de seda sobre las heridas. En unos minutos, las hemorragias de Ripred y Henry habían cesado.

Mientras Gregor aplicaba compresas de seda adicionales sobre el pelaje de Ripred, éste dijo entre dientes:

—Supongo que debería darte las gracias.

—Olvídalo —contestó Gregor—. Sólo lo he hecho porque te necesito. —No quería que Ripred pensara que eran amigos ni nada por el estilo.

—¿Ah, sí? Pues cuánto me alegro —dijo Ripred—. Me había parecido detectar en ti una inclinación por la justicia y el juego limpio. Algo muy peligroso en las Tierras Bajas, muchacho.

A Gregor le hubiera gustado que dejaran de una vez de decirle lo que era peligroso para él en las Tierras

Bajas. El lugar entero era un gran campo de minas. Hizo caso omiso del comentario de Ripred y siguió aplicando las telarañas. Detrás de él oyó a Luxa susurrarle a Henry:

—¿Por qué no nos dijiste nada?

—Para mantenerlos a salvo —le contestó éste en otro susurro.

«A salvo. Sí, seguro», pensó Gregor. Aunque volviera a las Tierras Altas, Gregor no creía que pudiera sentirse a salvo nunca más.

—No debes volver a hacerlo, Henry —le oyó decir a Luxa—. No puedes acabar con él tú solo.

—Podría haberlo hecho, si él no hubiera interferido —contestó Henry.

—No, el riesgo es demasiado grande, y podemos tal vez necesitarla —replicó Luxa—. Deja a esa rata en paz.

—¿Es una orden, majestad? —preguntó Henry, con una voz algo molesta.

—Si esa es la única forma de que hagas caso a mis consejos, entonces sí, lo es —dijo Luxa con severidad—. Controla tu espada hasta que entendamos mejor nuestra situación.

—Hablas exactamente igual que ese viejo loco de Vikus —dijo Henry.

—No, hablo como yo misma —contestó ella, dolida—. Y como hablaría alguien que quiere que ambos sobrevivamos.

Los primos se dieron cuenta entonces de que habían alzado tanto la voz que todos podían oírlos, de modo que dejaron de hablar. En medio del silencio, Ripred siguió royendo el hueso que llevaba consigo desde hacía un buen rato. El sonido de sus dientes ponía nervioso a Gregor.

—¿Podrías dejar de hacer eso, por favor? —le pidió Gregor a Ripred.

—Pues no, el caso es que no podría, no —contestó Ripred—. A las ratas nos siguen creciendo los dientes durante toda nuestra vida, por lo que necesitamos roer todo el rato para ir desgastándolos y que tengan así el tamaño adecuado. Si no royera a menudo, mis dientes inferiores crecerían tanto que me atravesarían el cráneo, y se me clavarían en el cerebro, provocándome, desgraciadamente, la muerte.

—Ah, está bien, bueno es saberlo —dijo Gregor, aplicando un último fragmento de tela sobre la herida. Luego apoyó la espalda sobre la pared de la cueva, y preguntó—: Y ahora, ¿qué?

—Bueno, pues como está claro que nadie quiere volver a soñar con los angelitos, lo mejor será que empecemos ya a buscar a tu padre —dijo Ripred poniéndose en pie rápidamente.

Gregor fue a despertar a Boots. Al tocarla se asustó muchísimo. La cara le ardía como un brasero.

—Oh, no, —dijo, sintiéndose desamparado—. Eh, Boots, eh, linda —la sacudió por el hombro suavemente. Ésta gimoteó algo entre sueños pero no se despertó.

—Luxa, tenemos un grave problema. Boots está enferma —dijo.

Luxa le tocó la frente con la mano.

—Tiene fiebre. Ha pescado alguna pestilencia de la tierra de las ratas.

Pestilencia. Gregor esperaba que no fuera tan grave como sonaba. Luxa rebuscó entre los frascos que les había dejado Solovet y eligió uno, aunque no parecía estar muy segura.

—Creo que éste es para la fiebre.

Ripred lo husmeó y arrugó la frente.

—No, ese mata el dolor. —Metió la cabeza en la bolsa y extrajo un frasquito de vidrio azul—. Éste es el que necesitas. Dale sólo unas gotas. Es muy pequeña y su organismo no aguantaría mucha cantidad.

Gregor no tenía muchas ganas de darle esa extraña medicina, pero Boots estaba ardiendo. Le echó unas cuantas gotas entre los labios, y le pareció que la niña se las tragaba. Trató de levantarla para meterla en la mochila, pero ella gimió de dolor. Gregor se mordió el labio.

—No puede viajar conmigo, le hace daño —dijo.

Tumbaron a Boots sobre una manta, y la colocaron encima de Temp. Gox tejió una tela para sujetar a la niña al caparazón del insecto.

Gregor se moría de preocupación.

Tras contar a los muertos ocho vivos serán los restantes.

No podía perder a Boots. De ninguna manera. Tenía que llevarla de vuelta a casa. Debería haberla dejado en Regalia. Nunca debería haber aceptado participar en la búsqueda. Si algo le ocurría a Boots, sería culpa suya.

La oscuridad del túnel le atravesó la piel y lo fue calando hasta los huesos. Quería gritar de dolor, pero las tinieblas lo ahogaban. Habría dado casi cualquier cosa por ver el sol, aunque sólo fuera un instante.

El grupo avanzaba despacio, trabajosa y recelosamente, inquietos todos por las mismas preocupaciones que nadie expresaba en voz alta. Incluso Ripred, que era con diferencia el más endurecido, parecía encogerse bajo el peso de la situación.

Esa desesperación general no fue sino una de las muchas razones por las cuales no detectaron a las ratas hasta que casi se hubieron topado con ellas. Ni el propio Ripred fue capaz de distinguir el olor en un lugar que apestaba a sus congéneres. Los murciélagos no pudieron detectarlas por la estrechez del túnel, y porque se estaban aproximando a un río, y el estruendo del agua era cada vez mayor. Los humanos no podían ver nada en la oscuridad.

Ripred los condujo fuera del túnel hacia una gigantesca cueva dividida por una profunda garganta por la que fluía un ancho y caudaloso río. Un puente colgante se extendía sobre éste, uniendo ambas orillas de la garganta. Se debió haber fabricado en tiempos mejores, con los esfuerzos conjuntos de varias especies. Unas gruesas bandas de seda tejidas por las arañas sujetaban delgadas losas de piedra cortadas por los humanos. Debieron de necesitar también las habilidades de vuelo de los murciélagos para construir un puente de esas características.

Cuando Gregor dirigió su linterna hacia arriba para ver cómo estaba sujeto el puente a la tierra, las descubrió: una veintena de ratas sentadas inmóviles encima de las rocas que bordeaban la entrada al túnel. Justo encima de sus cabezas. Esperando.

—¡Corre! —gritó Ripred pisándole literalmente los talones a Gregor. Éste dio un traspié y echó a correr por el puente, resbalando sobre las gastadas losas de piedra. Sentía en su cuello el aliento caliente de Ripred. Henry y Luxa volaban por encima de él, cruzando el río a toda velocidad.

Ya iba por la mitad del puente cuando recordó que Boots no estaba a su espalda. Había estado con él constantemente desde el principio del viaje, tanto que había empezado a pensar que eran inseparables. ¡Pero ahora iba a lomos de Temp!

Gregor dio bruscamente media vuelta para volver sobre sus pasos. Ripred, como si hubiera anticipado ese movimiento, le dio la vuelta de un empujón, y agarró la mochila entre sus dientes. Gregor se sintió levantado por los aires, mientras Ripred corría como un poseso hacia el otro extremo del puente.

—¡Boots! —gritó Gregor—. ¡Boots!

Ripred corría a la velocidad del rayo. Cuando llegó a la otra orilla, dejó a Gregor en el suelo y se unió a Luxa y a Henry, que trataban desesperadamente de hacer trizas las cuerdas de seda que sujetaban el puente.

Gregor alumbró con su linterna y vio que Gox ya había recorrido tres cuartas partes del puente. Detrás de ella, cargando con su hermana, Temp avanzaba trabajosamente. Lo único que separaba ahora a Boots de las veinte ratas asesinas que corrían por el puente era Tick.

—¡Boots! —gritó Gregor, lanzándose hacia el túnel. Ripred agitó la cola, golpeándolo con ella a la altura del pecho, y derribándolo al suelo, sin respiración. Gregor inspiró, tratando de llenarse de aire los pulmones, luego se puso a gatas y empezó a avanzar hacia el puente. Tenía que ayudarla. Tenía que hacerlo.

Gox recorrió como una flecha el resto del puente, y empezó a cortar las cuerdas con sus mandíbulas.

—¡No! —exclamó Gregor—. ¡Mi hermana! —se puso en pie justo a tiempo para recibir otro coletazo de Ripred.

Las cucarachas estaban como a tres metros de la orilla cuando las ratas las alcanzaron. No intercambiaron ni una sola palabra; era como si los insectos hubieran ensayado esa escena hacía tiempo. Temp se lanzó en un sprint final hasta el extremo del puente, y Tick se dio la vuelta para enfrentarse ella sola al ejército de ratas.

Cuando saltaron sobre ella, Tick se lanzó volando directamente sobre la cara de la que iba en cabeza. Ésta retrocedió, sorprendida. Hasta ese momento, Gregor ni siquiera se había dado cuenta de que las cucarachas tuvieran alas. Tal vez tampoco lo sabían las ratas. Pero no les llevó mucho tiempo reponerse de la sorpresa. La rata saltó hacia adelante y decapitó a Tick de un solo mordisco.

Temp se derrumbó sobre la orilla en el preciso instante en que el puente cedía. Veinte ratas, una de las cuales aún sostenía a Tick entre sus fauces, cayeron en picado al río. Como si esta imagen no fuera ya lo suficientemente espantosa, la superficie del agua se convulsionó mientras enormes pirañas emergían, devorando a las ratas que gritaban despavoridas.

Todo terminó en menos de un minuto. Cuando las aguas recuperaron la calma, ya no quedaba ni rastro de las ratas. Y Tick había desaparecido para siempre.

CAPÍTULO VIGESIMOTERCERO

Deprisa, deprisa, deprisa! —los apuró Ripred, conduciéndolos a todos desde la orilla hasta la entrada de un túnel, por el que los hizo avanzar durante unos minutos hasta que quedaron a salvo de la vista y el olfato de las ratas. Llegados a una pequeña cámara, les ordenó detenerse.

—Deténganse. Siéntense. Descansen.

Sin decir una palabra, los demás miembros de la expedición se desplomaron sobre el suelo del túnel. Gregor se sentó con Temp, dando la espalda a los demás. Recorrió el caparazón del insecto con la mano hasta encontrar los deditos calientes de Boots, y los rodeó con los suyos. Había estado a punto de perderla. De perderla para siempre. Boots nunca habría tenido la oportunidad de conocer a su padre, ni de volver a abrazar a su madre, ni de jugar con Lizzie o con él, ni de nada de nada.

No quería mirar a nadie. Todos habrían estado dispuestos a que Boots y los reptantes cayeran al agua con tal de detener a las ratas. No tenía nada que decirle a ninguno de ellos.

Y luego estaba Tick. La pequeña y valiente Tick, que se había enfrentado a un ejército de ratas para salvar a su hermanita. Tick, que nunca hablaba mucho. Tick, que compartía su comida con Boots. Tick, que después de todo no era más que una cucaracha. Una simple cucaracha que había sacrificado todo el tiempo que le quedaba sólo para que Boots pudiera tener más.

Gregor se llevó a los labios los deditos de Boots, y sintió que las lágrimas resbalaban por sus mejillas. No había llorado ni una sola vez en todo el tiempo que llevaba allá abajo, y eso que le habían pasado muchas cosas malas. Pero de alguna manera, el sacrificio de Tick había hecho pedazos la fina coraza que lo protegía del dolor. Desde ese momento, Gregor sentía una lealtad por las cucarachas que sabía que nunca se desvanecería. Nunca jamás volvería a quitarle la vida a una cucaracha. Ni en las Tierras Bajas, ni en las Tierras Altas, si es que por algún milagro conseguían regresar a casa.

Sintió que empezaba a temblar. Probablemente los demás lo encontraran ridículo, llorando ahí por la muerte de una cucaracha, pero le daba igual. Los odiaba. Los odiaba a todos.

Temp, cuyas antenas colgaban ahora miserablemente a ambos lados de su cabeza, extendió una de ellas y tocó a Gregor.

—Gracias. Gracias por llorar cuando Tick ha perdido tiempo.

—Boots también lloraría, si no estuviera... —Gregor no pudo terminar la frase pues otra oleada de sollozos lo asaltó. Se alegraba de que la niña no hubiera presenciado la muerte de Tick. Le habría impresionado mucho, y no lo habría entendido. Él tampoco lo entendía.

Gregor sintió una mano sobre su hombro, y se retorció para zafarse. Sabía que era Luxa, pero no quería hablar con ella.

—Gregor —susurró ésta con tristeza—. Gregor, debes de saber que habríamos recogido a Boots y a Temp si hubieran caído al vacío. También habríamos recogido a Tick, de haber habido una razón.

Gregor se apretó los párpados con los dedos para bloquear las lágrimas y asintió con la cabeza. Bueno, eso hacía que se sintiera un poquito mejor. Por supuesto que Luxa se habría lanzado a salvar a Boots si ésta hubiera caído. A los de las Tierras Bajas no les preocupaba caer al vacío tanto como a él, pues tenían siempre a sus murciélagos al lado.

—Está bien —dijo—. Lo sé. —Cuando Luxa se sentó junto a él, Gregor no se apartó—. Supongo que te debe parecer muy estúpido que llore por la muerte de una cucaracha.

—Aún no conoces a los habitantes de las Tierras Bajas si piensas que no derramamos lágrimas —dijo Luxa—. Lloramos. Lloramos, y no solamente por nosotros mismos.

—Sin embargo, no por Tick —dijo Gregor con una sombra aún de amargura.

—Yo no he llorado desde la muerte de mis padres —dijo Luxa despacio—. Pero por lo que respecta a eso, no se me considera normal.

Gregor sintió más lágrimas resbalando por sus mejillas cuando pensó en lo mucho que debía de haber sufrido una persona para perder la capacidad de llorar. En ese momento le perdonó todo a Luxa. Incluso olvidó por qué tenía que perdonarla.

—Gregor —dijo suavemente cuando éste hubo dejado de llorar—. Si regresas a Regalia y yo no... dile a Vikus que lo he entendido.

—¿Que has entendido qué? —preguntó Gregor.

—Por qué nos dejó con Ripred —dijo Luxa—. Teníamos que ir con un roedor. Ahora entiendo que estaba tratando de protegernos.

—Está bien, se lo diré —aseguró Gregor, sonándose la nariz. Permaneció un momento callado, y luego preguntó—. Bueno, ¿cada cuánto hay que darle a Boots la medicina? Todavía está muy caliente.

—Démosle una dosis ahora, antes de reanudar la marcha —dijo Luxa, acariciando la frente de la niña. Ésta murmuró algo en sueños, pero no despertó. Vertieron otras gotas más de medicina entre sus labios.

Gregor se puso en pie y trató de sacudirse de encima el dolor.

—Reanudemos la marcha —dijo sin mirar a Ripred. La rata había participado en montones de guerras. Probablemente habría visto morir a muchísimas criaturas. Le había dicho a Gox que se comiera a Treflex. Gregor estaba seguro de que la muerte de Tick le afectaba tan poco como... bueno, como a los neoyorquinos les afectaba matar a una cucaracha.

Pero cuando Ripred habló, su voz carecía de su habitual tonillo malicioso.

—Anímate, muchacho. Tu padre está cerca.

Gregor levantó la cabeza al oír esas palabras.

—¿Qué tan cerca?

—A menos de una hora de camino. Pero también lo están sus carceleros. Debemos avanzar con extrema cautela. Envuelvan sus pies en telarañas, no hablen y permanezcan juntos detrás de mí. Tuvimos una suerte poco común en el puente. No creo que nos acompañe allí adonde nos dirigimos ahora.

Gox, a quien Gregor apreciaba cada vez más conforme iba pasando el tiempo, les tejió rápidamente unos gruesos zapatos de seda para ahogar el ruido de sus pasos. Cuando Gregor alumbraba a Luxa con su linterna mientras se los ponía, la luz se apagó. Rebuscó en su bolsa y sacó las últimas dos pilas que quedaban.

—¿Cuánto tiempo más puede durarte la antorcha? —le preguntó a Luxa. Se había percatado de que se habían limitado a una sola antorcha tras el encuentro con Ripred, al parecer para ahorrar combustible. Ahora esa única antorcha tenía una llama muy débil.

—Poco tiempo —reconoció Luxa—. ¿Y qué pasó con tu palo luminoso?

—No lo sé —contestó Gregor—. Éstas son las últimas pilas que tengo, y no sé cuánta energía les queda.

—Una vez que rescatemos a tu padre, no necesitaremos luz. Ares y Aurora pueden llevarnos de vuelta a casa en la oscuridad —dijo Luxa para animarlo.

—No les va a quedar más remedio —dijo Gregor.

Los buscadores se reagruparon. Ripred iba a la cabeza, y lo seguían Temp y Boots. El túnel era lo suficientemente ancho como para que Gregor pudiera caminar a su lado. Detrás seguían Ares y Aurora, que avanzaban a pequeños vuelos, sin hacer ruido con las alas. Henry y Luxa cerraban la marcha a pie, espada en mano. Ripred les hizo un gesto con la cabeza y todos se adentraron, paso a paso, en territorio enemigo.

Avanzaban de puntillas, sin apenas atreverse a respirar. Gregor se quedaba petrificado de miedo cada vez que una piedrecita se movía bajo sus pies, pensando que había desencadenado otro ataque de las ratas. Tenía muchísimo miedo, pero una emoción nacía dentro de él, dándole las fuerzas necesarias para seguir poniendo un pie delante del otro. Era la esperanza. Fluía por su cuerpo, insistiendo en hacerle romper su norma. Su padre estaba cerca. Lo vería pronto. Si conseguían seguir avanzando sin que los descubrieran, lo vería pronto.

Cuando llevaban caminando sin ruido cerca de media hora, Ripred se detuvo de pronto en un recodo del túnel. Todo el grupo se inmovilizó a su vez. Ripred empezó a husmear el aire furiosamente y se acuclilló en el suelo.

Un par de ratas doblaron la esquina y se abalanzaron sobre ellos. Con un movimiento casi imposible de ejecutar, Ripred rebanó el cuello de una de ellas con los dientes, mientras golpeaba a la otra en los ojos con las patas traseras. Un instante después, ambas ratas yacían muertas en el suelo. Nadie había tenido tiempo de esbozar un solo gesto. La defensa de Ripred confirmaba lo que Gregor había sospechado la primera vez que lo había mirado a los ojos: incluso para los de su propia especie, Ripred era letal.

Ripred se limpió el hocico en el pelaje de uno de los cadáveres y dijo en un susurro:

—Éstos eran los centinelas de este túnel. Estamos a punto de entrar en un espacio abierto. Permanezcan pegados a la pared, en fila india, pues el suelo es inestable, y la caída al vacío, inconmensurable —todos asintieron medio atontados. Su ferocidad los había dejado anonadados—. Tranquilícense —añadió—. Y recuerden que estoy del lado de ustedes.

Al otro extremo del recodo del túnel se abría una gran explanada.

Ripred giró hacia la derecha, y todos lo siguieron en fila india. Un estrecho sendero bordeaba una profunda garganta. Cuando Gregor dirigió hacia allí la luz de su linterna, no vio nada más que un agujero negro. «Y la caída al vacío es inconmensurable», pensó.

El suelo bajo su pie izquierdo, el que estaba más cerca del precipicio, cedió bajo su peso, lanzando al vacío una pequeña avalancha de piedras y tierra. Gregor nunca la oyó tocar el fondo. Su único consuelo era que Ares y Aurora estaban en algún lugar detrás de él, listos para salvar a cualquiera que cayera al vacío.

Tras avanzar unos cien metros, llegaron a un terreno algo más sólido que se abría al otro lado de la garganta. Un arco de roca coronaba un ancho camino, cuyo suelo estaba desgastado por el paso de miles de ratas. Ripred tomó velocidad tan pronto como cruzó el arco, y Gregor sintió que la escasa protección que hasta entonces les ofrecía el entorno había desaparecido.

Ripred, Temp y Gregor echaron a correr a toda velocidad por el camino. Luxa y Henry habían levantado el vuelo instintivamente, a lomos de sus murciélagos. Gregor sentía como si miles de ratas los espiaran desde cada grieta de la roca.

El camino terminaba abruptamente en el borde de una profunda fosa circular con paredes lisas como el hielo. Una tenue luz brillaba en el fondo, revelando una criatura peluda acurrucada sobre una losa de piedra, toqueteando algo nerviosamente. Al principio Gregor levantó la mano en señal de advertencia pues pensó que se trataba de una rata.

Entonces, la criatura levantó la cabeza y Gregor reconoció lo que quedaba de su padre.

CAPÍTULO VIGESIMOCUARTO

El hombre que había desaparecido de la vida de Gregor hacía dos años, siete meses y una cantidad ya incontable de días era entonces la viva estampa de la salud. Era alto, fuerte y alegre, y la energía parecía manar de todos los poros de su piel. El hombre que los miraba desde el fondo de la fosa estaba tan delgado y tan débil que ni siquiera consiguió ponerse en pie. Cayó en cuatro patas, y tuvo que ayudarse con una mano para sostener su cabeza hacia atrás para poder verlos.

—¿Papá? —trató de articular Gregor, pero se le había quedado la boca completamente seca. Él también cayó en cuatro patas al borde de la fosa y extendió la mano inútilmente. Más de cinco metros lo separaban de su padre, pero aun así extendió la mano.

Luxa y Henry descendieron a la fosa, subieron a lomos de Aurora el lastimoso cuerpo del padre de Gregor, y lo sacaron de allí.

Todavía de rodillas, Gregor apretó las manos, antaño tan fuertes y capaces, de su padre. Cuando palpó sus nudillos, Gregor recordó que su padre solía cascar nueces con las manos.

—¿Papá? —articuló, y esta vez sí consiguió hacerse oír—. Papá, soy yo, Gregor.

Su padre frunció el ceño, como si estuviera tratando de recordar algo.

—Es la fiebre. Vuelvo a tener alucinaciones.

—No, papá, soy yo, estoy aquí. Y Boots también está aquí —dijo.

—¿Boots? —repitió su padre. Volvió a fruncir el ceño, y Gregor recordó entonces que nunca había visto a Boots. Ella había nacido después de su caída a las Tierras Bajas.

—Margaret —rectificó. Al poco tiempo de que su madre quedara embarazada, sus padres decidieron ponerle al bebé el nombre de Margaret en honor de la abuela de su padre.

—¿Margaret? —dijo su padre, completamente confundido. Se frotó los ojos. —¿Abuela?

La profecía había mencionado a «uno perdido antes», pero Gregor no se había imaginado que su padre estaría perdido hasta ese punto. Estaba esquelético y muy débil, ¿y qué había sido de su pelo y su barba? Estaban blancos como la nieve. Gregor tocó el hombro de su padre y se dio cuenta entonces de que estaba vestido con una túnica hecha de piel de rata. No era de extrañar que desde arriba le hubiera parecido un roedor.

—Quiero dormir —dijo su padre confusamente.

Eso era lo que más asustaba a Gregor. Había pensado que cuando encontrara a su padre, recuperaría a un adulto responsable. Y entonces, él podría dejar de tomar decisiones difíciles. Podría volver a ser un niño, sin más. Pero el hombre que tenía ante él era aún más desvalido que Boots.

Luxa extendió la mano, tocó la mejilla del padre de Gregor y frunció el ceño.

—Tiene fiebre, como tu hermana, y no le quedan fuerzas para combatirla. Por eso delira.

—Quizá si le hablo un minuto, lo recuerde todo. Tiene que recordar, Luxa —dijo Gregor desesperadamente.

—Ahora hemos de salir de aquí, Gregor —insistió Luxa, vertiendo un buen trago de la medicina contra la fiebre entre los labios del enfermo—. En Regalia lo curaremos como es debido. Henry, ayúdame a engancharlo a uno de los murciélagos. —Trató de sujetarlo a los lomos de Aurora con una banda de seda que Gox tejía rápidamente—. ¿Henry? —volvió a decir Luxa.

Pero Henry se mantenía alejado de ellos, sin ayudar, sin darse prisa, sin tan siquiera molestarse en fingir preocupación.

—No, Luxa, ya no debemos tener prisa.

Era una respuesta extraña. Nadie entendió lo que quería decir salvo Ripred. Una extraña expresión cruzó el semblante del animal.

—No, me imagino que Henry se ha ocupado de todo.

—Henry no ha tenido más remedio —contestó éste. Se llevó los dedos a la boca y emitió un largo silbido.

—¿Estás loco? ¿Qué estás haciendo? —le preguntó Gregor. Miró a Luxa, que parecía haberse convertido en una estatua. La cuerda de seda resbaló de entre sus dedos y cayó al suelo.

El ruido de muchos pasos de rata se hizo entonces audible. ¿Qué estaba ocurriendo? ¿Qué había hecho Henry?

—¿Ripred? —dijo Gregor.

—Parece que no soy el único espía del grupo, muchacho —dijo Ripred irónicamente—. Parece que tenemos también uno de sangre real.

—¿Quieres decir que Henry...? —Gregor nunca jamás hubiera creído que Henry pudiese ser un espía de las ratas. Éstas habían matado a sus padres, a su gente—. No puede ser —consiguió articular Gregor—. No puede ser un espía, porque ¿qué pasa entonces con Luxa? —ambos eran uña y carne.

—Lo lamento, prima —se apresuró a explicar Henry—. Pero no tenía elección. Con Vikus estábamos condenados a la perdición. Él quería aliarnos con los más débiles, cuando nuestra única posibilidad real de supervivencia es aliarnos con los más poderosos. Uniremos nuestras fuerzas a las de las ratas y reinaremos juntos, tú y yo.

Luxa habló con una serenidad que Gregor nunca le había visto.

—Ni ahora, ni nunca, Henry.

—Debes hacerlo, Luxa, no tienes elección. Debes unirte a nosotros, o perecer —dijo Henry fríamente, pero con un ligero temblor en la voz.

—Éste es un día tan bueno para morir como otro cualquiera —dijo Luxa—. Tal vez mejor, incluso —sus palabras sonaban como si tuviera mil años y estuviera a mil kilómetros de allí, pero no parecía asustada.

—De modo que te prometieron un trono, ¿no, es así? Vamos, Henry, no serás tan tonto como para pensar que cumplirán su palabra —dijo Ripred, irrumpiendo en una sonora carcajada.

—Sí que lo harán. Juntos echaremos a los reptantes y a los tejedores de las Tierras Bajas y nos repartiremos sus territorios —declaró Henry.

—¿Pero por qué? ¿Por qué quieres hacer eso? —quiso saber Gregor.

—Estoy cansado de tener a débiles y cobardes por aliados —contestó Henry—. Las ratas, por lo menos, no pecan de eso. Juntos nos protegeremos los unos a los otros. Juntos reinaremos. Juntos estaremos a salvo. Ya está decidido.

—Juntos, juntos —repitió Ripred con voz cantarina—. Cuánta camaradería estás planeando. Y cuánta soledad te aguarda. Ah, aquí están tus amigos.

Eran por lo menos cincuenta. Las ratas rompieron filas rápidamente y rodearon a los miembros de la expedición. Muchos reían, felices de haber capturado tantas presas de una vez.

Gregor miró a su alrededor. ¿Quién lucharía a su lado? Su padre estaba murmurando algo de un pez. Boots estaba tumbada sobre el caparazón de Temp, ajena a cuanto la rodeaba. Henry era un traidor, así que también podía descartar a Ares, pues ambos estaban vinculados. Sólo quedaban él, Luxa, Aurora, Gox, y... de repente no sabía qué pensar de Ripred. ¿Qué pasaba con Ripred? ¿En qué bando estaba realmente?

Gregor miró a Ripred, y éste le guiñó un ojo.

—Recuerda, Gregor, la profecía dice que sólo

cuatro de los doce morirán. ¿Crees que podemos acabar con ellos, tú y yo?

Qué bien, también podía contar con una rata sorprendente.

El círculo se agrandó, abriendo un espacio en el centro. Una enorme rata plateada avanzó para ocuparlo. Encasquetada sobre la oreja izquierda llevaba una corona dorada, claramente diseñada para una cabeza humana. Gregor oyó a Luxa respirar hondo, y comprendió entonces que esa corona había pertenecido a su padre o a su madre.

—Rey Gorger —dijo Ripred, haciendo una gran reverencia—. No esperaba el honor de contar con su presencia entre nosotros.

—Un desdichado reptante nos dijo que te ahogaste, Ripred —dijo el rey en voz baja.

—Sí, bueno, ése era el plan —dijo Ripred, asintiendo con la cabeza—. Pero a menudo los planes fracasan.

—Tenemos que darte las gracias por traer a nuestras garras al guerrero. Bueno, en realidad, eso ha sido mérito de Henry, pero qué más da, lo importante es que ahora está aquí. Quería asegurarme. Quería verlo con mis propios ojos antes de matarlo. ¿De modo que es él? —preguntó el rey Gorger, mirando a Gregor con atención—. Esperaba mucho más.

—Oh, no lo juzgues precipitadamente —dijo Ripred—. A mí se me ha antojado una deliciosa caja de sorpresas. —Recorrió el círculo de ratas, levantando de vez en cuando una pata delantera para rascarse el hocico. Cada vez que lo hacía, las ratas que estaban cerca de él se estremecían—. Clawsin... Bloodlet... oh, esto me parte el corazón, ¿eres tú, Razor? No te puedes ni imaginar cuánto me duele verte en compañía de su majestad.

La rata llamada Razor apartó la mirada de Ripred. ¿Estaría avergonzada? ¿Acaso podían las ratas sentir vergüenza?

Ripred se acercó a Henry por detrás y lo empujó hacia las ratas.

—Ve, ve, ve con tus amiguitos —Henry tropezó y recuperó el equilibrio junto al rey Gorger, pisándole el rabo. Las demás ratas se rieron, pero no el rey, que chasqueó la cola para liberarla del pisotón, partiendo en dos a la pobre Gox.

Las ratas dejaron de reír. Gregor vio la sangre azul que manaba del cuerpo de la araña, formando un pequeño charco en el suelo. Todo había sido tan rápido... En una décima de segundo había muerto un tercer miembro de la búsqueda.

—¿Por qué han dejado de reír todos? —preguntó el rey Gorger—. ¡Vamos, rían! —ordenó, y las ratas dejaron escapar un sonido que más parecía un balido de oveja. Luego, se tumbó sobre el suelo en una postura de relajación total, pero Gregor veía que sus músculos seguían tensos por la rabia.

—¿A quién le toca ahora? —preguntó el rey—. Vamos, no sean tímidos. ¿Qué tal si nos ocupamos del cachorro? De todas maneras no parece que le quede mucho tiempo. —Dirigió sus ojos de rata hacia Boots.

«Boots, no», pensó Gregor. «No mientras me queden fuerzas». Había algo que le rondaba por la cabeza. ¿Qué era? ¿Qué era lo que trataba de recordar? Y de repente, lo supo. Supo lo que querían decir los siguientes versos de la profecía.

El último en morir su bando elegirá.
El destino de los ocho en su mano estará.

«Soy yo», cayó en la cuenta Gregor. «Yo soy el último en morir». Estaba claro. Era Gregor a quien las ratas querían matar. Él era el guerrero. Él era la amenaza. Él era el que tenía que decidir cuál era su bando. Y, desde luego, no pensaba quedarse ahí de pie, viendo morir a quien amaba. Él era el guerrero, y los guerreros salvan vidas.

Una vez descubierto esto, el resto resultaba más fácil. Calculó la altura, corrió siete pasos, y saltó por encima del cuerpo plateado del rey Gorger.

Un aullido resonó a sus espaldas mientras corría. Por algunos chillidos de rata que siguieron, imaginó que Luxa, Aurora y Ripred se habrían puesto en movimiento para cubrirlo. Pero estaba seguro de que todas las demás ratas que pudieran hacerlo lo estarían persiguiendo. Bien. Así, con un poco de suerte, los otros podrían escapar. Salvo Henry y Ares. Le importaba un rábano lo que les ocurriera a esos dos.

El haz de luz de la linterna que sostenía en la mano se fue apagando, así que se deshizo de ella. De todas maneras, estaba entorpeciendo su carrera. Pero correr en la oscuridad no era buena idea. Podría tropezar, y tenía que llevar a las ratas lo más lejos posible de todos los demás. Entonces se acordó de la bombilla que tenía en el casco.

Había querido conservarla como último recurso. Si es que había un último recurso, era éste. Encendió el botón sin perder el paso, y el poderoso haz de luz le iluminó el camino.

¡El camino! ¡Había olvidado lo corto que era el camino! A menos de doscientos metros por delante de él ya aparecía la garganta, cuya profundidad, según había dicho Ripred, era «inconmensurable». No tendría la más mínima posibilidad si trataba de rodearla. Las ratas lo atraparían en cuestión de segundos.

No quería morir de esa manera. No quería darle a las ratas la satisfacción de devorarlo. Las oía a su espalda, oía su respiración y el sonido de sus dentelladas. El rey Gorger resoplaba furioso.

En un espantoso segundo, Gregor comprendió el resto de la profecía.

> 𝕽ogadle, pues, prudencia cuando con cautela salte,
> pues la vida puede ser muerte
> y la muerte, vida, en un instante.

Tenía que saltar, y con su muerte, los demás vivirían. Eso era. Eso era lo que Sandwich quería decir con su profecía, y en ese momento, Gregor lo creía.

Hizo un último sprint, como le había enseñado el entrenador de atletismo. Puso toda la carne en el asador. En los últimos pasos sintió un intenso dolor en la pantorrilla, y luego el suelo se hundió bajo sus pies.

Gregor de las Tierras Altas saltó.

CAPÍTULO VIGESIMOQUINTO

Gregor se lanzó al vacío, elevando su cuerpo al máximo. Sentía que la sangre resbalaba caliente por su pierna. Una de las ratas había conseguido pegarle un zarpazo justo antes de saltar.

«Estoy cayendo», pensó Gregor. «Como cuando caí a las Tierras Bajas». Sólo que ahora la caída era mucho más rápida. No había corrientes que lo sostuvieran desde abajo, únicamente el espantoso vacío que se abría bajo su cuerpo. Nunca había logrado entender del todo cómo había podido aterrizar sano y salvo la primera vez. Nunca había tenido un momento de calma y de serenidad para preguntárselo a Vikus. Y ahora, ya nunca lo sabría.

Tal vez todo formara parte del mismo sueño y ahora, por fin, se despertaría en su cama y podría ir a la habitación de su madre para contárselo. Pero Gregor sabía que no se trataba de un sueño. Estaba cayendo de verdad. Y cuando se estrellara contra el suelo, no se despertaría en su cama.

Pero algo no era igual que en su primera caída. Esta vez, a juzgar por el ruido, tenía mucha más compañía.

Gregor consiguió ladear su cuerpo en el aire. La bombilla de su casco iluminó una escena asombrosa. Las ratas que lo habían estado persiguiendo, que habían sido casi todas, estaban cayendo ahora tras él, en medio de una avalancha de piedras. El terreno inestable al borde del precipicio había cedido bajo el peso, sepultando con él a todo el ejército.

Muy impresionado, Gregor vio que entre las ratas había también un humano. Henry. Él también se había lanzado tras Gregor. Pero eso no podía ser. No podían morir los dos. La profecía sólo mencionaba un muerto más entre los buscadores.

El atisbo de un ala le dio a Gregor la respuesta. Por supuesto. Era Ares, el murciélago vinculado al traidor. Ares salvaría a Henry, y así se cumpliría la profecía. Pero también estarían a salvo los demás miembros de la búsqueda.

Gregor nunca había visto a Ares lanzarse en picado. Se dirigía hacia el suelo a una velocidad vertiginosa, esquivando a las ratas que trataban de agarrarse de él. Gregor empezó a dudar que el murciélago lograra remontar el vuelo antes de estrellarse. «Ha rebasado la velocidad necesaria», pensó Gregor mientras el murciélago dejaba atrás a Henry.

Entonces, Gregor escuchó la súplica desesperada de Henry: «¡Ares!».

En ese momento, Gregor se estrelló contra algo.

«Estoy muerto», pensó, pero no se sentía muerto porque le dolía muchísimo la nariz y tenía la boca llena de pelo. Luego tuvo la sensación de elevarse en el aire, y supo que estaba a lomos de Ares. Miró hacia abajo por encima del ala del murciélago y vio a las primeras ratas estrellándose sobre las rocas del fondo del precipicio. Gregor casi había tocado el suelo cuando Ares lo rescató. La visión de las ratas estrellándose era insoportable, aunque hubieran estado a punto de matarlo. Justo antes de que Henry chocara contra el suelo, Gregor escondió la cara entre el pelaje de Ares y se tapó los oídos.

Cuando se quiso dar cuenta, ya habían aterrizado. Luxa había montado a su padre sobre Aurora, y después Temp subió a lomos de Ares, detrás de él.

Ripred, ensangrentado, estaba con tres ratas que debían de haberse unido a él en el último momento. Le dedicó a Gregor una amarga sonrisa.

—Una deliciosa caja de sorpresas, eso eres tú.

—¿Qué vas a hacer ahora, Ripred? —le preguntó Gregor a la rata.

—Correr, chico. Correr como el viento. ¡Vuela alto, Gregor de las Tierras Altas! —dijo Ripred, antes de echar a correr por el camino.

—¡Vuela alto, Ripred! ¡Vuela alto! —gritó Gregor, mientras Ares y Aurora levantaban el vuelo por encima de la cabeza de la rata.

Sobrevolaron la garganta. En algún lugar por debajo de ellos yacían los cadáveres del rey Gorger, su ejército de ratas y Henry. La garganta llegó a su fin, y los murciélagos enfilaron por un ancho túnel que se alejaba de allí serpenteando.

Ahora que estaba a salvo, Gregor empezó a sentir retrospectivamente el pánico de su caída al abismo negro. Empezó a temblarle todo el cuerpo. Hundió el rostro en el pelaje de Ares, aunque así le doliera aún más la nariz. Oyó al murciélago susurrar:

—No lo sabía, Gregor. Te juro que no lo sabía.

—Te creo —le contestó Gregor con otro susurro. Si Ares hubiera estado al corriente del plan de Henry, ahora Henry estaría volando sobre su murciélago, y Gregor, sin lugar a dudas, estaría...

Entonces volvió a recordar las últimas palabras de la profecía.

El último en morir su bando elegirá.
El destino de los ocho en su mano estará.
Rogadle, pues, prudencia cuando con cautela salte,
pues la vida puede ser muerte
y la muerte, vida, en un instante.

De modo que hablaba no sólo de Gregor, sino también de Henry. Henry había resuelto que su bando era el de las ratas. Eso había decidido el destino de los otros ocho buscadores. No había saltado con cautela, no había mirado en absoluto dónde saltaba porque estaba demasiado enfrascado en ayudar a las ratas. Henry había muerto a causa de su decisión. Hasta sus últimos segundos de vida había pensado que Ares lo salvaría. Pero Ares había elegido salvar a Gregor.

—Gregor, tenemos problemas —susurró Ares, interrumpiendo sus pensamientos.

—¿Por qué? ¿Qué ocurre? —preguntó Gregor.

—Aurora y yo no sabemos qué dirección hay que tomar para llegar a Regalia —dijo el murciélago.

—¿Quieres decir que estamos perdidos? —dijo Gregor—. Creía que Luxa había dicho que podían llevarnos a casa a oscuras.

—Sí, podemos volar a oscuras, pero debemos saber en qué dirección hacerlo —explicó Ares—. Los voladores no tenemos mapas de esta zona.

—¿Qué piensa Luxa que debemos hacer? —preguntó Gregor.

Hubo un silencio. Gregor dio por hecho que Ares estaría comunicándose con Aurora. Entonces Ares dijo:

—Luxa no puede hablar.

«Luxa estará probablemente conmocionada», pensó Gregor. «Después de lo que le ha hecho Henry...».

—Y para complicar más las cosas, Aurora tiene un ala rota que se le debe curar pronto si queremos proseguir el vuelo —añadió Ares.

Gregor cayó de pronto en la cuenta de que era él quien estaba al mando.

—Pues entonces busca un lugar seguro donde aterrizar, ¿te parece?

El túnel serpenteante pronto se abrió sobre un ancho río. La fuente era una grandiosa cascada que manaba de un arco de piedra y caía doscientos metros, hasta mezclarse con las aguas del río. Por encima del arco había un saliente natural de piedra, de unos tres metros de ancho. Ares y Aurora descendieron hacia él y aterrizaron. Sus jinetes pusieron pie en la roca.

Gregor fue corriendo hacia Luxa, con la esperanza de poder trazar con ella algún plan, pero le bastó una mirada para saber que no podría ayudarlo en nada. Luxa tenía la mirada perdida y temblaba como una hoja. «¿Luxa? ¿Luxa?», la llamó. Como bien había dicho Aurora, no era capaz de pronunciar una sola palabra. Sin saber muy bien qué otra cosa podía hacer, Gregor la envolvió en una manta.

Después se volvió hacia Aurora. Su ala izquierda presentaba un largo desgarro del que manaba sangre.

—Puedo tratar de coserte esa herida —dijo Gregor, aunque la idea no le hacía mucha gracia. Sabía coser un poquito, poner botones y zurcir pequeños descosidos. Le angustiaba mucho la idea de perforar con una aguja la delicada ala del animal.

—Ocúpate primero de los demás —dijo Aurora. Luego, ésta se acercó volando hasta Luxa y rodeó a la chica con su ala sana.

Boots seguía dormida sobre el caparazón de Temp, pero su frente no estaba tan caliente como antes. La medicina también parecía haber calmado a su padre, pero Gregor seguía preocupado por lo frágil que se veía. Estaba claro que las ratas casi lo habían matado de hambre. Gregor se preguntó qué más cosas le habrían hecho.

Ares estaba acurrucado, en una postura que indicaba una tristeza tan extrema que Gregor decidió que era mejor dejarlo solo. El engaño de Henry casi había destruido al murciélago.

Salvo Aurora y él mismo, nadie parecía físicamente herido tras el enfrentamiento con el ejército del rey Gorger. Gregor abrió el botiquín y rebuscó en su interior. Si tenía que coser al murciélago, mejor sería hacerlo enseguida, antes de que le dieran ganas de cambiar de idea. Encontró un paquetito con agujas metálicas y escogió una al azar. En el botiquín también había varios ovillos de seda de los tejedores. Empezó a preguntarle a Gox cuál debía usar cuando recordó la sangre azul manando del cuerpo naranja sin vida. Eligió un hilo que le pareció delgado y resistente a la vez.

Limpió la herida de Aurora lo mejor que pudo, y luego le aplicó un ungüento que según le dijo ella serviría para anestesiar un poco la zona. Luego, con mucho miedo, empezó a coser el desgarrón. Le hubiera gustado proceder deprisa, pero coser aquella ala era una tarea lenta y meticulosa. Aurora trataba de permanecer inmóvil, pero una y otra vez reaccionaba involuntariamente al dolor.

—Lo siento, perdona —decía Gregor todo el rato.

—No, estoy bien —contestaba el animal. Pero Gregor se daba cuenta, por sus movimientos y gestos, de que le estaba haciendo mucho daño.

Cuando terminó, estaba bañado en sudor de tanta concentración. Pero el ala volvía a estar en su lugar, de una pieza.

—Trata de moverla —le dijo a Aurora, y ésta la extendió con cuidado.

—Está bien cosida —dijo—. Debería aguantar hasta que lleguemos a Regalia.

Gregor se sintió aliviado, y un poquito orgulloso de sí mismo por haberlo conseguido.

—Ahora debes ocuparte de tus propias heridas —le dijo Aurora—. Yo de todas formas no podré volar hasta que se me pasen los efectos del ungüento.

Gregor se limpió la herida de la pierna y se aplicó un poco de ungüento de un tarro de arcilla roja que recordaba haber visto utilizar a Solovet. Su nariz era harina de otro costal. Se limpió la sangre, pero seguía hinchada, tenía dos veces su tamaño normal. Lo más seguro era que estuviera rota, pero Gregor no sabía qué solían hacer los médicos con una nariz rota. Una nariz no se podía coser. No hizo nada, pues pensó que tocársela le haría más mal que bien.

Una vez que se hubo ocupado de las heridas de todos, Gregor no tenía ni idea de qué hacer a continuación. Trató de analizar su situación. Estaban perdidos. Tenían provisiones para tal vez una comida más. La antorcha de Luxa se había consumido, así que la única luz que tenían era la de su casco. Boots estaba enferma, su padre deliraba, Luxa estaba en estado de conmoción, Aurora, herida, y Ares, desesperado. Sólo quedaban Temp y él.

—¿Temp? —dijo Gregor—. ¿Qué te parece que tenemos que hacer ahora?

—No sé —contestó Temp, y en seguida agregó: — ¿Oyes a las ratas, las oyes?

—¿Cuando cayeron al vacío, te refieres? —preguntó Gregor—. Sí, sí, claro que lo oí, y fue horrible.

—No. ¿Oyes a las ratas, las oyes? —repitió Temp.

—¿Ahora? —Gregor sintió una oleada de náuseas—. ¿Dónde? —se acercó reptando hasta el borde del saliente de roca y echó un vistazo.

Centenares de ratas se estaban congregando a la orilla del río. Algunas estaban sentadas sobre las patas traseras, y con las garras de las delanteras arañaban las paredes rocosas que rodeaban la cascada. Un par de ratas trataron de trepar por ellas, pero resbalaron. Entonces empezaron a arañar la superficie rocosa, para crear muescas a las que poder agarrarse y trepar. Les llevaría cierto tiempo escalar la pared, pero Gregor sabía que al final lo conseguirían. Encontrarían la manera de llegar hasta arriba.

Retrocedió reptando hasta donde estaban los demás y se rodeó con fuerza las rodillas con los brazos. ¿Qué iban a hacer ahora? Volar, no había más remedio. Aurora tendría que, arreglárselas para hacerlo si las ratas trepaban hasta allí. Pero ¿volar adónde? La bombilla de su casco no podía durar eternamente. Cuando se apagara, estaría en la oscuridad más absoluta, con un puñado de inválidos. ¿Acaso habían sobrevivido a toda esa pesadilla para acabar pereciendo en la Tierra de la Muerte?

Tal vez Vikus les enviara ayuda. ¿Pero cómo podría saber dónde se encontraban? Y además, no imaginaba cómo estarían las cosas en Regalia. Gregor y Henry habían escenificado la última estrofa de la Profecía del Gris. ¿Pero significaba eso que los humanos habían ganado la guerra? No tenía ni idea.

Gregor cerró los ojos y apretó los párpados con fuerza, cubriéndoselos con las palmas de las manos. Nunca, en toda su vida, se había sentido tan desamparado. Trató de darse consuelo con la idea de que la Profecía del Gris decía que ocho de ellos sobrevivirían. «Bien, supongo que Ripred se las arreglará, pero si los que estamos aquí sentados sobre este saliente hemos de sobrevivir, vamos a necesitar un milagro», pensó.

Y fue entonces cuando ocurrió el milagro.

—¿Gregor? —dijo una voz perpleja. No estaba muy seguro de haberla oído—. Gregor, ¿eres tú?

Despacio, sin atreverse a creerlo, Gregor levantó los ojos hacia donde provenía el sonido. Su padre se había incorporado trabajosamente, apoyándose sobre un codo. Temblaba por el enorme esfuerzo y su voz era débil, pero en sus ojos había una expresión de reconocimiento.

—¿Papá? —pronunció Gregor—. ¿Papá?

—¿Qué estás haciendo aquí, hijo? —preguntó su padre, y Gregor supo entonces que su mente estaba lúcida.

Gregor no era capaz de moverse. Debería haber corrido a abrazar a su padre, pero de pronto tuvo miedo de ese desconocido vestido con pieles de rata y que se suponía que era su padre. ¿Estaba de verdad cuerdo ahora? ¿O cuando Gregor atravesara los metros de piedra que los separaban volvería a murmurar algo sobre un pez, y a abandonar a Gregor en la más absoluta oscuridad?

—¡Gue-go! —sonó una vocecita—. ¡Gue-go, quero salir! —dijo Boots. Gregor se dio la vuelta y la vio tratando de zafarse de la tela de araña que la sujetaba al caparazón de Temp. Corrió hasta ella y rasgó los hilos de seda. Era más fácil que ocuparse de su padre.

—Teno sed. Teno hambe —dijo Boots mientras Gregor la liberaba de sus ataduras.

Gregor sonrió. Si quería comer, tenía que ser porque se encontraba mejor.

—¿Galleta? —preguntó la niña esperanzada.

—Está bien, está bien —le dijo Gregor—. Pero mira quién está aquí, es papá —dijo, señalando a su padre. Si lo acompañaba su hermana, tal vez Gregor tuviera entonces el valor de hacerle frente a su padre.

—¿Papá? —preguntó Boots con curiosidad. Lo miró, y una gran sonrisa se dibujó en su rostro—. ¡Papá! —exclamó. Se retorció para zafarse de los brazos de Gregor y corrió directamente a los de su padre, derribando su frágil cuerpo al suelo.

—¿Margaret? —dijo éste, tratando de volver a incorporarse—. ¿Eres Margaret?

—¡No, soy Boots! —dijo la niña, halándole la barba hirsuta.

Bueno, tal vez el valor de Boots sólo contara cuando supiera contar, pero su capacidad de amar contaba siempre. Al contemplarla, Gregor sintió que su desconfianza empezaba a desaparecer. Se había enfrentado a ratas y arañas, y a sus más terribles temores sólo para reunirse con su padre. ¿Qué estaba haciendo ahora, ahí sentado, como si se hubiera comprado una entrada para contemplar el espectáculo?

—Conque Boots, ¿eh? —preguntó su padre. Estalló en una carcajada que sonó como si sus cuerdas vocales estuvieran completamente oxidadas.

La risa inundó a Gregor como una explosión de sol. Era él. ¡Era su padre de verdad!

—¡Papá! —Gregor corrió medio tropezándose hasta su padre, y se tiró a sus brazos.

—Oh, Gregor —dijo su padre, las lágrimas resbalando por sus mejillas—. ¿Cómo está mi niño? ¿Cómo está mi hombrecito?

Gregor se echó a reír cuando sintió que también sus ojos se llenaban de lágrimas.

—¿Qué estás haciendo aquí? ¿Cómo fuiste a parar a las Tierras Bajas? —preguntó su padre, que de repente parecía preocupado.

—De la misma manera que tú, supongo —contestó Gregor, que por fin había recuperado el habla—. Boots y yo caímos por el conducto de ventilación de la lavandería. Luego partimos en tu búsqueda, y aquí estás. —Dio unas palmaditas en el brazo de su padre, como para demostrarse a sí mismo que era cierto—. Aquí estás.

—¿Dónde es aquí exactamente? —preguntó su padre, esforzándose por mirar a su alrededor, a pesar de la oscuridad.

Gregor volvió de pronto a la realidad.

—Estamos encima de una cascada, en la Tierra de la Muerte. Unas cuantas ratas están tratando de escalar la pared rocosa. Muchos de nosotros estamos en mal estado, y nos encontramos totalmente perdidos —dijo. Al instante se arrepintió. Tal vez no debería haberle dicho lo desesperado de la situación. Tal vez todavía no pudiera soportarlo. Pero vio que la mirada de su padre se agudizaba, mientras se concentraba para reflexionar.

—¿A qué distancia están ahora las ratas de nosotros? —preguntó.

Gregor volvió a acercarse al borde y miró hacia el exterior. Se asustó al ver que las ratas ya estaban a medio camino de la pared.

—A unos quince metros, tal vez —dijo.

—¿Y cómo andamos de luz? —le preguntó entonces su padre.

—Sólo nos queda ésta —dijo Gregor, dándose unos golpecitos en el casco—. Y no creo que las pilas vayan a durar mucho más. —De hecho, la luz parecía volverse más tenue conforme hablaba.

—Tenemos que regresar a Regalia —declaró entonces su padre.

—Ya lo sé, pero ninguno de nosotros conoce el camino —dijo Gregor, sintiéndose impotente.

—Está al norte de las Tierras Bajas —dijo su padre.

Gregor asintió con la cabeza, aunque no entendía muy bien de qué les servía saber eso. No tenían sol, ni Estrella Polar, ni musgo sobre la parte norte del tronco de los árboles para guiarse. Estaban en un gran espacio negro.

Los ojos de su padre se posaron sobre el ala dañada de Aurora.

—¿Cómo le cosiste el ala a ese murciélago?

—Con aguja e hilo —contestó Gregor, preguntándose si su padre no estaría volviendo a delirar.

—¿Una aguja metálica? —preguntó su padre—. ¿Todavía la tienes?

—Sí, aquí está —dijo Gregor, sacando de nuevo el paquetito de agujas.

Su padre eligió una aguja y se sacó una piedrecita del bolsillo. Empezó a frotarla sobre la aguja, con rápidos movimientos.

—Consígueme un cuenco, o algo parecido. Vacía ese tarro de medicina si es necesario —le indicó su padre—. Y llénalo de agua.

Gregor obedeció rápidamente sus instrucciones, aunque todavía no entendía adónde quería llegar su padre.

—¿Qué estás haciendo? —le preguntó.

—Esta piedra es magnetita, una piedra imán. Había un montón en la fosa donde me tenían prisionero. Me guardé una en el bolsillo, por si acaso —le explicó su padre.

—¿Por si acaso qué? —quiso saber Gregor.

—Por si acaso conseguía escapar. Allí en la fosa también tenía algunos trozos de metal, pero ninguno del tamaño adecuado. Esta aguja es perfecta —dijo.

—¿Perfecta para qué? —le preguntó Gregor.

—Si froto la aguja con la piedra imán, la magnetizaré. Para que lo entiendas, lo que quiero decir es que la convertiré en una aguja como la de una brújula. Si podemos conseguir hacerla flotar sobre el agua sin romper la tensión de la superficie... —su padre depositó cuidadosamente la aguja dentro del agua. Flotaba. Entonces, para asombro de Gregor, la aguja describió un arco de cuarenta y cinco grados hacia la derecha, y luego permaneció inmóvil— ... nos indicará el norte.

—¿Indica el norte? ¿Igual que una brújula? —preguntó Gregor sin podérselo creer del todo.

—Bueno, tal vez se equivoque en unos cuantos grados, pero es lo suficientemente exacta —le dijo su padre.

Gregor sonrió contemplando el cuenco de agua. Todo iba a salir bien. Su padre había regresado.

El sonido de unas garras arañando la superficie de piedra le borró la sonrisa de la cara.

—¡Aurora! —llamó Gregor—. ¿Puedes volar?

—Creo que no tengo más remedio —dijo ésta, que sabía perfectamente lo cerca que estaban las ratas.

—Ares, si ahora te indico en qué dirección está Regalia, ¿puedes volar sin perder el rumbo? —preguntó Gregor, sacudiendo ligeramente al murciélago.

—Puedo mantener perfectamente el rumbo si conozco la dirección en la cual volar —dijo Ares, irguiéndose.

—¡A sus monturas! —ordenó Gregor, como había hecho Vikus al empezar la búsqueda—. ¡A sus monturas! ¡Regresamos a casa!

Todos lo obedecieron como pudieron. Gregor le dijo a Temp que montara con Luxa, para que pudiera cuidar de ella. Metió a Boots en la mochila, y ayudó a su padre a subir a lomos de Ares. Volvió a comprobar la dirección que marcaba la aguja dentro del cuenco y le dio la señal a Ares.

—Hacia allá está el norte. Ésa es la dirección que hay que tomar para llegar a Regalia —le dijo.

Gregor estaba a punto de guardar el cuenco cuando vio la primera garra de rata que había llegado a lo alto del saliente. Saltó sobre Ares y los murciélagos levantaron el vuelo, dejando a sus espaldas el cuenco y un puñado de ratas que los maldecían.

Ares enfiló el túnel que llevaba hacia el norte, y tras cerca de una hora de vuelo, le dijo a Gregor:

—Ahora ya sé dónde estamos.

Volaron entonces directo hacia Regalia, por espaciosas cuevas abiertas.

Por doquier yacían víctimas de la guerra. Gregor vio cuerpos de ratas, humanos, cucarachas, arañas, murciélagos y otras criaturas que ni siquiera sabía que vivieran en las Tierras Bajas, como ratones y mariposas. Ripred había mencionado mariposas alguna vez, pero Gregor había pensado que era porque las había visto en las Tierras Altas. Todos los cuerpos tenían el mismo aspecto. Se veían totalmente inmóviles. Fue para él casi un alivio cuando la luz de su casco se apagó por fin. Ya había visto demasiadas escenas de matanza. En medio de la oscuridad perdió toda noción del tiempo.

Gregor oyó los cuernos que anunciaban su llegada mucho antes de alcanzar la ciudad. Miró hacia abajo y vio a la gente que agitaba los brazos, gritando. Ni Luxa ni él respondieron al saludo.

Luxa ni siquiera miraba. Desde el momento en que levantaron el vuelo, había rodeado el cuello de Aurora con sus brazos, y había cerrado los ojos al mundo. Gregor no acertaba a imaginar lo que estaría sintiendo. Él había recuperado a su padre, y Boots estaba curada. Regresarían a las Tierras Altas y la familia volvería a estar reunida. Pero Henry era la familia de Luxa, y había preferido entregar a su prima a las ratas. ¿Qué sentimientos podía albergar ahora Luxa?

Las puertas del estadio se abrieron de par en par, y la ciudad apareció bajo sus pies. La multitud los aclamaba, agitando banderas. Divisaron entonces el palacio, y Ares se lanzó en picado hacia el Gran Salón.

Cuando ya estaban a pocos metros, los murciélagos, agotados, se desplomaron sobre el suelo, y se fueron deslizando sobre la superficie hasta detenerse por completo. Los habitantes de Regalia los rodearon en masa. En algún lugar entre la confusión de gente, Gregor vio a Dulcet cogiendo en brazos a Boots y alejándose deprisa del salón, seguida de la siempre fiel cucaracha. Dos personas extendieron a su padre sobre una camilla y se lo llevaron de allí. Los murciélagos apenas tenían fuerzas para protestar mientras también se los llevaban, pues estaban más necesitados de descanso que de cuidados médicos.

Gregor se resistió a los múltiples intentos de tumbarlo sobre una camilla, aunque sí aceptó un paño frío para aplicárselo sobre la nariz. Alguien tenía que contar la historia, y no le parecía que ahora mismo esa persona pudiera ser precisamente Luxa.

Ahí estaba la reina, pálida y perdida, ajena incluso al remolino de actividad que se afanaba a su alrededor. Sus preciosos ojos violetas estaban desenfocados, y sus brazos caían sin fuerza a ambos lados de su cuerpo. Gregor se situó a su lado, sin tocarla. Sólo quería que supiera que estaba junto a ella.

—Luxa, todo va a salir bien —le dijo, aunque sabía que sus palabras sonaban huecas.

La habitación quedó vacía, y Gregor vio a Vikus aproximarse corriendo hacia ellos. El anciano se detuvo a un metro escaso de donde se encontraban. La preocupación surcaba su rostro.

Gregor sabía que tenía que contarle lo que había ocurrido, pero lo único que acertó a decir fue:

—Henry estaba del lado de las ratas. Había hecho un trato con ellas para conseguir el trono.

Vikus miró a Luxa y abrió los brazos. Ésta permaneció de pie, aún petrificada, mirándolo como si fuera un perfecto desconocido.

—Luxa, es tu abuelo —le dijo Gregor. Le parecía lo mejor y lo más importante que podía decirle en ese momento—. Es tu abuelo.

Luxa entrecerró los ojos. Una lágrima diminuta se formó en ellos. En su rostro quedó reflejada entonces la batalla que estaba manteniendo con sus sentimientos, mientras trataba de impedir que afloraran a la superficie de su ser. Pero éstos ganaron la batalla y, para enorme alivio de Gregor, Luxa corrió a los brazos de Vikus.

CAPÍTULO VIGESIMOSEXTO

Al final, Gregor terminó contándole la historia a Solovet. Apareció poco después de Vikus y, tras besar las mejillas bañadas en lágrimas de Luxa, abrazó a Gregor. Aunque al chico no le preocupaban lo más mínimo sus heridas, a Solovet sí. Lo llevó inmediatamente a la enfermería del palacio para que lo curaran.

Mientras los médicos le limpiaban y cosían la herida de la pierna, y trataban de reducir la hinchazón de su nariz, Gregor le contó todo lo que había ocurrido desde su separación. El viaje a través de las malolientes cuevas, la llegada de las arañas, el intento de Henry de matar a Ripred, la fiebre de Boots, el sacrificio de Tick en el puente, el encuentro con su padre y la extraña serie de acontecimientos que habían hecho realidad la profecía de Sandwich.

Cuando terminó de hablar, se sintió como un globo que de pronto pierde todo el aire. Lo único que quería era ver a su padre y a Boots, e irse a dormir. Solovet lo llevó primero con Boots, que estaba en una enfermería con otros niños convalecientes. La habían bañado y le habían cambiado la ropa y, aunque seguía un poco caliente, Dulcet le aseguró que su enfermedad no era grave.

—Son muchas las cosas que no podemos curar, pero esto sí. No es más que un caso de fiebre de la humedad —le dijo para tranquilizarlo.

Gregor peinó con los dedos los ricitos de su hermana, y luego la dejó para ir a ver a su padre. Éste ya tenía mejor aspecto, y al verlo ahí dormido Gregor pensó que su rostro parecía más relajado. Los médicos no sólo lo habían bañado, sino que también le habían cortado el pelo y adecentado la barba. Habían sustituido las mugrientas pieles de rata por prendas de seda. Le habían dado de comer y le habían administrado un calmante.

—¿Y cuando despierte, estará bien del todo? —quiso saber Gregor.

—No se puede esperar que alguien que ha pasado años entre las ratas sobreviva intacto a esa experiencia —le dijo Solovet suavemente—. ¿Pero quieres saber si su mente y su cuerpo sanarán? Pienso que sí.

Gregor tuvo que contentarse con esa respuesta. Él mismo nunca volvería a ser el mismo después de lo que había vivido en las Tierras Bajas. Tenía que aceptar que su padre también cambiara en algunos aspectos.

Cuando salió de la enfermería, oyó una voz alegre que lo llamaba.

—¡Gregor! —Mareth lo envolvió en un gran abrazo de oso. Gregor se alegraba mucho de ver que Mareth estaba vivo, aunque mostrara heridas de batallas recientes.

—Hola, Mareth —le dijo—. ¿Qué tal va todo?

—Son tiempos oscuros, como siempre que estamos en guerra. Pero nos has devuelto la luz —le dijo con firmeza.

—¿En serio? —le preguntó Gregor. Se le había olvidado por completo esa parte de la profecía.

Un guerrero de las Tierras Altas, un hijo del sol,
podría devolvernos la luz, o tal vez no.

Así que al final lo había conseguido. Les había devuelto la luz. No estaba muy seguro de cómo lo había hecho, pero si Mareth lo decía, seguro que todos los demás habitantes de las Tierras Bajas también lo creían.

—¿Qué luz? —preguntó. Las imágenes que poblaban su mente eran implacablemente oscuras.

—Cuando las ratas se enteraron de la noticia de la muerte del rey Gorger, el caos se apoderó de todo el ejército. Los hicimos retroceder hasta lo más profundo de la Tierra de la Muerte. Sin cabecilla, su desorganización es total —explicó Mareth.

—Ah, bien —dijo Gregor—. Espero que dure.

Mareth lo llevó a la que había sido su habitación, la que había compartido con Boots. Se dio un breve baño, lo justo para librarse del olor a huevos podridos que se había pegado a su cuerpo en aquel túnel hediondo, y se desplomó sobre la cama.

Se despertó con la sensación de haber dormido mucho tiempo. Durante un par de minutos permaneció allí tumbado, en una modorra que le hacía sentirse seguro, sin recordar nada. Después todo cuanto había ocurrido asaltó su mente de repente, y no pudo permanecer en la cama ni un segundo más. Se dio otro baño y luego se comió los alimentos que alguien había dejado en su habitación mientras él se aseaba.

Gregor se disponía a ir a la enfermería cuando Luxa entró corriendo en su habitación. Sus ojos estaban rojos de haber llorado, pero volvía a parecer la Luxa de siempre.

—¡Gregor, tienes que venir! ¡Date prisa! —le dijo, jalándolo del brazo y obligándolo a seguirla.

Lo primero que pensó Gregor fue que habían atacado el palacio, pero no se trataba de eso.

—¡Es Ares! ¡Quieren desterrarlo! —le dijo Luxa con un hilo de voz mientras corrían por los pasillos—. ¡Él no sabía nada, Gregor! ¡Tenía tan poco conocimiento de la traición de Henry como yo misma!

—¡Ya lo sé! —le contestó Gregor.

Desembocaron en una habitación que Gregor no había visto nunca. Era como un círculo de dimensiones reducidas. Sobre unas gradas que bordeaban un escenario central, había sentados varios centenares de humanos y murciélagos. En primera fila se encontraban los miembros del Consejo de Regalia, entre ellos Vikus y Solovet. En el centro del escenario, solo y encorvado, estaba Ares.

Cuando Gregor y Luxa penetraron corriendo en la habitación, Aurora aleteó desde las gradas para reunirse con ellos.

—¡Quietos! —gritó Gregor, tratando de recuperar el aliento—. ¡No pueden hacer esto! —ignoraba por completo en qué consistía un destierro, pero sí recordaba haberle oído a Luxa decir que nadie sobrevivía mucho tiempo solo en las Tierras Bajas. Tal vez una rata como Ripred sí, pero él era extraordinario en todos los sentidos, y en cualquier situación.

Todos se pusieron en pie al ver aparecer a Gregor, y se inclinaron en señal de respeto.

—Bienvenido, guerrero, y muchas gracias por todo lo que nos has devuelto —le dijo Vikus tal y como mandaba el protocolo. Pero también le dedicó una sonrisa triste que le pareció mucho más personal.

—Sí, muy bien, de nada —contestó Gregor—. ¿Qué le están haciendo a Ares?

—Estamos a punto de votar para decidir su suerte —explicó Vikus—. Hemos sometido a un exhaustivo debate la cuestión de si tenía o no conocimiento de la traición de Henry.

—¡No sabía nada! —exclamó Gregor—. ¡Por supuesto que no sabía nada! De no ser así, yo no estaría aquí ahora. ¡Me salvó a mí, y dejó que Henry muriera cuando se dio cuenta de lo que estaba ocurriendo!

—Estaba vinculado a Henry —dijo un gran murciélago rojo—. Resulta difícil creer en su inocencia.

—¿Y qué hay de mi inocencia? —preguntó Luxa con voz tensa—. Nadie conocía tan bien a Henry como yo misma. ¿También piensas desterrarme a mí?

Un incómodo murmullo recorrió la habitación. Todos sabían lo unidos que habían estado los dos primos y, sin embargo, pese a todo, Luxa había sido el blanco de la traición de Henry.

—Aunque Ares fuera declarado inocente de la acusación de traición que sobre él pesa, queda aún la cuestión de que rompiera su vínculo —dijo el murciélago rojo—. Eso en sí es motivo de destierro.

—¿Incluso cuando descubres que estás vinculado a un tipo muy malo? —quiso saber Gregor—. A mí me parece que para esos casos debería haber una ley especial.

Algunos miembros del Consejo empezaron a rebuscar entre montones de viejos manuscritos, como si esperaran encontrar en ellos una respuesta a su pregunta. Pero otros eran claramente partidarios de que corriera la sangre.

—Poco me importa si lo desterramos por traición o por haber roto el vínculo. Sólo quiero que desaparezca. ¿Quién de nosotros podría volver a confiar en él? —gritó una mujer.

Hubo un gran alboroto en la sala. Ares pareció encogerse aún más, como aplastado por el peso de tanto odio.

Gregor no sabía qué hacer. No podía quedarse ahí parado, sin hacer nada, mientras desterraban a Ares a la Tierra de la Muerte a que se las arreglara solo. Pero, ¿cómo podía hacerles cambiar de opinión?

El murciélago rojo repitió las palabras de la mujer.

—Sí, ¡eso es! ¿Quién de nosotros podría volver a confiar en él?

—¡Yo! —gritó Gregor, haciendo callar a la multitud—. ¡Yo le confío mi vida! —y entonces supo lo que tenía que hacer.

Corrió junto a Ares y extendió la mano. El murciélago levantó la cabeza, perplejo, pero enseguida comprendió.

—Oh, no, Gregor —susurró el murciélago—. No soy digno de ello.

Gregor extendió la mano derecha y sujetó la garra izquierda de Ares. Se hizo un silencio tal que se podría haber oído volar a una mosca.

«Ares, yo me vínculo a ti,

Esto era todo cuanto recordaba de la promesa que Luxa le había recitado, pero ella se encontraba justo detrás, soplándole las palabras en voz baja.

nuestra muerte una son,
nosotros, dos.
En las tinieblas, en la luz, en la guerra, en la huida,

Gregor entonces recordó la última línea, sin necesidad de ayuda.

yo te salvaré a ti como a mi propia vida».

Ares parecía ahora más esperanzado. Que el guerrero se vinculara a él no le garantizaba que consiguiera escapar al destierro, pero tampoco era algo que se pudiera ignorar fácilmente. Pese a todo, vaciló.

—Dilo —le dijo Gregor en voz baja—. Por favor, dilo tú ahora.

Y Ares por fin obedeció, sustituyendo su nombre por el de Gregor.

«Gregor, yo me vínculo a tí,
nuestra vida y nuestra muerte una son,
nosotros, dos.
En las tinieblas, en la luz, en la guerra, en la huida,
yo te salvaré a tí como a mi propia vida».

Gregor dio un paso atrás para hacer frente a la multitud. Ares y él los miraban a todos, mano y garra aún entrelazadas. Gregor habló con una autoridad que le era del todo desconocida.

—Yo soy el guerrero. Yo soy el que ha llamado. ¿Quién de ustedes osa desterrar a Ares, mi vínculo?

CAPÍTULO VIGESIMOSÉPTIMO

Las palabras de Gregor fueron recibidas con enojo y dieron pie a un acalorado debate sobre la ley, pero al final el Consejo no pudo desterrar a Ares. El hecho de que Gregor se vinculara a él tuvo más peso del que se esperaba.

Un anciano seguía rebuscando furiosamente entre sus pergaminos hasta que Vikus le dijo:

—Oh, deja de agitar esos papeles, es obvio que no tenemos precedente para esto.

Gregor se volvió hacia su nuevo murciélago.

—Bueno, no creo que siga aquí mucho tiempo.

—No importa —le dijo Ares—. Mientras tenga fuerza para volar, siempre estaré a tu lado.

En cuanto las cosas se calmaron, Gregor se fue derechito a la enfermería. Se armó de valor antes de entrar en la habitación de su padre, por temor a que hubiera sufrido una recaída, pero cuando se decidió a entrar, lo esperaba una escena feliz. Su padre estaba sentado en la cama, riendo, mientras Boots trataba de darle de comer unas galletas.

—Hola, papá —lo saludó con una sonrisa.

—Oh, Gregor... —dijo su padre, devolviéndole la sonrisa. Le tendió los brazos, y Gregor corrió a acurrucarse en ellos, abrazándolo muy fuerte. Podría haber permanecido así para siempre, pero Boots los empujaba para separarlos.

—No, *Gue-go*, papá come galleta —dijo.

—La enfermera le ha dicho que me dé de comer, y se está tomando su tarea muy en serio —le explicó su padre sonriendo.

—¿Te encuentras bien? —le preguntó Gregor, sin dejar de abrazarlo.

—Oh, tras unas cuantas comidas como es debido, estaré como nuevo —dijo su padre. Ambos sabían que no sería tan sencillo. La vida nunca volvería a ser igual, pero por lo menos volvían a tener una vida, y podían disfrutarla juntos.

Gregor se pasó las siguientes horas con su padre y su hermana, y con Temp, que vino a ver cómo se encontraba la princesa. Gregor no se atrevía a pedirle a su padre que le contara por todo lo que había pasado, pero él parecía deseoso de hablar.

—Aquella noche, la noche de mi caída, no podía dormir. Bajé a la lavandería para tocar un poco el saxofón. No quería despertar a nadie.

—¡Nosotros también caímos por allí! —exclamó Gregor—. Por el conducto de ventilación.

—Eso es. La rejilla metálica empezó a abrirse y cerrarse, haciendo mucho ruido —comentó su padre—. Cuando me acerqué a ver qué pasaba, la corriente de aire me aspiró, y fui a parar aquí abajo. ¿Sabes?, es un fenómeno extraño éste de las corrientes de aire... —Y su padre se lanzó en una explicación de veinte minutos sobre los aspectos científicos de las corrientes de aire. Gregor no sabía de qué estaba hablando, pero era genial escucharlo de todos modos.

—Estuve en Regalia un par de semanas, pero los extrañaba tanto a todos que estaba perdiendo el juicio. De modo que una noche traté de escapar con un par de linternas y una escopeta de aire comprimido que encontré en el museo. Las ratas me alcanzaron antes de que pudiera llegar al Canal —contó su padre, con un gesto de fatalismo.

—¿Y cómo es que te perdonaron la vida? —preguntó Gregor.

—No fue por mí, sino por la escopeta. Cuando se me acabó la munición, me rodearon. Una de ellas me preguntó por el arma, así que me puse a hablar de ella sin parar. Las convencí de que sabía fabricarlas, y por eso decidieron mantenerme con vida. Me pasé el tiempo fabricando armas que yo podía utilizar, pero que se rompían en cuanto las ratas las tocaban. Una ballesta, una catapulta, un ariete... Apareciste en el momento más oportuno; creo que estaban empezando a sospechar que nunca iba a fabricarles nada que no se rompiera al primer uso —le contó su padre.

—No sé cómo pudiste soportarlo —dijo Gregor.

—Porque nunca dejé de creer que conseguiría regresar a casa —le contestó su padre. Entonces su semblante se ensombreció, y le costó mucho trabajo formular la pregunta siguiente—. Bueno, ¿y cómo está tu madre?

—Pues ahora mismo no debe de estar muy bien —dijo Gregor—. Pero se recuperará en cuanto volvamos todos a casa.

Su padre asintió con la cabeza y luego le preguntó:

—¿Y tú?

Gregor no le habló de lo mal que la había pasado, sino sólo de las cosas de las que no le resultaba difícil hablar. Le habló de sus entrenamientos de atletismo, de la escuela y de cómo había tocado el saxofón en el Carnegie Hall. No mencionó ratas ni arañas, ni lo mal que estaba desde que su padre había desaparecido.

Pasaron la tarde jugando con Boots, comiendo y, muchas veces, sin motivo especial, alargando la mano para tocarse el uno al otro.

Al final apareció Dulcet e insistió en que Boots y su padre necesitaban descansar, de modo que Gregor fue a dar un paseo por el palacio, sintiéndose más feliz de lo que se había sentido en dos años, siete meses y ya no le importaba cuántos días. No estaba dispuesto a seguir respetando su norma. Nunca más. Aunque volvieran malos tiempos, ya nunca más se negaría a sí mismo la posibilidad de ser feliz en el futuro aunque el presente fuera doloroso. Se permitiría a sí mismo soñar.

De camino a su habitación pasó por delante de la sala en la que lo habían encerrado como prisionero la noche en que había tratado de escapar de Regalia. Vikus estaba sentado a la mesa solo, rodeado por pilas de pergaminos y mapas. Su semblante se iluminó al ver a Gregor, y le indicó con un gesto que entrara.

—Pasa, pasa, aún no hemos tenido ocasión de hablar desde tu regreso —le dijo animadamente—. ¿Cómo se encuentra tu padre?

—Mejor. Mucho mejor —dijo Gregor, sentándose frente a Vikus.

—¿Y la princesa? —preguntó el anciano con una sonrisa en su rostro.

—Está bien. Ya no tiene fiebre.

Se quedaron ahí sentados un minuto sin decir nada, sin saber por dónde empezar a hablar.

—Bien, guerrero... al final saltaste—dijo Vikus.

—Sí, lo hice —dijo Gregor con una sonrisa de oreja a oreja—. Tuve suerte de que estuviera ahí Ares.

—También tuvo suerte Ares —dijo Vikus—. Todos tuvimos suerte. ¿Sabías que las ratas se están batiendo en retirada?

—Me lo ha dicho Mareth —asintió Gregor.

—Pienso que la guerra terminará pronto —dijo Vikus—. Las ratas han empezado a enfrentarse entre ellas por el trono.

—¿Y qué hay de Ripred? —quiso saber Gregor.

—Me han llegado noticias suyas. Está congregando en la Tierra de la Muerte a un grupo de ratas partidarias de su causa. No será tarea fácil asumir el liderazgo de las ratas. Primero ha de convencerlas de que la paz es deseable, y eso en sí será una larga lucha. Con todo, no es una rata que se deje amilanar —dijo Vikus.

—De eso estoy seguro —dijo Gregor—. Incluso las demás ratas tienen miedo de enfrentarse a él.

—Y con razón. Nadie puede defenderse de él —comentó Vikus—. Ah, eso me recuerda que tengo algo para ti. En varias ocasiones en el viaje hiciste constar que no tenías espada. El Consejo de Regalia me ha pedido que te haga entrega de ésta.

Vikus metió la mano por debajo de la mesa y extrajo un objeto alargado envuelto en una tela de seda muy gruesa. Gregor desenrolló la tela y encontró una espada increíblemente hermosa, con incrustaciones de piedras preciosas.

—Perteneció al propio Bartholomew de Sandwich. Es deseo expreso de mi pueblo que ahora sea tuya —declaró Vikus.

—No puedo aceptarla —dijo Gregor—. Quiero decir que es demasiado para mí, y además mi madre ni siquiera me deja tener una navaja. —Eso era cierto. Cuando Gregor cumplió diez años, su tío le regaló una navaja de bolsillo con más de quince accesorios, pero su madre se la quitó y dijo que la guardaría hasta que fuera mayor de edad.

—Entiendo —dijo Vikus. Observaba a Gregor con atención—. Tal vez si tu padre te la guardara, tu madre estaría de acuerdo.

—Tal vez. Pero hay otra cosa... —empezó a decir Gregor. Pero no sabía cómo explicar esa otra cosa, y era la razón principal por la que no quería ni tocar el objeto que tenía ante sí. Tenía que ver con Tick, Treflex y Gox; tenía que ver con todas las criaturas que había visto yacer sin vida en su camino de vuelta a Regalia. Tenía incluso que ver con Henry y con las ratas. Tal vez no fuera lo suficientemente inteligente para comprenderlo, pero Gregor tenía la sensación de que tenía que haber habido otra manera de arreglar las cosas que hubiera podido evitar todas esas muertes.

—Fingí ser el guerrero para poder recuperar a mi padre. Pero yo no quiero ser un guerrero —dijo Gregor—. Yo quiero ser como usted.

—Yo he participado en muchas guerras, Gregor —dijo Vikus con cautela.

—Ya lo sé, pero usted no va por ahí provocándolas. Primero trata de arreglar las cosas de cualquier otra manera posible. Incluso con las arañas. Y con Ripred —explicó Gregor—. Incluso cuando los demás creen que se equivoca, usted lo sigue intentando.

—En ese caso, Gregor, sé qué regalo me gustaría darte, pero sólo podrás encontrarlo tú mismo —dijo Vikus.

—¿Qué es? —le preguntó Gregor.

—La esperanza —contestó el anciano—. Habrá momentos en que te será muy difícil hallarla. Momentos en que será mucho más fácil optar mejor por el odio. Pero si quieres encontrar la paz, primero tendrás que ser capaz de esperar que esa paz sea posible.

—¿Y es que usted no piensa que yo sea capaz? —dijo Gregor.

—Al contrario, tengo grandes esperanzas de que lo seas —dijo Vikus sonriendo.

Gregor deslizó la espada por encima de la mesa para devolvérsela al anciano.

—Dígales que le dije que gracias, pero que no puedo aceptarla.

—No puedes imaginar lo feliz que estoy de transmitir ese mensaje —dijo Vikus—. Y ahora, debes descansar. Mañana te espera un viaje.

—¿Ah, sí? ¿Adónde? Espero que no tenga que volver a la Tierra de la Muerte, ¿no? —dijo Gregor, un poco mareado.

—No. Creo que es hora de que te enviemos de regreso a casa —dijo Vikus.

Aquella noche pusieron otra cama en la habitación de su padre para que pudieran dormir los tres juntos. Ahora que ya iba a regresar a casa, Gregor dejó que acudieran a su mente imágenes de Lizzie, de su abuela y, sobre todo, de su madre. ¿Seguirían todas bien cuando él regresara? Recordó su conversación con Vikus, y trató de tener esperanza.

En cuanto Boots y su padre se despertaron, los condujeron al muelle desde el que Gregor había escapado la primera noche. Un grupo de ciudadanos de las Tierras Bajas se había congregado para decirles adiós.

—Ares los llevará a la puerta que hay sobre el Canal —explicó Vikus—. De allí hasta su casa la distancia no es grande.

Mareth le dio un puñado de papeles. Gregor se dio cuenta de que era dinero.

—Lo he cogido del museo. Vikus dijo que tal vez lo necesitarás para viajar por las Tierras Altas.

—Gracias —le dijo Gregor. Se preguntaba cómo de lejos de su apartamento quedaría la entrada que comunicaba el Canal con las Tierras Altas. Se imaginó que pronto lo descubriría.

—El camino está ahora despejado de peligros, pero no se demoren. Como ya saben, en las Tierras Bajas las cosas pueden cambiar de la noche a la mañana —les dijo Solovet.

De repente, Gregor cayó en la cuenta de que jamás volvería a ver a ninguna de esas personas. Le sorprendió darse cuenta de lo mucho que iba a echarlas de menos. Habían vivido muchas experiencias juntos. Gregor se despidió de todo el mundo con un abrazo. Cuando llegó a Luxa, pensó que tal vez debía conformarse con estrecharle la mano, pero aun así le dio un abrazo a ella también. Y de hecho, ella se lo devolvió. Estaba un poco rígida, porque, claro, al fin y al cabo era una reina.

—Bueno, si alguna vez te pasas por las Tierras Altas, ven a casa a visitarnos —le dijo Gregor.

—Tal vez te volvamos a ver aquí algún día —le contestó Luxa.

—Oh, no lo sé. Seguro que al volver a casa no me la acabo —dijo Gregor.

—¿Qué quiere decir «no me la acabo»? —quiso saber Luxa.

—Que mi madre me castigará sin salir del apartamento nunca más —explicó Gregor.

—Eso no es lo que dice la Profecía de la Destrucción —comentó Luxa pensativamente.

—¿Qué? ¿Qué es eso? —preguntó Gregor, sintiendo que lo atenazaba el pánico.

—¿No te lo mencionó Vikus? Sigue a la Profecía del Gris —dijo Luxa.

—Pero yo no salgo en ella, ¿verdad? ¿Verdad que no, Vikus? —quiso saber Gregor.

—Ah, debes partir enseguida si quieres aprovechar la corriente —dijo Vikus, poniéndole a la espalda la mochila con Boots dentro y empujándolo hasta Ares, a lomos del cual ya estaba su padre.

—¿Qué me está usted ocultando? ¿Qué es la Profecía de la Destrucción? —insistió Gregor mientras lo levantaban en volandas para depositarlo sobre el murciélago.

—Ah, eso —dijo Vikus como sin darle importancia—. Es algo muy confuso. Nadie ha sido capaz de encontrarle una explicación en siglos y siglos. Vuela alto, Gregor de las Tierras Altas. —Vikus le hizo una señal a Ares y éste desplegó las alas.

—Pero, ¿de qué se trata? ¿Qué dice la profecía? —gritó Gregor desde el aire.

—¡Adiós, Temp! ¡Hasta *ponto!* —dijo Boots agitando la manita alegremente.

—¡No, Boots, no! ¡No vamos a volver! —le dijo Gregor con convicción.

Lo último que vio Gregor mientras se alejaban del palacio fue a Vikus agitando la mano en señal de despedida. No estaba seguro, pero le pareció oír que el anciano decía «¡Hasta pronto!».

Gregor volvía a ir río abajo, pero esta vez lo hacía sobrevolando las aguas agitadas sobre el fuerte lomo de Ares. Pronto llegaron a la playa donde se había topado con

Fangor y Shed. Descubrió la tierra ennegrecida, allí donde habían prendido fuego.

Diez minutos después, el río desembocó en lo que parecía un mar, o el lago más grande que Gregor había visto en su vida. Unas olas gigantescas agitaban la superficie del agua y se estrellaban sobre playas de rocas.

Entonces aparecieron dos guardias montados en sendos murciélagos y los escoltaron por encima del agua. Gregor no veía ratas por ninguna parte, pero quién sabe qué otras criaturas habría por ahí, buscando algo que echarse a la boca. Gregor vislumbró entonces durante un segundo una cola con púas, de unos seis metros de largo, que emergía del agua para volver a sumergirse enseguida. «No pienso siquiera preguntar qué era eso», se dijo a sí mismo.

Los centinelas se pusieron en guardia mientras Ares empezaba a ascender por el interior de un amplio cono de piedra. En su base, la superficie tenía por lo menos un kilómetro de diámetro. Un extraño viento neblinoso parecía empujarlos hacia arriba. «Esto deben de ser las corrientes», pensó Gregor.

Ares volaba en círculos cada vez más pequeños conforme iba ascendiendo. Tuvo que replegar las alas para poder pasar a través de la abertura que había en la cúspide del cono.

Después enfilaron a toda velocidad túneles que le resultaban familiares. No estaban hechos de piedra, sino de cemento, por lo que Gregor se imaginó que ya estarían cerca de casa. El murciélago aterrizó en la base de una escalera desierta y les señaló el final de la misma con un gesto de cabeza.

—Yo no puedo ir más lejos —dijo—. Ése es el camino para llegar a tu casa. Vuela alto, Gregor de las Tierras Altas.

—Vuela alto, Ares —dijo Gregor. Durante un momento, apretó fuertemente la garra de Ares con su mano. Luego la soltó, y el murciélago desapareció en la oscuridad.

Gregor tuvo que ayudar a su padre a subir la larga escalera. Arriba, en el techo, había una losa de piedra. Cuando Gregor la abrió, una ráfaga de aire fresco lo golpeó en la cara. Se trepó al exterior y sus manos palparon la hierba.

—Caray —dijo, apresurándose en ayudar a su padre—. Caray, mira esto.

—Luna —dijo Boots alegremente, señalando con su dedo índice hacia el cielo.

—Sí, linda, es la luna. ¡Mira, papá, es la luna! —su padre estaba demasiado agotado a causa de la subida por la larga escalera para poder contestar. Durante unos minutos permanecieron sentados en la hierba, contemplando la belleza del cielo nocturno. Gregor miró a su alrededor y por el horizonte de rascacielos vio que estaban en Central Park. Desde detrás de una hilera de árboles le llegaba el ruido del tráfico. Volvió a colocar la losa de piedra para tapar la abertura y ayudó a su padre a ponerse en pie.

—Venga, vamos a tomar un taxi. ¿Quieres ir ya con mi mamá, Boots? —preguntó.

—¡Síiii! —dijo Boots entusiasmada—. *Quero* ir ya con mi mamá.

Debía de ser ya muy tarde. Aunque algunos restaurantes seguían abiertos, no había nadie por la calle.

Tanto mejor, pues tenían una pinta bien rara, vestidos los tres con la pintoresca ropa de las Tierras Bajas.

Gregor paró un taxi y los tres se acomodaron en el asiento de atrás. El taxista no reparó en lo extraño de su aspecto, o no le importaba en absoluto. Probablemente ya había visto de todo.

Gregor apoyó la cara contra la ventanilla, bebiéndose los edificios, los coches, ¡y las luces! ¡Todas esas luces tan bonitas! El trayecto hasta su casa se le hizo cortísimo. Le pagó al taxista y añadió una gran propina.

Cuando llegaron al portal, su padre se sacó del bolsillo el llavero, el que le había hecho Gregor. Extendió las llaves con dedos temblorosos y encontró la que buscaba. Por una vez el ascensor no estaba averiado, y subieron hasta su planta.

Abrieron sin ruido la puerta del apartamento, para no despertar a nadie. Gregor vio a Lizzie dormida en el sofá. Desde la habitación oía a su abuela murmurando en sueños, así que ella también estaba bien.

Había una luz encendida en la cocina. Su madre estaba sentada a la mesa, totalmente inmóvil. Tenía las manos entrelazadas, y miraba fijamente una pequeña mancha en el mantel. Gregor recordaba haberla visto tantas noches así desde la desaparición de su padre... No sabía qué decir. No quería asustarla, ni sorprenderla, ni hacerla sufrir aún más de lo que ya había sufrido.

Así que entró en la cocina y dijo las únicas palabras que sabía que su madre estaba deseando oír.

—Hola, mamá. Ya estamos en casa.

AGRADECIMIENTOS

En primer lugar, quiero dar las gracias al maravilloso autor de literatura infantil James Proimos, sin cuyo aliento y generosidad nunca habría tenido el deseo de escribir libros. Le debo mucho por presentarme a nuestra agente, Rosemary Stimola. Según me dicen los editores, es la mejor profesional de este gremio, y no tengo motivos para ponerlo en duda. Durante muchos años antes de conocerla, mi abogado, Jerold Couture, me guió sabiamente por los entresijos del negocio del entretenimiento, por lo cual le estaré eternamente agradecida.

Quiero hacer aquí mención especial de Jane y Michael Collins, mis padres y, casualmente, el mejor equipo de investigación del mundo. Con todo mi cariño, les agradezco su ayuda a la hora de guiarme tanto en la vida como en los libros.

Tengo que destacar también en particular a dos amigos escritores por sus contribuciones específicas. Una primera conversación con Christopher Santos resultó de vital importancia para el enfoque final de este libro. Richard Register, confío en ti tanto y en tantas cuestiones, que tendré que conformarme con hacerte llegar un agradecimiento general por todo lo que haces.

Estoy tratando de encontrar las palabras adecuadas para expresar lo afortunada que me siento por haber dado con Kate Egan como editora. Le sobra talento, inteligencia y paciencia, y no concibo la posibilidad de desarrollar este libro con ninguna otra persona. Muchas gracias también a Liz Szabla por su experto asesoramiento y su ayuda, y al gran equipo de Scholastic Press.

Escribí la mayor parte de este libro en casas ajenas. Dixie y Charles Pryor, Alice Rinker, y Deb y Greg Evans, no estoy segura de cuándo habría terminado este libro —ni si lo hubiera conseguido terminar siquiera— si no me hubieran abierto sus hogares, dejándome compartir la tranquilidad de su espacio.

Gregor de las Tierras Altas es ante todo y sobre todo, la historia de una familia. Yo he tenido la suerte de nacer en una grande, donde reina el amor. Así que quiero dedicar esta novela a los clanes de los Collins, los Brady, los Pryor, los Rinker, los Pleiman, los Carmosino, los Evans, los Davis y los Owen, por ser pilares constantes en este mundo tan inestable.

Y hablando de familia, mi mayor agradecimiento va para Cap, mi marido, y para mis hijos, Isabel y Charlie, que me devuelven la luz todos los días.

ÍNDICE

Este libro se terminó de imprimir en los talleres
gráficos de HCI Printing and Publishing, Inc. en U.S.A .
en el mes de noviembre de 2007.